The Cultures of Globalization

Post-Contemporary Interventions

Series Editors   Stanley Fish and Fredric Jameson

Duke University Press   Durham and London   1998

THE

CULTURES

OF

GLOBALIZATION

Edited by Fredric Jameson and Masao Miyoshi

Fifth printing, 2003

© 1998 Duke University Press

All rights reserved

Printed in the United States of America on acid-free paper ∞

Typeset in Adobe Garamond by Keystone Typesetting, Inc.

Library of Congress Cataloging-in-Publication Data appear on the

last printed page of this book.

To Edward Said

Contents

Acknowledgments

The Globalization and Culture conference was sponsored by Duke University (the Office of the President, the Dean of Trinity College, the School of the Environment, the Graduate School, the Office of the Provost, the Dean of the Faculty of Arts and Sciences, the Center for International Studies, and the Institute for the Arts) and the University of California, San Diego (the Office of the President, the Organized Research Project in the Humanities). We are deeply grateful for their support. We also thank the Organized Research Project in the Humanities, the University of California, for funding editorial expenses. We thank Joan McNay and Pam Terterian for their generous help during the conference and for the manuscript preparation. Eric Cazdyn rescued us out of an unexpected rush during the preparation of the manuscript, and we are grateful to him. Shelton Waldrep served as assistant editor in the earlier stage, taking welcome charge of a major portion of clerical work as well as significant editorial details. Finally, we are in debt to Reynolds Smith of Duke University Press for his warm enthusiasm and expert advice.

Preface

Globalization falls outside the established academic disciplines, as a sign of the emergence of a new kind of social phenomenon, fully as much as an index of the origins of those disciplines in nineteenth-century realities that are no longer ours. There is thus something daring and speculative, unprotected, in the approach of scholars and theorists to this unclassifiable topic, which is the intellectual property of no specific field, yet which seems to concern politics and economics in immediate ways, but just as immediately culture and sociology, not to speak of information and the media, or ecology, or consumerism and daily life. Globalization—even the term itself has been hotly contested—is thus the modern or postmodern version of the proverbial elephant, described by its blind observers in so many diverse ways. Yet one can still posit the existence of the elephant in the absence of a single persuasive and dominant theory; nor are blinded questions the most unsatisfactory way to explore this kind of relational and multileveled phenomenon.

In this situation, in which the concept has no firm disciplinary home or privileged context, it would seem only natural to be pressed initially for a definition. Such requests are both comprehensible and suspicious: Nietzsche famously warned about the inevitable recursiveness of definitions. In much the same way, one often has the feeling that the call for a definition of globalization, preliminary to any discussion of the thing itself, betrays a certain bad faith; and that those who insist on it already know what it is in the first place, at the same time seeking to prove its nonexistence by way of the confusion of the hapless definer. In my own contribution to this volume, I will try to show that as a concept, "globalization" knows its own internal slippages among various zones of reference. Nonetheless, it is worth trying to formulate some provisional starting point.

Clearly enough, the concept of globalization reflects the sense of an immense enlargement of world communication, as well as of the horizon of a world market, both of which seem far more tangible and immediate than in earlier stages of modernity. Roland Robertson, surely one of the most ambitious theorists of the matter, has formulated the dynamic of globalization as "the twofold process of the particularization of the universal and the universalization of the particular."[1] This is a valuable lead, even though Robertson is intent on offering something like a utopian vision of "globality," of some new global ethic and consciousness in the world today, rather than a structural account of the forms globalization takes in the various realms of the political, the economic, and the cultural. I believe that it is necessary to add a dose of negativity to his formula, and to insist on the relations of antagonism and tension between these two poles. I thus propose to "define" globalization as an untotalizable totality which intensifies binary relations between its parts— mostly nations, but also regions and groups, which, however, continue to articulate themselves on the model of "national identities" (rather than in terms of social classes, for example). But what we now need to add to the other qualifications implicit in the formulation—binary or point-to-point relations already being rather different from some plural constellation of localities and particulars—is that such relations are first and foremost ones of tension or antagonism, when not outright exclusion: in them each term struggles to define itself against the binary other. We must therefore now add that such relationships (between a state claiming universality, for example, such as the United States or the West, and another claiming local particu- larity; or between particulars; or between universals) are necessarily symbolic ones, which express themselves in a range of collective Imaginaries. This does not of course mean that they are somehow *merely* cultural, let alone unreal: for such symbolic transmission requires the preexistence of economic and communicational channels and preestablished circuits. What emerges world- wide are then patterns of negative and positive exchanges which resemble those of class relations and struggles within the nation-state, even though, as I have insisted, they do not (yet) define themselves in that way and currently remain fixed and thematized at the level of the spatial and the geopolitical. I should add that, even in this provisional "definition," the status of the older nation-state under globalization remains a topic for heated debate: it will be more productive to keep this matter open, and in particular to insist that the definition does not imply any transcendence of the older form of the nation- state, nor even a form that might be thought eventually to replace it (world government, world culture, or whatever). Indeed, the purpose of the "defini- tion" is precisely to encourage disagreement and debate about just this ques- tion, along with many others.

For it turns out that the intellectual space of "globalization" involves the intersection of a number of different conceptual axes (my essay makes an attempt to model these patterns of opposition on the classic philosophical

debates they seem to articulate). At one level, it is the evaluation of globalization that is itself at stake: Is it a matter of transnational domination and
uniformity or, on the other hand, the source of the liberation of local culture
from hidebound state and national forms? For this second position, the
transnational rejoins the regional and the local and substitutes NGOs (nongovernmental organizations) for the corrupt and ossified one-party state.
This marks a return to the ideal of civil society, as that was first theorized
during the emergence of bourgeois society from feudalism. But "civil society"
is an idea that has two distinct levels, which it sometimes slyly substitutes for
one another in a kind of ideological prestidigitation. For it can mean the
political "freedom" of the various social groups to negotiate their political
contract, or the economic "freedom" of the marketplace itself, as a plural
space of innovation and production, distribution and consumption. The
authority of the work of Néstor García Canclini (whose absence from our
conference was greatly regretted) reinforces this dual vision of freedom, and
celebrates the creativity and vitality of peasant markets as an augury of a new
political freedom to come (not the least interest of *Hybrid Cultures*'s account
of peasant markets, by the way, lies in his demonstration of the globalization,
avant la lettre, of peasant artisinal production).[2]

Manthia Diawara's essay in this collection makes a strong case for this
vitality on the local level, although the restoration of the concrete African
setting with all its constraints makes his account something other than a mere
ideological celebration of the market. Ioan Davies rehearses the intellectual
vitality and variety of African cultural life by contrasting two theorists of
African "identity," Valentin Mudimbe and Anthony Appiah. Meanwhile, on
another continent and in a quite different transcolonial situation, Walter
Mignolo comes to cultural variety by way of the multiplicity of indigenous
Latin American languages and the emergence of local peasant political movements. Alberto Moreiras, finally, theorizes a new philosophical defense of this
local emergence of difference in his account of the emergence of the category
of "specificity" as over against the old universalism that so often merely
underwrote an imperial knowledge/power system; with this essay, however,
the dialectical view that some new transnationality served to liberate the local
and the regional from specifically national constraints seems on the point of
turning over into a critique of globalization as a new power system.

But Diawara's celebration of local culture did not exclude the observation
of negative features of transnationality; in particular, he rejoins Sherif Hetata

in a more somber evaluation of the deleterious effects of the U.S. dollar as a new world currency standard (along with the worldwide spread of American mass culture that accompanies it). Subramani chronicles in the case of Fiji the difficulties any regional culture meets in achieving autonomy, while Barbara Trent offers the unfamiliar perspective of a left-wing new world film market. These reflections find their sociological underpinnings in Leslie Sklair's identification of an essentially American consumerism as a new worldwide ideology, with its effects on local movements and local culture, while Masao Miyoshi, after a review of the transformations brought about by the new transnational corporations, turns to the question of critique and resistance on the part of intellectuals, and offers a bleak view of the effects of globalization on the university system.

But these perspectives find themselves modified when, between the level of the new transnational system (whether it be welcomed for its liberatory effects or denounced for its increasing standardization and control) and the level of the local and regional, the third term of the individual nation-state is introduced. The critique of the nation-state, identified with a virulent "nationalism" (that can extend all the way to local ethnic violence), was a stock-in-trade of internationalism all the way back to the end of World War II, when the vision of the United Nations was opposed to the supposedly nationalist expansionism of the defeated fascist powers. This critique only occasionally developed as far as a projection of some new value of federalism, on a world or regional scale. Nor has the evolution—in full globalization today—of vaguely "federalist" regional blocs gone unnoticed, along with the immense hinterlands they drain: Latin America for the United States, the former Soviet bloc for the European community, and a new East Asia Co-Prosperity Sphere for Japan. At the same time, the palpable evidence of a crisis of the very idea of federalism has been less often addressed: something that might lead the disinterested observer (if there could be one) to characterize the upheavals of the present age less in terms of the death of communism or socialism than in the very agony of the various federalist experiments themselves, and not only in the Soviet Union and Yugoslavia, but also in Canada and Spain.

However, when one positions the model at a somewhat different angle, everything changes and it is no longer the bureaucratic state apparatus that restricts the burgeoning of local cultures and local political freedoms, but rather the transnational system itself that menaces national autonomy, and that on all levels: socially, by way of Sklair's "culture-ideology of consumerism"; culturally, by way of American mass culture; politically, by the emergence of a world policing system; and economically, through the demands of IMF and the structural requirements of the "free market." Under those conditions, the older idea of a national project and a national culture reemerges as an oppositional value. Liu Kang reminds us of the uniqueness of the Chinese experience, and the various recent Chinese theorizations of possibilities that might still be realized within its framework. But it is with speakers from other Asian civilizations (which had to coexist with and to develop against imperial occupations and a capitalist system) that it remains to reassert the role that the national "collective project" may still have to play today. Paik Nak-chung reminds us of the oppositional power of a national literature in the uniquely beleaguered situation of Korea, while Geeta Kapur offers a comprehensive view of the social power of a national art and cinema in India. These interventions suggest that the modernist project itself—repudiated by a certain postmodernity in speakers who celebrate the conjunction of the global and the local—is still alive and well in some parts of the world today, and they remind us of the energizing and enabling claims of an older modernism to reinvent the collectivity and to change the world and the self, claims now so often dismissed as evoking a repressive unity and a stifling of social and regional difference. They suggest that alongside a multiple and postmodern postcoloniality, there also exists a modernist one, for which the "liberation" brought by Americanization and American mass culture and consumption can also be experienced as a threat and a force of disintegration of traditions from which new and alternative possibilities might otherwise have been expected to emerge. It is a modernism very different from the older traditionalisms, and also from the Westernizing "modernisms" that once struggled against them.

A further ambiguity in this play of different axes of opposition in the globalization debate turns on the way in which the new global system is identified. For there result very different emphases when it is philosophically characterized in terms of Eurocentrism and when it is economically identified in terms of an essentially American worldwide capitalism. This is the moment to evoke Enrique Dussel's astonishing proposal for the construction of a new non-Eurocentric world historiography, and also Noam Chomsky's detailed but impassioned account of the impact of Reaganite and Thatcherist market "deregulations" and restructuring on a hitherto flourishing and semi-autonomous national space (New Zealand).

But there are other global dilemmas that seem to lie outside these frameworks, and this symposium has scarcely been able to touch on all of them: the conflicted strategies of feminism in the new world-system, for example; or the politics of AIDS on a worldwide scale; the relationship between globalization and identity politics, or ethnicity, or religious fundamentalism; the impact on science and the academic disciplines. As for ecology, however, an area in which a truly global strategy has seemed both urgent and realizable, the very rich essays of Joan Martinez-Alier and David Harvey implacably criticize the oversimplifications and naïve fantasies often associated with contemporary ecological movements, while at the same time making modest yet tangible and productive proposals. Martinez-Alier dispels the traditional opposition between ecological thought and Marxism or socialism, while Harvey patiently unmasks the unspoken contradictions and wishful thinking of current middle-class ecological programs.

These essays therefore offer the picture of a mobile exchange of perspectives on globalization today; indeed, they show this area up, not as a new field of specialization, but rather as a space of tension, in which the very "problematic" of globalization still remains to be produced. It would therefore not be desirable to emerge from those shifting theoretical models and oppositions with anything like a new and definitive concept of globalization, or even some new theory of its possibilities and dilemmas, although we have chosen to conclude the debate with a series of reactions by younger scholars and graduate students that can serve to suggest both the actuality of these questions and also future lines of explorations. What seems clear is that the state of things the word *globalization* attempts to designate will be with us for a long time to come; that the intervention of a practical relationship to it will be at one with the invention of a new culture and a new politics alike; and that its theorization necessarily uniting the social and the cultural sciences, as well as theory and practice, the local and the global, the West and its Others, but also postmodernity and its predecessors and alternatives, will constitute the horizon of all theory in the years ahead.

Fredric Jameson

Notes

1   Roland Robertson, *Globalization: Social Theory and Global Culture* (London, 1992), 177–178. Robertson's most intriguing (and "Weberian") idea in this book is the proposition that it was precisely the syncretism and eclecticism of Japanese religion that prepared Japan uniquely for a privileged role in the current state of globalization. See also, for a full and useful review of current theories on globalization, Frederick Buell, *National Culture and the New Global System* (Baltimore, 1994).

2   Néstor García Canclini, *Hybrid Cultures: Strategies for Entering and Leaving Modernity,* trans. Christopher L. Chippari and Silvia L. López (Minneapolis, 1995).

I GLOBALIZATION

AND PHILOSOPHY

Beyond Eurocentrism:

The World-System and the Limits of Modernity

Two opposing paradigms, the Eurocentric and the planetary, characterize the question of modernity. The first, from a Eurocentric horizon, formulates the phenomenon of modernity as *exclusively* European, developing in the Middle Ages and later on diffusing itself throughout the entire world.[1] Weber situates the "problem of universal history" with the question: "to what combination of circumstances should the fact be attributed that in *Western civilization,* and in Western civilization only,[2] cultural phenomena have appeared which (as *we*[3] like to think) lie in a line of development having *universal* significance and value."[4] According to this paradigm, Europe had exceptional *internal* characteristics that allowed it to supersede, through its rationality, all other cultures. Philosophically, no one expresses this thesis of modernity better than Hegel: "The German Spirit is the Spirit of the new World. Its aim is the realization of absolute Truth as the unlimited self-determination (*Selbst-bestimmung*) of Freedom—*that* Freedom which has its own absolute form itself as its purport."[5] For Hegel, the Spirit of Europe (the German spirit) is the absolute Truth that determines or realizes itself through itself without owing anything to anyone. This thesis, which I call the Eurocentric paradigm (in opposition to the world paradigm), has imposed itself not only in Europe

3

and the United States, but in the entire intellectual realm of the world periphery. The chronology of this position has its geopolitics: modern subjectivity develops spatially, according to the Eurocentric paradigm, from the Italy of the Renaissance to the Germany of the Reformation and the Enlightenment, to the France of the French Revolution;[6] throughout, Europe is central. The "pseudo-scientific" division of history into Antiquity (as antecedent), the Medieval Age (preparatory epoch), and the Modern Age (Europe) is an ideological and deforming organization of history; it has already created ethical problems with respect to other cultures. Philosophy, especially ethics, needs to break with this reductive horizon in order to open itself to the "world," the "planetary" sphere.

The second paradigm, from a planetary horizon, conceptualizes modernity as the culture of the *center* of the "world-system,"[7] of the first world-system, through the incorporation of Amerindia,[8] and as a result of the *management* of this "centrality." In other words, European modernity is not an *independent, autopoietic, self-referential* system, but instead is *part* of a world-system: in fact, its *center*. Modernity, then, is planetary. It begins with the *simultaneous* constitution of Spain with reference to its "periphery" (first of all, properly speaking, Amerindia: the Caribbean, Mexico, and Peru). Simultaneously, Europe (as a diachrony that has its premodern antecedents: the Renaissance Italian cities and Portugal) will go on to *constitute* itself as center (as a super-hegemonic power that from Spain passes to Holland, England, and France) over a growing periphery (Amerindia, Brazil, slave-supplying coasts of Africa, and Poland in the sixteenth century;[9] the consolidation of Latin Amerindia, North America, the Caribbean, and eastern Europe in the seventeenth century;[10] the Ottoman Empire, Russia, some Indian reigns, the Asian subcontinent, and the first penetration into continental Africa in the first half of the nineteenth century[11]). Modernity, then, in this planetary paradigm is a phenomenon proper to the system "center-periphery." Modernity is not a phenomenon of Europe as an *independent* system, but of Europe as center. This simple hypothesis absolutely changes the concept of modernity, its origin, development, and contemporary crisis, and thus, also the content of the belated modernity or postmodernity.

In addition, we submit a thesis that qualifies the previous one: the centrality of Europe in the world-system is not the sole fruit of an internal superiority accumulated during the European Middle Ages over against other

cultures. Instead, it is also the fundamental effect of the simple fact of the discovery, conquest, colonization, and integration (subsumption) of Amerindia.
This simple fact will give Europe the determining *comparative advantage* over
the Ottoman-Muslim world, India, and China. Modernity is the fruit of
these events, not their cause. Subsequently, the *management* of the centrality of the world-system will allow Europe to transform itself in something
like the "reflexive consciousness" (modern philosophy) of world history; the
many values, discoveries, inventions, technologies, political institutions, and
so on that are attributed to it as its exclusive production are in reality effects of
the *displacement* of the ancient center of the third stage of the interregional
system toward Europe (following the diachronic path of the Renaissance to
Portugal as antecedent, to Spain, and later to Flanders, England, etc.). Even
capitalism is the fruit and not the cause of this juncture of European planetar-
ization and centralization within the world-system. The human experience of
4,500 years of political, economic, technological, and cultural relations of the
interregional system will now be hegemonized by a Europe—which had never
been the "center," and which, during its best times, became only a "periphery." The slippage takes place from central Asia to the eastern, and Italian,
Mediterranean; more precisely, toward Genoa, toward the Atlantic. With
Portugal as an antecedent, modernity begins properly in Spain, and in the
face of the impossibility of China's even attempting to arrive through the
Orient (the Pacific) to Europe, and thus to integrate Amerindia as its periphery. Let us look at the premises of the argument.

Expansion of the World-System

Let us consider the movement of world history beginning with the rupture,
due to the Ottoman-Muslim presence, of the third stage of the interregional
system, which in its classic epoch had Baghdad as its center (from A.D. 762 to
1258), and the transformation of the interregional system into the first *world-*
system, whose center would situate itself up to today in the North Atlantic.
This change in the center of the system will have its prehistory in the thirteenth through the fifteenth centuries and before the collapse of the third
stage of the interregional system; the new, fourth stage of the world-system
originates properly in 1492. Everything that had taken place in Europe was
still a moment of *another* stage of the interregional system. Which state

originated the deployment of the world-system? The answer is the state that will annex Amerindia, and from it, as a springboard or "comparative advantage," will go on to achieve superiority by the end of the fifteenth century. The candidates are China, Portugal, and Spain.

1

Why not China? The reason is very simple. It was impossible for China[12] to discover Amerindia (a nontechnological impossibility; that is to say, empirically, but not historically or geopolitically, possible), for it had no interest in attempting to expand into Europe. For China the center of the interregional system (in its third stage) was in the East, either in Central Asia or in India. To go toward completely "peripheral" Europe? This could not be an objective of Chinese foreign commerce.

In fact, Cheng Ho, between 1405 and 1433, was able to make seven successful voyages to the center of the system (he sailed to Sri Lanka, India, and even eastern Africa[13]). In 1479, Wang Chin attempted the same, but the archives of his predecessor were denied to him. China closed in upon itself, and did not attempt to do what, at precisely that very moment, Portugal was undertaking. Its internal politics—perhaps the rivalry of the mandarins against the new power of the merchant eunuchs[14]—prevented its exit into foreign commerce. Had China undertaken it, however, it would have had to depart *toward the west* to reach the center of the system. The Chinese went east and arrived at Alaska and, it appears, even as far as California, and still to its south, but when they did not find anything that would be of interest to its merchants, and as they went further away from the center of the interregional system, they most probably abandoned the enterprise. China was not Spain for geopolitical reasons.

However, to refute the old "evidence," which has been reinforced since Weber, we still need to ask: Was China culturally *inferior* to Europe in the fifteenth century? According to those who have studied the question,[15] China was neither technologically,[16] nor politically,[17] nor commercially, nor even because of its humanism,[18] inferior. There is a certain mirage in this question. The histories of Western science and technology do not take strictly into account that the European "jump," the technological *boom* begins to take place in the sixteenth century, but that it is only in the seventeenth century that it shows its multiplying effects. The *formulation* of the modern technological paradigm (in the eighteenth century) is confused with the origin of modernity, without leaving time for the crisis of the medieval model. No notice is taken that the scientific revolution—discussed by Kuhn—departs from a modernity that has already begun, the result of a "modern paradigm."[19] It is for that reason that in the fifteenth century (if we do not consider the later European inventions) Europe does not have any superiority over China. Needham allows himself to be bewitched by this mirage, when he writes: "The fact is that the spontaneous autochthonous development of Chinese society did not produce any drastic change paralleling the *Renaissance and the scientific revolution* of the West."[20]

To treat the Renaissance and the scientific revolution[21] as being *one and the same event* (one from the fourteenth century and the other from the seventeenth century) demonstrates the distortion of which we have spoken. The Renaissance is still a European event of a peripheral culture in the third stage of the interregional system. The scientific revolution is the result of the formulation of the modern paradigm that needed more than a century of modernity to attain its maturity. Pierre Chaunu writes: "Towards the end of the XV century, to the extent to which historical literature allows us to understand it, the far East as an entity comparable to the Mediterranean . . . does not result under any inferior aspect, at least superficially, to the far West of the Euro-Asiatic continent."[22]

Let us repeat: Why not China? Because China found itself in the easternmost zone of the interregional system, whence it looked to the center: to India in the west.

2

Why not Portugal? For the same reason: that is, because it found itself in the farthest point west of the same interregional system, and because *it also looked, and always, toward the center:* toward India in the east. Columbus's proposal (the attempt to reach the center through the West) to the king of Portugal was as insane as it was for Columbus to claim to discover a new continent (since he *only and always* attempted, and could not conceive another hypothesis, to reach the center of the third stage of the interregional system[23]).

The Italian Renaissance cities are the farthest point west (peripheral) of the interregional system, which articulated anew, after the Crusades (which failed in 1291), continental Europe with the Mediterranean. The Crusades ought to be considered a frustrated attempt to connect with the center of the system, a link that the Turks ruptured. The Italian cities, especially Genoa (which rivaled Venice's presence in the eastern Mediterranean), attempted to open the western Mediterranean to the Atlantic, in order to reach once again through the south of Africa the center of the system. The Genoese placed all their experience in navigation and the economic power of their wealth at the service of opening for themselves this path. It was the Genoese who occupied the Canaries in 1312,[24] and it was they who invested in Portugal and helped the Portuguese to develop their navigational power.

Once the Crusades had failed, and because the Europeans could not foresee the expansion of Russia through the steppes (who, advancing through the frozen woods of the North, reached the Pacific and Alaska[25] in the seventeenth century), the Atlantic was the only European door *to the center of the system*. Portugal, the first European nation already unified in the eleventh century, will transform the reconquest[26] against the Muslims into the beginning of a process of Atlantic mercantile expansion. In 1419, the Portuguese discover the Madeiras Islands, in 1431 the Azores, in 1482 Zaire, and in 1498 Vasco da Gama reaches India (the center of the interregional system). In 1415, Portugal occupies the African-Muslim Ceuta, in 1448 El-Ksar-es-Seghir, in 1471 Arzila. But all of this is the *continuation* of the interregional system whose connection is the Italian cities: "In the twelfth century when the Genoese and the Pisans first appear in Catalonia, in the thirteenth century when they first reach Portugal, this is part of the efforts of the Italians to draw the Iberian peoples into the international trade of the time. . . . As of 1317, according to Virginia Rau, 'the city and the port of Lisbon would be the great centre of Genoese trade. . . .'"[27]

A Portugal with contacts in the Islamic world, with numerous sailors (former farmers expelled from an intensive agriculture), with a money economy, in "connection" with Italy, once again opened peripheral Europe to the interregional system. But despite this it did not stop being on the periphery. Not even the Portuguese could pretend to have abandoned this situation, for although Portugal could have attempted to dominate the commercial exchange in the sea of the Arabs (the Indian sea[28]), it never could produce the commodities of the East (silk fabrics, tropical products, sub-Saharan gold, etc.). In other words, it was an intermediary and always peripheral power of India, China, and the Muslim world.

With Portugal we are in the anteroom, but still neither in modernity nor in the world-system (the fourth stage of the system, which originated, at least, between Egypt and Mesopotamia).

3

Why does Spain begin the world-system, and with it, modernity? For the same reason that it was prevented in China and Portugal. Because Spain could not reach the center of the interregional system that was in Central Asia or India, could not go east (since the Portuguese had already anticipated them, and thus had exclusivity rights) through the south Atlantic (around the coasts of Western Africa, until the cape of Buena Esperanza was discovered in 1487), Spain had only one opportunity left: to go toward the center, to India, through *the Occident,* through the West, by crossing the Atlantic Ocean.[29] Because of this Spain bumps into, finds without looking, Amerindia, and with it the entire European medieval paradigm enters into crisis (which is the paradigm of a peripheral culture, the farthest western point of the third stage of the interregional system), and thus inaugurates, slowly but irreversibly, the first *world* hegemony. This is the only world-system that has existed in planetary history, and this is the modern system, European in its center, capitalist in its economy.

This essay situates itself explicitly (is it perhaps the first practical philosophy that attempts to do so "explicitly"?) within the horizon of this modern world-system, taking into consideration not only the center (as has been done *exclusively* by modern philosophy from Descartes to Habermas, thus resulting in a *partial,* provincial, regional view of the historical ethical event), *but also* its periphery (and with this one obtains a *planetary* vision of the human experience). My position is not informative or anecdotal: it is sensu stricto philosophical. I have already treated the theme in another work,[30] in which I showed Columbus's existential impossibility, as a Renaissance Genoese, of convincing himself that what he had discovered was not India. He navigated, according to his own imagination, close to the coasts of the fourth Asiatic peninsula (which Heinrich Hammer had already drawn cartographically in Rome in 1489[31]), always close to the Sinus Magnus (the great gulf of the Greeks, territorial sea of the Chinese) when he transversed the Caribbean. Columbus died in 1506 without having superseded the horizon of stage 3 of the interregional system.[32] He was not able subjectively to supersede the interregional system—with a history of 4,500 years of transformations, beginning with Egypt and Mesopotamia—and to open himself to the new stage of the world-system. The first one who suspected a *new* (the *last* new) continent was Amerigo Vespucci, in 1503, and therefore, he was existentially and subjectively the first Modern, the first to unfold the horizon of the Asian-Afro-Mediterranean system as world-system, which for the first time incorporated Amerindia.[33] This revolution in the Weltanschauung of the cultural, scientific, religious, technological, political, ecological, and economic horizon is the *origin* of modernity, seen from the perspective of a world paradigm and not solely from a Eurocentric perspective. In the world-system, the accumulation in the center is for the first time accumulation on a world scale.[34] Within the new system everything changes qualitatively and radically. The very medieval European peripheral subsystem changes internally as well. The founding event was the discovery of Amerindia in 1492.[35] Spain is ready to become the first modern state;[36] through the discovery it begins to become the center of its first periphery (Amerindia), thus organizing the beginning of the slow shifting of the center of the older, third stage of the interregional system (Baghdad of the thirteenth century), which from peripheral Genoa (but the western part of the system) had begun a process of reconnection first with Portugal and now with Spain, with Seville to be precise. Genoese and other Italian wealth suddenly flows into Seville. The "experience" of the eastern Renaissance Mediterranean (and through it, of the Muslim world, of India and even China) is thus articulated with the imperial Spain of Charles V (who reaches into the central Europe of the bankers of Augsburg, to the Flanders of Amberes, and later, to Amsterdam, with Bohemia, Hungary, Austria, and Milan, and especially the kingdom of the Two Sicilies,[37] of the south of Italy, namely Sicily, Sardinia, the Baleares, and the numerous islands of the Mediterranean). But because of the economic failure of the political project of the world empire, the emperor Charles V abdicates in 1557. The path is left open for the world-system of mercantile, industrial, and, today, transnational capitalism.

To demonstrate, let us make a comparative analysis, (among the many that may be analyzed—we would not want to be criticized as being a reductive economist because of the example that we have adopted!). It is not a coincidence that twenty-five years after the discovery of the silver mines of Potosí in Peru and the mines in Zacateca in Mexico (1546)—from which a total of 18,000 tons of silver arrived in Spain between the years 1503 and 1660[38]—

thanks to the first shipments of this precious metal, Spain was able to pay for, among the many campaigns of the empire, the great armada that defeated the Turks in 1571 in Lepanto. This led to the dominance of the Mediterranean as a connection with the center of the older stage of the system. However, the Mediterranean died as the road of the center toward the periphery in the west, because now the Atlantic was structuring itself as the center of the new world-system![39]

Wallerstein writes: "Bullion was desired as a preciosity, for consumption in Europe and even more for trade with Asia, but it was also a necessity for the expansion of the European economy."[40] I have read, among the many unpublished letters of the General Indian Archive of Seville, the following text of July 1, 1550, signed in Bolivia by Domingo de Santo Tomás: "It was four years ago, to conclude the perdition of this land, that a mouth of hell[41] was discovered through which every year a great many people are immolated, which the greed of the Spaniards sacrifice to their god that is gold,[42] and it is a mine of silver which is named Potosí."[43] The rest is well known. The Spanish colony in Flanders will replace Spain as a hegemonic power in the center of the recently established world-system; it liberates itself from Spain in 1610. Seville, the first modern port (along with Amberes), after more than a century of splendor, will cede its place to Amsterdam[44] (the city where Descartes in 1636 will write *Le Discours de la Méthode,* and where Spinoza will live[45]), the new port controlling naval, fishing, and crafts power; to which flow agricultural exports and great expertise in all branches of production; the city that will, in many respects, bankrupt Venice.[46] After more than a century, modernity was already visible in this city's definitive physiognomy: its port; the channels that as commercial ways reached to the houses of the bourgeoisie and the merchants (who used their fourth and fifth floors as cellars, from which boats were directly loaded with cranes); and a thousand other details of a capitalist metropolis.[47] From 1689 on, England will challenge and will end up imposing itself over Holland's hegemony—which, however, it will have to share with France, at least until 1763.[48]

Amerindia, meanwhile, constitutes the fundamental structure of the first modernity. From 1492 to 1500 approximately 50,000 square kilometers are colonized (in the Caribbean, and farm land from Venezuela to Panama).[49] In 1515 these numbers will reach 300,000 square kilometers, with about 3 million dominated Amerindians; by 1550 Spain has colonized more than 2 million

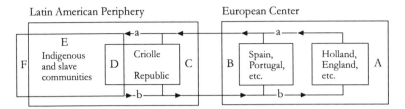

Figure 1. An Example of the Center-Periphery Structure in the Center and Colonial Periphery of the 18th Century

Notes: Arrow a: domination and export of manufactured goods; arrow b: transfer of value and exploitation of labor; A: power of the center; B: semiperipheral nations; C: peripheral formations; D: exploitation of Amerindian labor or slaves; E: indigenous communities; F: ethnic communities who retained a certain exteriority to the world-system

Source: Enrique Dussel, *Historia General de la Iglesia en América Latina* (Salamanca, 1983), 223.

square kilometers (an area greater than the whole of Europe of the center) and more than 25 million (a low figure) indigenous peoples,[50] many of whom are integrated into a system of work that produces value (in Marx's strict sense) for the Europe of the center (in the *encomienda, mita,* haciendas, etc.). We would have to add, from 1520 onward, the plantation slaves of African provenance (about 14 million until the final stage of slavery in the nineteenth century, including those in Brazil, Cuba, and the United States). This enormous space and population will give to Europe, center of the world-system, the *definitive comparative advantage* with respect to the Muslim, Indian, and Chinese worlds. It is for this reason that in the sixteenth century: "The periphery (eastern Europe and Hispanic America) used forced labor (slavery and coerced cash-crop labor [of the Amerindian]). The core, as we shall see, increasingly used free labor."[51]

For the goals of this philosophical work, it is of interest to indicate solely that with the birth of the world-system, the *"peripheral* social formations"[52] were also born: "The form of *peripheral* formation will depend, finally, at the same time on the nature of the accumulated pre-capitalist formations and the forms of external aggression."[53] These will be, at the end of the twentieth century, the Latin American peripheral formations,[54] those of the African Bantu, the Muslim world, India, Southeast Asia,[55] and China; to which one must add part of Eastern Europe before the fall of socialism (see fig. 1).

Modernity as "Management" of the Planetary Center and Its Contemporary Crisis

We have thus arrived at the central thesis of this essay: that modernity was the fruit of the "management" of the centrality of the first world-system. We now have to reflect on what this implies.

There are, at the least, two modernities: the first is a Hispanic, humanist, Renaissance modernity, still linked to the old interregional system of Mediterranean, Muslim, and Christian.[56] In this, the "management" of the new system will be conceived from out of the older paradigm of the interregional system. That is, Spain "manages" centrality as domination through the hegemony of an integral culture, a language, a religion (and thus, the evangelization process that Amerindia will suffer); as military occupation, bureaucratic-political organization, economic expropriation, demographic presence (with hundreds of thousands of Spaniards and Portuguese who forever will inhabit Amerindia), ecological transformation (through the modification of the fauna and flora), and so on. This is the substance of the world empire project, which, as Wallerstein notes, failed with Charles V.[57] Second, there is the modernity of Anglo-Germanic Europe, which begins with the Amsterdam of Flanders and which frequently passes as the *only* modernity (this is the interpretation of Sombart, Weber, Habermas, and even the postmoderns, who will produce a "reductionist fallacy" that occludes the meaning of modernity and, thus, the sense of its contemporary crisis). This second modernity, to be able to manage the immense world-system suddenly opening itself to tiny Holland,[58] which from being a Spanish colony now places itself as the center of the world-system, must accomplish or increase its efficacy through *simplification*. It is necessary to carry out an abstraction (favoring *quantum* to the detriment of *qualitas*) that leaves out many valid variables (cultural, anthropological, ethical, political, and religious variables; aspects that are valuable even for the European of the sixteenth century) that will not allow an adequate, "factual"[59] or technologically possible management of the world-system.[60] This *simplification* of complexity[61] encompasses the totality of the life-world (*Lebenswelt*), of the relationship with nature (a new technological and ecological position that is no longer teleological), of subjectivity itself (a new self-understanding of subjectivity), and of community (a new intersubjective and political relation). A new economic attitude (practico-productive) will now establish itself: the capitalism.

The first, Hispanic, Renaissance, and humanist modernity produced a theoretical and philosophical reflection of the highest importance, which has gone unnoticed by so-called modern philosophy (which is only the philosophy of the second modernity). The theoretical-philosophical thought of the sixteenth century has contemporary relevance because it is the first, and only, that lived and expressed the originary experience during the period of the constitution of the first world-system. Thus, out of the theoretical "recourses" that were available (the scholastic-Muslim-Christian and Renaissance philosophies), the central philosophical ethical question that obtained was the following: What right has the European to occupy, dominate, and manage the recently discovered cultures, conquered by the military and in the process of being colonized? From the seventeenth century on, the conscience (*Gewissen*) of the second modernity did not have to wrestle with this question: it had already been answered in fact. From Amsterdam, London, and Paris (in the seventeenth century and from the eighteenth century onward), "Eurocentrism" (the superideology that will establish the legitimacy, without falsification, of the domination of the world-system) will *no longer* be questioned, until the end of the twentieth century—among other movements, by liberation philosophy.

In another work I have touched on this ethical question.[62] Here I will only examine the theme in general. Bartolomé de las Casas demonstrates in his numerous works, using an extraordinary bibliographic apparatus, rationally and carefully grounding his arguments, that the constitution of the world-system as European expansion in Amerindia (in anticipation of the expansion in Africa and Asia) does not have any right; it is an unjust violence, and cannot have any ethical validity:

> The common way mainly employed by the Spaniards who call themselves Christian and who have gone there to extirpate those pitiful nations and wipe them off the earth is by unjustly waging cruel and bloody wars. Then, when they have slain all those who fought for their lives or to escape the tortures they would have to endure, that is to say, when they have slain all the native rulers and young men (since the Spaniards usually spare only the women and children, who are subjected to the hardest and bitterest servitude ever suffered by man or beast), they enslave any survivors. . . . Their reason for killing and destroying such an infinite number of souls is that the Christians have an ultimate aim, which is to acquire gold, and to swell

themselves with riches in a very brief time and thus rise to a high estate disproportionate to their merits. It should be kept in mind that their insatiable greed and ambition, the greatest ever seen in the world, is the cause of their villanies.[63]

Later, philosophy will no longer formulate this problematic, which showed itself unavoidable at the origin of the establishment of the world-system. For the ethics of liberation, this question remains fundamental.

In the sixteenth century, then, the world-system is established in Seville, and philosophy questions, from out of the old philosophical paradigm, the praxis of domination, but it does not reach the formulation of the *new paradigm*. However, the origin of the new paradigm ought not to be confused with the origin of modernity. Modernity begins in 1492, more than a century before the moment in which the paradigm, adequate to its own new experience, is formalized, using Kuhn's terminology; the formulation of the new modern paradigm takes place in the first half of the seventeenth century.[64] This new paradigm corresponds to the exigencies of *efficacy*, technological "factibility" or governmentalism of the management of an enormous world-system in expansion; it is the expression of a necessary process of *simplification* through "rationalization" of the life-world, of the subsystems (economic, political, cultural, religious, etc.). Rationalization, as construed by Werner Sombart,[65] Ernst Troeltsch,[66] and Max Weber,[67] is *effect* and not cause. But the effects of that *simplifying rationalization* to *manage* the world-system are perhaps more profound and negative than Habermas or the postmoderns imagine.[68]

The corporeal Muslim-medieval subjectivity is *simplified:* subjectivity is postulated as an *ego,* an I, about which Descartes writes: "Accordingly this 'I'—that is, the soul by which I am what I am—is *entirely* distinct from the body, and indeed is easier to know than the body, and would not fail to be whatever it is, even if the body did not exit."[69] The body is a mere machine, *res extensa,* entirely foreign to the soul.[70] Kant himself writes: "The human soul should be seen as being linked in the present life to two worlds at the same time: of these worlds, inasmuch as it forms with the body a personal unity, it feels but only the material world; on the contrary, as a member of the spirit world (*als ein Glied der Geisterwelt*) [without body] it receives and propagates the pure influences of immaterial natures."[71] This dualism—which Kant will apply to his ethics, inasmuch as the maxims ought not to have any empirical or "pathological" motives—is posteriorly articulated through the negation of practical intelligence, which is replaced by instrumental reason, the one that will deal with technical, technological "management" (ethics disappears before a *more geometric* intelligence) in the *Critique of Judgment.* It is here that the conservative tradition (such as that of Heidegger) continues to perceive the *simplifying* suppression of the organic complexity of life, now replaced by a technique of the "will to power" (critiques elaborated by Nietzsche and Foucault). Galileo, with all the naïve enthusiasm of a great discovery, writes: "Philosophy is written in this grand book, the universe, which stands continually open to our gaze. But the book cannot be understood unless one first learns to comprehend the language and read the letters in which it is composed. It is written in the *language of mathematics,* and its characters are triangles, circles and other geometric figures, without which it is humanly impossible to understand a single word of it; without these, one wanders about in a dark labyrinth."[72]

Heidegger said that the "*mathematical* position"[73] one must take before entities is to have the mathematics already known, "ready-to-hand" (in the axioms of science, for example), and to approach the entities only to use them. One does not "learn" a weapon, for instance, but instead one learns to make "use" of it, because one already knows what it is: "The *mathemata* are the things insofar as we take cognizance of them as what we already know them to be in advance, the body as the bodily, the plant-like of the plant, the animal-like of the animal, the thingness of the thing, and so on."[74] The "rationalization" of political life (bureaucratization), of the capitalist enterprise (administration), of daily life (Calvinist asceticism or puritanism), the decorporalization of subjectivity (with its alienating effects on living labor, criticized by Marx, as well as on its drives, analyzed by Freud), the nonethicalness of every economic or political gestation (understood only as technical engineering, etc.), the suppression of practical-communicative reason, now replaced by instrumental reason, the solipsistic individuality that negates the community, and so on, are all examples of the diverse moments that are negated by this *simplification,* apparently necessary for the management of the centrality of a world-system that Europe found itself in need of perpetually carrying out. Capitalism, liberalism, dualism (without valorizing corporeality), and so on are *effects* of the management of this function which corresponded to Europe as center of the world-system: effects that are constituted through mediations in systems that end up totalizing themselves.

Capitalism, mediation of exploitation and accumulation (effect of the world-system), is later on transformed into an *independent system* that from out of its own self-referential and autopoietic logic can destroy Europe and its periphery, even the entire planet. And this is what Weber observes, but reductively. That is to say, Weber notes part of the phenomenon but not the horizon of the world-system. In fact, the formal procedure of *simplification* that makes the world-system *manageable* produces formal rationalized subsystems that later on do not have internal standards of self-regulation within its own limits of modernity, which could be redirected at the service of humanity. It is in this moment that there emerge critiques from within the center (and from out of the periphery, such as is mine) of modernity itself. Now one (from Nietzsche to Heidegger, or with the postmoderns) attributes to *reason* all culpable causality (as object "understanding" that takes place through analysis and disintegration)—this culpability can be traced back as far as Socrates (Nietzsche) or even Parmenides himself (Heidegger). In fact, the modern *simplifications* (the dualism of an *ego*-alma without a body, teleological instrumental reason, the racism of the superiority of one's own culture, etc.) have many similarities with the *simplification* that Greek slavery produced in the second interregional system. The Greek Weltanschauung was advantageous to the modern man—not without complicity does he resuscitate the Greeks, as was done through the German romantics.[75] The subsumptive supercession (*Aufhebung*) of modernity will mean the critical reconsideration of *all* these simplifying reductions produced since its origin—and not only a few, as Habermas imagines. The most important of these reductions, next to that of solipsistic subjectivity, without community, is the negation of the corporeality of this subjectivity—to which are related the critiques of modernity by Marx, Nietzsche, Freud, Foucault, Levinas, and the ethics of liberation.

Because of all this, the concept that one has of modernity determines, as is evident, the claim to its realization (such as in Habermas), or the type of critique one may formulate against it (such as that of the postmoderns). In general, no debate between rationalists and postmoderns overcomes the Eurocentric horizon. The crisis of modernity (already noted by, as we have remarked frequently, Nietzsche and Heidegger) refers to internal aspects of Europe. The peripheral world would appear to be a passive spectator of a thematic that does not touch it, because it is a "barbarian," a "premodern," or, simply, still in need of being "modernized." In other words, the Eurocentric view reflects on the problem of the crisis of modernity solely with the

European–North American moments (or now even Japanese), but it minimizes the periphery. To break through this "reductivist fallacy" is not easy. We will attempt to indicate the path to its surmounting.

If modernity begins at the end of the fifteenth century, with a Renaissance premodern process, and from there a transition is made to the properly modern in Spain, Amerindia forms part of "modernity" since the moment of the conquest and colonization (the mestizo world in Latin America is the only one that is as old as modernity[76]), for it contained the first "barbarian" that modernity needed in its definition. If modernity enters into crisis at the end of the twentieth century, after five centuries of development, it is not a matter only of the moments detected by Weber and Habermas, or by Lyotard or Welsch,[77] but also of those moments of a "planetary" description of the phenomenon of modernity.

To conclude, if we situate ourselves, instead, within the planetary horizon, we can distinguish at least two positions in the face of the formulated problematic. First, on the one hand, there is the "substantialist" developmentalist[78] (quasi-metaphysical) position that conceptualizes modernity as an *exclusively European* phenomenon that *expanded from the seventeenth century on* throughout all the "backward" cultures (the Eurocentric position in the center and modernizing in the periphery); thus, modernity is a phenomenon that must be concluded. Some who assume this first position (for example, Habermas and Apel), defenders of reason, do so critically, because they think that European superiority is not material, but formal, thanks to a new structure of critical questions.[79] On the other hand, there is the conservative "nihilist" position (of Nietzsche or Heidegger, for instance), which denies to modernity positive qualities and proposes practically an annihilation without exit. The postmoderns take this second position (in their frontal attack on "reason" *as such,* with differences in the case of Levinas[80]), although, paradoxically, they also defend parts of the first position, from the perspective of a developmentalist Eurocentrism.[81] The postmodern philosophers are admirers of postmodern art, of the *media,* and although they theoretically affirm *difference,* they do not reflect on the origins of these systems that are the fruit of a rationalization proper to the management of the European centrality in the world-system, before which they are profoundly uncritical, and, because of this, they do not attempt to contribute valid alternatives (cultural, economic, political, etc.) for the peripheral nations, or the peoples or great majorities who are dominated by the center and/or the periphery.

The second position, from the periphery, is the one we defend. It considers the process of modernity as the already indicated rational management of the world-system. This position intends to recoup what is redeemable in modernity, and to halt the practices of domination and exclusion in the world-system. It is a project of liberation of a periphery negated from the very beginning of modernity. The problem is not the mere superseding of instrumental reason (as it is for Habermas) or of the reason of *terror* of the postmoderns; instead, it is a project of overcoming the world-system itself, such as it has developed for the past 500 years until today. The problem is the exhaustion of a "civilizing" system that has come to its end.[82] The overcoming of *cynical managerial reason* (planetary administrative), of capitalism (as economic system), of liberalism (as political system), of Eurocentrism (as ideology), of machismo (in erotics), of the reign of the white race (in racism), of the destruction of nature (in ecology), and so on presupposes the liberation of diverse types of the oppressed and/or excluded. It is in this sense that the ethics of liberation defines itself as transmodern (because the postmoderns are still Eurocentric).

The end of the present stage of civilization is heralded by three limits of the "system of 500 years," as Noam Chomsky calls it. These limits are, first, the ecological destruction of the planet. From the very moment of its inception, modernity has constituted nature as an "exploitable" object, with the increase in the rate of profit of capital[83] as its goal: "For the first time, nature becomes purely an object for humankind, purely a matter of utility; it ceases to be recognized as a power for itself."[84] Once the earth is constituted as an "exploitable object" in favor of *quantum,* of capital, that can defeat all limits, all boundaries, the "great civilizing influence of capital" is revealed: nature now reaches its unsurmountable limit, where it is its own limit, the impassable barrier for ethical-human progress, and we have arrived at this moment: "The universality towards which it [nature] irresistibly strives encounters barriers in its own nature, which will, at a certain state of its development, allow it to be recognized as being itself the greatest barrier to this tendency, and hence will drive towards its own suspension."[85] Given that nature is for modernity only a medium of production, it runs out its fate of being consumed, destroyed, and, in addition, accumulating geometrically upon the earth its debris, until it jeopardizes the reproduction or survival of life itself. Life is the absolute condition of capital; its destruction destroys capital. We have arrived at this state of affairs. The "system of 500 years" (modernity or capitalism) confronts its first absolute limit: the death of life in its totality, through the indiscriminate use of an anti-ecological technology constituted progressively through the sole criterion of the *quantitative* management of the world-system in modernity: the increase in the rate of profit. But capital cannot limit itself. In this lies the utmost danger for humanity.

The second limit of modernity is the destruction of humanity itself. "Living labor" is the other essential mediation of capital as such; the human subject is the only one that can "create" new value (surplus value, profit). Capital that defeats all barriers requires incrementally more absolute time for work; when it cannot supersede this limit, then it augments productivity through technology; but this increase decreases the importance of human labor. It is thus that there is *superfluous* (displaced) *humanity*. The unemployed do not earn a salary, that is, money; but money is the only mediation in the market through which one can acquire commodities to satisfy needs. In any event, work that is not employable by capital increases, thus increasing unemployment and the proportion of needing subjects who are not solvent, including clients, consumers, and buyers—as much in the periphery as in the center.[86] The result is poverty, poverty as the absolute limit of capital. Today we know how misery grows throughout the entire planet. It is a "law of modernity": "Accumulation of wealth at one pole is, therefore, at the same time accumulation of misery, the torment of labour, slavery, ignorance, brutalization and moral degradation at the opposite pole. . . ."[87] The modern world-system cannot overcome this essential contradiction. The ethics of liberation reflects philosophically from this planetary horizon of the world-system, from this double limit that configures the terminal crisis of the civilizing process: the ecological destruction of the planet and the extinguishing in misery and hunger of the great majority of humanity. Before these co-implicating phenomena of planetary magnitude, the projects of many philosophical schools would seem naïve and even ridiculous, irresponsible, irrelevant, cynical, and even complicitous (certainly in the center, but even worse in the periphery, in Latin America, Africa, and Asia), for they are closeted in their "ivory towers" of sterile Eurocentric academicism. Already in 1968 Marcuse had asked, referring to the opulent countries of late capitalism:

> why do we need liberation from such a society if it is capable—perhaps in the distant future, but apparently capable—of conquering poverty to a greater degree than ever before, or reducing the toil of labour and the time

of labour, and of raising the standard of living? If the price for all goods delivered, the price for this comfortable servitude, for all these achievements, is exacted from people far away from the metropolis and far away from its affluence? If the affluent society itself hardly notices what it is doing, how it is spreading terror and enslavement, how it is fighting liberation in all corners of the globe?[88]

The third limit of modernity is the impossibility of the subsumption of the populations, economies, nations, and cultures that it has been attacking since its origin and has excluded from its horizon and cornered into poverty. This is the theme of the exclusion of African, Asian, and Latin American alterity and their indomitable will to survive. There is more to say on this theme, but for now I want to emphasize that the globalizing world-system reaches a limit with the exteriority of the alterity of the Other, a locus of "resistance" from whose affirmation the process of the negation of negation of liberation begins.

Translated by Eduardo Mendieta

Notes

This essay is part of chapter 2 of *Etica de la Liberacion* (Ethics of liberation), a work in progress.

1 As a "substance" that is invented in Europe and that subsequently "expands" throughout the entire world. This is a metaphysical-substantialist and "diffusionist" thesis. It contains a "reductionist fallacy."

2 The English translation is not adequate to the expression Weber uses, "Auf dem Boden," which means *within* its regional horizon. We want to establish that "in Europe" really means the development in modernity of Europe as the "center" of a "global system," and not as an *independent* system, as if "only-from-within itself" and as the result of a solely *internal* development, as Eurocentrism pretends.

3 This "we" is precisely the Eurocentric Europeans.

4 Max Weber, *The Protestant Ethic and the Spirit of Capitalism,* trans. Talcott Parsons (New York, 1958), 13; emphasis added. Later on Weber asks: "Why did not the scientific, the artistic, the political, or the economic development there [in China and India] enter upon that path of *rationalization* which is peculiar to the Occident?" (25). To argue this, Weber juxtaposes the Babylonians, who did not mathematize astronomy, and the Greeks, who did (but Weber does not know that the Greeks learned it from the Egyptians); he also argues that science

emerged in the West, but not in India or China or elsewhere, but he forgets to mention the Muslim world, from whom the Latin West learned Aristotelian "experiential," empirical exactitude (such as the Oxford Franciscans, or the Marcilios de Padua, etc.), and so on. Every Hellenistic, or Eurocentric, argument, such as Weber's, can be falsified if we take 1492 as the ultimate date of comparison between the supposed superiority of the West and other cultures.

5   Georg Wilhelm Friedrich Hegel, *The Philosophy of History,* trans. J. Sibree (New York, 1956), 341.

6   Following Hegel, in Jürgen Habermas, *Der philosophische Diskurs der Moderne* (Frankfurt, 1988), 27.

7   The world-system or planetary system of the fourth stage of the same interregional system of the Asiatic-African-Mediterranean continent, but now—correcting Frank's conceptualization—factually "planetary." See André Gunder Frank, "A Theoretical Introduction to 5000 Years of World System History," *Review* 13, no. 2 (1990): 155–248. On the world-system problematic, see Janet Abu-Lughod, *Before European Hegemony: The World System A.D. 1250–1350* (New York, 1989); Robert Brenner, "Das Weltsystem: Theoretische und Historische Perspektiven," in *Perspektiven des Weltsystems,* ed. J. Blaschke (Frankfurt, 1983), 80–111; Marshall Hodgson, *The Venture of Islam* (Chicago, 1974); Paul Kennedy, *The Rise and Fall of the Great Powers* (New York, 1987); William McNeil, *The Rise of the West* (Chicago, 1964); George Modelski, *Long Cycles in World Politics* (London, 1987); Michael Mann, *The Sources of Social Power: A History of Power from the Beginning to A.D. 1760* (Cambridge, UK, 1986); L. S. Stavarianos, *The World to 1500: A Global History* (Englewood Cliffs, NJ, 1970); William Thompson, *On Global War: Historical-Structural Approaches to World Politics* (Columbia, SC, 1989); Charles Tilly, *Big Structures, Large Processes* (New York, 1984); Immanuel Wallerstein, *The Modern World-System* (New York, 1974); Immanuel Wallerstein, *The Politics of the World-Economy* (Cambridge, UK, 1984).

8   On this point, as I already mentioned, I am not in agreement with Frank on including in the world-system the prior moments of the system, which I call interregional systems.

9   Wallerstein, *Modern World-System,* chap. 6.

10 Ibid., chaps. 4, 5.

11 Ibid., chap. 3.

12 See Owen Lattimore, *Inner Asian Frontiers of China* (Boston, 1962), and Morris Rossabi, ed., *China among Equals: The Middle Kingdom and Its Neighbors, 10th–14th Centuries* (Berkeley, 1983). For a description of the situation of the world in 1400, see Eric Wolf, *Europe and the People without History* (Berkeley, 1982).

13 In the museum of Masamba, a port city of Kenya, I have seen Chinese porcelain, as well as luxurious watches and other objects of similar origin.

14 There are other reasons for this nonexternal expansion: the existence of "space" in the neighboring territories of the empire, which needed all its power to "conquer the South" through the cultivation of rice and its defense from the "barbarian

North." See Wallerstein, *Modern World-System*, 24, which has many good arguments against Weber's Eurocentrisms.

15 For example, see the following works by Joseph Needham: "The Chinese Contributions to Vessel Control," *Science* 98 (1961): 163–168; "Commentary on Lynn White's *What Accelerated Technological Change in the Western Middle Ages?*," in *Scientific Change*, ed. A. C. Crombie (New York, 1963), 117–153; and "Les contributions chinoises à l'art de gouverner les navires," *Colloque International d'Histoire Maritime* (Paris, 1966): 113–134. All of these discuss the control of shipping, which the Chinese had dominated since the first century after Christ. The Chinese use of the compass, paper, gunpowder, and other discoveries is well-known.

16 Perhaps the only disadvantages were the Portuguese caravel (invented in 1441), used to navigate the Atlantic (but which was not needed in the Indian Ocean), and the cannon, which, although spectacular, outside naval wars never had any real effect in Asia until the nineteenth century. Carlo Cipolla, in *Guns and Sails in the Early Phase of European Expansion, 1400–1700* (London, 1965), 106–107, writes: "Chinese fire-arms were at least as good as the Western, if not better."

17 The first bureaucracy (as the Weberian high stage of political rationalization) is the state mandarin structure of political exercise. The mandarin are not nobles, or warriors, or aristocratic or commercial plutocracy; they are *strictly* a bureaucratic elite whose examination system is *exclusively* based on the dominion of culture and the laws of the Chinese empire.

18 William de Bary indicates that the individualism of Wang Yang-ming, in the fifteenth century, which expressed the ideology of the bureaucratic class, was as advanced as that of the Renaissance (*Self and Society in Ming Thought* [New York, 1970]).

19 Through many examples, Thomas Kuhn in *The Structure of Scientific Revolutions* (Chicago, 1962) situates the modern scientific revolution, fruit of the expression of the new paradigm, practically with Newton (seventeenth century). He does not study with care the impact that events such as the discovery of America, the roundness of the earth (empirically proved since 1520), and others could have had on the science, the "scientific community," of the sixteenth century, since the structuration of the first world-system.

20 Needham, "Commentary on Lynn White," 139.

21 A. R. Hall places the beginning of the scientific revolution in the 1500s (*The Scientific Revolution* [London, 1954]).

22 Pierre Chaunu, *Séville et l'Atlantique (1504–1650)* (Paris, 1955), 50.

23 *Factually*, Columbus will be the first Modern, but not *existentially* (because his *interpretation of the world* remained always that of a Renaissance Genoese: a member of a peripheral Italy of the third interregional system). See Paolo Emilio Taviani, *Cristoforo Colombo: La genesi della scoperta* (Novara, 1982), and Edmundo O'Gorman, *La Invención de América* (Mexico, 1957).

24 See J. Zunzunegi, "Los orígenes de las misiones en las Islas Canarias," *Revista Española de Teología* 1 (1941): 364–370.

25   Russia was not yet integrated as periphery in the third stage of the interregional system (nor in the modern world-system, except until the eighteenth century with Peter the Great and the founding of St. Petersburg on the Baltic).

26   Already in 1095 Portugal had the rank of empire. In Algarve in 1249, the reconquest concluded with this empire. Enrique the Navigator (1394–1460) as patron introduced the sciences of cartography and astronomy and the techniques of navigation and shipbuilding, which originated in the Muslim world (he had contact with the Moroccans) and the Italian Renaissance (via Genoa).

27   Wallerstein, *Modern World-System,* 49–50. See also Charles Verlinden, "Italian Influence in Iberian Colonization," *Hispanic Historical Review* 18, no. 2 (1953): 119–209, and Virginia Rau, "A Family of Italian Merchants in Portugal," in *Studies in Honor of Armando Sapori,* ed. C. Cisalpino (Milan, 1957), 715–726.

28   See K. N. Chaudhuri, *Trade and Civilisation in the Indian Ocean: An Economic History from the Rise of Islam to 1750* (Cambridge, UK, 1985).

29   My argument would seem to be the same as in J. M. Blaut, ed., *1492: The Debate on Colonialism, Eurocentrism, and History* (Trenton, NJ, 1992), 28, but in fact it is different. It is not that Spain was "geographically" closer to Amerindia: distance was only one criterion. Spain had to go *through* Amerindia not only because it was closer, but because this was the necessary route to the center of the system, a point that Blaut does not deal with. Gunder Frank (in Blaut, *1492,* 65–80) makes the same error, because for him 1492 represents only a secondary, internal change in the same world-system. However, if it is understood that the interregional system, in its stage prior to 1492, is the "same" system but not yet a "world" system, then 1492 assumes a greater importance than Frank grants it. Even if the system *is the same,* there exists a qualitative jump, which, in other respects, is the origin of capitalism proper, to which Frank denies importance because of his prior denial of relevance to concepts such as *value* and *surplus value;* in fact, he equates *capital* with *wealth* (use-value with a virtual possibility of transforming itself into exchange-value, but not capital accumulated in stages 1 through 3 of the interregional system). This is a grave theoretical error.

30   Enrique Dussel, *The Invention of the Americas* (New York, 1995).

31   See ibid., appendix 4, where the map of the fourth Asiatic peninsula is reproduced (after the Arabian, Indian, and Malaccan), certainly a product of Genoese navigations, where South America is a peninsula attached to the south of China. This explains why the Genoese Columbus would hold the opinion that Asia would not be so far from Europe (South America = fourth peninsula of China).

32   This is what I call, philosophically, the "invention" of Amerindia seen as India, in all of its details. Columbus, existentially, neither "discovered" nor reached Amerindia. He "invented" something that was nonexistent: India in the place of Amerindia, which prevented him from "discovering" what was in front of him. See ibid., chap. 2.

33   This is the meaning of the title of chapter 2, "From the *Invention* to the *Discovery* of America," in my *Invention of the Americas.*

34 See Samir Amin, *L'accumulation à l'échelle mondiale* (Paris, 1970). This work is not yet developed on the world-system hypothesis. It would appear as though the colonial world were a *rear* or *subsequent* and *outside* space to European medieval capitalism, which is transformed "in" Europe as modern. My hypothesis is more radical: the fact of the discovery of Amerindia, of its integration as periphery, is a *simultaneous* and *coconstitutive* fact of the restructuration of Europe *from within* as center of the only new world-system that is, only now and *not before,* capitalism (first mercantile and later industrial).

35 I refer to Amerindia, and not America, because during the entire sixteenth century, the inhabitants of the continent were thought to be "Indians" (wrongly called because of the mirage that the interregional system of the third stage still produced in the still-being-born world-system. They were called Indians because of India, center of the interregional system that was beginning to fade). Anglo-Saxon North America will be born slowly in the seventeenth century, but it will be an event "internal" to a growing modernity in Amerindia. This is the *originating* periphery of modernity, constitutive of its first definition. It is the "other face" of the very same phenomenon of modernity.

36 Unified by the marriage of the Catholic king and queen in 1474, who immediately founded the Inquisition (the first ideological apparatus of the state for the creation of consensus); by a bureaucracy whose functioning is attested to in the archives of the Indies (Sevilla), where everything was declared, contracted, certified, archived; by a grammar of the Spanish language (the first national language in Europe), written by Nebrija, who in his prologue warns the Catholic kings of the importance for the empire of *only one language;* by Cisneros's edition of the Complutensian Polyglot Bible (in seven languages), which was superior to Erasmus's because of its scientific care, the number of its languages, and the quality of the imprint, begun in 1502 and published in 1522; by military power that allowed it to recoup Granada in 1492; by the economic wealth of the Jews, Andalusian Muslims, Christians of the reconquest, the Catalans with their colonies in the Mediterranean, and the Genoese; by the artisans from the antique caliphate of Cordoba, and so on. Spain in the fifteenth century is far from being the semiperipheral country that it will become in the second part of the seventeenth century—the only picture of Spain with which the Europe of the center remembers it, as Hegel or Habermas do, for example.

37 The struggle between France and the Spain of Charles V, which exhausted both monarchies and resulted in the economic collapse of 1557, was played out above all in Italy. Charles V possessed about three-fourths of the peninsula, allowing Spain to transfer through Italy to its own soil the links with the system. This was one of the reasons for all the wars with France: for the wealth and the experience of centuries were essential for whoever intended to exercise new hegemony in the system, especially if it was the first planetary hegemony.

38 This produced an unprecedented increase of prices in Europe, which was convergent with an inflation of 1000 percent during the sixteenth century. Externally

this will liquidate the wealth accumulated in the Turkish-Muslim world, and will even transform India and China internally (see Earl Hamilton, *El florecimiento del capitalismo y otros ensayos de historia económica* [Madrid, 1948]; Earl Hamilton, *International Congress of Historical Sciences* [Stockholm, 1960], 144–164; and D. Ingrid Hammarström, "The *Price Revolution* of the Sixteenth Century," *Scandinavian Economic History* 1 [1957]: 118–154). Furthermore, the arrival of Amerindian gold produced a complete continental hecatomb of Bantu Africa because of the collapse of the kingdoms of the sub-Saharan savannah (Ghana, Togo, Dahomey, Nigeria, etc.) that exported gold to the Mediterranean. To survive, these kingdoms increased the selling of slaves to the new European powers of the Atlantic, with which American slavery was produced. See Pierre Bertaux, *Africa: Desde la prehistoria hasta los Estados actuales* (Madrid, 1972); V. M. Godinho, "Création et dynamisme économique du monde atlantique (1420–1670)," *Annales ESC* (1950): 10–30; Pierre Chaunu, *Séville et l'Atlantique (1504–1650)* (Paris, 1955), 57; F. Braudel, "Monnaies et civilisation: De l'or du Soudan à l'argent d'Amérique," *Annales ESC* (1946): 12–38. The whole ancient third interregional system is absorbed slowly by the modern world-system.

39 All of the subsequent hegemonic power will remain until the present on their shores: Spain, Holland, England (and France partly) until 1945, and the United States in the present. Thanks to Japan, China, and California in the United States, the Pacific appears for the first time as a counterweight. This is perhaps a novelty of the next century, the twenty-first.

40 Wallerstein, *Modern World-System*, 45.

41 This is the entrance to the mine.

42 For the past thirty years this text has kept me alert to the phenomenon of the fetishism of gold, of "money," and of "capital." See Enrique Dussel, *Las metáforas teológicas de Marx* (Estella, Spain, 1993).

43 *Archivo General de Indias* (Seville), 313. See also Enrique Dussel, *Les évêques latinoaméricains defenseurs et evangelisateurs de l'indien (1504–1620)* (Wiesbaden, 1970), 1, which was part of my doctoral thesis at the Sorbonne in 1967.

44 Wallerstein, *Modern World-System*, 165.

45 It should be remembered that Spinoza (Espinosa), who lived in Amsterdam (1632–1677), descended from an Ashkenazi family from the Muslim world of Granada, who were expelled from Spain and exiled to the Spanish colony of Flanders.

46 Wallerstein, *Modern World-System*, 214.

47 Ibid., chap. 2, "Dutch Hegemony in the World-Economy," where he writes: "It follows that there is probably only a short moment in time when a given core power can manifest *simultaneously* productive, commercial, and financial superiority *over all other core powers*. This momentary summit is what we call hegemony. In the case of Holland, or the United Provinces, that moment was probably between 1625–1675" (39). Not only Descartes, but also Spinoza, as we already indicated, constitute the philosophical presence of Amsterdam, world center of

the system (and—why not?—of the self-consciousness of humanity *in its center,* which is not the same as a mere *European* self-consciousness).

48 See ibid., chap. 6. After this date, British hegemony will be uninterrupted, except in the Napoleanic period, until 1945, when it loses to the United States.

49 See Pierre Chaunu, *Conquête et exploitation des nouveaux mondes (XVIe siècle)* (Paris, 1969), 119–176.

50 Europe had approximately 56 million inhabitants in 1500, and 82 million in 1600 (see C. Cardoso, *Historia económica de América Latina* [Barcelona, 1979], 114).

51 Wallerstein, *Modern World-System,* 103.

52 See Samir Amin, *El desarrollo desigual: Ensayo sobre las formaciones sociales del capitalismo periférico* (Barcelona, 1974), 309.

53 Ibid., 312.

54 The colonial process in Latin America ends, for the most part, at the beginning of the nineteenth century.

55 The colonial process of these formations ends, for the most part, after the so-called World War II (1945), given that the North American superpower requires neither military occupation nor political-bureaucratic domination (proper only to the old European powers, such as France and England), but rather the management of the dominion of economic-financial dependence in its transnational stage.

56 *Muslim* here means the most "cultured" and civilized of the fifteenth century.

57 I think that *management* of the new world-system according to old practices had to fail because it operated with variables that made the system unmanageable. Modernity *had begun,* but it had not given itself a new way to manage the system.

58 Later on, it will also have to manage the system of the English island. Both nations had limited territories, with small populations in the beginning, without any other capacity than their creative "bourgeois attitude" to existence. Because of their weakness, they had to greatly reform the management of the planetary metropolitan enterprise.

59 The technical "factibility" will become a criterion of truth, of possibility, of existence; Vico's "verum et *factum* conventuntur."

60 Spain, and Portugal with Brazil, undertook as states (world empire) (with military, bureaucratic, and ecclessiastical resources, etc.) the conquest, evangelization, and colonization of Amerindia. Holland, instead, founded the East India Company (1602), and later that of the "Western Indies." These companies (as well as the subsequent British, Danish, etc.) are capitalist enterprises, secularized and private, which function according to the "rationalization" of mercantilism (and later of industrial capitalism). This highlights the difference between the rational management of the Iberian companies and the management of the second modernity (a world-system not managed by a world empire).

61 In every system, complexity is accompanied by a process of "selection" of elements that allow, in the face of increase in such complexity, for the conservation of the "unity" of the system with respect to its surroundings. This necessity of

selection-simplification is always a "risk" (see Niklas Luhmann, *Soziale Systeme: Grundriss einer algemeinen Theorie* [Frankfurt, 1988]).

62 See Dussel, *The Invention of the Americas,* chap. 5. During the sixteenth century there were three theoretical positions before the fact of the constitution of the world-system: (1) that of Gines de Sepulveda, the *modern* Renaissance and humanist scholar, who rereads Aristotle and demonstrates the natural slavery of the Amerindian, and thus confirms the legitimacy of the conquest; (2) that of the Franciscans, such as Mendieta, who attempt a utopian Amerindian Christianity (a "republic of Indians" under the hegemony of the Catholic religion), proper to the third Christian-Muslim interregional system; and (3) Bartolomé de las Casas's position, *the beginning of a critical "counterdiscourse" in the interior of modernity* (which, in his work of 1536, a century before *Le Discours de la Méthode,* he titles *De unico modo* [The only way], and shows that "argumentation" is the rational means through which to attract the Amerindian to the new civilization). Habermas speaks of "counterdiscourse," suggesting that it is only two centuries old (beginning with Kant). Liberation philosophy suggests, instead, that this counterdiscourse begins in the sixteenth century, perhaps in 1511 in Santo Domingo with Anton de Montesinos, decidedly with Bartolomé de las Casas in 1514 (see Dussel, *The Invention of the Americas,* 17–27).

63 Bartolomé de las Casas, *The Devastation of the Indies: A Brief Account,* trans. Herma Briffault (Baltimore, 1992), 31. I have placed this text at the beginning of volume 1 of my work *Para una ética de la liberación latinoamericana* (Buenos Aires, 1973), because it synthesizes the general hypothesis of the ethics of liberation.

64 Frequently, in the contemporary histories of philosophy, and of course of ethics, a "jump" is made from the Greeks (from Plato and Aristotle) to Descartes (1596–1650), who takes up residence in Amsterdam in 1629 and writes *Le Discours de la Méthode,* as we indicated above. That is, there is a jump from Greece to Amsterdam. In the interim, twenty-one centuries have gone by without any other content of importance. Studies are begun by Bacon (1561–1626), Kepler (1571–1630), Galileo (1571–1630), and Newton (1643–1727), and Campanella writes *Civitas Solis* in 1602. Everything would seem to be situated at the beginning of the seventeenth century, the moment I have called the second moment of modernity.

65 See Werner Sombart, *Der moderne Kapitalismus* (Leipzig, 1902), and W. Sombart, *Der Bourgeois* (Munich, 1920).

66 See Ernst Troeltsch, *Die Soziallehren der christlichen Kirchen und Gruppen* (Tübingen, 1923).

67 See Jürgen Habermas, *Theorie des kommunikativen Handelns* (Frankfurt, 1981). Habermas insists on the Weberian discovery of "rationalization," but he forgets to ask after its cause. I believe that my hypothesis goes deeper and further back: Weberian rationalization (accepted by Habermas, Apel, Lyotard, etc.) is the apparently necessary mediation of a deforming simplification (by instrumental reason) of practical reality, in order to transform it into something "manageable,"

governable, given the complexity of the immense world-system. It is not only the internal manageability of Europe, but also, and above all, *planetary* (center-periphery) management. Habermas's attempt to sublate instrumental reason into communicative reason is not sufficient because the moments of his diagnosis on the *origin itself of the process of rationalization* are not sufficient.

68 The postmoderns, being Eurocentric, concur, more or less, with the Weberian diagnosis of modernity. That is, they underscore certain rationalizing aspects or media (means of communication, etc.) of modernity; some they reject wrathfully as metaphysical dogmatisms, but others they accept as inevitable phenomena and frequently as positive transformations.

69 René Descartes, *Le Discours de la Méthode* (Paris, 1965).

70 See Enrique Dussel, *El dualismo en la antropología de la Cristiandad* (Buenos Aires, 1974), and Enrique Dussel, *Método para una Filosofía de la Liberación* (Salamanca, 1974). Current theories of the functions of the brain definitively put in question this dualistic mechanism.

71 Immanual Kant, *Kants Werke* (Darmstadt, 1968), 940.

72 Stillman Drake, *Discoveries and Opinions of Galileo* (New York, 1957), 237–238.

73 See Enrique Dussel, *Para una de-strucción de la historia de la ética* (Mendoza, 1973).

74 Martin Heidegger, *What Is a Thing?*, trans. W. B. Barton (Chicago, 1967), 73.

75 See Martin Bernal, *Black Athena: The Afroasiatic Roots of Classical Civilization* (New Brunswick, NJ, 1989), 224.

76 Amerindia and Europe have a premodern history, just as Africa and Asia do. Only the hybrid world, the syncretic culture, the Latin American *mestiza* race that was born in the fifteenth century has existed for 500 years; the child of Malinche and Hernán Cortés can be considered as its symbol. See Octavio Paz, *El laberinto de la soledad* (Mexico City, 1950).

77 See, among others, Jean-François Lyotard, *La condition postmoderne* (Paris, 1979); Richard Rorty, *Philosophy and the Mirror of Nature* (Princeton, NJ, 1979); Jacques Derrida, "*Violence et métaphysique,* essai sur la pensée d'Emmanuel Levinas," *Revue de Métaphysique et Morale* 69, no. 3 (1964): 322–354; Jacques Derrida, *L'Ecriture et la Différence* (Paris, 1967), and *De la Grammatologie* (Paris, 1967); Odo Marquart, *Abschied vom Prinzipiellen* (Stuttgart, 1981); Gianni Vattimo, *La fine della Modernità* (Milan, 1985).

78 This Spanish word, *desarrollismo,* which does not exist in other languages, points to the fallacy that pretends the same development (the word *Entwicklung* has a strictly Hegelian philosophical origin) for the center as for the periphery, not taking note that the periphery is not *backward* (see Franz Hinkelammert, *Ideologías del desarrollo y dialéctica de la historia* [Santiago, 1970], and his *Dialéctica del desarrollo desigual: El caso latinoamericano* [Santiago, 1970]). In other words, it is not a temporal *prius* that awaits a development similar to that of Europe or the United States (like the child/adult), but instead it is the asymmetrical position of the dominated, the *simultaneous* position of the exploited (like the free lord/

slave). The "immature" (child) could follow the path of the "mature" (adult) and get to "develop" herself, while the "exploited" (slave), no matter how much she works, will never be "free" (lord), because her own dominated subjectivity includes her "relationship" with the dominator. The "modernizers" of the periphery are developmentalists because they do not realize that the relationship of planetary domination has to be overcome as a prerequisite for "*national* development." Globalization has not extinguished, not by the least, the "national" question.

79 See Habermas, *Theorie des kommunikativen Handelns,* along with his debates with P. Winch and A. MacIntyre.

80 We will see that Levinas, the "father of French postmodernism" (from Derrida on), neither is postmodern nor negates reason. Instead, he is a critic of the *totalization* of reason (instrumental, strategic, cynical, ontological, etc.). Liberation philosophy, since the end of the decade of the 1960s, studied Levinas because of his radical critique of domination. In the preface to my work, *Philosophy of Liberation* (New York, 1985), I indicated that the philosophy of liberation is a "postmodern" philosophy, one that took its point of departure from the "second Heidegger," but also from the critique of "*totalized* reason" carried out by Marcuse and Levinas. It would seem as though we were "postmoderns" *avant la lettre.* In fact, however, we are critics of ontology and modernity from (*desde*) the periphery, which meant and *still* means something entirely different, as we intend to explain.

81 Up to now, the postmoderns remain Eurocentric. The dialogue with "different" cultures is, for now, an unfulfilled promise. They think that mass culture, the *media* (television, movies, etc.), will impact peripheral urban cultures to the extent that they will annihilate their "differences," in such a way that what Vattimo sees in Turin, or Lyotard in Paris, will be shortly the same in New Delhi and Nairobi; and they do not take the time to analyze the *hard* irreducibility of the hybrid cultural horizon (which is not *absolutely* an exteriority, but which for centuries will not be a univocal interiority to the globalized system) that receives those information impacts.

82 See Fredric Jameson, *Postmodernism, or, The Cultural Logic of Late Capitalism* (Durham, NC, 1991).

83 In Stalinist "actually existing" socialism, the criterion was the "increase in the rate of production," measured, in any event, by an approximate market value of commodities. It is a question at the same time of fetishism. See F. Hinkelammert, *Crítica a la razón utópica* (San José, Costa Rica, 1984), 123.

84 Karl Marx, *Grundrisse,* trans. Martin Nicolaus (New York, 1973), 410.

85 Ibid.

86 Pure necessity without money is no market, it is only misery, growing and unavoidable misery.

87 Karl Marx, *Capital* (New York, 1977), 799. Here we must remember that the *Human Development Report, 1992* (New York, 1992) has demonstrated in an

incontrovertible manner that the richest 20 percent of the planet consumes today (as never before in global history) 82.7 percent of goods (incomes) of the planet, while the remaining 80 percent of humanity only consumes 17.3 percent of the goods. Such concentration is the product of the world-system we have been delineating.

88 Herbert Marcuse, "Liberation from the Affluent Society," in *To Free a Generation: The Dialectics of Liberation,* ed. David Cooper (New York, 1967), 181.

Walter D. Mignolo

Globalization, Civilization Processes,

and the Relocation of Languages and Cultures

1

Globalization, in transnational corporate lingo, is conceived as the last of three stages of global transformation since 1945. In a more sociohistorical vocabulary, globalization could be linked with Western expansion since 1500 and cast in terms of either Immanuel Wallerstein's world-system[1] or in Norbert Elias's "civilizing process."[2] Whereas Wallerstein's model allows for a rereading of modernity as a global economic system (see Dussel in this volume), Elias's research tells the story of a growing awareness in the emerging European consciousness of its mission to Christianize and civilize the world. The very self-description by European intellectuals of the notion of "civilization," which will become then the foundation of the colonial "civilizing mission," is basically a construction of the European Enlightenment. However, the general idea (as Elias amply demonstrates) is already at work in the European Renaissance. It is a paradoxically and highly ethnocentric move, indeed, to assume that from 1500 Europe has to civilize the world, when other civilizations (such as the Chinese, Indian, Islamic, Incan, Aztec, and Mayan) have been in place, so to speak, for centuries before a group of ascending barbarous communities began to posit themselves as a new center (which for them was the center) of the world, in the name of Christianity and of Europe.[3] The very concept of "civilization" gained a universal scope once Europe began to expand all over the planet and, as such, repressed the already existing self-conceptualization of highly sophisticated social organizations (e.g., China, the Islamic world, Inca, and Mexico). "Civilization" then became a trademark of Christian Europe and a yardstick by which to measure other societies. The comparison was, on the one hand, a series of forced understanding and, on the other, a justification to carry and implant civilization in the rest of the planet, which had been declared either lacking some properties or having them in excess. It will take us too far away from the topic to describe the equivalent of the European notion of "civilization" among communities that much earlier reached the level of social sophistication that Elias describes as the European "civilizing process."

When in 1959, for example, J. Needham and L. Wang published their monumental *Science and Civilization in China,* they were still writing within the double bind of the very concept of "civilization": on the one hand, something that belonged to Europe as a treasure that shall be enjoyed by the entire planet; on the other hand, "civilization" was something that other cultures and communities had as an "object" to be studied by those who not only invented the idea of the "civilizing mission" but also, and concomitant with it, a discipline called "civilizational studies." "Civilization" then has a double edge: the ideological justification of European economic expansion and the foundation of a field of study that located Europe as the locus of enunciation and other civilizations of the planet as the locus of the enunciated. In what follows, I will first explore the complicities between the conception of languages and literatures, the boundaries of the humanities and the cultures of scholarship in the past five hundred years, a period we identify as modernity and also as globalization enacted in the very constitution and expansion of the Western world-system (see Dussel in this volume). In this process, Latin American independence from Spain and Portugal, in the nineteenth century, created the conditions for the articulation—in the very process of nation-building—of the dichotomy civilization/barbarism (*Facundo: Civilization and Barbarism,* 1845, by Domingo Faustino Sarmiento, Argentinian intellectual and later president, 1872–78). Sarmiento's formula became a canonical figure of Latin American culture and, at the same time, a justification for internal colonialism. Second, I will make an effort to identify the instances where the civilizing mission began to crack and the oppositions civilization/barbarism, first world/third world, and developed/undeveloped are superseded by the self-relocation and restitution of thinking and theorizing within and by barbarians, third-world people, the underdeveloped, women, and people of color. I will close by exploring the significance of Brazilian "anthropologian" (*antropologador,* as he calls himself) Darcy Ribeiro's work, mainly in two of his books: *O processo civilizatorio* (1968) and *Las Américas y la civilización* (1969). I will propose that these two books are a displacement of Elias's concept of "civilizing process" and Sarmiento's internal colonialist version of the civilizing mission as well as of the connivance between disciplinary foundations and colonial powers (mainly in the case of anthropology). Elias describes the differences in the use of "civilization" first in England and France to indicate a sense of national pride and then in Germany, where the same feeling was expressed by the word *culture.* Furthermore, "civilization" is self-conceived as a process, and "culture," a product. "Civilization" can be carried and expanded all over the planet, but not "culture." This distinction was dramatic for intellectuals of the colonized world, such as Sarmiento in Argentina, who assumed that the local culture had to be improved by the growing and expanding European civilization.

The distinction between civilization and culture, as process and product, contributed to the internal colonialism enacted by intellectuals from colonized areas who fought against the "barbarism" of their culture in pro of the European civilization. The current relocation of languages and cultures in the last stage of globalization is contributing to redress and rearticulate a distinction that for centuries worked out so well that it was even supported by intellectuals in the periphery who were being self-colonized in the name of self-determination. Darcy Ribeiro's work—as we shall see at the end of this article (as well as in Dussel in this volume)—sets the stage for a decentering of theoretical practice and its foundation in local histories.[4] More recently, the publication in extended version and in book form of Samuel P. Huntington's *The Clash of Civilizations and the Remaking of World Order*[5] has located the debate in the context of globalization. The following section addresses, from a different perspective, Huntington's analysis of languages, cultures and globalization.

2

A few decades before the emergence of an unknown (from the perspective of European observers) continent and unknown people inhabiting it, geographical boundaries coincided with the boundaries of humanity. Outlandish creatures with two heads, three arms, and the like, were supposed to inhabit that region beyond known geographical boundaries. The limits of geography coincided with the limits of humanity. In a matter of two or three decades, however, both boundaries (of the world and of humanity) began to be transformed radically. The outlandish creatures once inhabiting the unknown corners of the world were replaced by the savages (or cannibals) inhabiting the New World. Geographical boundaries and the boundaries of humanity were relocated by both the transformation of knowledge generated through cross-cultural interactions among people who until then had been unaware of one another, as well as by the growing awareness of the earth's expansion beyond the limits of the known. The cannibals and the savages were located in a space that began to be conceived as a New World (figure 1).

Toward the end of the nineteenth century, however, spatial boundaries were transformed into chronological ones. In the early modern period, a transformation took place between geographical and human boundaries; at the end of the nineteenth century, savages and cannibals in space were converted into primitives and exotic Orientals in time. Whereas the sixteenth century was the scene of a heated debate about the boundaries of humanity—having Las Casas, Sepulveda, and Victoria as main characters in that controversy—toward the nineteenth century the question was no longer whether primitives or Orientals were human but, rather, how far removed from the present and civilized stage of humanity they were. Lafitau (*Moeurs des sauvages americains comparées aux moeurs des premiers temps*, 1724) has been credited as being one of the landmark thinkers in this process of converting the savages/cannibals into primitives/Orientals and in relocating them in a chronological scale as opposed to a geographical distance. The "denial of coevalness"[6] was the end result of relocating people in a chronological hierarchy rather than in geographical places. The relocation of languages, peoples, and cultures in time rather than in space, found in Hegel's *Philosophy of History* (1822), its most systematic formulation, had not been contested until the past fifty years by intellectuals engaged with the movements of liberation

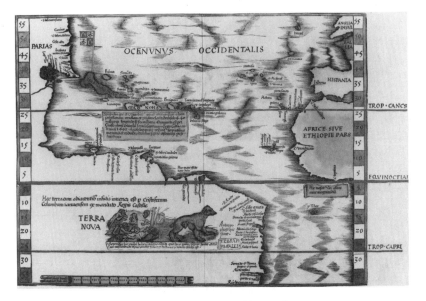

Figure 1. *Tabula Terre Nova* (1513) by Martin Waldseemüller

and decolonization. Today, Hegel's *Philosophy of History* is a common reference for intellectuals in / from Africa, Asia, Latin America, and the Caribbean, writing to cast out Hegel's arrangements of cultural differences in a time frame having the European idea of civilization and Western Europe as a point of arrival. The current stage of globalization, driven by transnational corporations, is nonintentionally contributing to the restitution of space and location and to the multiplication of local histories. That is, the current stage of globalization and its emphasis on the market is contributing to the denial of the denial of coevalness, a strategic principle of the three previous stages of globalization under the banners of Christianization (Spanish Empire), Civilizing Mission (British Empire and French Colonization), and Development / Modernization (U.S. Imperialism).

The denial of the denial of coevalness, as a project and a desire for intellectual decolonization, today has to confront the new version of the savages, cannibals, and primitives of yesterday, recast in terms of the underdeveloped. Although savages / cannibals were people to be converted to Christianity, primitives to be Civilized and Orientals to be Westernized, Underdeveloped people instead have to be Modernized. Progress and Modernity replaced the Christian mission of Spain and Portugal, the civilizing mission of France and

England, and became the new goal of the U.S. imperial version of previous colonialisms. However, old ideas and prejudices did not vanish: they survive in the present, recast in a new vocabulary. The three stages of globalization enacted by Western expansion previous to the transnational and global marketplace that I am presupposing here are not to be seen in a Hegelian linear chronology but, rather, in a spatial coexistence of memory (see below), and as diachronic contradictions. Paradoxically, the last stage of globalization (transnational corporations [TNCs] and technoglobalism) is creating the conditions to think spatially rather than chronologically. Spatialization brings to the foreground the fact that there are no people in the present living in the past (as the Hegelian model of universal history proposed), but that the present is a variety of chronological circles and temporal rhythms. Thus, economic globalization is facilitating the intellectual task of denying the denial of coevalness, in the removal of the civilizing mission and in the conceptualization of the civilizing process as one to which the entire humanity contributed and is contributing.

The links between languages and the boundaries of humanity shaped the idea of literature, cultures of scholarship, and civilization in European modernity. Modernity, the period of globalization that today is witnessing a radical transformation, is characterized by and shaped from a particular articulation of languages (English, French, German, Italian), literatures of these languages (with their legacy in Greek and Latin), and cultures of scholarship (mainly in English, French, and German). Italian remains the foundation for Renaissance studies and maintains its clout from its close relation with Latin. Wallerstein has noted about cultures of scholarship that "At least 95 percent of all scholars and all scholarship from the period of 1850 to 1914, and probably even to 1945, originates in five countries: France, Great Britain, the Germanies, the Italies, and the United States. There is a smattering elsewhere, but basically not only does the scholarship come out of these five countries, but most of the scholarship by most scholars is about their own country. . . . This is partly pragmatic, partly social pressure, and partly ideological: *these are the important countries, this is what matters, this is what we should study in order to learn how the world operates.*"[7] In other words, the languages and the scholarship of the countries came from where the civilizing mission spread. Notice that Spain and Portugal are no longer part of the languages and scholarship of the modern European world.

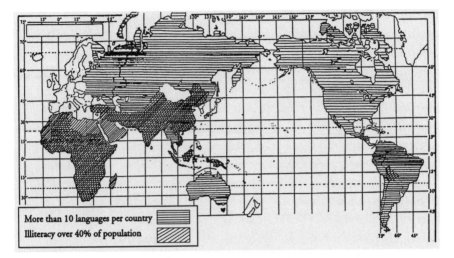

Figure 2. Relationship of illiteracy to countries with more than ten languages
Source: Florian Coulmas, *Linguistic Minorities and Literacy* (Berlin, 1984).

Let's press this issue further by exploring once more the conversion of the
human differences in space into the human differences in time, and by
introducing two new players to the game: languages and literacies, on the one
hand, and the links among the boundaries of humanity, linguistic maps, and
the processes of civilization on the other. The complicities between languages
and the boundaries of humanity have been clear since the beginning of
Western expansion in the early modern period. If we dig into the archives, we
can find similar examples in which languages were taken as one of the foundations upon which to enact identity politics; language served to define
the boundaries of a community by distinguishing it from other communities. The connivance among certain languages, alphabetic writing, and the
boundaries of humanity was not new in the Renaissance/early modern period.[8] What was new was the planetary proportion and the long duration in
which such complicities began to be articulated.

The linguistic map shown in figure 2 will give a better idea of the correlation between geographical locations and theoretical production. First, you
can see the correlation between geocultural and geolinguistic locations of
modernity (white on the map) and the geocultural domains where European
modernity was not relevant or was received (willingly or not), as a foreign
element to be incorporated or resisted from the perspective of vernacular

languages and cultures. Second, you can see (horizontal lines) that the majority of the planet (with the exception of European countries) comprises geocultural areas with more than ten languages each. Although this situation is in the process of being corrected, the fact remains that if European countries were not counted as countries with more than ten languages, it was because imperial and national languages were the only ones to count as such; the rest were counted as dialects. The discourse of the civilizing mission was double-sided: one for nation-building, the other for colonial expansion. The map also shows (diagonal lines) that in most areas of the world (with the exception of European countries), more than 40 percent of the population is illiterate. All sorts of conclusions can be drawn from this statistic. One of them could entail, for instance, celebration of the low illiteracy rate in European countries and the linking of this achievement with the natural intellectual development of the people living in that particular area of the planet, where the agents and the agency of the civilizing mission were located. On the other hand, one could link lower linguistic diversity and lower illiteracy rates in Europe to the process of colonial and global expansion since 1500. This date could also be used to locate the process in which intellectuals living in the part of the planet that began to be self-constructed as Europe, and as a territory where human civilization attained its highest mark, put a heavy premium on the "letter" as a distinctive sign of the concept of civilization that Renaissance and Enlightenment intellectuals forged for themselves:[9] Guizot, for instance, apparently believed and explicitly stated that "civilization" was a pure European phenomenon (*Histoire de la civilization en Europe*, 1828; *Histoire de la civilization en France*, 1830).

Turning now to the complementary statistics in figure 3, we can see that there are about one hundred languages accounting for 95 percent of the world population. Of these one hundred, 75 percent of the world population speaks twelve. Of those twelve, six are colonial and, therefore, the languages of European modernity. Their ranking by quantity of speakers is English, Spanish, German, Portuguese, French, Italian. Chinese is the most spoken language on the planet, above English. Although English enjoys the power of being accompanied and supported by the geocultural location of capitalism during the period of the British Empire and, in the past half-century, in the United States, Spanish, although displaced as a relevant language of modernity (dominated by French, German, and English), has more speakers than French and German. Russian, the second displaced language from European modernity,

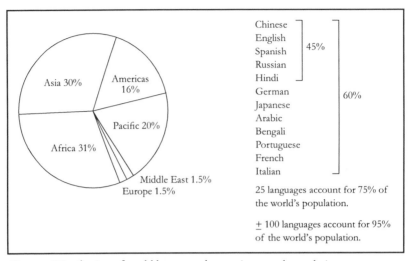

Figure 3. Distribution of world languages by continent and population
Source: Florian Coulmas, *Linguistic Minorities and Literacy* (Berlin, 1984).

managed, nevertheless, to have a marginal presence through literature and has more speakers than German. Hindi is between Russian and German. Finally, Japanese, Arabic, and Bengali are languages whose number of speakers exceeds that of Portuguese, French, and Italian. But that is not all. Globalization and the enactment of the civilizing mission through the agency of colonial languages made it possible for these languages to be spoken far beyond their place of "origin." Thus, the delinking between languages and territories, the double-sided politics of languages (one for the nation, one for the colonies), and, finally, the increasing massive migrations made possible by the very industrial revolution and the means of transportation, reveal the splendors and miseries of the colonial languages: on the one hand, the story of their planetary scope; on the other, the story of their impossible control by their respective academies of national languages. In the meantime, the three languages of high modernity (English, German, French) remain the hegemonic languages of scholarship and world literature. Certainly, well-established languages such as Chinese, Japanese, Arabic, and Hebrew were not suppressed by modern colonial languages, as was the case of less-established ones such as Quechua, Aymara, or Nahuatl, which suffered the impact of Latin and Spanish, supported by the infrastructure of what Darcy Ribeiro called "mercantile empires with a salvation mission" to distinguish Spanish (as well as Portuguese and Russian) empire(s) from "colonial-capitalistic mercantilism" (Holland

Table 1   Speakers of Major Languages (Percentages of World Population*)

Language	1958	1970	1980	1992
Arabic	2.7	2.9	3.3	3.5
Bengali	2.7	2.9	3.2	3.2
English	9.8	9.1	8.7	7.6
Hindi	5.2	5.3	5.3	6.4
Mandarin	15.6	16.6	15.8	15.2
Russian	5.5	5.6	6.0	4.9
Spanish	5.0	5.2	5.5	6.1

*Total number of people speaking languages spoken by 1 million or more people
Source: Samuel P. Huntington, *The Clash of Civilizations and the Remaking of World Order* (New York, 1996). Percentages calculated from data compiled by Professor Sidney S. Culbert, Department of Psychology, University of Washington, Seattle, on the number of people speaking languages spoken by 1 million people or more and reported annually in the *World Almanac and Book of Facts*. His estimates include both "mother-tongue" and "nonmother tongue" speakers and are derived from national censuses, sample surveys of the population, surveys of radio and television broadcasts, population growth data, secondary studies, and other sources.

and England, seventeenth century) and from the "industrial imperialism" enacted by England in the nineteenth century and the United States in the second half of the twentieth century.

Let's now turn toward Huntington's comment on language and civilization in this global era (see tables 1 and 2). Huntington's main argument is to disprove that English is (becoming) a universal language, the language of a unified civilization. He is right to say that when a Korean businessman and a Chinese banker speak in English they are not carrying in that conversation the weight of English/American civilization. Furthermore, there are far more speakers of Mandarin than English speakers. As a matter of fact, the totality of speakers of languages spoken in China is almost equal to the totality of speakers of colonial languages (see table 2). If we add to this the number of speakers of Hindi, Russian, Bengali, and Arabic, the number of speakers of noncolonial languages largely outweighs the number of speakers of colonial languages.

But the question is not so much the number of speakers as it is the hegemonic power of colonial languages in the domain of knowledge, intellectual production, and cultures of scholarship. In the domain of literature, for instance, one can write in English and still add to it the density of Spanish/Latin American memories, as Latino/as are doing in this country.

Table 2   Speakers of Principal Chinese and Western Languages

Language	1958		1992	
	No. of Speakers (in millions)	Percentage of World	No. of Speakers (in millions)	Percentage of World
Mandarin	444	15.6	907	15.2
Cantonese	43	1.5	65	1.1
Wu	39	1.4	64	1.1
Min	36	1.3	50	0.8
Hakka	19	0.7	33	0.6
Chinese languages	581	20.5	1119	18.8
English	278	9.8	456	7.6
Spanish	142	5.0	362	6.1
Portuguese	74	2.6	177	3.0
German	120	4.2	119	2.0
French	70	2.5	123	2.1
Western languages	684	24.1	1237	20.8
World total	2845	44.5	5979	39.4

Source: Samuel P. Huntington, *The Clash of Civilizations and the Remaking of World Order* (New York, 1996). Percentages calculated from language data compiled by Professor Sidney S. Culbert, Department of Psychology, University of Washington, Seattle, and reported in the *World Almanac and Book of Facts* for 1959 and 1993.

English in postpartition India doesn't carry the same memory as national English in Britain; in the same way that English spoken in England by Third World immigrants doesn't carry the same cultural and ideological weight as the King's English. In other words, what the current stage of globalization is enacting is (unconsciously) the uncoupling of the "natural" link between languages and nations, languages and national memories, languages and national literature. Thus, it is creating the condition for and enacting the relocation of languages and the fracture of cultures. Indeed, the very concept of culture (and civilization in Huntington's perspective) is difficult to sustain as homogenous spaces for people of common interests, goals, memories, languages, and beliefs. It is true, as Huntington underlines, that after decolonization "native" languages are gaining ground as they are linked either to state politics or to social movements and in literature. Cultures of scholarship are also being relocated. Thus, if English is becoming the universal language of scholarship, English is not carrying with it the conceptual weight and value of Western scholarship. My contention is that something similar to what happens in literature is happening in cultures of scholarship: a border gnoseology is emerging at the intersection of Western epistemology and non-Western knowledge, characterized as "wisdom" by the former.

In June of 1996 a World Conference on Language Rights took place in Barcelona, Spain, and more than one hundred NGOs attended. One of the main goals of the conference was to approve a universal declaration of language rights, which intends to be a complimentary resolution to the declaration of human rights. The final goal is to have this declaration approved by the OUN. The conference was presided over by Rigoberta Menchú, the well-known Maya-Quiche intellectual and activist from Guatemala. This event, I submit, is the consequence of a radical transformation of those colonial beliefs that linked languages with the boundaries of humanity from the early stages of modernity and globalization. Toward the 1970s, the power of national states began to be eroded by the configuration of transnational economic alliances (the years of OPEC, of Japan entering the world market, the consolidation of the TNC). The weakening of the state was counterbalanced by the strengthening of communities that had been repressed precisely during the years of nation-building and state consolidation. Asia and Africa were the locations of decolonization movements. Latin Americans experienced a revival of indigenous movements for their rights, their lands, their languages.[10] Rigoberta Menchú emerges from these processes. What all this amounts to, among other important consequences, is the clear and forceful articulation of a politics and philosophy of language that supplants the (al)location to which minor languages had been attributed by the philosophy of language underlying the civilizing mission and the politics of language enacted by the state both within the nation[11] and in the colonies.[12]

In Latin America, the increasing influence and internationalization of indigenous organizations[13] had a remarkable impact on the politics of language and education. The rise of what began to be called "new ethnicity" did not emerge all at once, of course. Behind this development there was a long tradition of rebellions, resistances, and adaptations controlled either by colonial or national powers (or both) and omitted in the teaching of national histories, cultures, and national literary practices.[14] Spanish, a subaltern language in the European modernity, became the official and hegemonic language in areas with a dense Amerindian population such as the Andes (Bolivia, Peru,

Ecuador) and Mesoamerica (Mexico, Guatemala). From the point of view of the Amerindian population, languages were critical in maintaining a sense of continuity from colonial times through the nation-building period and up to the end of the twentieth century. The changes witnessed in the 1970s, the emergence of a new Indian consciousness, were propelled by Indians who had been employed by the state, either as community development workers or as schoolteachers. They were looking not only for a new Indian identity but also for the chance to put pressure on those in positions of power and in government in order to influence the future of Indian polity. On the other hand, technological globalization contributed to the process, because indigenous activists and their international supporters could be linked through the web of transnational information networks. One of the paradoxes of globalization is that it allows subaltern communities within the nation-state to create transnational alliances beyond the state to fight for their own social and human rights. The right to have and use languages located in a subaltern position by the discourse of the civilizing mission and the public policy of the state is one of the restitutions claimed under language and human rights. That is, the links between languages and the boundaries of humanity are entering into a process of disintegration whose consequences we may not yet foresee.

Parallel to social movements and the premium placed on the language issue was the emergence of intellectuals of Amerindian descent for whom their "mother tongue" was naturally an Amerindian language (Aymara, Quechua, Maya, Nahuatl). The emergence of a new community of intellectuals in the cultural landscape of Latin America fits Gramsci's description of the "organic intellectual": "Every social group, coming into existence on the original terrain of an essential function in the world of economic production, creates together with itself, organically, one or more strata of intellectuals which give it homogeneity and an awareness of its own function not only in the economic but also in the social and political fields."[15] For historical reasons, related to the history of colonialism itself, intellectuals of Amerindian descent in Latin America do not have the influence in the public spheres that African American or Latino/a intellectuals have in the United States. One area where they have been active and influential is education and in contesting the state ideology regarding language and memories.[16] More than a restitution of an authentic past, the intellectual articulation of history and education shall be understood in the process of nation-building and colonial and imperial world order. To make a long story short, at the end of the nineteenth century, when the institutionalization of national languages was at its height[17] and the cannibals of the early colonial period were converted into the primitives of the era of colonial expansion and the standard of civilization was also stipulated among the major European powers,[18] the civilizing mission and the concept of "civility" became a regulative principle in interstate, imperial, and neocolonial discourses in the Americas.

A case in point is the notion of "frontier" at the end of the century in the United States as well as in Argentina: the frontier was the movable (westward) landmark of the march of the civilizing mission, the line dividing civilization from barbarism. The frontier, however, was not only geographic but epistemologic as well: the location of the primitive and the barbarian was the "vacant land," from the point of view of economy, and the "empty space" of thinking, theory, and intellectual production.[19] As Barran persuasively states it: "The subjugation of the 'barbarian' sensibility was simplified by the fact that it (the barbarian sensibility) was ill-adapted to theorize itself, since theory was precisely its negation. That absence of self-theoretical reflection did not make possible the formation of a 'barbarian' counterculture, consciously programmed. Theory and pre-elaborated plans were, instead, the essence of 'civilization' and their agents were the intellectuals of the new society."[20] Thus, the organic intellectuals of the Amerindian social movements (as well as Latino, African American, and women's) are precisely the main agents of the moment in which "barbarism" appropriates the theoretical practices and elaborated projects, engulfing and superseding the discourse of the civilizing mission and its theoretical foundations. The "frontier of civilization" in the late nineteenth century has become the "borderland" of the end of the twentieth century. Borderlands, contrary to frontiers, are no longer the lines where civilization and barbarism meet and divide, but the location where a new consciousness, a border gnosis, emerges from the repression subjected by the civilizing mission.[21] Border gnosis is not a counterculture, but the denial of the denial of "barbarism"; not a Hegelian synthesis, but the absorption of the "civilizing" principles into the "civilization of barbarism": a "phagocythosis" of civilization by the barbarian (as Argentinian philosopher Rodolfo Kusch will have it), rather than the barbarian bending and entering civilization. It is also an act of "anthropofagia," as Brazilian writer Mario de Andrade and Brazilian poet and literary critic Haroldo de Campos word it. What we are facing here is no longer spaces in between or hybridity, in the convivial images of contact zones, but the forces of "barbarian" theorizing and rationality, to which this paper would like to contribute, integrating and superseding the restrictive logic behind the idea of "civilization" by giving rise to what the civilizing mission suppressed: the self-appropriation of all the good qualities that were denied to the barbarians. "Border gnoseology" (rather than epistemology) in all its complexity (geocultural, sexual, racial, national, diasporic, exilic, etc.) is a new way of thinking that emerges from the sensibilities and conditions of everyday life created by colonial legacies and economic globalization.[22]

At this point I need to come back to Wallerstein's observation about cultures of scholarship between 1850 and 1945 and to the distribution of the scientific labor at the moment of high modernity and capitalist global expansion,[23] and to pursue their transformation after 1945, when the center of the cultures of scholarship began to be relocated in the United States. But before looking at the transformation of scholarly labor after 1945, let's briefly go back to Elias to establish the links between the two periods mentioned above. According to his neo-Marxist model, there is a moment in the evolution of the human species in which the "warrior" and the "man of wisdom" emerged as particular social roles. It is also, according to Elias, when the community became organized and survived on food surplus instead of on production and preservation. If we now make a quantum leap and link the simple version of the model to the danger of nuclear war (Elias's latest concern)[24] and to cultures of scholarship (the topic I am introducing now), we are forced to face once again the complicity between the civilizing mission articulated in colonial discourse and the civilizing process(es) articulated as an object of study of the human sciences in complicity with the ideology of the civilizing mission: that is, a configuration of knowledge whose power consisted in denying epistemological possibilities to the barbarians. Cultures of scholarship were precisely what people outside Europe either lacked (like the Aztecs and the Incas) or, if they happened to possess them (like China, India, and the Islamic world), they became an object of study (e.g., the rise of "Orientalism"). Over the five hundred years of Western expansion and the creation of colleges and universities in colonized areas since the beginning of the sixteenth century, this belief became so strong as to make people doubt their own wisdom, when that wisdom was not articulated in Western educational institutions and languages. When comparative studies of civilization became a prestigious discipline within European research institutions, a distinction was made between civilizations that were converted into objects of study and civilizations that had the necessary frame of mind and cultures of scholarship to be the place from where to study other civilizations. Cultures of scholarship after WWII were recast under these legacies, although they adapted to the new needs of the third stage of globalization.

At the inception of what I have called the third stage of globalization (since 1945), decolonization went hand in hand with the cold war and the division of the world into three ranked areas (first, second, and third worlds). Such a geocultural division also implied a division of scientific and scholarly labor. Once countries were located as being (a) technologically advanced and free of ideological constraints, (b) technologically advanced but encumbered by an ideological elite, preventing utilitarian thinking, and (c) traditionally, economically, and technologically underdeveloped, with a traditional mentality obscuring the possibility of utilitarian and scientific thinking, the loci of scientific and scholarly enunciation were also established. Thus the map of scholarly production between 1850 and 1945 traced by Wallerstein: scholarship was located in Europe and the rest of the world was either the scene of interesting human achievements to study and understand, but frozen in time and antimodern, or of cultures where the civilizing mission had precisely the mission to civilize. The first was the province of civilizational studies (e.g., Orientalism), the second the province of anthropology. The dominant colonial cultures of scholarship were in France, England, and Germany. After 1945, the previous landscape was redressed slightly.

Once the new world order was accepted (first, second, and third worlds), the distribution of scientific labor was reorganized accordingly.[25] *Culture* and no longer *civilization* was the term used to locate a huge area of the planet within the premodern, that is, the third world. The third world became a space, geographic as well as epistemological, where "culture" rather than "science" was produced. The second world had, indeed, achieved a level of technological and scientific status comparable with the first. However, the discourse of universal scientific and scholarly knowledge was produced in the first, underlying the "ideological" shortcoming of the second world, which kept them apart from an ideal neutrality of scientific knowledge, tied up with the political ideal of democracy. Thus, the first world also became the locus of disciplinary and scholarly enterprise that made the second world an object of study. In summary, and according to the scientific division of labor, one group of social scientists was set apart to study the pristine state of under-developed countries and their interactions with the Western world (e.g., the North Atlantic). This task was mainly placed in the hands of anthropologists. Other clans (sociologists, political scientists, and economists) also studied the third world in its process of modernization and contributed to setting guide-lines to modernize (instead of Christianize or civilize) backward countries, although the main province of this group of social scientists remained in the self-study of the first world and no longer in specific countries. Wallerstein's dictum about the social sciences between 1850 and 1914 can be recast in the new world order after 1945: "basically not only does the scholarship come out of these five countries [to which it is necessary to add the United States, after 1945], but most of the scholarship by most scholars is about their own coun-try."[26] If we change "country" to "first world" and we add the United States to the original picture, we have a map of the correspondence between distribu-tion of scientific labor and areas of study instead of country. In fact, "area of study" is an invention that corresponds to the last stage of globalization and cuts across the study of "civilization" and "culture" before 1945.

The humanities were not alien to such a distribution of labor, although they did not occupy a central place in it. To take just one example: the study of languages and literatures was cast within the same epistemological frame. The languages of literature were mainly the colonial languages of the modern period with their distinguished legacies, Greek and Latin. Literary studies remained within that tradition. Literature in the modern period was in-creasingly cast as "national literature," and, of course, written in a national language. Literary studies, in their historico-philological foundation before 1945 as well as in their structuralist and poststructuralist formulations of the 1970s, focused on the literature of the five countries of scholarship mentioned by Wallerstein. I am sure we all noticed that Spain was not among the five countries of modern scholarship. And, of course, Spanish did not count as a language of scholarship. This imperial rift of the modern period put Spain and Spanish in an ambiguous place between "Eastern Civilizations" and "Modern Europe." When it comes to Latin America, the location of Spain between the Arabic world of North Africa and the European world of West-ern Europe becomes further complicated because of the relations during the modern period between Spanish and Amerindian languages, and by the fact that Andean and Mesoamerican civilizations were not part of civilizational studies in the nineteenth century.[27] Latin America became, then, of particular interest to understanding the question of languages, literatures, and literary studies in the changing distribution of scientific labor and cultural practices since 1850. The Spanish language, in Latin America, was twice subaltern: it was no longer the Spanish of Spain, while at the same time, Spain and Spanish became marginal to European modernity since the seventeenth century. On the other hand, Amerindian languages, in their complex and rich relations between the oral and the written,[28] were not part of reflections on languages and literatures, but of pre-Columbian studies (a particular version of civilizational studies framed within the history and legacies of Spanish colonialism), of folklore and ethnohistory or, more recently, of colonial cultural studies.[29] In summary: languages and literary studies were maintained within the epistemological framework of cultural practice and scholarship of North Atlantic modernity and the cultural configuration shaped by the idea of civilization and the civilizing mission, together with the process of economic globalization.

I have suggested that the economic conditions created by globalization contributed to the rise of "barbarian theorizing" as border gnoseology, not as an opposition to "civilian" (in the double meaning of both civilization and citizenship) "theorizing" but as a displacement and a new departure. The comparison between Norbert Elias's and Darcy Ribeiro's studies of civilization process could be helpful in this regard. There are three aspects of the comparison I would like to highlight. First, whereas Elias conceives the civilization process as a particular European phenomenon of the past five hundred years, Ribeiro conceives it as a long, diverse, and complex set of processes of the human species. Second, whereas Elias focuses on the civilizing process, which is at the same time the consolidation of (Western) Europe as a world hegemonic power, Ribeiro looks at Europe as a recent outcome of human civilizing processes that were preceded by previous hegemonic power and will also be transformed and dissolved in a future governed by what Ribeiro calls "the thermonuclear revolution and future societies." Third, although both Elias and Ribeiro are still prisoners of the temporal arrangement of human histories implanted in modernity, Ribeiro's concern with colonization and European expansion allows him to open the doors to a spatial conceptualization of civilization processes and of local histories arranged around successive and surviving centers of world hegemony. Fourth, and finally, the fact that Ribeiro's geocultural focus and concerns are the Americas and not Europe (as in the case of Elias's) makes it impossible for him not to analyze the process of European civilization as a process of sub-alternization of world cultures: "Nothing in the world," Ribeiro states,

> was left out by the forces liberated by the European expansion. In it we detect the foundation of the reorganization of nature, whose flora and fauna were normalized all over the planet. It (European colonial expansion) is the main agency for the disappearance of thousands of ethnic communities, for racial mixtures and for the linguistic and cultural extension of European people. In the process of this expansion, modern technologies as well as forms of social organization and bodies of cultural values relevant in and for Europe, were disseminated and generalized. The outcome of this process is the modern world, unified by commerce and communication, activated by the same technology, inspired by a basic and common system of values.[30]

This, in a nutshell, is Ribeiro's view of what Elias called the "civilizing process."

Now, what is relevant in this comparison to understand "barbarian theorizing" as border epistemology emerging from the conditions created by the last and perhaps most radical stage of globalization is the possibility (for someone like Ribeiro) of theorizing from the border (border as threshold and liminality, as two sides connected by a bridge, as a geographical and epistemological location); that is, of having both the formation in "civilized theorizing" and the experience of someone who lives and experiences, including the training in "civilized theorizing," in communities that have been precisely subalternized and placed in the margins by the very concept and expansion of European civilization. Thus an *anthropologador:* someone who was trained as an anthropologist and at the same time was part of the "other." The common knowledge that Ribeiro is a "Third World theoretician," as implied by Meggers[31] in her introduction to the first edition of *O Proçesso Civilizatorio,* was clearly stated by Sonntag in his preface to the German edition: "The sheer fact of being a theory *from/of* the Third World *for* the Third World, the censured one, are those who continue to believe that the belly of the world is someplace in between Vienna, Berlin, Bonn, Moscow, Washington or Rome. The fact that Ribeiro doesn't attribute to the First World a relevant role in the formation of 'future societies' . . . implies clearly a challenge which has to be confronted by critical theory of the developed world (e.g., 'civilian theorizing'), immediately and seriously, if it doesn't want to run the risk of disappearing."[32] The only change I would make to this paragraph is that Ribeiro's theory of the civilizing process is certainly a theory *from/of* the third world, but *not only for the third world.* Sonntag, with plenty of good will, maintains the regional scope of third-world theorizing for the third world, as a kind of "barbarian counterculture" to which still first-world theorizing has to react and accommodate itself. Third-world theorizing is also *for* the first world in the sense that critical theory is subsumed and incorporated in a new geo-cultural and epistemological location.

To close, then, the main thrust of this article was, first, that globalization is creating the conditions for spatializing the civilization process and, by so doing, of denying the denial of coevalness as one of the main epistemological strategies of colonial/imperial expansion and creating the conditions for "barbarian theorizing": theorizing from/of the third world (the expression used metaphorically here) for the (first/third) entire planet. The second purpose of this article was to identify some of the instances (social movements and language rights, emergence of new sites of thinking in between disciplines and in between languages, e.g., the self-restitution of barbarism as a theoretical locus, and a progressive force offering valuable correctives to the abuses of post-Enlightenment reason, science, and disciplinarity), in which the denial of the denial of coevalness materializes itself by redressing and implementing long-lasting forces, sensibilities, and rationalities repressed by the one-sided ideology of the civilizing mission/process. The relocation of languages and cultures, finally, is creating the conditions for the emergence of an epistemological potential (e.g., border gnoseology) at the multiple intersections and interstices of the "West and the rest" in Huntington's new world order.[33]

Notes

1 Immanuel Wallerstein, *The Modern World System* (New York, 1974).

2 Norbert Elias, *The Civilizing Process* (1937), Vol. 1, *The History of Manners* (New York, 1978), Vol. 2, *State Formation and Civilization* (New York, 1982).

3 Joseph Fontana, *Europa Ante el Espejo* (Barcelona, 1994); Denys Hay, *Europe: The Emergence of an Idea* (Edinburgh, 1957); Edgar Morin, *Penser l'Europe* (Paris, 1987).

4 It is worth noting that Sigmund Freud's *Das Unbehagen in der Kultur* was translated into English as *Civilization and Its Discontents.*

5 Samuel P. Huntington, *The Clash of Civilizations and the Remaking of World Order* (New York, 1996).

6   Johannes Fabian, *Time and the Other: How Anthropology Makes Its Object* (New York, 1983).

7   Immanuel Wallerstein, "Open de Social Sciences," ITEMS 50, no. 1 (1996): 3.

8   Walter D. Mignolo, "On the Colonization of Amerindian Languages and Memories: Renaissance Theories of Writing and the Discontinuity of the Classical Tradition," *Comparative Studies in Society and History* 34, no. 2 (1992): 301–330.

9   Ernst-Robert Curtius, *L'idée de civilisation dans la conscience française*, trans. from German by Henri Jourdan (Paris, 1929); W. Mignolo, "Nebrija in the New World: The Question of the Letter, the Colonization of Amerindian Languages, and the Discontinuity of the Classical Tradition," *L'Homme* 122–124 (1992): 187–209; Robert J. C. Young, *Colonial Desire: Hibridity in Theory, Culture and Race* (New York, 1995), 29–54.

10 R. Stavenhagen and D. Iturralde, eds. *Entre la ley y la costumbre. El derecho cosuetudinario indigena en America Latina.* (Mexico, 1990). Stefano Varese, ed., *Pueblos indios, soberania y globalismo* (Quito, 1996).

11 Pierre Bourdieu, *Language and Symbolic Power*, ed. John B. Thompson (Boston, 1991), 37–65; Bruce Mannheim, *The Language of the Inka since the European Invasion* (Austin, 1991), 1–112.

12 Shirley Brice Heath, *Telling Tongues: Language Policy in Mexico, Colony to Nation* (London, 1972).

13 M. Jansen and T. Leymour, eds., *The Indian of Mexico in Pre-Columbian and Modern Times: An International Colloquium* (Leiden, 1981); Donna Lee Van Cott, *Indigenous Peoples and Democracy in Latin America: Inter-American Dialogue* (New York, 1994).

14 Heath, *Telling Tongues*.

15 Antonio Gramsci, *Prison Notebooks* (New York, 1994), 5.

16 Intellectuals of indigenous descent have been active, mainly in Bolivia, Ecuador, and Guatemala, both as scholars and political leaders. Victor Hugo-Cárdenas, the current vice president of Bolivia, is a case in point. Joanne Rappaport, *The Politics of Memory: Native Historical Interpretation in the Colombian Andes* (New York, 1990), studied the life and deeds of several intellectuals of indigenous descent. Historian Roberto Choque is one distinguished figure currently in Bolivia, together with Humberto Mamani, Esteban Ticona, and others (see the collection *Educación Indígena: Ciudadanía o colonización?* [La Paz, 1992], with prologue by Victor Hugo-Cárdenas.) In the Islamic world, a similar concern is being explored by scholars and intellectuals of Islamic/Muslim descent. See Tomas Gerholm, "Two Muslim Intellectuals in the Postmodern West: Akbar Ahmed and Ziauddin Sardar," in *Islam, Globalization and Postmodernity* (New York, 1990), 194–212.

17 E. J. Hobsbawm, *Nations and Nationalism since 1780: Programme, Myth, Reality* (Cambridge, UK, 1990).

18 G. W. Gong, *The Standard of "Civilization" in International Society* (Oxford, 1984); Roland Robertson, " 'Civilization' and Civilizing Process: Elias, Global-

ization and Analytic Synthesis," in *Cultural Theory and Cultural Change*, ed. M. Featherstone (London, 1992), 211–228.

19 Jose Pedro Barran, *Historia de la Sensibilidad en Uruguay*, Vol. 2, *El disciplinamiento, 1860–1920* (Montevideo, 1990).

20 Ibid., 18.

21 Gloria Anzaldúa, *Borderlands: La Frontera* (San Francisco, 1987).

22 I do not have time to elaborate on this topic. To avoid the possible surprise of the reader, I can say that what I am working toward is in the articulation of what we can call "postcolonial reason" (a way of critical thinking from the histories of various colonialisms, rather than from the history of modernity, as in the case of the Frankfurt School). Postcolonial thinkers, instead of being Jews, like the members of the Frankfurt School, are people who have experienced colonial legacies. Furthermore, I am not trying to find a niche for postcolonial critical thinking within a discipline, as does Craig Calhoun (*Critical Social Theory: Culture, History and the Challenge of Difference* [Oxford, 1995]), who brilliantly attempts to find in sociology a niche for transdisciplinary critical thinking (e.g., feminism) within the tradition of the Frankfurt School. On the contrary, I am trying to reveal the complicities among imperial languages, colonial expansion, and disciplinary foundations in the social sciences and the humanities. In other words, I am trying to state that postcolonial critical thinking is, to intellectuals who have experienced colonial legacies, what critical theory (à la Frankfurt) is to those who have experienced the limits of modern reason and the racial persecution of the Jews.

23 Frederick Engels and Karl Marx, *On Colonialism* (Moscow, 1959).

24 Norbert Elias, "The Retreat of Sociologists into the Present," *Theory, Culture and Society* 4, nos. 2–3 (1987): 23–30.

25 Carl E. Pletsch, "The Three Worlds, or the Division of Social Scientific Labor, circa 1950–1975," *Comparative Study of Society and History* 23, no. 4 (1981): 565–590.

26 Wallerstein, "Open de Social Sciences," 3.

27 Michael D. Coe, *Breaking the Maya Code* (New York, 1992).

28 Elizabeth Hill Boone and Walter D. Mignolo, eds., *Writing without Words: Alternative Literacies in Mesoamerica and the Andes* (Durham, NC, 1994).

29 Walter D. Mignolo, "The Darker Side of the Renaissance: Colonization and the Discontinuity of the Classical Tradition," *Renaissance Quarterly* 45, no. 4 (winter 1992): 808–828.

30 Darcy Ribeiro, *Las Américas y la civilización: Proçesso de formación y causas del desarrollo desigual de los pueblos americanos* (Caracas, 1992), 57.

31 Betty J. Meggers, "Prologo a Ediçao Norte-Americana," reprinted in Ribeiro's *O Proçesso Civilizatorio: Etapas da Evoluaçáo Socio-Cultural* (Petropolis, 1991).

32 Heinz Rudolf Sonntag, "Epilogo a Ediçao Alema," reprinted in Ribeiro's *O Proçesso Civilizatorio*, 216.

33 Huntington, *The Clash of Civilizations*, 183–206.

Notes on Globalization as a Philosophical Issue

1

Four positions on our topic seem logically available. The first affirms the opinion that there is no such thing as globalization (there are still the nation-states and the national situations; nothing is new under the sun). The second also affirms that globalization is nothing new; there has always been global-ization and it suffices to leaf through a book like Eric Wolf's *Europe and the People without History*[1] to see that as far back as the neolithic trade routes have been global in their scope, with Polynesian artifacts deposited in Africa and Asian potsherds as far afield as the New World.

Then I suppose one should add two more: one that affirms the relationship between globalization and that world market which is the ultimate horizon of capitalism, only to add that the current world networks are only different in degree and not in kind; while a fourth affirmation (which I have found more interesting than the other three) posits some new or third, multinational stage of capitalism, of which globalization is an intrinsic feature and which we now largely tend, whether we like it or not, to associate with that thing called postmodernity.

Meanwhile, above and beyond all this, there are the judgments: one can deplore globalization or celebrate it, just as one welcomes the new freedoms of the postmodern era and the postmodern outlook, and in particular the new technological revolutions, or on the other hand, elegiacally laments the passing of the splendors of the modern: the glories and possibilities of modernism in the arts, the disappearance of History as the fundamental element in which human beings exist, and, not least, the end of an essentially modernist field of political struggle in which the great ideologies still had the force and the authority of the great religions in earlier times. But I do think we have an interest in at least provisionally separating this now familiar postmodern debate from the matter of globalization, all the while understanding only too well that the two issues are deeply intertwined and that positions on the postmodern are bound to make their way back in eventually.

Let's start from the principle that we already somehow know what globalization is, and try rather to focus on the concept of globalization, on its ideological structure, if you like (it being understood in advance that the word ideology is unpejorative, and that a concept can be ideological and also correct or true all at once). I believe that globalization is a communicational concept, which alternately masks and transmits cultural or economic meanings. We have a sense that there are both denser and more extensive communicational networks all over the world today, networks that are on the one hand the result of remarkable innovations in communicational technologies of all kinds, and on the other have as their foundation the tendentially greater degree of modernization in all the countries of the world, or at least in their big cities, which includes the implantation of such technologies.

But the communicational focus of the concept of globalization is essentially incomplete: I defy anyone to try to think it in exclusively media or communicational terms; and we can find a point of contrast and distinction in the images of the media in the earlier twentieth century, that is to say, in the modernist period. There did then seem to be a certain semiautonomy about the development of the media: radio did seem to penetrate for the first time into remote areas (both at home and abroad); the progress of film around the world was both swift and startling, and seemed to bring some new kind of mass consciousness with it; journalism and reporting, meanwhile, were somehow at their outer reaches heroic acts, which shed new light and brought back new information. No one can feel that the cybernetic revolution is like that, if only because it builds on those first, already established networks. The communicational development today is no longer one of "enlightenment" in all its connotations, but rather of new technologies.

This is why, along with the communicational concept of globalization, one always finds other dimensions smuggled in. Thus, if the newer phenomenon essentially distinguishes itself from the older, modern one by technology rather than by information (even though this term is then itself reappropriated and ideologically developed today on a grand scale), what happens is that the technology and what the computer people call information begin to slip insensibly in the direction of advertisements and publicity, of postmodern marketing, and finally of the export of TV programs, rather than the return of startling reports from remote places. But this is to say that the surface concept, the communicational one, has suddenly acquired a whole cultural dimension: the communicational signifier has been endowed with a more properly cultural signified or signification. Now the positing of an enlargement of communicational nets has secretly been transformed into some kind of message about a new world culture.

But the slippage can also take another direction: the economic. Thus, in our attempt to think this new, still purely communicational concept, we begin to fill in the empty signifier with visions of financial transfers and investments all over the world, and the new networks begin to swell with the commerce of some new and allegedly more flexible capitalism (I have to confess that I have always found this a ludicrous expression). We begin remembering that the newly flexible production was made possible precisely by computerization (a loop back to the technological again), and we also remember that computers and their programs and the like are themselves among the most hotly exchanged forms of goods among the nations today. In this variant, then, the ostensibly communicational concept has secretly been transformed into a vision of the world market and its newfound interdependence, a global division of labor on an extraordinary scale, new electronic trade routes tirelessly plied by commerce and finance alike.

Now I think we are better equipped to understand the flows of debate and ideology around this slippery concept, whose twin and not altogether commensurable faces now seem to produce two distinct types of position, which are however themselves reversible. Thus, if you insist on the cultural contents of this new communicational form, I think you will slowly emerge into a postmodern celebration of difference and differentiation: suddenly all the cultures around the world are placed in tolerant contact with each other in a kind of immense cultural pluralism which it would be very difficult not to welcome. Beyond that, beyond the dawning celebration of cultural difference, and often very closely linked to it, is a celebration of the emergence of a whole immense range of groups, races, genders, ethnicities, into the speech of the public sphere; a falling away of those structures that condemned whole segments of the population to silence and to subalternity; a worldwide growth of popular democratization—why not?—which seems to have some relationship to the evolution of the media, but which is immediately expressed by a new richness and variety of cultures in the new world space.

If, on the other hand, your thoughts turn economic, and the concept of globalization becomes colored by those codes and meanings, I think you will find the concept darkening and growing more opaque. Now what comes to the fore is increasing identity (rather than difference): the rapid assimilation of hitherto autonomous national markets and productive zones into a single sphere, the disappearance of national subsistence (in food, for example), the forced integration of countries all over the globe into precisely that new global division of labor I mentioned before. Here what begins to infuse our thinking of globalization is a picture of standardization on an unparalleled new scale; of forced integration as well, into a world-system from which "delinking" (to use Samir Amin's term) is henceforth impossible and even unthinkable and inconceivable. This is obviously a far more baleful prospect than the preceding joyous vision of heterogeneity and difference, but I'm not sure that these visions are logically incompatible; indeed, they seem somehow to be dialectically related, at least on the mode of the unresolvable antinomy.

But now, having achieved these first twin positions, having in some first moment rotated the concept in such a way that it takes on these distinct kinds of content, its surface now glittering in light, and then obscured again by darkness and shadow—now it is important to add that the transfers can begin. Now, after having secured these initial structural possibilities, you can project their axes upon each other. Now, in a second moment, the baleful vision of Identity can be transferred onto the cultural realm: and what will be affirmed, in some gloomy Frankfurt School fashion, is the worldwide Americanization or standardization of culture, the destruction of local differences, the massification of all the peoples on the planet.

But you are equally free to do the inverse, and to transfer the joyous and celebratory Difference and multiple heterogeneities of the first, cultural dimension onto the economic sphere: where, as you may well imagine, the rhetoricians of the market pop up and feverishly reassure us as to the richness and excitement of the new free market all over the world: the increase in sheer productivity that open markets will lead to, the transcendental satisfaction that human beings have finally begun to grasp exchange, the market, and capitalism as their most fundamental human possibilities and the surest sources of freedom.

Such are the multiple structural possibilities and combinations made available by this most ambiguous ideological concept and its alternating contents, through which we may now provisionally explore a few paths.

2

One obvious path is the sense in which globalization means the export and import of culture. This is, no doubt, a matter of business; yet it also presumably foretells the contact and interpenetration of national cultures at an intensity scarcely conceivable in older, slower epochs.

It is enough to think of all the people around the world who watch exported Northamerican television programs to realize that this cultural intervention is deeper than anything known in earlier forms of colonization or imperialism, or simple tourism. A great Indian filmmaker once described the ways in which the gestures and the allure of walking of his teenage son were modified by watching American television: one supposes that his ideas and values were also modified. Does this mean that the rest of the world is becoming Americanized? and if so, what do we think about that; or perhaps one should ask, what does the rest of the world think about that, and what might Americans think about it?

For I must now add here a basic point about cultural pluralism and diversity, even about linguistic pluralism and diversity. We have to understand, in this country, something that is difficult for us to realize: namely, that the United States is not just one country, or one culture, among others, any more than English is just one language among others. There is a fundamental dissymmetry in the relationship between the United States and every other country in the world, not only third-world countries, but even Japan and those of Western Europe, as I will suggest in a moment.

This means that there is a kind of blindness at the center, which reflection on globalization may help us partly correct. American blindness can be registered, for example, in our tendency to confuse the universal and the cultural, as well as to assume that in any given geopolitical conflict all elements and values are somehow equal and equivalent; in other words, are not affected by the disproportions of power. I happen to think this poses interesting and relatively new philosophical problems, but I want to illustrate the consequences in more concrete terms.

Take, for example, the question of languages in the new world-system: Are they all equal, and can every language group freely produce its own culture according to its own needs? The speakers of the smaller languages have always protested against that view; and their anxieties can only be heightened by the emergence of a kind of global or jet-set transnational culture in which a few international hits (literary or cultural) are canonized by the media and given a heightened circulation inconceivable for the local products they tend in any case to squeeze out. Meanwhile, it is important for us here to realize that for most people in the world English itself is not exactly a culture language: it is the lingua franca of money and power, which you have to learn and use for practical but scarcely for aesthetic purposes. But the very connotation of power then tends in the eyes of foreign speakers to reduce the value of all forms of English-language high culture.

By the same token, American mass culture, associated as it is with money and commodities, enjoys a prestige that is perilous for most forms of domestic cultural production, which either find themselves wiped out—as with local film and television production—or co-opted and transformed beyond recognition, as with local music. We do not here sufficiently notice—because we do not have to notice—the significance, in the Gatt and Nafta negotiations and agreements, of the cultural clauses, and of the struggle between immense U.S. cultural interests, who want to open up foreign borders to American film, television, music, and the like, and foreign nation-states who still place a premium on the preservation and development of their national languages and cultures and attempt to limit the damages—both material and social—caused by the leveling power of American mass culture: material on account of the enormous financial interests involved; social because of the very change in values likely to be wrought by what used to be called—when it was a far more limited phenomenon—Americanization.

3

All of which suggests that we need to open a long parenthesis on the significance of the Gatt and Nafta agreements, which constitute stages in a long American attempt to undermine a politics of cultural subsidies and quotas in other parts of the world but primarily in Western Europe.

French resistance to this American pressure has mostly been presented over here as a cultural eccentricity, like frogs' legs. I want to argue, however, that it sets a fundamental agenda for all culture workers in the next decade and may be an adequate focus for reorganizing the equally old-fashioned or eccentric notion of cultural imperialism and indeed of imperialism generally, today, in the new late-capitalist world-system.

The becoming cultural of the economic, and the becoming economic of the cultural, has often been identified as one of the features that characterizes what is now widely known as postmodernity. In any case, it has fundamental consequences for the status of mass culture as such. The Gatt talks are there to remind us that American film and television fall under base and superstructure alike, as it were; they are economics fully as much as they are culture, and are indeed, along with agribusiness and weapons, the principal economic export of the United States—an enormous source of sheer profit and income. This is why American insistence on opening the quota barriers on film in foreign countries should not be seen as a Northamerican cultural eccentricity, such as violence or apple pie, but rather a hardheaded business necessity—a formal economic necessity irrespective of the frivolous cultural content.

Our Gatt cultural policy must thus also be seen as a drive for economic expansion—the logic of capital generally being an irresistible drive for expansion, or positing a requirement for enlarged accumulation that cannot be slowed or arrested, suspended or reformed, without mortal damage to the system itself. It is in particular important ironically to distance the rhetoric of freedom—not merely free trade, but free speech, the free passage of ideas and intellectual "properties"—which accompanies this policy. The material side of ideas or cultural items always lay in the institutions of reproduction and transmission; those are today, however, everywhere visible as enormous corporations based on a monopoly of the relevant information technology: so the freedom of those corporations (and their dominant nation-state) is scarcely the same thing as our individual freedom as citizens. Meanwhile, the accompanying politics of copyright, patent, and intellectual property indissociable from the same international politics reminds us sharply that the sought-after freedom of ideas is important because the ideas are private property and designed to be sold in great and profitable quantities. I won't discuss this important feature of the latter any more (which has its ecological equivalent in the attempt to patent chemicals derived from third-world rain forests and the like), but will return to the free market later on.

The other side of this particular freedom I do want to comment on, however, is that it is literally a zero-sum game in which my freedom results in the destruction of other people's national culture industries. Those of you who think the politics of socialism is dead—those of you now inveterately prejudiced against the intervention of the state, and fantasizing about the possibilities of nongovernmental organizations (NGOS)—might do well to reflect on the necessity of government subsidies in the creation of any independent or national film industry: West Germany's Länder have long been a model for the subsidizing of avant-gardes; France has had intricate and valuable provisions for supporting younger filmmakers out of commercial film profits; England's current new wave, around Channel Four and the BFI, would not exist without the government and its older BBC and socialist traditions; Canada finally (along with Québec) offers a range of precedents for a really productive and stimulating role of the state in culture and even cultural politics. The point is that the Gatt talks were designed, at least in the eyes of the American state lobbyists, to dismantle all these local and national subsidies as forms of "unfair" international competition; these subsidies were direct and explicit targets of the currently suspended free-trade-in-entertainment drive; and I hope it is also obvious that success in this area would at once mean the tendential extinction of new national cultural and artistic production elsewhere, just as the free movement of American movies in the world spells the death knell of national cinemas elsewhere, perhaps of all other national cinemas as distinct species. To talk about this in terms of a telos or an intention may seem conspiratorial, but surely the two sides go together: your own securing of advantage and the destruction of your enemy's; in this particular instance, the new freer market emphatically does not result in an increase in your competitor's business as well. Already, as long ago as the Marshall Plan, American aid to the postwar Western European countries was accompanied by foresightful provisions about the quantities of American film to be lawfully admitted to the European markets; in several instances, the English, the German, and the Italian most notably, this flooding of the theaters by American films effectively killed off the respective national industries, which had to specialize or go third-world to survive at all. It is no accident that the French industry alone retained its national character, and that it should therefore be in France that the greatest consciousness of these dangers is to be found.

This destruction of a national film production—and along with it, potentially, that of national or local culture as a whole—is what can be witnessed everywhere now in the third and second worlds. It should be understood that the triumph of Hollywood film (from which I won't here separate out television, which is today just as important or even more so) is not merely an economic triumph, it is a formal and also a political one. It was a significant theoretical event, I think, when in their 1985 book, *The Classical Hollywood Cinema,* Bordwell, Thompson, and Staiger pronounced the death of the various '60s and '70s filmic experiments all over the world and the universal hegemony of the classic Hollywood form.[2] This is, of course, in another sense a relatively final death of the modern, insofar as independent filmmakers all over the world could be seen to be guided by a certain modernism; but it is also the death of the political, and an allegory of the end of the possibility of imagining radically different social alternatives to this one we now live under. For political film in the '60s and '70s still affirmed that possibility (as did modernism in general, in a more complex way), by affirming that the discovery or invention of a radically new form was at one with the discovery or invention of radically new social relations and ways of living in the world. It is those possibilities—filmic, formal, political, and social—that have disappeared as some more definitive hegemony of the United States has seemed to emerge.

Now it will be said that there is a good reason for all this, namely, that people like Hollywood films and that they can probably also be expected eventually to like the American way of life, insofar as it can be extended to them. Why do Hungarian and Russian audiences flock to Hollywood films rather than what remains of their own once prestigious national film production? Why is it to be feared that with privatization the hitherto sealed and protected film culture of India will begin to melt away like snow, despite the extraordinary size and popularity of traditional Hindi comedy? The rapidity of the editing of American films and the sensuous attractions of its essential violence can be appealed to as explanations; but in that form such explanations still sound rather moralizing. It is easy to become addicted to Hollywood films and television; indeed, I imagine most of us are; but it would be preferable to look at it the other way around and measure the degree to which each national culture and daily life is a seamless web of habits and habitual practices, which form a totality or a system. It is very easy to break up such traditional cultural systems, which extend to the way people live in their bodies and use language, as well as the way they treat each other and nature. Once destroyed, those fabrics can never be recreated. Some third-world nations are still in a situation in which that fabric is preserved. The violence of American cultural imperialism and the penetration of Hollywood film and television lie in imperialism's destruction of those traditions, which are very far from being precapitalist or quasi-religious traditions, but are rather recent and successful accommodations of the old institutions to modern technology.

The point is therefore that, alongside the free market as an ideology, the consumption of the Hollywood film form is the apprenticeship to a specific culture, to an everyday life as a cultural practice: a practice of which commodified narratives are the aesthetic expression, so that the populations in question learn both at the same time. Hollywood is not merely a name for a business that makes money but also for a fundamental late-capitalist cultural revolution, in which old ways of life are broken up and new ones set in place. But if these other countries want that . . . ? it will still be asked. The implication is that it is in human nature; and further, that all history has been moving toward American culture as its apotheosis. But it is rather a matter of whether we want that ourselves; because if we can imagine nothing else, then obviously we have nothing to warn other cultures about either.

4

We must thus now return to the American standpoint, and stress the point of fundamental dissymmetry between the United States and other cultures. There can, in other words, never be parity in these areas: in the new global culture there are no take-off stages; other languages will never come to equal English in its global function, even if they were systematically tried out; just as other local entertainment industries are most unlikely to supplant Hollywood in any global or universally successful form, particularly owing to the way in which the American system itself undertakes to incorporate exotic elements from abroad—samurai culture here, South African music there, John Woo films here, Thai food there, and so forth.

This is indeed the sense in which the new explosion of world culture has seemed to so many to be an occasion for celebration; nor is it desirable to choose between the two very different views of the matter, but rather to intensify their incompatibility and opposition such that we can live this particular contradiction as our own historic form of Hegel's "unhappy consciousness." On the one hand, there is the view according to which globalization essentially means unification and standardization. By the intermediaries of the great, mostly American-based transnational or multinational corporations, a standard form of American material life, along with Northamerican values and cultural forms, is being systematically transmitted to other cultures. Nor is this simply a matter of machinery and buildings, which increasingly make all the places of the world look alike. It is not only a matter of values either—although Americans always find it shocking when foreigners suggest that human rights, feminist values, and even parliamentary democracy are not necessarily to be seen as universals, but rather merely local American cultural characteristics that have been exported as practices valid for all peoples in the world.

That kind of shock is good for us, I want to say; but I have not yet mentioned the supreme form in which American economic interest and American cultural influence coincide to produce the export of a way of life itself. People often evoke "corrosive individualism" and also consumerist "materialism" as a way of accounting for the destructiveness of the new globalization process. But I think these moralizing concepts are inadequate to the task, and do not sufficiently identify the destructive forces that are North American in origin and result from the unchallenged primacy of the United States today and thus the "American way of life" and American mass media culture. This is *consumerism* as such, the very linchpin of our economic system, and also the mode of daily life in which all our mass culture and entertainment industries train us ceaselessly day after day, in an image and media barrage quite unparalleled in history. Since the discrediting of socialism by the collapse of Russian communism, only religious fundamentalism has seemed to offer an alternative way of life—let us not, heaven help us, call it a lifestyle—to American consumerism. But is it certain that all of human history has been, as Fukuyama and others believe, a tortuous progression toward the American consumer as a climax? And is it meanwhile so sure that the benefits of the market can be extended so far as to make this new way of life available for everyone on the globe? If not, we will have destroyed their cultures without offering any alternatives; but it has also been argued that all the other recrudescences of what people think of as local and nationalist violence are themselves reactions and defense mechanisms in the face of heightened globalization. Here is, for example, Giovanni Arrighi:

> Entire communities, countries, even continents, as in the case of sub-Saharan Africa, have been declared "redundant," superfluous to the changing economy of capitalist accumulation on a world scale. Combined with the collapse of the world power and the territorial empire of the USSR, the unplugging of these "redundant" communities and locales from the world supply system has triggered innumerable, mostly violent feuds over "who is more superfluous than whom," or, more simply, over the appropriation of resources that were made absolutely scarce by the unplugging. Generally speaking, these feuds have been diagnosed and treated not as expressions of the self-protection of society against the disruption of established ways of life under the impact of intensifying world market competition—which for the most part is what they are. Rather, they have been diagnosed and treated as the expression of atavistic hatreds or of power struggles among local bullies, both of which have played at best only a secondary role.[3]

Whatever the validity of Arrighi's diagnosis here, he at least gives us a strong lesson in thinking about current events in terms of the current situation of globalization, rather than in culturalist terms (which generally end up being racist ones).

It is hard to give voice now to more positive views after such catastrophic visions without trivializing the other side of the coin: the celebration of globalization and postmodernity. But this is also a very persuasive view that I think many of us, particularly in the United States, tend to share unconsciously and practically to the degree to which we are ourselves the recipients of the new world culture. Our conference is indeed itself a sign that we are now in a position to benefit from globalization in the activation of a host of new intellectual networks and the exchanges and discussions across a variety of national situations which have themselves become standardized by globalization to the degree to which we can now speak to each other. My sense is that the old and fundamental opposition, in the colonized world, between Westernizers and traditionalists, has almost completely disappeared in this new postmodern moment of capitalism. That opposition was, so to speak, a modernist one, and it no longer holds for the very simple reason that tradition in that form has everywhere been wiped out. Neo-Confucianism and Islamic and Hindu fundamentalism themselves are new, are postmodern inventions, not survivals of ancient ways of life. In that sense also the opposition between the metropolis and the provinces has also disappeared, both nationally and on a global scale; and this not necessarily for a very good reason either, as it is essentially standardization that effaces the difference between the center and the margins. And although it may be an exaggeration to claim that we are all marginals now, all decentered in the current good senses of those words, certainly many new freedoms have been won in the process whereby globalization has meant a decentering and a proliferation of differences. You see how this view grasps the arrival of globalization in exactly the opposite way from the pessimistic one, for which it meant unification and standardization; yet these are indeed the two antithetical features of that elephant we are here blindly attempting to characterize.

In the realm of culture, no one has given a more powerful expression to the celebratory picture of globalization than the Mexican theorist Néstor García Canclini in his conception of culture as hybridization:[4] in his view, the eclectic contacts and borrowings enabled by globalization are progressive and healthy, they positively encourage the proliferation of new cultures (and indeed, I think it is implied by this view that in any case culture always functioned this way, by impure and disorderly combinations, and not by situations of isolation and regulated tradition). García Canclini's work thus gives ammunition to the most vital utopian visions of our own time, of an immense global urban intercultural festival without a center or even any longer a dominant cultural mode. I myself think this view needs a little economic specificity and is rather inconsistent with the quality and impoverishment of what has to be called corporate culture on a global scale.

But its clash with the previous pessimistic view of the globalization process is the shock from which I hope the sparks will fly, and in any case, this is surely one of the most important debates of the current period.

(The other very important and surely related opposition is that which obtains between the older values of autonomy and self-sufficiency—both in culture and economics—and current visions of systemic interdependence in which we are all points in a net or global web. There, too, powerful cases can be made on both sides, but I mention this particular debate only in passing and in order to read it onto some enlarged agenda.)

But now I need to move back to the trilateral possibility, and say why, if García Canclini proves to be wrong about the continuing cultural vitality and production of the so-called third world, we might not continue to expect a counterbalance to Americanization in the two other great world centers of Europe and Japan.

In the present context, I would rather present that as a problem than a mere opinion: namely, whether, in our time, the relationship between culture and economics has not fundamentally altered. At any rate, it does seem to me that fresh cultural production and innovation—and this means in the area of mass-consumed culture—are the crucial index of the centrality of a given area and not its wealth or productive power. This is why it was extraordinarily significant when the ultimate Japanese moves to incorporate the U.S. entertainment industry—Sony's acquisition of Columbia Pictures and Matsushita's buyout of MCA—both failed: it meant that despite immense wealth and technological and industrial production, even despite ownership itself and private property, the Japanese were unable to master the essentially cultural productivity required to secure the globalization process for any given competitor. Whoever says the production of culture says the production of everyday life—and without that, your economic system can scarcely continue to expand and implant itself.

As for Europe—more wealthy and culturally elegant than ever, a glittering museum to a remarkable past, most immediately the past of modernism itself—I want also to suggest that its failure to generate its own forms of mass cultural production is an ominous sign. Is it possible that the death of modernism also meant a certain end for a certain type of hegemonic European art and culture? I happen to find the effort, stimulated by the EEC, to conjure up a new European cultural synthesis, with Milan Kundera substituting for T. S. Eliot, an equally ominous, if more pathetic, symptom. The emergence of a host of local popular and ethnic or oppositional cultures all over Europe is a welcome bonus of postmodernity, as it is everywhere in the world, but by definition renounces the old European hegemonic project.

By the same token, the former socialist countries have seemed largely unable to generate an original culture and a distinctive way of life capable of standing as an alternative, while, as I have already suggested, in the third world the older traditionalisms are equally enfeebled and mummified, and only a religious fundamentalism seems to have the strength and the will to resist Americanization. But here the operative word is surely *seems;* for we have yet to see whether these experiments offer positive social alternatives, or merely reactive and repressive violence.

5

The celebration of market "freedom" has so often seemed to place these ominous developments in a wholly new and positive light that it seems worthwhile, in conclusion, to interrogate this concept in its turn, and to determine the interference of philosophical categories activated by the identification of globalization with the market as such. These inner conceptual contradictions can at first be registered as so many conflations of otherwise distinct and differentiated "levels" of social life.

Thus, in a splendid work to which I have often referred, A. O. Hirschman documents the ways in which the earliest Renaissance pamphlets and treatises about the benefits of commerce and of what was shortly to develop into capitalism itself celebrated *la douceur du commerce:* the beneficent influence of trade on savage or violent, barbaric mentalities, the introduction of cosmopolitan interests and perspectives, the gradual implantation of the civil among rude peoples (not least those of feudal Europe itself, I may add).[5] Here already we have a conflation of two levels: that of exchange is conflated with that of human relations and everyday life (as we would now say today), and an identity between them affirmed. Meanwhile in our own time, the ineffable Hayek has proposed a similar identification, but on a grander political scale: the identity between free enterprise and political democracy. Lack of the latter is supposed to impede development of the former; and therefore it must follow that development of the latter—democracy—is dependent on development of the free market itself. It is a syllogism enthusiastically developed by the Friedmanites, and most recently brandished by all those carpetbagging Free World economists who raced to the benighted countries of the former East after 1989 to offer advice on how to build this particular better mousetrap.[6] But even within this system of ideological identifications there is a more basic ambiguity, and it concerns the market itself: the use of Marx's own categories suggests that this very "idea" or ideologeme involves the illicit conflation of two distinct categories, that of distribution and that of production (there may also be a slippage into consumption itself at various points in the rhetorical operation).

For capitalist production is what is generally being defended here, but in the name and under the guise of distribution—the extraordinary and heterogeneous varieties of market exchange—of which we know that precisely one of the fundamental crisis points in capitalism always comes when those things do not function in sync: overproduction, piling up in warehouses of goods that nobody can buy, and so on and so forth. Meanwhile, the libidinalization of the market, if I may put it that way—the reason so many people now feel that this boring and archaic thing is sexy—results from the sweetening of this pill by all kinds of images of consumption as such: the commodity, as it were, becoming its own ideology, and in what Leslie Sklair calls the new transnational "culture-ideology of consumption" changing traditional psychic habits and practices and sweeping all before it into something allegedly resembling the American Way of Life.

Suppose, however, that what are here identified as so many levels of the same thing were in reality in contradiction with each other; for example, suppose that consumerism were inconsistent with democracy, that the habits and addictions of postmodern consumption block or repress possibilities of political and collective action as such? We may remember, for example, that historically the invention of mass culture as a component of Fordism was the very source of the famous American exceptionalism: that is to say, that what permitted a federalism, a melting pot, a management of class struggle, in the United States, as against most other countries in the world, was precisely our unique system of mass culture and consumption as that displaced energies in new consensus-governed directions. It becomes ironic, then, when mass culture is offered as a space of democratization, let alone resistance, as many participants in the globalization debate have tended to do.

But some of these confusions can be clarified by the situations themselves, others by the disentanglement of levels I have been proposing here. Let's look more closely at the celebration of the liberating effects of commercial mass culture, particularly as that has been expressed with special emphasis in the Latin American areas, by scholars and theorists such as George Yúdice, and particularly in the area of popular music (and in Brazil, of television).[7] In literature, language protects the great modern literary productions—the Latin American Boom, for example—which in many ways reverse the direction and conquer Northamerican and European markets. In music, the point is made, not only that local music wins out over imported or Northamerican kinds, but also and even more importantly, that the transnationals actually invest in these, in the local music and recording industries (and also, in Brazil, in the local television networks). Here, then, mass culture would seem to offer a mode of resistance to a general absorption of local and national production into the orbit of transnational business, or at least, in the latter case, a way of co-opting and deflecting that to your own local and national advantage. On the other hand, even this particular national success story does not constitute the rule rather than the exception, given the way in which television in some other (not merely third-world) countries is almost wholly colonized by imported Northamerican shows. It is no doubt proper to distinguish between economic and cultural dependency as a rule of thumb: what I want to point out is that even such a banal distinction reintroduces the philosophical dilemmas, and in particular the problems of category and level, I have stressed here. What is indeed the justification for distinguishing these two levels of the economic and the cultural, when in the United States today, as we have already seen, the cultural—the entertainment business—is, along with food, one of our most important economic exports, and one the American government is prepared to go to great lengths to defend, as witness the struggles within the Gatt and Nafta negotiations?

From a different kind of theoretical point of view, meanwhile, the theory of postmodernity affirms a gradual de-differentiation of these levels, the economic itself gradually becoming cultural, all the while the cultural gradually becomes economic. Image society and advertising can no doubt document the gradual transformation of commodities into libidinal images of themselves, that is to say, into well-nigh cultural products; whereas the dissolution of high culture and the simultaneous intensification of investment in mass cultural commodities may be enough to suggest that, whatever was the case at earlier stages and moments of capitalism (where the aesthetic was very precisely a sanctuary and a refuge from business and the state), today no enclaves—aesthetic or other—are left in which the commodity form does not reign supreme.

The proposition, therefore, that the cultural realm can in certain circumstances (Brazilian television) enter into conflict with the economic realm (dependency), though neither illogical nor unthinkable, needs further elaboration, one feature of which would no doubt lie in Brazil's unique status as an immense market of virtually continental dimensions, an explanation I prefer to the more traditional ideas of cultural difference, national and linguistic tradition, and the like, which themselves need to be translated back into materialist terms.

Yúdice's proposition, however, remains to be examined: that under certain circumstances, culture—but now let's restrict it to popular music to simplify matters—can serve as a proving ground for democracy by offering new conceptions and exercises of something like citizenship; in other words, that there are practices of consumer choice and personal autonomy that train the otherwise subaltern individual in a new kind of freedom that can be seen (as Schiller did long ago)[8] as a preparation for political freedom. This is clearly to posit a "fusion" of the levels of culture and politics with a vengeance, and our restriction to music (not just contemplative bourgeois listening, but dance and musical practice in general) makes the proposition far more plausible than it sounds when a John Fiske, for example, rehearses it for commercial television.[9] Nor should we forget that the great and (alas) abortive utopian blueprints for the changes French socialism never made when it came to power were patterned specifically and explicitly on the model of music by their principal theoretician, Jacques Attali, himself a musician and an economist (who frequently stressed the kinship between these two "levels").[10] But it is perhaps Stuart Hall who has most persuasively spoken out for a new conception of culture, particularly in his recent "new times" (I hesitate to call it postmodern) period or turn; leaving aside the question of Hall's Marxism or socialism today, his account of the way in which the new musical culture of postmodernity functions to overcome the subalternities of the various minority groups in Britain is a powerful one, and goes a long way toward restoring political potentialities to art in a different sense than we have been accustomed to thinking about them.[11] This cultural multiplicity is, however, no doubt aimed at two forms of unity or oneness: the oneness of the racist state and the unity of the white (Protestant) citizens represented by that state. (We're talking now about the antagonistic structure of Imaginary relations, and not necessarily about the empirical social realities of this or that locality in Britain.)

It is a model that can now clarify the widespread theoretical and political emphasis on culture and the market in Latin America as well. For it is often stressed (by no one so forcefully as by García Canclini himself) that everywhere in Latin America culture and its support are identified with the state; in Mexico, with the postrevolutionary state. Power in these countries is itself identified with the state rather than, as in so-called first-world countries, with capitalism itself. Thus, an emphasis on commerce and trade in a situation of state power amounts precisely to a privileging of the moment of multiplicity as a place of freedom and resistance: the market in the sense of exchange and commerce thus functions in Latin America very much as do the so-called NGOs in Asia and Africa, as what also escapes the unenlightened domination of the state itself. But in the Anglo-American first world, I'm tempted to say, the state can still be a positive space: its powers are what must be protected against the right-wing attempts to dissolve it back into private businesses and operations of all kinds. The state is the place of welfare and social legislation, the source of the safety net of a whole range of crucial legislative powers (over employment, health, education, and the like), which must not be surrendered to the fragmenting and disintegrating effects of American business.

Yet, there is a way in which these two radically different situations can be compared: in the one, Latin America, multiplicity is celebrated against an oppressive unity; in the other, North America, a positive unity is defended against an oppressive multiplicity. But these simply change the valences on the terms; the mode of evaluation remains the same. Such changes and similarities are, I believe, to be grasped as structural peculiarities, not yet of globalization as such, but rather of the older international system: in other words, a level of abstraction and interrelationship in which what holds at a national level is reversed at a distance. If that sounds exceedingly obscure, let me cite the most dramatic example of it I have found, from C. L. R. James's great history of the Haitian revolution, which he significantly entitled *The Black Jacobins*.[12] The title is itself the paradox I have in mind: because what transpires in James's narrative is that so-called subjects of history play very different roles across the international network. We have been taught, indeed, that the most radical force in the French Revolution was the sansculottes: not yet a proletariat exactly, but a mixture of petty bourgeois, apprentices, students, lumpens, and the like. These constituted the army of the Jacobin movement and of Robespierre. What James shows us is that in Haiti the sansculottes (along with their revolutionary culture exported from France) become the forces of reaction, the principal forces who oppose the revolutionary movement and the enemies of Toussaint Louverture. It is too easy to evoke simple racism in this situation: I propose that it be read rather as a dialectical reversal which is itself determined by the coming into being of relationships that are no longer internal national ones (I hesitate to use a word like transnational, which for all its literal applicability has much more recent connotations; just as I hesitate to pronounce the word imperialism, which is also anachronistic; nor can slavery be thought of in simple colonial terms either). And I think the dialectical shift from positive to negative in this matter of unity and multiplicity, in the differences between the Northamerican and the Latin American situations, is also to be theorized in something of the same way.

But now I want to develop this dialectic a little more broadly. We have in this particular instance observed the endowment of the abstract opposition of Identity and Difference with a specific content of unity versus multiplicity. Yet it is also possible to transcode all this into the terms of the current postmodern debates; in the Latin American case, I believe that the positive force of culture is not meant to designate mass or popular culture exclusively, but rather includes high culture and very specifically the national literature and language: samba, let's say, is opposed to Guimarães Rosa, but identified with his literary achievement and enveloped within the more general pride of an autonomous national culture as such. Yet one can also identify national situations—and I use this clumsy circumlocution deliberately, to forestall the usual endless debates about whether there still are such things as "nations" and what their relationship to that other mysterious thing called "nationalism" might be—in which the defense of national autonomy takes the form of what may seem a more traditional modernism: the defense of the powers of art and high culture, the deeper kinship between such artistic modernism and the political power of the collectivity itself, now however conceived as a unified political power or collective project rather than a dispersal into democratic multiplicities and identity positions.

India is a vast and multiple place indeed, and one finds both modernisms and postmodernisms in full development there. But I have been thinking in particular of a specific vision that unites the social democratic project of the older Congress Party and Nehru's fellow-traveling nonalignment with a whole aesthetic and artistic politics that is quite different from the cultural studies politics (if I may put it that way) which we have touched on in the Latin American situation. But is this just the older modernism belated and warmed over? Does it really amount to a defense of Identity over against Difference, and in that sense does it reinforce the attacks on modernism current everywhere, which always seem to have the effect of discarding a modernist politics along with a modernist art, and thereby leaving us politically aimless, as so many people complain today?

It is not out of any wish to mediate, to resolve all these differences and turn theoretical debates and battles into harmony—but rather because I want to stage the powers and benefits of the dialectic itself—that I would propose the following hypothesis: that these differences do not have to do with Difference so much as with where it is located or positioned. Who could be against Difference on the social or even the political levels? Indeed, behind many of these essays stands the validation of a new democratic politics (in the first as well as in the third world) stimulated by the vitality of markets as such, peasant and otherwise: it is a more exotic sociological variant of that age-old defense of commerce and capitalism in terms of exchange and political freedom that has already been mentioned. Yet everything depends on the level at which a malign and standardizing or despotic identity is discerned. If this is to be found in the existence of the State itself, as a national entity, then to be sure, a more micropolitical form of difference, in markets and culture, will be affirmed over against it as a force for the resistance to uniformity and power: here, then, the levels of the cultural and the social are summoned to stand in radical conflict with the level of the political. And at certain key moments in arguments of this kind, something like an affirmation of federalism is invoked as a future ideal, notwithstanding recent historical developments, about which one might also affirm that they document the failure and death, not of communism, but rather precisely of federalism as such (the USSR, Yugoslavia, even Canada).

However, when one positions the threats of Identity at a higher level globally, then everything changes: at this upper range, it is not national state power that is the enemy of difference, but rather the transnational system itself, Americanization and the standardized products of a henceforth uniform and standardized ideology and practice of consumption. At this point, nation-states and their national cultures are suddenly called upon to play the positive role hitherto assigned—against them—to regions and local practices in the preceding paradigm. And as opposed to the multiplicity of local and regional markets, minority arts and languages, whose vitality can certainly be acknowledged all over the world uneasily coexisting with the vision of doom, of their universal extinction, it is striking to witness the resurgence—in an atmosphere in which the nation-state as such, let alone "nationalism," is a much maligned entity and value—of defenses of national culture on the part of those who affirm the powers of resistance of a national literature and a national art. Such defenders identify the levels of art and politics by linking the vitality of a national and a modernist culture (here, perhaps, one could indeed oppose to Gramsci's "national-popular" strategy a genuine "national-modernist" one, despite the fact that Gramsci himself was probably also a modernist in such matters) to the possibility of a great collective or national political project such as was envisioned on the Left and on the Right during the modernist period.

This position presupposes that it is only by way of such a possibility that the encroachments of the world market, of transnational capitalism along with the great capital-lending power centers of the so-called first world, can be opposed. That in the process it must also oppose the dispersals of a postmodern mass culture then places it in contradiction with those for whom only the activation of a truly grassroots culture of multiplicities and differences can oppose, first the national state itself, and then presumably what lies beyond it in the outside world (even though, paradoxically, it is often elements of that outside and transnational mass culture that are appropriated for such resistances: Hollywood films being sometimes the source of resistance to internal hegemony as well as the form external hegemony ultimately takes).

Now I have little enough time to summarize what may seem to have been a never-ending series of paradoxes; such an impression would already mark a useful beginning, insofar as it awakens the suspicion that our problems lie as much in our categories of thought as in the sheer facts of the matter themselves. And that would be, I think, the meaning and function of a return to Hegel today, as over against Althusser. The latter is surely right about his materialistic dialectic, his semiautonomous levels, his structural causality, and his overdetermination: if you look for those things in Hegel you find what everybody knew all along, namely, that he was simply an idealist. But the right way of using Hegel is not that way; it lies rather in precisely those things he was capable of exploring because he was an idealist: namely, the categories themselves, the modes and forms of thought in which we inescapably have to think things through, but which have a logic of their own to which we ourselves fall victim if we are unaware of their existence and their in-forming influence on us. Thus, in the most famous chapter of the Greater *Logic*, Hegel tells us how to handle such potentially troublesome categories as those of Identity and Difference.[13] You begin with Identity, he says, only to find that it is always defined in terms of its Difference with something else; you turn to

Difference and find out that any thoughts about that involve thoughts about the "identity" of this particular category. As you begin to watch Identity turn into Difference and Difference back into Identity, you grasp both as an inseparable Opposition, you learn that they must always be thought together. But after learning that, you find out that they are not in opposition, but rather, in some other sense, one and the same as each other. At that point, you have approached the Identity of identity and nonidentity, and in the most momentous single reversal in Hegel's entire system, suddenly Opposition stands unveiled as Contradiction.

This is always the point we want to reach in the dialectic: we want to uncover phenomena and find their ultimate contradictions behind them. And this was Brecht's notion of dialectic: to hold fast to the contradictions in all things, which make them change and evolve in time. But in Hegel, Contradiction then passes over into its Ground, into what I would call the situation itself, the aerial view or the map of the totality in which things happen and History takes place. I like to think that it is something like this movement of the categories—producing each other, and evolving into ever new viewpoints—that Lenin saw and learned in Hegel, in his momentous reading of him during the first weeks and months of World War I.[14] But I would also like to think that these are lessons we can still put to use today, not least in our attempts to grasp the still ill-defined and ever-emerging effects of that phenomenon we have begun to call globalization.

Notes

1   Eric Wolf, *Europe and the People without History* (Berkeley, 1982).
2   David Bordwell, Kristin Thompson and Janet Staiger, *The Classical Hollywood Cinema: Film Style and Mode of Production to 1960* (New York, 1985), 381–385.
3   Giovanni Arrighi, *The Long Twentieth Century* (London, 1994), 330–331.
4   Néstor García Canclini, *Culturas Híbridas* (Mexico City, 1989).
5   Albert O. Hirschman, *The Passions and the Interests* (Princeton, NJ, 1977).
6   But see Maurice Meisner's *The Deng Xiaoping Era* (New York, 1996) for powerful evidence about the possibilities for capitalist development offered by so-called "nondemocratic" systems.
7   George Yúdice, "Civil Society, Consumption, and Governmentality in an Age of Global Restructuring" *Social Text* 45 (1995): 1–25.
8   Friedrich Schiller, *On the Aesthetic Education of Man,* trans. E. M. Wilkinson and L. A. Willoughby (Oxford, 1967).

9   John Fiske, *Television Culture* (London, 1987).

10 Jacques Attali, *Les Trois Mondes* (New York, 1983).

11 Stuart Hall and Martin Jacques, *New Times: The Changing Face of Politics in the 1990's* (New York, 1991).

12 C. L. R. James, *The Black Jacobins* (New York, 1963).

13 G. W. F. Hegel, *The Science of Logic,* trans. A. V. Miller (London, 1969), bk. 2, sect. 1, chap. 2: "The Essentialities or Determinations of Reflection."

14 Kevin Anderson, *Lenin, Hegel and Western Marxism* (Urbana, IL, 1995).

II ALTERNATIVE LOCALITIES

Global Fragments: A Second Latinamericanism

The Immigrant Imaginary

The battle between the local and the global is also a struggle for or against the planetary imposition of a system of control based upon hierarchically organized homogenization and administered difference. Area studies either will help, through the supply of epistemic tools and in other ways, in the construction and implementation of said system of control, or will hinder it. This essay is a programmatic contribution to the latter task, understood from my own position as a Latinamericanist living and working in the United States.

Western universities are not just purveyors of globalization at the technical level, but also significant sites of theorization for nonglobal practices and experiences. On the one hand, by virtue of its institutional mission in the reproduction of the global system, the Western university is an overwhelming machine for the colonizing and dismantling of singular practices. Disciplinary knowledge, for instance, can only advance in the sense of a more and more thorough subjection of its object of study to the global epistemological power/knowledge grid. Even when disciplinary knowledge attempts to understand antiglobal or heterogenizing movements in its object, it cannot but proceed to subject its object to an ever more thorough disciplinary ideological interpellation. Disciplinary knowledge is a globalizing machine.

At the same time, the university is also the theoretical site of enunciation for any number of singularizing practices: of feminist practices, of gay and lesbian practices, of calls for the cultural survival of threatened or disappearing human communities and calls for solidarity with the poor, of theories of racial consciousness, of resistance to colonial discourse, and of a certain enactment of postcolonial discourse. The university remains one of the sites for a tradition of thinking whereby critical theoretical reflection takes place, even if not necessarily attached to immediate political practices in the larger public sphere. Although it may be true that democratization initiatives at the local, national, or transnational levels are not first developed at the university, the university welcomes them and contributes to their theorization. The university, in view of the shrinking of the intellectual public sphere, has become one of the last institutional sites where a critical practice is not just theoretically possible, but also practically existing.

James Petras and Morris Morley's 1990 harsh indictment of the Latin American institutional intellectual (defined as one who "writes for and works within the confines of other institutional intellectuals, their overseas patrons [i.e., funding institutions], their international conferences, and as political ideologues establishing the boundaries for the liberal political class")[1] is unfair only insofar as it limits itself to the Latin American intellectual. Those are in fact the general conditions of global academic thinking, at least in the West and in Western-dominated areas. There is consequently a need to develop a coherent theoretical framework under which reflection on current political constraints can give way to reflection on political possibilities. Some of those possibilities are to be found in the space afforded by the apparent contradiction between tendential globalization and regional theory. Within the United States, the most obvious institutional stage for that conflict is the academic area studies establishment.

Area studies were never conceived to be a part of antiglobal theory. On the contrary, as Vicente Rafael retells the story, "since the end of World War II, area studies have been integrated into larger institutional networks, ranging from universities to foundations, that have made possible the reproduction of

a North American style of knowing, one that is ordered toward the proliferation and containment of Orientalisms and their critiques."[2] The project
followed an integrationist logic whereby "the 'conservative' function of area
studies, that of segregating differences, is made to coincide with their 'progressive' function, that of systematizing the relationship among differences
within a flexible set of disciplinary practices under the supervision of experts
bound by the common pursuit of total knowledge."[3] A secret imperial project
comes then to join the more apparently epistemic one: "the disciplined study
of others ultimately works to maintain a national order thought to be coter-
minous with a global one."[4]

For Rafael, however, the practice of area studies as traditionally understood
is today threatened by the arrival upon the scene of what he calls "an immigrant imaginary," one of the immediate consequences of which is to problematize the spatial relationships between center and periphery, between
home and abroad, between the locality of knowledge production and its site
of intervention: "Since decolonization, and in the face of global capitalism,
mass migrations, flexible labor regimes, and spreading telecommunications
technologies, it has not been possible for area studies to be, or merely to be, a
colonial undertaking that presumes the metropole's control over its discrete
administrative units."[5]

U.S. Latinamericanism is certainly conditioned, although perhaps not yet
to a sufficient degree, by the drastic demographic changes and the massive
Latin American immigration to the country in recent decades. U.S. Latinamericanism can no longer pretend merely to be an epistemic concern with
the geographic other south of the border. Instead, the borderlands have
moved northward and within. The immigrant imaginary must necessarily
affect an epistemic practice that used to be based upon a national-imperial
need to know the other, insofar as that other is now pretty much ourselves, or
an important part of ourselves. As Rafael puts it, "the category of the immigrant—in transit, caught between nation-states, unsettled and potentially
uncanny—gives one pause, forcing one to ask about the possibility of a
scholarship that is neither colonial nor liberal nor indigenous, yet constantly
enmeshed in all these states."[6]

This hybrid scholarship has been theorized by a number of critics under
the name of postcolonial studies. Postcolonial Latinamericanism is therefore
a Latinamericanism informed by the immigrant imaginary—by the Latin

American within. Insofar as this academic practice arises out of a politics of location, or rather, out of a counterpolitics of location, as location was already thoroughly inscribed in previous practices; and insofar as this counterpolitics fixates upon differential localities of enunciation in their difference with respect to the smooth space of hegemonic, metropolitan enunciation, postcolonial Latinamericanism conceives of itself as a form of antiglobal epistemic practice geared toward the articulation and/or production of difference through the expression of an always irreducible if shifting distance from the global.

The immigrant imaginary thus opens the possibility of Latinamericanist counterimaginings to historically constituted Latinamericanism. Through them, Latinamericanism attempts to become an instance of antiglobal theory, insofar as it opposes the imperial formation of knowledge that has accompanied the move of capital toward universal subsumption in globalization. But what is to be decided is whether or not antiglobality can remain strong enough to counter effectively the controlling force of historically constituted Latinamericanism as the latter moves to reconstitute itself through the immigrant imaginary, by taming it and reducing it to a contingent position or a set of mobile positions within new social paradigms. In other words, there is no guarantee that the immigrant difference will not be ultimately assimilated—indeed, has not already been assimilated—by the global apparatus and its constant recourse to the homogenization of difference.

A question arises in that connection. Perhaps homogenizing disciplinary developments and the new role of the global university in the reproduction and servicing of the global system are not really in opposition to the academic theorization of heterogenizing, singularizing drives. Perhaps the latter is just the other side of the former, or in a sense necessary to it, necessary for the further expansion of global homogenization, a form of self-produced feed. In any case, even if homogenization and heterogenization are not really antinomical but stand in some sort of dialectical relationship, the relationship between them, as actually existing, remains an important site of political engagement. From the point of view of intellectual institutional politics insofar as they relate to global citizenship today, such a relationship might appear to be the proper region for reflection on new kinds of work in area studies. Although the following remarks are meant to refer to area studies in general, let me frame them as a question about the possibility of a second Latinamericanism.

Two Kinds of Latinamericanism

In the middle of the recent debate concerning CIA involvement in the Central American counterinsurgency apparatus, the *New York Times* published an article, signed by Catherine S. Manegold, which might be taken to stand as an archetypical example of the way the Western imaginary regulates and controls its engagement with alterity in post–cold war times: "the most improbable of intimacies."[7] The article embodies a powerful although fundamentally reactive narrative whose subtext sets up Latinamericanist solidarity work against the backdrop of obscure jungle desire or some heart-of-darkness fascination:

> Jennifer Harbury was 39 when she first saw Efraín Bamaca Velázquez. She was a lawyer working on a book about the women in Guatemala's rebel army, following an idiosyncratic path that led her deeper and deeper inside a well-hidden, war-hardened society of guerrilla fighters. She had traveled from Texas to Mexico City to the jungles of western Guatemala in her research. She was there to tell their story. She made no pretense of objectivity. She did not see gray and did not want to.[8]

Harbury's guerrilla romance with the younger and beautiful Maya comandante, described as "a fawn" in subliminar allusion to Walt Disney's Bambi, becomes a plausible and tendentially exhaustive explanation for an entanglement in social and political struggles that would otherwise seem utterly inappropriate for the Harvard Law graduate: "The prospect of death ordered his days. A fear of banality ordered hers."[9] Death appears as the figure of some exotic authenticity, and simultaneously therefore as the source of a perverse longing—a longing for negation that won't take itself for what it is. Through Harbury's paradigmatic story, the engagement of an American citizen with Central American revolutionary social movements is shown to amount to little more than a deluded orientalism of the heart: "Ms. Harbury tells it as a love story, her first, though she was married once before to a Texas lawyer whom she lived with only briefly."[10]

Orientalism of the heart is undoubtedly the mythical other side of the kind of global politics the CIA itself, together with the FBI, the DEA, and other U.S. law enforcement agencies would rightfully pursue, according to their criteria, for higher reasons involving global security and transnational terrorism. Within this discourse, orientalism of the heart comes close to being the only possible explanation for an opening to alterity in global times. Through Harbury, an entire class of Latinamericanist solidarity workers and left-wing intellectuals, as well as melodramatic citizens in general, are indicted at the level of affect: their desire, it can always be said, is only obscure love, and therefore neither epistemologically nor politically viable: "She made no pretense of objectivity. She did not see gray and did not want to."[11]

Globalization is essentially related to the sovereign pull of capital, to sovereignty as not only the foundation but also the apotheosis of empire. What Kenneth Frampton has called the "optimizing thrust of universal civilization" is perhaps no longer dependent upon the imperial projections of this or that national formation, or of a given set of them.[12] Theories of postmodernity tell us that it instead follows the flow of capital into a tendential saturation of the planetary field. Totality affects metropolitan self-understanding, as it affects peripheral or intermediate localities, by constantly reducing their claims to a differential positioning regarding universal standardization. Global difference may indeed be in an accelerated process toward global identity, to be accomplished by means of some monstrous, final dialectical synthesis after which there will be no possibility of negation.[13] And yet negation occurs, if only as a residual instance doomed to self-understanding through death. "The prospect of death ordered his days," says Manegold of the Maya comandante, as if only death could compensate for, or at least present a limit to, the desperate banality of the global standard.

I'll define Latinamericanism as the set or the sum total of engaged representations providing a viable knowledge of the Latin American object of enunciation.[14] Latinamericanist desire can claim to have a powerful association with death in at least two ways: on the one hand, Latinamericanism, as an epistemic machine in charge of representing the Latin American difference, seeks its own death by way of an integration of its particular knowledge into what Robert B. Hall, in one of the founding documents of area studies as we know them today, called "the fundamental totality" and "the essential unity" of all knowledge.[15] In this first sense, Latinamericanist knowledge aspires to a particular form of disciplinary power that it inherits from the imperial state apparatus. It works as an instantiation of global agency, insofar as it ultimately wants to deliver its findings into some totality of allegedly neutral, universal knowledge of the world in all its differences and identities. Born out of an ideology of cultural difference, its fundamental thrust is to capture the Latin American difference in order to release it into the global epistemic grid. It therefore works as a machine of homogenization, even where it understands itself in terms of promoting or preserving difference. Through Latinamericanist representation, Latin American differences are controlled and homogenized and put at the service of global representation. It is thus that Latinamericanist knowledge, understood in this first sense, ultimately seeks its own death, as it endeavors to transfigure itself into its own negation and to dissolve into the panopticon.

On the other hand, Latinamericanism can also conceivably expect to produce itself as an antirepresentational, anticonceptual apparatus whose main function would be that of arresting the tendential progress of epistemic representation toward total articulation. In this sense, Latinamericanism does not primarily work as a machine of epistemic homogenization, but rather against it: a disruptive force, or a wrench, in the epistemological apparatus, an anti-disciplinary instance or Hegelian "savage beast" whose desire does not go through an articulation of difference or identity, but rather through their constant disarticulations, through a radical appeal to an epistemic outside, to an exteriority that will not be turned into a mere fold of the imperial interior. In this sense, Latinamericanism seeks an articulation with alternative localities of knowledge production to form an alliance against historically constituted Latinamericanist representation and its attendant sociopolitical effects.

In the first case, Latinamericanism aims toward its own dissolution in its apotheosic completion: the day when Latinamericanist representation will finally be able to release itself into the final, apocalyptic integration of universal knowledge. In the second case, Latinamericanism engages its own death by operating a thorough critique of its own representational strategies regarding the Latin American epistemic object. But this critical, antirepresentational practice depends upon its previous formation and can be taken to be nothing but its negative or its very form of negation. It could even be argued that this critical, second Latinamericanist practice only comes into focus precisely at the moment when the first Latinamericanism starts to offer the first signs of its radical success, which is also its dissolution as such. However, this may not be entirely the first Latinamericanism's own merit: something else has happened, a social change that has radically altered the stakes in the game of knowledge production.

Commenting on Gilles Deleuze's idea that "we have recently experienced a passage from a disciplinary society to a society of control," Michael Hardt makes the following argument:

> The panopticon, and disciplinary diagrammatics in general, functioned primarily in terms of positions, fixed points, and identities. Foucault saw the production of identities (even "oppositional" or "deviant" identities, such as the factory worker and the homosexual) as fundamental to the functions of rule in disciplinary societies. The diagram of control, however, is not oriented toward position and identity, but rather mobility and anonymity. It functions on the basis of "the whatever," the flexible and mobile performance of contingent identities, and thus its assemblages or institutions are elaborated primarily through repetition and the production of simulacra.[16]

If the first Latinamericanism was one of the institutional avatars of the way disciplinary society understood its relationship to alterity, a window in the panopticon, as it were, the second Latinamericanism might be conceived to appear as a form of contingent epistemic performativity arising out of the shift to a society of control. No longer itself caught in the search and capture of "positions, fixed points, identities," the second Latinamericanism finds in this unexpected releasement the possibility of a new critical force. This is so only to the extent that the second Latinamericanism can articulate itself in the rift, as it were, of a historical disjunction: that which mediates the change from discipline to control.

If societies of control assume the final collapse of civil society into political society, and thus the coming into being of the global state of the real subsumption of labor under capital, what is then the mode of existence of nonmetropolitan societies in global times? Presumably, it would have to be defined by a quantitatively larger presence in their midst of elements from previous social configurations, themselves in the process of vanishing, but at a slower pace. In other words, "the whatever" is active in peripheral societies still only as a dominant horizon, not a social given.

It may already hold true for metropolitan societies that, in Hardt's words,

> instead of disciplining the citizen as a fixed social identity, the new social regime seeks to control the citizen as a whatever identity, or rather an infinitely flexible placeholder for identity. It tends to establish an autonomous plane of rule, a simulacrum of the social—separate from the terrain

of conflictive social forces. Mobility, speed, and flexibility are the qualities that characterize this separate plane of rule. The infinitely programmable machine, the ideal of cybernetics, gives us at least an approximation of the diagram of the new paradigm of rule.[17]

But this "paradigm of rule" is not yet, I think, naturalized in peripheral societies. In the meantime, in the time lag that separates peripheral discipline and metropolitan control, there the second Latinamericanism announces itself as a critical machine whose function for the time being is twofold: on the one hand, from its disjointed, shifting position from the diagram of discipline to the diagram of control, to engage Latinamericanist representation as obsolete metropolitan disciplinary epistemics; on the other hand, from its disjointed, residual connection with Latin American disciplinary social formations, to engage Latinamericanist representation as it evolves into the new paradigm of epistemic rule. The second form of Latinamericanism, which grows out of epistemic disjunctures, can then use its problematic status alternatively or simultaneously against paradigms of discipline and against paradigms of control. Thus announced, it remains no more than a logical and political possibility whose conditions and determinations must then be further, even systematically, explored.[18]

Hardt ends his essay in reference to the possibilities of political practice that the shift from societies of discipline to societies of control necessarily opens: "The networks of sociality and forms of cooperation embedded in contemporary social practices constitute the germs of a new movement, with new forms of contestation and new conceptions of liberation. This alternative community of social practices (call it, perhaps, the self-organization of concrete labor) will be the most potent challenge to the control of postcivil society, and will point, perhaps, to the community of our future."[19] The second Latinamericanism, nothing but a form of academic social practice, understands itself as fully within the gaze of this alternative community.

If it is fair to say that the first Latinamericanism operates under the assumption that alterity can always, and indeed must always, be theoretically reduced, the second Latinamericanism understands itself in epistemic solidarity with the residual voices, or silences, of Latin American alterity. But it does not do so without risk. Insofar as there should remain some linkage between solidarity practices and third-world, or colonial, localities of enunciation, globalization turns solidarity, epistemic or not, into an orientalist poetics of the residually singular, the tendentially vanishing, the obscurely, if beautifully, archaic, as represented in the *New York Times* piece: "he looked almost like a fawn."[20]

Globalization, once accomplished, dispenses with alternative localities of enunciation and reduces politics to the administration of sameness. Within accomplished globalization, as was said above, there is only room for repetition and the production of simulacra; even so-called difference is nothing more than homogenized difference, a difference that responds to always already predefined "lexicons and representations, . . . [and] systems of conflicts and responses."[21] However, insofar as globalization is not yet accomplished, insofar as the time lag, or the difference between societies of discipline and societies of control, has not closed in upon itself, the possibility of alternative localities of enunciation will remain dependent upon an articulation with the singular, the vanishing, the archaic.

But whatever can still speak in singularly archaic ways can only be a messianic voice. It is a singularly formal voice, in that it only and endlessly says "Listen to me!" It is a prosopopoeic voice, in the sense that it is a voice from the dead, from the dying, a voice of mourning, like all messianic voices. Latinamericanism can only be open to the messianic intimations of its object through an active affirmation of solidarity. Solidarity has epistemic force insofar as it understands itself to be in critical resistance to old and new paradigms of social-epistemic rule. A Latinamericanist epistemic politics of solidarity is therefore an extension into metropolitan academic practices of counterdisciplinary or countercontrol movements arising in principle from the Latin American social field.

Solidarity politics needs to be conceived, in at least one of its faces, as a counterhegemonic response to globalization, an opening to the trace of the messianic in the global world. Metropolitan-located solidarity politics, insofar as it represents a specific articulation of political action with claims for redemption originating in a nonhegemonic other, is not the negation of globalization: it is, rather, the recognition, within globalization, within the frame of globalization or within globalization as frame, of an always vanishing and yet persistent memory, an immemoriality sheltering the singular affect, sheltering singularity, even if that singularity must be understood in reference to a given community or to a given possibility of communal affiliation.

There is then another possibility for reading Manegold's story: Harbury does not indulge in orientalism, but, through her politics of solidarity with the dead and the dying, she opens herself up to the possibility of preservation of what is immemorial, and therefore to a new thinking beyond memory: a postmemorial thinking, aglobal, coming to us from the singularity that remains, residually. If thinking is always a thinking of the singular secret, a thinking of affective singularities, there is no such thing as globalized thinking; and yet, globalization reveals that which globalization itself destroys, and by so doing gives it as a matter for thinking: a thinking of mourning singularity, from singularity-in-mourning, a thinking of what is revealed in destruction. This is not to say that such a thinking has been given to us as yet, only that its possibility may be there. As possibility, a possibility that I cipher in the notion of a second Latinamericanism, it prefigures an epistemological break, with all sorts of implications for a revision of cultural geopolitics, including a revision of area studies and of its articulation with identity politics.

The Singular Dream

Globalization in the cultural-ideological sphere follows in the wake of the subjection of the citizenry to homogenizing drives mostly deriving from what Leslie Sklair has called "the culture-ideology of consumerism."[22] But even consumerism itself is effective at the individual level by calling for an antiglobal, always local and localized appropriation of the product. As George Yúdice has argued, if citizenship is to be defined fundamentally in terms of participation, and if participation is not to be thought, today, outside the frame of consumerist ideology, then citizenship and the consumption of goods, whether material or phantasmatic, go hand in hand. Those parameters presuppose that civil society cannot be understood, today, as in any sense outside the global economic and technological conditions that contribute to the production of our experience; indeed, those global conditions would be the fundamental producers of experience. As Yúdice puts it, "theories of civil society based on experiences of struggles of social movements against or despite the state, which captured the imagination of social and political theorists in the 1980s, have had to rethink the concept of civil society as a space apart. Increasingly, there is an orientation toward understanding political and cultural struggles as processes that take place in the channels opened up by state and capital."[23]

Arjun Appadurai makes what I will read as a similar point about civil society when he describes "the conditions under which current global flows occur" as produced by "certain fundamental disjunctures between economy, culture, and politics."[24] For Appadurai, "global cultural process[es] today are products of the infinitely varied mutual contest of sameness [homogeniza-tion] and difference [heterogenization] on a stage characterized by radical disjunctures between different sorts of global flows and the uncertain land-scapes created in and through these disjunctures."[25] Appadurai's "radical disjunctures" disarticulate and rearticulate social actors in unpredictable and therefore uncontrollable ways (in "radically context-dependent ways," as Ap-padurai adds rather euphemistically);[26] they are, today, the purveyors of experience, not the objects of it.

If, as Yúdice says, the culture-ideology of consumerism is ultimately re-sponsible, in the global system, for the very articulation of oppositional social and political claims, in other words, if consumerist globality not only abso-lutely circumscribes but even produces resistance to itself as yet another possibility of consumption; or if "the fundamental disjunctures between economy, culture, and politics," in Appadurai's words, are responsible for a global administration of experience that no social agency can control and no public sphere can check, then it would seem that intellectuals are fundamen-tally conditioned to be little more than purveyors of a more or less smooth incorporation of the global system into itself, along with the whole array of workers in the cultural-ideological sphere. There is no cultural-ideological praxis that is not always already produced by the movements of transnational capital, which is to say, we are all factors of the global system, even if and when our actions misunderstand themselves as desystematizing ones.

Ideology, then, in a certain strong sense, following the movement of capi-tal, is no longer produced by a given social class as a way to assert its hege-mony; it is not even to be solely understood as the instrument of transclass hegemonic formations, but it has come to function, unfathomably, through the very gaps and disjunctures of the global system, as the ground on which social reproduction distributes and redistributes a myriad of constantly over-determined, constantly changing subject positions. Under those conditions, even the Gramscian notion of the progressive organic intellectual as someone with a "direct link to anti-imperialist and anticapitalist struggles" would seem to appear as an ideologically packaged product for subaltern consumption. Petras and Morley's "new generation" of would-be organic intellectuals have a tough job cut out for them indeed.[27]

If there is tendentially no conceivable exterior or outside of the global system, then all our actions are seemingly condemned to reinforce it. So-called oppositional discourse runs the most unfortunate risk of all: that of remaining blind to its own conditions of production as yet another kind of systemic discourse. And yet, what would insight accomplish? In other words, what good is it to engage in a metacritics of intellectual activity if that very metacritics is ultimately destined to become absorbed in the systemic apparatus whose functioning it was once thought designed to disrupt? Even the willed metacritical singularity of our discourses, whether it is to be thought in conceptual terms or in terms of style, voice, or mood, is to be incessantly reabsorbed into the frame that alone enables it, producing the site for its expression.

This notion may only be new in terms of its concrete articulation. A number of contemporary theorists have made similar points, and they all have a Hegelian genealogy: Louis Althusser talking about the ideological state apparatus and Fredric Jameson on capital in its third stage, and their discourse is not so drastically different in this respect from the quasi-totalizing parameters Jacques Lacan set in reference to the unconscious, Martin Heidegger and Jacques Derrida regarding Western ontotheology and the age of planetary technology, or Michel Foucault regarding the radically constituting sway of the power/knowledge grids. All of these thinkers come to the far side of their thinking by opening up, usually in a most ambiguous manner, the possibility of a thinking of the outside that will then become a redemptive or salvific region. Such a possibility seems to be an imperative for Western thinking, even the essential site for its constitution: an ineffable disjuncture at its origin, or the trace of the messianic in it, which Derrida has recently thought of, in his book on Marx, as just another name for deconstruction.[28] This messianic trace, which turns up in contemporary thinking as the compulsive need to find the possibility of an outside to the global system, a point of articulation permitting the dream of an oppositional discourse, has been expressing itself, ever since Hegelian dialectics, as the very power of the metacritical or self-reflective instance in the thinking apparatus. If it is true, on the one hand, that metacritics will always be reabsorbed by the system that first opens up its possibility, it seems as if it were also true that at some point, at some place of utmost ineffability or ambiguity, metacritics could throw a wrench into the reabsorption machine, arresting it or paralyzing it even if only temporarily. Such is, perhaps, the utopian dream of Western thinking in the age of mechanical reproduction.

But the age of mechanical reproduction, the age of the global system and the planetary technologization of (disjunctive) experience is also the age in which the question as to whether or not there is something other than a thinking that must be called Western retrieves a new legitimacy. The question itself comes from such Western thinking, for only Western thinking is sufficiently naturalized within the global system that constitutes it that it can legitimately, as it were, dream of an alternative singularization of thinking. But it is a special question, in that in it Western thinking wants to find an end of itself as a response to itself. This end would not necessarily have to come from non-Western geopolitical spaces; it would suffice, I think, to find the end internally, as perhaps a fold in the question about the end itself.

The end of thinking was paradoxically articulated by Theodor Adorno in terms of the ultimately irrepressible historical victory of instrumental reason. The radical negation of negativity itself, understanding the latter as the force of alienation, was for him the motor of a critical thinking that could then not stop short of negating the very possibility of critical thinking as a thinking of always insufficient negativity, always running the risk of a positive reification of its negative impulse. Adorno's melancholy abandonment of hope in the face of what he understood to be the fundamental but also fundamentally inescapable error of totality, which is also total alienation, would still find redemption in an always receding utopian countermove insofar as the latter could still be at all imagined, although never articulated.

Martín Hopenhayn has shown up to what point Adornian pessimism was conditioned by his metropolitan location, and by his more or less unconscious assumption of a particular historical standpoint that was then naturalized as universal. Hopenhayn argues that it is today quite possible, indeed even necessary, from the standpoint of Latin American new social movements and other emergent oppositional practices, to understand and use the full force of a critical theory-inspired thinking of negativity insofar as the global system is concerned, *and* at the same time use such gained knowledge toward the concrete affirmation "of that which negates the whole (interstitial, peripheric)."[29] This would be a thinking of historical disjuncture, where a dialectical relationship between negation and affirmation may not quite obtain. Globality may not be overcome or arsoned by "interstitial sparks," but spaces of coexistence may be implemented, folds within the global system, where an exterior to totality emerges as the site of a possible, concrete freedom: "Negation does not liberate from the negated—the general order—but it acknowledges spaces where that order is resisted. From this perspective, an *absolute* cooptation by dominant reason does not exist, even though micro-spatial, counter-hegemonic logics may not be able to engage in a process of general overcoming of dominant reason. [But this] critical function of social knowledge [preempts] . . . the total closure of the world by the dominant order."[30]

Hopenhayn's interstitial or peripheric spaces are disjunctive sites, of which it is affirmed that they hold the possibility of a singularization of thinking beyond negativity. With negative thinking they share the notion that there will be no historical closure insofar as the historicity of any system can still be understood as historicity, that is, insofar as something other than it can still be imagined. These interstitial spaces, however, are not postponed, as they might have been for Adorno, to the improbable but still ever more dimly perceivable future of utopian redemption; they are instead found in alternative presents, in the different temporality of alternative spatial locations. Hopenhayn quotes an Adornian sentence that might in fact define the negativity aspect of the new thinking of the singular: "Only s/he who is not totally caught up in the self-movement of the object is at all able to follow it."[31] Beatriz Sarlo opens her *Escenas de la vida postmoderna* with a similar statement: "Whatever is given is the condition of a future action, not its limit."[32] But a singular thinking must then establish its own positivity.

"Negation does not liberate from the negated—the general order—but it acknowledges spaces where that order is resisted."[33] If Latinamericanism could find in negativity a possibility of recognition of alternative knowledges, Latinamericanism would still not be a thinking of the singular, but it would have opened itself to the singular event and thus to the possibility of an exteriority to the global. In Latinamericanism, then, an end of thinking comes into operation which is also the stated goal of Latinamericanist thinking: the preserving and effecting of a Latin American singularity that would arrest "the total closure of the world by the dominant order."

Neo-Latinamericanism and Its Other

We are not yet outside the region defined by what Jameson has called the "temporal paradox" of postmodernity, which, when thought of on a global scale, takes on spatial overtones as well. In its first formulation, the paradox reads: "the equivalence between an unparalleled rate of change on all the levels of social life and an unparalleled standardization of everything—

feelings along with consumer goods, language along with built space—that would seem incompatible with just such mutability."[34]

If Latinamericanism could once generally think of itself as the set of interested representations in charge of preserving, no matter in how contradictory or tense a manner, an idea of Latin America as the repository of a cultural difference that would resist assimilation by Eurocentric modernity, for Jameson such an enterprise would today have been voided of social truth, for that specific countermodernity would have, at least tendentially, "everywhere vanished from the reality of the former Third World or colonized societies."[35] The Latinamericanist emphasis on cultural difference must then be understood in the context of neotraditional practices: "a deliberate political and collective choice, in a situation in which little remains of a past that must be completely reinvented."[36]

This particular kind of postmodern epistemic constructivism, which is in itself providing a powerful if perhaps residual possibility of revival to area studies as historically constituted, stands in a paradoxical relationship to the critical function that modernity envisaged as proper to the intellectual. The modern intellectual, again in Jameson's formulation, "is a figure that has seemed to presuppose an omnipresence of Error, variously defined as superstition, mystification, ignorance, class ideology, and philosophical idealism (or 'metaphysics'), in such a way that to remove it by way of the operations of demystification leaves a space in which therapeutic anxiety goes hand in hand with heightened self-consciousness and reflexivity in a variety of senses, if not, indeed, with Truth as such."[37]

The risk of Latinamericanism today is to engage in a neotraditional production of difference that could then no longer be interpreted as having a fundamentally demystifying character. The Latin American nonmodern residual, as invoked in journalistic, cinematic, and even academic discourse, is today frequently no more than an already-itself-constructed pretext for an epistemic invention by means of which metropolitan postmodernity narrates itself to itself via the detour of some presumed heterogeneity, which is in turn nothing but the counterpart of the thorough universal standardization, the stuff upon which the latter feeds in order to produce itself. If Catherine Manegold's rendering of Jennifer Harbury's story has revelatory power, it is because it reveals the deep structure of such epistemic constructionism. If its power is fundamentally reactive, it is because it reinforces it rather than attempting to modify it or to counter it.

One of the main (negative) functions of a second, antirepresentational, critical Latinamericanism would be that of arresting the tendential progress of epistemic representation toward total articulation. This second Latinamericanism is to be conceived as a kind of contingent epistemic performativity arising out of, and dwelling in the time lag between, the shift from a disciplinary society, in the Foucauldian sense, to a society of control, following Hardt's critical use of the Deleuzian notion. This second Latinamericanism would understand itself as an epistemic social practice of solidarity, with singular claims originating within whatever in Latin American societies still remains in a position of vestigial or residual exteriority, that is, whatever actively refuses to interiorize its subalternization with respect to the global system. In fact, this second Latinamericanism emerges as a critical opportunity through the metacritical realization that the first, or historical, Latinamericanism has come to a productive end in the end of the disciplinary paradigm of rule that understood the progress of knowledge as the panoptic search and capture of "positions, fixed points, and identities."[38]

Historically constituted Latinamericanism seeks to reformulate itself at the service of the new paradigm of rule through an epistemic constructivism that homogenizes difference in the very process of interpellating it, and for which this construction of neodifference is no more than a post–civil society detour toward the goal of universal subsumption of knowledges into the global standard. It is this new avatar of Latinamericanism, whose direct genealogy is historical Latinamericanism, that should be understood as neo-Latinoamericanism properly so-called (thus falling within the purview of Jameson's critique).

Against neo-Latinoamericanism, then, as its negation and secret possibility, another Latinamericanism, whose possibility dwells in the gap between the rupture of disciplinary epistemics (and its constant recourse to "positions, fixed points, and identities") and its reformulation as an epistemics of control (and its recourse to "the whatever" as the infinitely contingent placeholder for an identity that can never go beyond its frame and must therefore continuously produce itself as simulacrum and repetition). Between discipline and control, then, lies the always contingent performativity of a thinking of the Latin American singular, against discipline, against control. This Latinamericanism can only be announced here, in view of the programmatic determination of this essay. Its limit, which is therefore also the condition of its actions for the future, in Sarlo's phrase, might be given in the notion of preempting the total closure of the world by the dominant. It does not seem possible to find a way in which Latinamericanism can offer anything but a construed heterogeneity when attempting to think the Latin American singular; in other words, the Latin American singular, on being interpellated by Latin-americanism, cannot but become a Latinamericanist singular; by the same token, however, a radical opening to extradisciplinary heterogeneity through the work of negation remains the mark of this critical and antirepresenta-tional Latinamericanism, which self-reflexivity only prepares.

Opposite Numbers

Catherine Manegold's account of Jennifer Harbury's story has a neoracist sub-text. Etienne Balibar's precise definition of the phenomenon allows it to be understood as the reactive counterpart to Rafael's immigrant imaginary. Bali-bar explicitly mentions immigration, "as a substitute for the notion of race and a solvent of 'class consciousness,' " as a first clue toward the understanding of contemporary transnational neoracism.[39] Neoracism is the sinister coun-terpart to the cultural politics of difference that the immigrant imaginary, and other nonimmigrant but nevertheless subaltern social groups, generally in-voke as their emancipatory banner. Neoracism works in effect as the mirror image of identity politics, that is, as an identity politics of the dominant, insofar as "it is a racism whose dominant theme is not biological heredity but the insurmountability of cultural differences, a racism which, at first sight, does not postulate the superiority of certain groups or peoples in relation to others but 'only' the harmfulness of abolishing frontiers, the incompatibility of life-styles and traditions; in short, . . . a differentialist racism."[40]

Balibar makes the point that differentialist racism takes the antiracist argu-mentation of culturalism at its word, promoting a curious and effective "turn-about effect": for the neoracist, "if insurmountable cultural difference is our 'natural milieu,' . . . then the abolition of that difference will necessarily" create problems, such as "defensive reactions, interethnic conflicts and a general rise in aggressiveness," that would be best avoided by preempting, through exclusion in the form of some minor or major ethnic-cleansing procedure, too close a contact between the different human groups.[41] Mane-gold's understated ridicule of Harbury's involvement with the Maya guerrilla as a form of orientalism of the heart or romantic third-worldism is, con-sciously or unconsciously, meant to promote precisely that need for cultural separation. The result of all this is what Balibar calls a naturalization of racist conduct, in the sense that neoracism ideologically conceives of itself as trying to avoid racist conduct by eliminating the conditions that would lead to its "inevitable" manifestation.

Neoracism is, insofar as it affects, for instance, the Latino population in the United States, the opposite social and political number of the immigrant imaginary. What I am calling the "second" Latinamericanism fundamentally orients itself against the culturalist ground of neoracism. If, "from the logical point of view, differentialist racism is a meta-racism, or what we might call a 'second-position' racism, which presents itself as having drawn the lessons from the conflict between racism and anti-racism, as a politically operational theory of the causes of social aggression,"[42] then second-position Latinamericanism is, from the logical and the political point of view, also a meta-Latinamericanism that has understood the culturalist dangers of neo-Latinamericanism and its co-optation of difference. But it is above all a meta-Latinamericanism that understands itself as the social, political, and epistemic opposition to a historically reconstituted Latinamericanism in the context of the society of control—whether historically reconstituted Latinamericanism is posited as neo-Latinamericanism, in its liberal variant, or, in its extreme version, as an ideological formation at the service of a globalized technopolitics of selective inclusion and hierarchically organized distribution of planetary resources. In this, as in other things, we do not see gray, and we do not really want to.

Notes

"Latinamericanism," a term modeled on Edward Said's "Orientalism," was first used by Enrico M. Santí in "Latinamericanism and Restitution," *Latin American Literary Review* 40 (1992): 88–96. See also my "Restitution and Appropriation in Latinamericanism," *Journal of Interdisciplinary Literary Studies* 7, no. 1 (1995): 1–43.

1 James Petras and Morris Morley, "The Metamorphosis of Latin America's Intellectuals," in *U.S. Hegemony under Siege: Class, Politics and Development in Latin America* (New York, 1990), 152.
2 Vicente Rafael, "The Cultures of Area Studies in the United States," *Social Text* 41 (winter 1994): 91.
3 Ibid., 96.
4 Ibid., 97.
5 Ibid., 98, 103.

6 Ibid., 107.

7 Catherine S. Manegold, "The Rebel and the Lawyer: Unlikely Love in Guatemala," *New York Times,* 27 March 1995, A1.

8 Ibid. See also Catherine S. Manegold, "A Woman's Obsession Pays Off—At a Cost," *New York Times,* 26 March 1995, sec. 4, pp. 1, 4, for more of the same if from a different angle. For rich treatments of recent U.S. representations of Latin Americans along similar lines, see George Yúdice's comments on Joan Didion's *Salvador* in "Testimonio and Postmodernism," *Revista de crítica literaria latinoamericana* 36 (1992): 15–31, and Fredric Jameson's analysis of Robert Stone's *A Flag for Sunrise* in "Americans Abroad: Exogamy and Letters in Late Capitalism," in *Critical Theory, Cultural Politics, and Latin American Narrative,* ed. Steven Bell, Albert H. Le May, and Leonard Orr (Notre Dame, IN, 1993), 35–60.

9 Manegold, "Rebel," A1.

10 Ibid., A5.

11 Ibid., A1.

12 Kenneth Frampton, *Modern Architecture: A Critical History* (London, 1985), 327.

13 Jameson asks the question "Is global Difference the same today as global Identity?" at the end of his analysis of Frampton's proposal for a critical regionalism in architecture. Jameson wonders whether "pluralism and difference are not somehow related to [late capitalism's] own deeper internal dynamics" (*The Seeds of Time* [New York, 1994], 205, 204). Frampton's notion is relevant to this essay to the extent that Latinamericanism, or any area studies for that matter, can also be conceived from a certain perspective as a kind of critical regionalism. In fact, what Frampton says about modern architecture can sometimes be rather uncannily applied to geopolitical epistemics: "Critical Regionalism tends to flourish in those cultural interstices which in one way or another are able to escape the optimizing thrust of universal civilization. Its appearance suggests that the received notion of the dominant cultural centre surrounded by dependent, dominated satellites is ultimately an inadequate model by which to assess the present state of modern architecture" (Frampton, *Modern Architecture,* 327).

14 I take the notion of "engaged representation" from Stephen Greenblatt. Commenting about early European responses to the New World, Greenblatt remarks: "The responses with which I am concerned—indeed the only responses I have been able to identify—are not detached scientific assessments but what I would call engaged representations, representations that are relational, local, and historically contingent. Their overriding interest is not knowledge of the other but practice upon the other; and . . . the principal faculty involved in generating these representations is not reason but imagination" (*Marvelous Possessions: The Wonder of the New World* [Chicago, 1991], 12–13). Greenblatt's observation also applies, in my opinion, to later Latinamericanist representations.

15 Robert B. Hall, *Area Studies: With Special Reference to Their Implications for Research in the Social Sciences, Social Science Research Council Pamphlet 3* (May 1947), 2, 4.

16 Michael Hardt, "The Withering of Civil Society," *Social Text* 45, no. 14 (1995): 34, 36. The essay by Deleuze that Hardt refers to is "Postscript on the Societies of Control," *October* 59 (1991): 3–7.

17 Hardt, "Withering," 40–41.

18 I attempt to initiate such systematic exploration in my book in progress, *The Exhaustion of Difference.* My use of the notion of time lag is indebted to Homi Bhabha's invention of the term as a powerful tool of postcolonial studies: "in each achieved symbol of cultural/political identity or synchronicity there is always the repetition of the sign that represents the place of psychic ambivalence and social contingency . . . [the] time-lag [is] an iterative, interrogative space produced in the interruptive overlap between symbol and sign, between synchronicity and caesura or seizure. . . ." ("Postcolonial Authority and Postmodern Guilt," in *Cultural Studies,* ed. Lawrence Grossberg, Cary Nelson, and Paula Treichler [New York, 1992], 59). See also Walter Mignolo, typescript 27–29, in *Dimensions of Postcolonial Studies,* ed. Kalpana Sheshadri-Crooks and Fawzia Afzal-Khan, forthcoming, for further references and articulations.

19 Hardt, "Withering," 41.

20 Manegold, "Rebel," A5.

21 Daniel Mato, "On the Complexities of Transnational Processes: The Making of Transnational Identities and Related Political Agendas in 'Latin' America," typescript 32, in *Transnational Processes, Nation-States, and Cultures,* ed. Cristina Szanton Blanc, N. Glick Schiller, and L. Basch, forthcoming.

22 In one of Sklair's formulations, "the culture-ideology of capitalism proclaims, literally, that the meaning of life is to be found in the things that we possess. To consume, therefore, is to be fully alive, and to remain fully alive we must continually consume" (*Sociology of the Global System* [Baltimore, 1991], 41). But what is to be consumed is not necessarily only objects: identities are in fact consumable products as well, for instance. "Global capitalism does not permit cultural neutrality. Those cultural practices that cannot be incorporated into the culture-ideology of consumerism become oppositional counter-hegemonic forces, to be harnessed or marginalized, and if that fails, destroyed physically. Ordinary so-called 'counter-cultures' are regularly incorporated and commercialized and pose no threat, indeed through the process of differentiation (illusory variety and choice), are a source of great strength to the global capitalist system" (42).

23 George Yúdice, "Consumption and Citizenship," typescript 8. See his essay "Globalización y nuevas formas de intermediación cultural," in *Mundo, región, aldea: Identidades, políticas culturales e integración regional,* ed. Hugo Achúgar and Gerardo Caetano (Montevideo, 1994), 134–57, for these and related issues.

24 Arjun Appadurai, "Disjunction and Difference in the Global Cultural Economy," in *The Phantom Public Sphere,* ed. Bruce Robbins (Minneapolis, 1993), 280, 275.

25 Ibid., 287.

26 Ibid., 292.

27 One does not quite know whether Petras and Morley are talking out of wishful thinking or out of something else when they say "the incapacity of the institutional intellectual to provide adequate responses to the pressing problems confronting liberal-democratic regimes has already set in motion the formation of nuclei of young intellectuals with ties to the political and social movements. . . . The current crisis in Latin America may force members of the new generation of intellectuals who cannot be or choose not to be absorbed by the system to fight against it and to reconstitute themselves through organic ties to popular movements" ("Metamorphosis," 156).

28 "The necessary disjointure, the de-totalizing condition of justice, is indeed here that of the present—and by the same token the very condition of the present and of the presence of the present. This is where deconstruction would always begin to take shape as the thinking of the gift and of undeconstructible justice, the undeconstructible condition of any deconstruction, to be sure, but a condition that is itself *in deconstruction* and remains, and must remain (that is the injunction) in the disjointure of the *Unfug* . . . in the waiting and calling for what we have nicknamed here without knowing the messianic" (Jacques Derrida, *Specters of Marx: The State of the Debt, the Work of Mourning, & the New International* [New York, 1994], 28). See Jameson's comments on the Derridean messianic toward the end of "Marx's Purloined Letter," *New Left Review* 209 (1995): 75–109.

29 Martín Hopenhayn, *Ni apocalípticos ni integrados: Aventuras de la postmodernidad en América Latina* (Santiago, 1994), 155.

30 Ibid.

31 Ibid., 133.

32 Beatriz Sarlo, *Escenas de la vida postmoderna: Intelectuales, arte y videocultura en la Argentina* (Buenos Aires, 1994), 10.

33 Hopenhayn, *Apocalípticos,* 155.

34 Jameson, *Seeds,* 15.

35 Ibid., 20.

36 Ibid.

37 Ibid., 12–13. But see, for instance, Homi Bhabha, *The Location of Culture* (New York, 1994), or Rey Chow, *Writing Diaspora: Tactics of Intervention in Contemporary Cultural Studies* (Bloomington, IN, 1993), for different accounts of intellectual work in the context of postcolonial reason. See also Bruce Robbins, *Secular Vocations: Intellectuals, Professionalism, Culture* (London, 1993), in reference to the contemporary "professional" intellectual.

38 Hardt, "Withering," 36.

39 Etienne Balibar, "Is There a 'Neo-Racism'?," in Balibar and Immanuel Wallerstein, *Race, Nation, Class: Ambiguous Identities* (New York, 1991), 20.

40 Ibid., 21.

41 Ibid., 22.

42 Ibid.

Toward a Regional Imaginary in Africa

There is a globalized information network that characterizes Africa as a continent sitting on top of infectious diseases, strangled by corruption and tribal
vengeance, and populated by people with mouths and hands open to receive
international aid. The globalization of the media, which now constitutes a
simultaneous and unified imaginary across continents, also creates a vehicle
for rock stars, church groups, and other entrepreneurs in Europe and America
to tie their names to images of Afro-pessimism for the purpose of wider and
uninterrupted commodification of their name, music, or church. Clearly, the
media have sufficiently wired Africa to the West, from the public sphere to
the bedrooms, to the extent that Africans are isolated from nation to nation
but united in looking toward Europe and America for the latest news, politics, and culture.

The purpose of this paper is to present African perspectives on globalization in the form of public criticism generated by African cultural workers,
elites of the nation-state, and gossips in the marketplaces. Individuals in these
three social domains are in opposition, but they are united in their resistance
to the kind of globalization I have outlined above, going as far as to describe it

as the recolonization of Africa by international financial institutions such as the World Bank and the International Monetary Fund.

The Crisis of the CFA Devaluation

On January 20, 1994, European and American financial institutions imposed an expected but long-resisted currency devaluation on Francophone Africa that rendered export goods and labor in the region cheaper and more attractive to international corporations. Nigeria, Zaire, and Ghana, before Francophone Africa, had gone through the same process in the 1980s. Such "structural adjustment programs," the World Bank and other financial experts argue, by attracting investors to devalued products and people, create business roles for Africans who have been excluded for decades from the scene of global economics.

Before the devaluation occurred, countries like Congo, Côte d'Ivoire, and Cameroon were already suffering from the low prices offered for their export goods by the Clubs of Paris, London, and New York. Furthermore, it is difficult to understand how the devaluation will help Africans to repeat the economic success of the "Asian Dragons" (Hong Kong, Taiwan, and South Korea), given the historical differences between Africa's and Asia's experience with Western slavery, forced labor, and colonialism. During the independence movements, Francophone Africans were closely allied with the French Left and the labor unions, a fact that now makes it possible for Africans to take for granted the rights of workers, and that complicates the emergence of an organized cheap labor market in Africa as a means toward development.

The currency devaluation constitutes, therefore, the most serious economic and cultural crisis in Franco-African relations since the 1960s, when most African countries assumed their independence from France. It defines two things for the collective imaginary of Francophone Africans. First, it identifies France, the World Bank, and "weak" African leaders as the enemies of the people, the demons on whom to blame people's daily sufferings. Second, the devaluation provides people with new reflections about their own lives, about their relation to their leaders, political institutions, and globalization. In a sense, one can say that devaluation has united Francophone Africa inside and outside. From within, it mobilizes an inter-African imaginary for self-determination against the recolonization of the continent. From without, it links Africa to the West by cheapening the cost of raw material, and this has induced the worst economic crisis yet.

Like an earthquake that spares the house neither of the rich nor the poor, and against which there is no insurance policy, people from Dakar (Senegal) to Douala (Cameroon) feel the impact of the devaluation every hour, every day, and every month. Imagine the farmer being told that his harvest is only worth half of its real value, or the head of a household of sixteen having now to spend for the equivalent of thirty-two people. In the urban enclaves, where small entrepreneurs, the middle class and the underclass conglomerate, the devaluation, also referred to as "devalisation" (a pun on *dévaliser*, to rob), has the impact of a bush fire in a dry Harmattan season. In Dakar, the price of a sack of rice has doubled, producing a swarm of beggars in the streets. The devaluation wiped out what little resources the middle class used to display to distinguish itself from the underclass. The restaurants, movie theaters, clothing stores, and nightclubs are left to tourists and foreign businesspeople. Gasoline has become so precious that cab drivers wisely wait in front of hotels for customers. Universities have been closed in Senegal, Mali, Gabon, and Côte d'Ivoire. Fire departments, the police, and hospitals are barely functional in these countries, where people seem to be more preoccupied by the elusive daily bread for themselves and their families.

Everywhere in Africa, new social movements are sprouting with a view to wrest the nation away from what are perceived as incompetent leaders, or to liberate it from a second colonization by France, the World Bank, and the International Monetary Fund. In Dakar recently, I found myself discussing the issue of structural adjustment and Africa's second colonization with crew members of Ethiopian Airlines. Unsurprisingly, a young flight attendant said with pride that Ethiopia, unlike the other African states, had never been colonized. The copilot took a contrary attitude and asked rhetorically if the World Bank or the International Monetary Fund were not in Ethiopia. In his view, that was enough to prove that Ethiopia, too, had joined the ranks of colonies.

In Mali, students who played the central role in overthrowing the military dictatorship are once again agitating and vowing to overthrow the democratic government. Because of the recent structural adjustment programs and the devaluation, they are being treated to reduced scholarships, higher admission standards, school closures, and the lack of jobs after graduation. In Mali,

Senegal, Côte d'Ivoire, and many other countries, there are hints of privatizing education, something that even military dictators had not dared to do before. Many West Africans are longing again for the day and the heroes that will turn the tide of misery and humiliation suffered under structural adjustment and the devaluation. Students at the University of Dakar walked out of the negotiation to end the year-long strike in 1994, when they heard that the World Bank was behind the plans to restructure the university. Resistance is also mounting in such local newspapers as *Sopi, Le Sud, Wal Fadjri: L'Aurore,* and *Le Cafard Enchaîné.* They ask on whose side are the International Monetary Fund and the World Bank when they take into consideration economic factors only and when they insist on closing down state-owned factories and institutions. The press sees such structural adjustment as strategies designed to undermine the nation-state and to destroy the sociocultural base of African lives. The name of the World Bank now connotes more failure than success in Africa, and people are blaming structural adjustment programs for the recent crises in Sudan, Somalia, Rwanda, Zaire, and Nigeria.

Many conversations in Dakar's streets involve expert analyses of the investment activities of the World Bank in Africa. An unemployed schoolteacher may, for example, dominate the discussion during tea time with his pet theory about how the Bank has refinanced the debts owed to the industrial countries in order to impose structural adjustment on African states, while making sure that they owe an even bigger sum than before. The unfamiliar theory confuses many of his listeners—precisely what the schoolteacher was hoping for. He then goes on to explain that the interest payment on the Bank's loans absorbs revenues from coffee and oil exports that are necessary for the development of the continent. Or that the Bank only gives a small portion of the loans at a time, investing the biggest chunk in Western banks, and forcing Africans to pay interest on the total package.

A cab driver told me that he learned one lesson from the devaluation: African leaders are not real presidents, they are mere ambassadors who do what the "real presidents" in France and America tell them to do. He insisted that to be president is not to be ordered around like an ambassador. If African presidents had been in charge, they would have responded to the devaluation by uniting and creating their own currency. How can you be independent if you do not have your own money, he asked me rhetorically. He then said that Mali and Senegal were once one country and that they became divided all because Senghor was listening too much to de Gaulle. People feel that any change in Africa must first begin with leadership: African governments should not be run according to the needs and concerns of Europe and America. People do not understand why such issues as structural adjustment, pollution and other environmental concerns, population control, the need to preserve "authentic African cultures," and many more similar obsessions of European specialists have come to dominate the lives of Africans, pushing to the back the concerns for survival, modernization, and the good life in Africa. There is much admiration for Japanese and Chinese leaders, and regrets that African leaders did not follow their example. The saying goes that the West respects Japan, Hong Kong, China, and Taiwan today because these countries did not wait for the advice of the white man to jump into their own style of modernity. Africans, too, must find their own way in the modern world.

African leaders themselves view the devaluation as the end of an era that was characterized by personal friendships with the successive French presidents. Gone are the days when African leaders could count on France as a strong "father" who would defend them against the "bullies" of the World Bank and the International Monetary Fund. With the devaluation, African presidents have been dealt a humiliating blow that can be neither effaced by a promise of economic recovery nor concealed by long speeches on national television. This is all the more devastating because some people associate the power of the leaders with the wholeness of their public image. The Griots used to sing a popular song in Mali, called "Patron," to remind the masses that the president's power can be seen in the million CFA francs clothes he wears, in the car he drives, and in the way he speaks French. But now that the CFA is devalued, the exchange rate of the president's clothes is also devalued, damaging his symbolic capital in the process.

Most people in West Africa believe that France approved the devaluation for two reasons. First, it came because Houphouet Boigny, commonly known as *Le vieux* (the Old Man), died. Rumors have it that Mitterand promised Houphouet not to cheapen the value of the currency in his lifetime. Such a move would have meant a personal affront to the Old Man, after all that he had done for France. Had not Houphouet conspired with de Gaulle to isolate Sekou Toure after the latter's insulting "No" to France during the referendum of 1958? It was after Guinea's dramatic break with France that de Gaulle used the Old Man and Leopold Sedar Senghor of Senegal to prevent Guinea from participating in the economic and cultural activities of the region. Cornered like a wild animal, Sekou Toure then turned against his own people and became the worst dictator of West Africa. Many people believe that such sanctions would not have succeeded without Houphouet Boigny, who was respected by everyone in the region.

Because of the Old Man, Côte d'Ivoire became the privileged partner of France, which was anxious to display it as a success model against Guinea and Mali, which opted for socialism and looked to the Soviet Union, Cuba, and China for help. For years, France continued to invest in Côte d'Ivoire, making it the envy of the region. In his last years, the Old Man was clearly in a good position to take credit for the rapid and relatively peaceful modernization of his country, while economic crisis, dictatorships, and military coups were rampant throughout Africa. France remained loyal to Houphouet Boigny even during the economic crisis of the 1980s, coming to his rescue when oil and coffee prices fell. The Old Man became an undisputed leader in Francophone Africa, garnering votes for France at the United Nations and buffering the region against American and Soviet influences. It was the Old Man himself then, who appealed to Mitterand not to devaluate the CFA. It was said that the Old Man believed that devaluation, of all the elements of a crisis, was the one that affected people the most at the individual level, and therefore was the most likely to tarnish the popular image of a president. France wisely waited until the Old Man died to devalue the CFA by 100 percent.

The second reason the CFA was devalued had to do with France's position in Europe. France has to choose between a role in the European Economic Community (EEC), which had global economic implications, and a role as the lone superpower in Francophone Africa. The emergence of the EEC as a European supernation has began to erode not only France's power to protect certain national rights like those of its own traditionally strong unions, but also its power to sustain bilateral economic and political relations with Francophone Africa and to keep them away from the influence of the political culture of the EEC. To save face, France has often attempted to integrate Francophone Africa into the political culture of the EEC by shifting projects for African development from Paris to Brussels. The strategy is not only a money-saving device for France, but it also does not challenge in the immediate run the older-brother image of France in Africa and the unequal nature of

Franco-African relations; furthermore, France's role of intermediary between Africa and Europe boosts Francophony at the European level. This is no small gain in view of the fact that Germany, the United Kingdom, and France are all jockeying for linguistic dominance in the EEC.

It is clear that other EEC members want a distinction drawn between those interests that are germane to the particular identity of France and Francophony, and those that are of consequence to the EEC's role in the global market. Some EEC members, conscious of the need to create a European economic hegemony in Africa, unlike France, which places priority on Francophone Africa, are seeking to diversify aid among Anglophone, Francophone, and Lusophone African countries. Clearly, France can no longer ignore the realities of the global economy and resist injunctions of the EEC and the World Bank to stop overrating, for political reasons only, the value of the currency in Francophone Africa.

In August 1994, seven months after the devaluation of the CFA, the prime minister of France, Edouard Balladur, toured Francophone countries to reassure them that France had not abandoned them. While in Dakar, he stressed the common ties that bind France and Francophone Africa and France's commitment to those ties. He declared that France was ready to support Africa during this difficult time by giving financial aid that could cushion the impact of the devaluation and by underwriting the cost of certain pharmaceutical products to keep their price from doubling. Balladur also pointed out that the devaluation was not a bad thing; its aim was to bring Africa back into the world economy, and it had done that. Francophone Africa was now exporting more goods to Europe, America, and Asia than before; the lowered cost of the currency had also the potential to attract investors and to create jobs in Africa. Visibly, Balladur's optimism was shared by Côte d'Ivoire's new president, Henri Konan Bedié, who believed that his country had put the devaluation behind itself and was ready to compete, as the "African Elephant," against the "Asian Dragons." In Burkina Faso, Mali, and Senegal, the governments also tried to make a patriotic issue out of the devaluation by launching campaigns in favor of consuming national products and by demonizing imported goods such as cheese, ice cream, certain brands of rice, designer clothes, and perfumes. It is true that these political campaigns on radio and television are greeted by nationalist feelings, but the masses also feel anger toward the leaders and the elite who consume these goods in the first place. Some people point out that consumption is not the issue, the devaluation is, which means that people no longer have enough money to consume either local or imported goods.

Culture and Nationalism as Resistance to Globalization

I still remember my high school entrance exam because of drawing. I had prepared well for the important subjects: math, French, history, geography, and biology. Drawing, physical education, and music were not as important because the grades received in these disciplines were not weighted by a multiple factor in the final grade, as was the case with math and French. But that year we were asked to draw a *blason,* and I did not know what the word meant. I knew that, although drawing could not hurt me much, it could help me. We weren't supposed to talk to the examiner, so I looked intently in his eyes to show that I needed help. He came toward me and said to me: "Draw something, just anything, with something on it." I took my chances and drew a fisherman casting a net in the river, with fish visible in the water and the sun glowing in the background. When I went home that day, my uncle asked me how I did in the exam. I said that everything went well except for drawing. I asked him what a *blason* was. He did not know the meaning of the word either. I was disappointed. He told me that he was sure that I did well.

After the exam results were posted, I found out that I did well in drawing. This surprised me, but I did not think much of it, as I went on to high school. I now associate this event with two other incidents in my life. The first one took place around 1968 with the news that the national cigarette factory was on fire. I had a cousin who was very hip then. He was "in the wind," as we used to say, with his Honda motorcycle, his collection of records by Johnny Halliday and James Brown, his Elvis Presley navy cap, and white jeans. My cousin attended the Ecole normale d'administration, where they trained our new leaders. When he heard that the factory was on fire, he rushed there on his Honda. He came back later all covered with ash and dirt. He kept walking up and down in the yard, and everyone who came in asked him what had happened to his clothes. "I was at the national factory, helping to put out the fire," he said. I wondered then what took him so long to go to the bathroom and wash up, but I did not make much of that either.

The second incident happened in 1969, after the coup d'état. The military regime unleashed a campaign of privatization including an accusation against the national factories for draining the resources of the peasants, inducing drought, famine, and corruption. The soldiers promised that once we privatized everything, the French, the Americans, the World Bank, and the International Monetary Fund would help us, and foreign companies would invest in our country. I was not too bothered by this argument, for there were things about the old regime that I didn't particularly care for, such as the fact that we could not buy the latest records by the Beatles, the Jackson Five, and James Brown. I also resented that my peers in Côte d'Ivoire and Senegal had access to new movies from Europe and rock concerts. I definitely did not like the neighborhood policing, the curfews, and the imposition of Russian and Chinese in our school curriculum.

I was surprised, therefore, to see people marching to the National Assembly with banners and shouting "Ne touchez pas aux acquis du peuple. Yankee! Go Home. Jan Smit, au poteau." They were marching against capitalist invasion and appropriation of our national culture and economy. Because it was the thing to do, I joined the march until the tanks came and chased us away. Later, whenever we talked about that march, we linked it to another event that took place in the National Soccer Stadium. The president of the military regime had appointed one of the organizers of the rally to his cabinet. When the privatization issue came up again, the man waited for a big gathering at the stadium; he stood up and sang the national anthem, stated his opposition to privatization, and handed his resignation to the president. The man's courage made him an instant national hero; some versions of the event had tears dropping from his eyes as he sang the national anthem. That man is Alpha O. Konaré, the new president of Mali. Looking back at my high school drawing, I realized now that I was participating in the creation of a national structure of feeling with my *blason*.

Before the devaluation, globalization was viewed in two ways in Africa. Some people perceived it as the new colonialism of cultural forms of life in Africa by transnational corporations in complicity with Western governments and corrupt African leaders. Others viewed it as an opportunity for African artists and entrepreneurs to leave the periphery and join the metropolitan centers in Europe and America. The first paradigm relies on Fanonian theories of resistance and nationalist consciousness, whereas the second is based on performance and competition in the global village. As the applications of structural adjustment programs began to take their toll on national institutions like education, health care, state-owned factories, and the department of labor, people who felt that these were symbols of national autonomy engaged in cultural and social forms of protest and resistance. The Boy Scouts movements that started in the 1960s to construct a patriotic sentiment among the youth, and to draft them into the projects of nation-building, changed in the 1970s and 1980s into social movements of protest in high schools and universities, against the government's decreased commitment to education.

In the 1960s, mass education was part of the independence movement that presented schools as the road to Africa's development and self-determination. People felt that the meaning of independence lay in the possibility of everyone's having admission to free schools, unlike colonialism, which denied access to education. School therefore becomes a necessary symbol of national sovereignty, and students who fight to keep the institution from deviating from its original purpose are the new national heroes.

Souleymane Cisse's *Finye* (1982) is a classical deployment of narrative that constructs students as national heroes struggling for self-determination, democracy, and equal right to education. The film tells the story of Bah and Oumou, two high school sweethearts from different class formations. Oumou's father is a member of the ruling junta and governor of the region. Bah lives with his grandparents in an impoverished section of the city; his parents were presumably killed by the junta. The conflict involves the elite, powerful enough to buy exams and scholarships for their children abroad, and the masses, who are victims of educational reforms. Naturally, Oumou passes her exam, but Bah and other students with similar backgrounds fail, leading to the creation of a student movement to protest against the military dictatorship. The film ends with the mobilization of the whole country and the international press behind the students. Bah dies a national hero, and a civilian governor replaces the colonel. *Finye,* first inspired from the many student strikes in Francophone Africa, has become a prophetic film that continues to influence the youth movement against neocolonialism and military dictatorships in West Africa. A few years after the film was released, a student leader by the name of Cabral was killed by a soldier in an attempt to break a strike. The name Cabral was, incidentally, borrowed from Amilcar Cabral, the revolutionary leader of Guinea Bissau who was assassinated by the Portuguese army. Cabral, the student, like his namesake in the liberation struggle, and like Bah, the character in Cisse's film, has become a martyr who inspired other Malian students to continue the struggle until the military was defeated. By 1992, democracy finally arrived in Mali after a bloody confrontation between students, supported by their parents and other social groups, and the military. It was just like in *Finye*.

For those who believe in the second paradigm of globalization, good African art means a self-exiled art from the continent, in search of an eager clientele and economic success in the metropolitan centers of Europe, America, and Asia. Paris, New York, London, and Brussels become the outlets of the latest African music, films, theater, fashion, and literature. It is after acclaim has been heaped on the artist in Europe or America that he or she returns to Africa to display the laurels. Some artists return when the metropole no longer has use for their work. In other words, Africa is considered a secondary or marginal market for African art.

The plot of Sembene Ousmane's *Gelwaar* (1993) revolves around conflicts between Muslims and Christians about the corpse of Pierre Henry Thioune, a.k.a. Gelwaar, a Christian and political activist, who is buried in a Muslim cemetery and must be exhumed and given a proper Christian burial. It turns out that Gelwaar was killed because he exposed the negative effects of international aid on his country and incited people to rebel. For Sembene, the political culture in Africa has become so dependent on aid that it has lost the capacity to reproduce anything but a generation of beggars. In a controversial and powerful scene, the film contrasts mendacity to prostitution to illustrate that the prostitute's task is nobler than the beggar's because the prostitute supports herself and the beggar depends on donors. This is a new thinking insofar as it changes the cultural significance of begging in predominantly Muslim and animist West African societies, where beggars are seen as humble and honest people and as intermediaries between God and those who want to be absolved from a sin.

At the end of the film, a group of young people, inspired by Gelwaar's words, stop a truck full of sacks of flour donated by international organizations and spill the flour on the road rather than let it reach its destination. When an elderly man tells them that it is a sacrilege to pour food on the ground, Gelwaar's wife replies that what really constitutes a defilement of culture is to continue receiving this aid from foreigners.

With *Gelwaar*, Sembene returns to utopian narratives of self-determination that he explored in such early novels as *O Pays mon beau peuple* and *Les Bouts de bois de dieu* (*God's Bits of Wood*), and which he later abandons in his films in favor of the criticism of postindependence regimes, satire, and socialist realism. By describing itself in the generic as a legend of the twenty-first century, *Gelwaar* draws attention to the African fin de siècle, when the youth will break away from old paradigms of Afro-pessimism and take their destinies into their own hands.

National passion, in Africa as elsewhere, is built through soccer matches, star musicians, athletes, filmmakers, and writers that the nation appropriates. Countries that are predominantly Islamic find national unity by identifying with Arab nations that are successful through the grace of Allah, and against Christian demons and imperialists. Christianized Africans, on the other hand, think that they have a monopoly on modernity and find unity in labeling Islamic Africans as backward nations. But Africans themselves contributed to the shaping of national structures of feeling. Writers such as Sembene Ousmane and Ngugi Wa Thiongo tie the rise of national consciousness in Africa to World War II, in which Africans fought next to white people against fascism, xenophobia, and racism. In *O Pays mon beau peuple,* one of Sembene's characters argues that the war was more important for Africans than education, because it demystified white men for black people who traveled to Europe and saw white people as normal human beings, capable of evil and good, and fear and courage.

The nation in Africa is defined in opposition to other African states. Guineans despised Malians because they were poor and were invading Guinea to steal precious resources. People in Côte d'Ivoire blamed Ghanaians for the increase in prostitution and other crimes in their country. In Guinea, where I was at the time of independence, I remember that when the Malian national soccer team won a game, our joy was mixed with fear. There were fights in the streets, and for some time my young friends refused to play with me.

Market Corruption and the Resistance to Globalization

West African markets, traditionally the centers of international consumption and cross-cultural fertilization, provide a serious challenge to the scheme of globalization and structural adjustment fostered by the World Bank and other multinational corporations that are vying to recolonize Africa. All sorts of merchandise from a variety of origins are on display in traditional markets, which makes it impossible for the nation-states to control the flow of goods, currency exchange rates, and the net worth of the markets. Everything from computers, fax machines, and brand-name shoes to gold jewelry is found covered with dust in the marketplace. Merchants who specialize in currency exchange carry large sums in Japanese yens, Deutsche Marks, British pounds, French francs, and U.S. dollars in the deep pockets of the billowing trousers they wear under their long and loose gowns. In the markets are also well-traveled businesspeople who speak English, Spanish, and German, in addition to French and several African languages.

Markets occupy an important place in the collective unconscious of people in West Africa. In other words, every market is surrounded by legends and ghost stories. West African folktales abound with market stories in which human beings conduct transactions during the daytime and spirits take over at night. For some criminals and vandals these stories function as powerful deterrents, making modern stores, with their alarm systems, safer targets than the markets that are said to be crowded with ghosts at night. There are at least two other reasons why people keep away from traditional markets at night. It is believed that most merchants resort to the magic power of medicine men and Marabouts to protect themselves and their belongings. Markets are also where some outcasts and deranged people find refuge at night.

The history of markets in West Africa is also the history of the slave trade and the movement transcending tribal isolationism toward the mixing of cultures, customs, and languages: in other words, the movement toward globalization. Medieval towns in West Africa such as Timbuktu, Ganem, Araouane, Kumbi Saleh, Bornu, and Niani prospered through their markets, where Arab traders bartered salt, beads, dates, and domestic animals for slaves and gold. The disappearance or decline of some of these historic cities may also have been anticipated by the ban on slave trade or the displacement of some commodities by others in the marketplace.

West African markets continued to develop and support cities during the European slave trade and colonialism, cementing ties among diverse tribes around market goods and commercial languages such as Dioula and Hausa. The long-distance trips of kola merchants from Mali to Côte d'Ivoire, the regional roaming of Hausa spice and medicine dealers, and the forays of the slave traders between the interior of the continent and the coasts constitute the first efforts at creating a regional imaginary where faithful consumers waited to receive commodities and cultures from greedy and crafty merchants. What makes these traditional schemes of globalization special is the structural continuity they maintain with contemporary markets in opposition to the forms and structures of modernism that the nation-states have put in place in West Africa since the 1960s. It is for this reason that some may dismiss the markets as conservative and primitive forms of transaction that are opposed to the structured development plans of the nation-states.

What strikes the visitor to a market in West Africa is the seeming disorder implied by the display of commodities in discord: tomatoes and lettuce stand next to a colorful layout of fabrics from Holland and Hong Kong. The markets are cluttered and crowded with curvilinear paths that seem more to indicate the way out of the confusion than to lead to the merchandise of one's choice. If there is a vendor of mangoes, bananas, and oranges at the east entrance of the markets, there is likely to be one at the north, west, and south entrances as well. In fact, most merchants prefer to be on the periphery of the markets, or at the doors, instead of being grouped according to merchandise or affinity or occupying the center areas. Disorder is also implied by the manner in which merchants fight over shoppers and cut prices to outbid one another. The visitor to these markets may also be a little startled by the sight of deranged people, nearly naked, moving naturally among the crowd.

In West Africa today, traditional markets still pose the strongest obstacle to the nation-states and their plans for modernization. They also challenge the World Bank and other global institutions that consider the nation-states the only legitimate structure with which to conduct business in Africa. The local banks and treasuries compete with the markets for the money, and it is not uncommon nowadays to hear that all the money has vanished into the market and that the banks and the government coffers are empty.

Many state officials depend on the markets to cope with the crisis. Official employees often take foreign currency out of the banks to deliver to merchants in the market where they get more local money in exchange. Customs officers and tax collectors supplant their low wages with bribes from the merchants, which come in the form of brand-new cars, villas, and large sums in cash. The ministers in the government and the generals in the army receive equally valuable gifts in return for their friendship and protection.

The traditional markets can also serve as sources of emergency cash for the politicians in power. Merchants are often asked to contribute when the president's office needs money for a prestige trip to the United Nations or the Organization of African Unity. In the worst case scenario, when the banks run out of money and the president's office must have it, the tax collectors may suddenly remember an uncollected tax and threaten to close shops in the market until the amount needed is collected. All of this may seem grotesque to the outsider, or at least an abuse of the merchants by the state, but the market accepts it as normal because it increases the state's indebtedness to a system it officially dismisses as artisanal, primitive, and corrupted.

The competition between the markets and the nation-states and their multinational allies over the control of economic culture in West Africa has led to the politicization of merchants, who see in the new schemes of democratization and globalization nothing more than taking business away from the markets and delivering it to Lebanese- and French-run stores. On the other hand, African governments and the World Bank blame the failure of development projects on the markets, where corrupt merchants peddle smuggled goods at very low prices and prevent the rise of legitimate entrepreneurs who pay taxes.

Recently, the World Bank threatened to suspend a loan delivery to Mali until it was able to reduce significantly the flow of illegal merchandise in the Grand Marche de Bamako. The market of Bamako subsequently caught fire, which led people to speculate that it was the work of government arsonists. The Kermel market in Dakar burned under similarly suspicious circumstances in 1993, and it was rumored that the state's fire department, which was alerted at two in the morning, did not arrive at the site until six, by which time the place had been completely swallowed up in flame and smoke.

One must bear in mind that since the Arab and European conquests of Africa, many aristocrats from declining empires transformed themselves into powerful merchants in the marketplace and created a link between court nobility and economic capital, not to mention cultural capital. They elevated commerce to the highest level of distinction, comparing modern merchants with medieval warriors and powerful landlords, and contrasting their merchants' "authentic" nobility to that of colonial army officers and state functionaries who were relegated to the lower class.

Clearly, therefore, West African markets have been structuring economic fields of power and social spaces in the cities and provinces that engaged the colonial system in a competition for the reproduction of public spheres. At the time of independence, the nation-states, like the colonial system, regarded the markets as backward and failed to share with them the responsibility for the production of the elites of the modern state. From the onset, therefore, we have in West Africa two antagonistic systems, the market and the nation-state, competing for economic and cultural capital.

The markets' nobility is articulated not only by the distinction between the richest merchants and the poorest ones, but also through the accumulation of what Pierre Bourdieu calls symbolic capital, that is, a set of behaviors—such as lowering the price of goods for certain people, a readiness to help the needy, a reputation as a good Moslem, remembering one's origins and not being blinded by money, being clean, well-dressed, and courteous—which mask the merchants' monetary motivations by linking them to recognizable and accepted practices of the family, kinship, and the market. State functionaries are viewed with distrust because they always arrive in the market to take something and never give anything back; they are viewed as men without honor; they feed off the merchants' sweat. Students are also perceived with suspicion because, like baby snakes that grow into big and dangerous snakes, students will turn into functionaries one day. In West Africa, the majority of pickpockets and other petty criminals are dropouts from schools, a lumpenproletariat that is alienated from the values of the market, yet not good enough to join the service of the nation-state.

On the other hand, the state selects the members of its own nobility from among those who can read and speak French. Schools and armies are the principal sources of this new African elite, which considers the merchants the most uncivilized, the most corrupt and backward of all men. Yet, a more intelligent scenario of nation-building would have been to put the traditional market economy at the base of the political culture of the state, and to undertake at the same time to transform progressively the merchants into modern business bureaucrats and entrepreneurs. In other words, the West African governments should have worked in the interest of the markets with their age-old tradition of Hausa, Soninke, Yoruba, Fulani, Serere, Mandinka, and Dioula traders.

But the West African states became the accomplices of their European partners, and not of the merchants of the marketplace who were considered too primitive to be included in the category of the "new man" à la Frantz Fanon. The problem here, contrary to what Axelle Kabou and others seem to believe, is not that African traditions are closed to the outside influences that are necessary to modernization. West African merchants were familiar with faraway and forbidden metropolises like Paris, New York, Hong Kong, Tokyo, and Johannesburg before African students set foot in those places. There is a saying in West Africa that when the Americans reached the moon, they found Soninkes and Hausas there, looking for diamonds. The problem is that the nation-state believed too much in the new man and confused him with the European man and his culture, which could be acquired in West Africa at the expense of the market woman and man and their cultures.

The concept of Western technology involves a masked essentialism and immanence that cement the relationship between the European and modern technology and posits that any participation in the technological revolution must necessarily import European culture. The implications of this ideology, which refuses to place science in a historical context and to see the evolution of Europe as a particular moment of that history, have been devastating to cultures in Africa, which are usually viewed in binary opposition to Western culture and technology. The states in Africa have surrendered to the notion of the superiority of European rationality and internalized the stereotype of African experiences in the market as discontinuous with the interest of the new man. Yet, if the Japanese had listened to Europeans, they would be laughing at themselves today, and the scientific world would be worse off.

West African merchants are struggling against the homogenization of the world markets and cultures by doing what they have done from the Middle Ages to the present: traveling to faraway places to bring the goods that will keep them competitive in the market, and resisting attempts at a takeover by Lebanese and Europeans; resorting to cultural strategies of price breaking, tax evasion, and corruption of state agents, while denigrating the same civil servants for being too Westernized and against the prosperity of the market. Far from remaining closed to outside influences, the merchants are the first to introduce radios, sunglasses, watches, televisions, and Mercedes cars to the remote places of West Africa. They revitalize traditional cultures through the introduction of these new elements in the market, resist the takeover of businesses by multinational corporations, and compete with the agents of the state for the role of modernizing the masses.

African intellectuals and European expatriates, blinded by an essentialized notion of Western technology versus African traditions, consider the consumer culture of the market alienating. They unleash a plethora of arguments emanating from anthropology, Marxism, and nationalism, against Moslem and Christian fundamentalism, which attempt to shield the African in his or her authenticity, pure relation to production, and clean communion with God from the exploitation, alienation, and splitting of his or her identity by the consumer goods from the West. Although the alienation thesis may have been a meaningful argument during the early phases of nation-building in

Africa, or during colonialism, it has lost some of its explanatory power in the era of globalization. For instance, it is possible to see a valid theory of alienation in Fanon's discovery that the French used culture-specific radio dramas to destabilize the Algerian family structure during the liberation war. For Fanon, the French deliberately used the radio to strike at the core of the Algerian resistance movement, as, for example, when a Moslem family had to listen to an enticing love story on the radio in the presence of in-laws. Fanon's critique of alienation was extended to television and newspapers to show that Africans utilize European culture as their reference for news, fashion, and definition of reality.

African filmmakers have unsparingly deployed this Fanonian concept of alienation to define their own positions against cultural imperialism. Films denounce it under whatever form it presents itself: the preference of some Africans for the French language over local languages in *Xala* (1974) and *Gelwaar* (1993) by Sembene Ousmane; their habit of watching television as an escape or source of identity formation in *The Garbage Boys* (1986) by Cheick Oumar Sissoko, *The Shadow of the Earth* (1978) by Taieb Louhichi, *Zan Boko* (1988) by Gaston Kabore, and most recently in *Bab El Oued City* (1994) by Merzak Alouache, a powerful film about Moslem fundamentalism in Algeria. The last film opens with a loudspeaker declaring that "we must clean our city of the filth coming from outside." The allusion is to European cultural imperialism, which stands between Algerians and their Moslem identity. Imported goods, particularly goods associated with France such as Camembert cheese, alcoholic beverages, television soap operas, and makeup for women, come under attack, forcing into clandestinity those who consume them. But, as the film shows, with globalization and the homogenization of taste, goods imported from Europe and elsewhere may be the only goods that some Algerians know. Clearly, by placing a ban on the consumption of these products, the advocates of the alienation thesis may be involved not only in regulating taste and encouraging the consumption of local and culturally authentic goods, but also in a decision that may lead to the physical and mental starvation of people.

The markets in West Africa, on the contrary, give back to people what the state and the multinational corporations take away from them, that is, the right to consume. The slow death of many African nations is the result of the many forms of structural adjustment, including the devaluation of the CFA franc, which exclude the people from the spaces of consumption. As postmodern reality defines historicity and ethics through consumption, those who do not consume are left to die outside of history and without human dignity. The traditional markets are the only places where Africans of all ethnic origins and classes, from the country and the city meet and assert their humanity and historicity through consumption. People find unity in their lives through the consumer culture of the market. If their existences are denied daily by the devaluation and other forms of structural adjustment, at least in the market they buy, sell, exchange news about the crisis, help each other out, and, in the process, find themselves. When state functionaries are discharged because of budget cuts, they have the market to turn to for self-renewal; when peasants leave their villages for the city, they get "modernized" in the marketplace; women discover their self-worth in the market as their entrepreneurial skills raise them to the same rank as rich male merchants. Markets thus become a meeting place for the employed and the unemployed, the young and the old, women and men, the intellectual and the peasant; they are a place for new generative forces, a transfiguration of old concepts, and revitalization; a place that provides not only the basis for a challenge to structural adjustment, but also, as C. L. R. James discovered in his analysis of the Accra market in 1946, a basis for revolutionary action.

Markets in West Africa clearly undermine official forms of globalization according to which a nation-state attracts the investments of multinational corporations after undergoing a measure of structural adjustment, that is, devaluation. By producing disorder through pricing, pirating, smuggling, and counterfeiting, they participate in the resistance to multinational control of the national economy and culture. In this sense, it is possible to argue that markets are engaged in a struggle to keep the life-world in Africa from being recolonized by multinational systems which have an eye only for cheap labor, cheap natural resources, and devalued cultures. For example, as a challenge to the monopoly of Thai rice in Senegal, the merchants smuggle rice from neighboring countries, which they sell on credit to loyal consumers, who are convinced by necessity and through market gossip that Thai rice is sticky and choppy and therefore not good for the national dish, *cebu-jen*.

This brings up the charges of counter-systematicity cast at West African markets. I have already argued above that the states should have given a modern structure to the markets, not by trying to create a tabula rasa new man, but by channeling the economic and cultural capital of the market into a modern political culture of the state. This would have entailed the transformation of some merchants into new elites of banking, entrepreneurship, and government bureaucracy. The states in Africa instead turned against merchants and demonized them with epithets of tribalists, the uncivilized, and feudalists. Blinded by their commitment to Euro-modernism, which has long fixed African cultures as its antipodal enemy, African states and intellectuals have no other recourse than to view markets as chaotic, incoherent, and precapitalist modes of exchange; in other words, corrupt and conservative.

Clearly, the charges of disorder and the seeming arbitrariness of prices emanate from a complete misunderstanding of the way markets participate in the African culture of call and response and compete to absorb discordant consumers, from black American tourists looking for a bargain and the "real" thing at the same time, to African women shopping for the latest "super wax" cloth, to servants of the middle class buying condiments and young people trying on the latest Adidas and Nike shoes, to the nouveaux riches being persuaded to buy sinks and toilet seats for their new villas. The markets have an order that is one of inclusion, regardless of one's class and origin, whether one is a buyer or a flaneur. Markets, aside from being the best reflection of West African societies, are the places where Africa meets Europe, Asia, and America; as they say in West Africa, "Visit the market and see the world."

What about the corruption charges against the markets? I believe that they too have to be put in the context of the war of position between the markets on the one hand, and the states and their Eurocentric vision of modernization on the other. I have already discussed the honor system and the way in which symbolic capital is accumulated by individuals in the marketplace. This honor system, like every other system, has its internal and external rules according to which government functionaries, just like the former colonizers, are not to be trusted. From this perspective, the corruption of the civil servants, or, to put it in another way, the "buying" of customs agents, army and police officers, the ministers, and even the president, is a step toward winning the war, or at least prolonging the life of the market.

The nation-states have yet to convince the powerless in West Africa of a reason to support them, other than by intimidation by the army and the police. Most people cannot send their children to school and do not have access to health services, electricity, running water, and dependable roads from one city to another. For these disenfranchised people, all the states seem to be good for is hosting international organizations and channeling foreign aid through the leaders' own families. The government leaders constantly sign deals with foreign corporations to exploit gold, oil, and other raw materials. Meanwhile, hard-working merchants and farmers encounter roadblocks at the entrance of every city or state, with the aim of preventing them from shopping and selling freely within national borders. It is in this sense that one can argue that "buying" civil servants to circumvent roadblocks and keep the markets alive is a way of resisting the recolonization of the life-world in Africa.

Crucially, therefore, one must distinguish the corruption of the state from that of the market. The state corruption is the result of a liberal attitude in favor of bilateral and multilateral relations with Europe and other advanced countries, against the masses in Africa. Only the elites benefit from this type of corruption, which, in a sense, prevents the states from building a broad-based and democratic political capital. Aside from undermining the politics of self-determination launched by the independence struggles of the 1960s, state corruption also fosters tribalism and military dictatorship. Market corruption, on the other hand, benefits the masses by increasing the variety of goods in the marketplace, lowering prices, and making consumption possible. This role of the market is often overlooked by African political scientists who, in their desire to become advisers to the World Bank, ignore the role of European governments and international institutions in the corruption of the state and blame African traditions for failing to embrace modernization because of their innate predisposition to debauchery.

One must also consider the particular historical context of Africa today to understand market corruption as a critique of the nation-states and the World Bank for taking jobs away from people, reducing their power to consume, and devalorizing their worth in society. The markets have survived because the nation-states could not satisfy the people's demand for goods, and they lacked inclusive economic programs. Now that the nation-states are no longer considered the best modernizers and the multinational corporations have assumed that role, the markets are again the focus of attention. Instead of emphasizing the functions of markets as agents of globalization and homogenization, the World Bank and other financial and political institutions use nation-states to stem the circulation of goods in the markets. It is in this sense that the marketplace becomes a site of resistance to any globalization that does not take into account social agents in West Africa who constitute patterns of consumption and political positions as determined by their social spaces.

Conclusion

The argument that the markets are conservative and against the nation-state renders invisible their competitive and revitalizing nature. When the nation-states emerged in Africa in the 1960s, they were greeted as the proper structures of modernization, with national education, health, army, and sports systems, national factories and cooperatives. As stated, these nation-states went to war against the markets, which were considered either artisanal or corrupt. In socialist states like Guinea-Conakry, the markets were completely emptied, and the state became the only supplier of goods.

As the fin de siècle draws nearer, it becomes clear that the nation-state, for which many Africans still fight, kill, and die, is no longer viable as a cultural and economic unit. With nation-states as the paradigm of political, cultural, and economic development, Mali, Guinea, Côte d'Ivoire, Burkina Faso, Gambia, and Senegal, for example, are pushed into a competition against one another over the production and ownership of the "authentic" Mande music and culture. Clearly, West African musicians, filmmakers, and artists are the losers when their arts are confined to just one country. The narrow frontiers and visa requirement of the nation-states also affect the markets and consumers, who are not free to drive across borders to shop. Typically, Malians have relatives in Guinea, Senegal, Burkina Faso, Côte d'Ivoire, and Niger. But the nation-state is built in such a way that Malians define their belonging to Mali through opposition to other nation-states in the same region. To survive in the postmodern world dominated by new regional economic powers and information systems, West African states, too, must adopt a regional imaginary and promote the circulation of goods and cultures that are sequestered or fragmented by the limits that the nation-state imposes on them. What is urgent in West Africa today is less a contrived unity based on an innate cultural identity and heritage, but a regional identity in motion that is based on linguistic affinities, economic reality, and geographic proximity, as defined by the similarities in political and cultural dispositions grounded in history and patterns of consumption. For example, it ought to be possible to draw a new map of West Africa with Côte d'Ivoire, Burkina Faso, Niger, Nigeria, Ghana, Togo, Benin, Mali, Senegal, Guinea-Conakry, Guinea-Bissau, Sierra Leone, Liberia, and Gambia with Dioula (also known as Mande, Bambara, Mandinka, and Wangara), English, French, Hausa, and Yoruba as the principal languages of business, politics, and culture.

Negotiating African Culture:

Toward a Decolonization of the Fetish

Écoutez le monde blanc
horriblement las de son effort immense
ses articulations rebelles craquer sous les étoiles dures
ses raideurs d'acier bleu transperçant la chair mystique
écoute ses victoires proditoires trompter ses défaites
écoute aux alibis grandioses son piètre trébuchement

Pitié pour nos vainqueurs omniscients et naïfs![1]

Of Gods and Philosophers

The debate around the origins and history of religion is at the heart of the reexamination of the idea of Africa, as Mudimbe's book of that name, as well as two others and several novels, make clear. And yet, in what way is the exercise central to understanding the culture of the present? At one level, that of the sense of the essence of African identity, it is, of course, crucial to know that we have had other identities than the ones we appear to have now. This is an exercise that is common to all societies and all cultures. It is an exercise that is necessary in understanding how culture has been misread, misappropriated, deliberately distorted so that those who were active in the making of history were displaced from that history. Much of the rethinking of history during the latter part of the twentieth century in Africa and elsewhere is precisely about reconstructing how the narratives were put together. But such an act has its own complications. Is the rethinking being done in the name of ethnicity, religion, class, gender, nation? And against which hegemonies? In Mudimbe's account, at least three stories are interwoven: rethinking the genesis of civilization in terms of the commonality of myths (Greek, Christian,

African); rethinking the particularly European concept of Africa, in which, he argues, "the will to truth . . . seems to espouse perfectly a will to power"; and, finally, the value of certain kinds of European philosophy in posing the contradictions between the claims to universalism of European thought and the apparent particularism of the African.[2] In this exercise, Mudimbe is wonderfully eclectic. Lévi-Strauss, Sartre, Foucault, Deleuze and Guattari, Marx, and Evans-Pritchard are critically invoked either because there is usefulness in some of their conceptualizations or because they have become part of the "colonial library" and thus the resource of ideas that Africans are bound to explore. In telling these "stories," Mudimbe is concerned both to weave a narrative of how different approaches to the study of Africa came together or, through fissiparity, produced new forms of thought, and to fight against any essentialism that might reduce "Africanness" to a common denominator. Because Mudimbe's education has been Catholic and in French (he is a Zairean-born former Benedictine monk), the discourse leans heavily on Central African, Catholic, and French sources, though in *The Invention of Africa* he surely provides some of the most succinct overviews found anywhere. This Catholic French emphasis, however, provides the basis for raising a strategic issue about the direction that Mudimbe seems to be taking us.

The religious affiliation that nurtured Mudimbe is one that is popular over wide tracts of Africa (primarily French-, Italian-, and Portuguese-speaking, but not entirely so). In fact, in Mudimbe's own reading, it is interesting to note that he has little problem dealing with English-speaking African political, sociological, and anthropological writings, although the arguments of non-Catholic Christians (including Ethiopians) and Islamic scholars are dealt with parenthetically. The observation is not one on which one wishes to base a contestation, but rather to further explore the tension that he himself outlines in discussing an article by the Ghanaian philosopher Kwasi Wiredu.[3] After saying that he suspects "empiricism for being a kind of simplification of the phenomenon it comments on," Mudimbe goes on to argue: "Wiredu is speaking a 'British language.' I am reading it in 'French.' What does this imply for both the Akan worldview in particular and 'African' philosophy in general? The concept of alienation to which he refers in his invitation for a conceptual decolonization could be used *à propos* of our difficult dialogue. Yet it is perhaps a wonderful trap. What is at stake here seems more a question of method. It is, I would suspect, a question about our respective subjective choices for thinking the philosophical practice in Africa."[4]

In establishing his own stance for "thinking the philosophical practice in Africa," Mudimbe leaves open a door to other philosophical practices, and, needless to say, this opening is much more generous and more sophisticated than some of the earlier discussions of ethnophilosophy and Egyptology. The opening that Mudimbe suggests to Wiredu is one that requires a response that might be a Ghanaian-Akan-Protestant-English-empiricist response, in which "I wish very much that Wiredu would speak more explicitly from his own existential locality as subject." In this, Mudimbe may have been conjuring up Appiah's book (though Appiah, too, is Catholic), which is existential and which emerges out of a different tradition, though one that is conscious of Mudimbe's own. But *In My Father's House*[5] is not quite the response that Mudimbe might have wished. Though, as with *The Invention of Africa*, it deals largely with the development of debates around African philosophy, but from a distinctly different stance, and although the sense of place and individuals is woven throughout it, an element enters into Appiah's narrative that takes it in a direction that is not present in Mudimbe's concerns. If Mudimbe, thinking about politics, deals with it discursively, as theoretical positions, Appiah confronts it as event, movement, theater. His Ghana is described from his father's house, through to the Asante, to the emergence of an independent Ghana and the rise and fall of Nkrumah, to the evolution of Ghanaian politics over the subsequent years. If in some ways the chapter "Altered States" reads like an intrusion, reading through the book one realizes that most of the theorizing and accounts of philosophical developments is done precisely to help Appiah come to terms with himself in the context of his country's political changes. Apart from occasional references to Christianity, religion plays a small part in these explorations.

Appiah's collection of essays helps us to begin to place the differences between reading African and Western philosophy. Mudimbe cannot avoid being hermeneutical, placing text on text to unravel a sense of meaning. The central feature of philosophy is to work through or talk to a viable living one, which offers a coherence to the various ways by which we are dominated. Mudimbe's philosophy is both deconstructive and reconstitutive, in which everything that has ever been written about Africa, and as much of the talking that has been recorded, becomes an occasion for establishing, in the best way, a set of critical African problematics. If Mudimbe is everywhere concerned with the everyday as the negotiable presence, it is a concern that is directly related to the textuality, the facticity of the everyday. When he deals with art, it is a discourse swathed in text, in the establishment of creative and critical schools, and in the assignation of meaning and purpose to artists and art objects: "To academic rules of representation and techniques of arriving at 'the beautiful,' popular artists propose an opposing vision. They want to transmit a clear message; they claim the virtue of sociological and historical truth; and they try to name even the unnameable and the taboo. Here technical flaws become marks of originality. The artist appears as the 'undisciplinable' hero, challenging social institutions, including art practices, particularly academic ones. Yet this 'deviant,' who sometimes attacks both a tradition and its modern currents, incarnates clearly the locus of their confrontations."[6]

Mudimbe's work is that of the schoolman who writes as if the turmoils of the world can be reconstructed as discourse. It is a world where the chaos might be understood, engaged in, as part of a structured whole, where the maker of batiks in Kenya or the mermaid artist in Zaire can be seen as part of an ongoing pattern of meaning. Even the discussion with the anthropologist Peter Rigby, critical as it is, brings Marxism as a research endeavor into the search for a totalizing schema.

In contrast, Appiah provides us with a perspective that drives us to consider the current crises in different parts of Africa and how they interlock with the crises in the rest of the world. This is not to claim that Appiah is particularly radical in anything he says, but rather that his approach to issues essentially similar to those Mudimbe confronts displays a difference of sensibility. Mudimbe's article "Reprendre" appeared in a catalogue for an exhibition, *Africa Explores,* curated by Susan Vogel at the Center for African Art in New York in 1991. Appiah attended an earlier exhibition, also curated by Susan Vogel at the same Center, in 1987. It is instructive to note how Appiah saw the exhibition. Where Mudimbe theorized *over* the exhibition to provide meanings to the objects (he was not the only commentator: there were five other contributors, all of them Western, to the catalogue, with Vogel providing the narrative connections), Appiah deconstructs the exhibition, its place, its sponsors, *their* write-overs. *This* specific gallery space is the occasion for theorizing. Thus, we move from the auspices of the exhibition and the manifest absurdities of "[David] Rockefeller's easy movement between considerations of finance, of aesthetics and of decor"[7] to the objects and artists themselves and their treatment as commodity. From this Appiah takes us to James Baldwin's choice, and discussion, of a Nigerian piece called *Man with a*

Bicycle and hence to a lengthy discussion on postcolonial and postmodern culture, and in particular to a discussion of the African novel, culminating with Mudimbe's novel *Entre les eaux.* The details of Appiah's analysis need not concern us here. Much more telling is the form and the consciousness that the world inhabited by Africans is a world that is bound up with that of the Other, that the fate of the African intellectual, marginalized in Africa as protocolonial products, is to become "Otherness-machines," and that "our only distinction in the world of texts to which we are latecomers is that we can mediate it to our fellows." The African intellectual/philosopher is therefore caught in the middle ground, as Other in both worlds. "And what happens will happen not because we pronounce on the matter in theory, but out of the changing practices of African culture."[8]

These authors suggest two existential routes for African philosophy. For Mudimbe, the "colonial library" must be restocked, rethought, reanimated: "Moving in my imaginary library, which includes the best and the worst books about the idea of Africa, I chose my own path. It led me beyond the classically historical boundaries (in terms of references and texts) and, at the same time, maintained me firmly in what is a line of desolation."[9] For Appiah, the libraries matter less than the practices: "I am grateful to James Baldwin for his introduction to the 'Man with a Bicycle': a figure who is, as Baldwin rightly saw, polyglot—speaking Yoruba and English, probably some Hausa and a little French for his trips to Contonou or Cameroon; someone whose 'clothes do not fit him too well.' He and the other men and women amongst whom he mostly lives suggest to me that the place to look for home is not just the postcolonial novel . . . but to the all-consuming vision of this less-anxious creativity. It matters little who it was made *for*; what we should learn from is the imagination that produced it."[10] Within this dichotomy, there is surely a common thread that runs through the concerns of both Appiah and Mudimbe. Any search for the new Africa will hardly succeed unless the essential cultural eclecticism is recognized and unless the absolute marginality of its intellectuals (most of whom can only seriously live and work outside their countries of origin) is taken as an operating fact. To the former I return below, but of the latter it is perhaps worth considering the ongoing thematic of Homi Bhabha's collection of essays *Nation and Narration,* in which identity is seen as necessarily hybrid, between the "inside" and the "outside," and the "turning of boundaries and limits into the *in-between* spaces through which the meanings of cultural and political authority are negotiated."[11] If Bhabha and many of the contributors to his collection see this as a promising space, creating a transnational culture from an anti-nationalist nation-space, the problem remains that this culture may be as elitist as that of the Imperial Chinese literati and that the agency for its transmission may be through movements and organizations (unlike in China) that are not of the literati's choosing.

An alternative reading of religion and culture is found in *Beyond the Rivers of Ethiopia,* published in Ghana and written by Mensa Otabil, pastor of the International Central Gospel Church in Accra, with a congregation of six thousand. Dr. Otabil's auspices are clear. The book has an introduction by Dr. Leonard Lovett (who grew up "as an African-American child . . . in Pompano Beach, Florida"), professor of Religion and Society at Oral Roberts University in Tulsa, Oklahoma, from which university Dr. Otabil received one of his two doctorates. The aim of the book is also clear: to retrace within the Bible (the King James version, no less) "the purposes of God for the Black Race." Thus, we have an exegetical exercise in which the Bible is rethought in terms of Abraham's third wife, Keturah, of Moses' father-in-law, of the Midianites, of the Cushites, of the Cyrenians, of Simon the cross-bearer, of some of the early Church elders. If the book falls short of saying that the Children of Israel and the Apostles were black (and it does not, of course, question the authenticity of the texts themselves), it does completely shift the emphasis of a textual reading of biblical continuity and intent by searching for a subtext or at least a parallel reading of the existing text. The important element in this reading is not that it displaces the white or the semitic man, nor does it glorify Egypt (for that would surely provide a real dichotomy), but that it rediscovers the black presence in the existing text. It operates in the "in-between spaces" to create a narrative continuity. This is not simply saying that we were there before, but that we have been continuously present whenever God needed us. And the message for the present is quite explicit: "We need to know our history so that we can know the future. We have to move backwards in order to move forwards. When we trace black history, we do not trace it in a narrow cultural sense. . . . Whenever the world has been in a crisis the black man has always appeared on the scene."[12]

Thus, there is a different international intellectual community, spreading from Oklahoma to Accra and beyond. Its audience is in the millions and its practice is the hermeneutical reading of text to give hope to the present. What was missing, perhaps, in Mudimbe's plea for dialogue with Wiredu's rationalism or in Appiah's practical culture was this other discourse. At the end of Mudimbe's novel *Entre les eaux,* the central figure, Pierre Landu, a revolutionary priest, is saved from execution and sent off to a contemplative monastery: "l'humilite de ma bassesse, quelle gloire pour l'homme."[13] Mudimbe's character's pessimism is that, both Marx and Aquinas having failed him, the only personal solution is that of quietistic retreat. The Protestant solution, backed as it is now with the black Christians of the American diaspora, is much more cunning. By seeing blacks everywhere always as operating between the cracks, the texts can move from being hegemonic to interstitial. "By the rivers of Babylon" and *Beyond the Rivers of Ethiopia* are, ultimately, the same text.

The Languages of Culture

> I have nothing against English, French, Portuguese, or any other language for that matter. They are all valid as far as they are languages and in as far as they do not seek to oppress other nations, nationalities, and languages. But if Kiswahili or any other African language were to become the language for the world, this would symbolize the dawn of a new era in human relations between the nations and peoples of Africa and those of other continents.[14]

Ngugi's brave plea will not be taken up seriously, of course (where is the forum to make it practical?), though Wole Soyinka[15] and others have backed the campaign in different ways. The point of his critique, however, is not flippant: of all African writers he has addressed the issue of the dominant and subordinate languages in the most precise manner. Ngugi's detention in and ultimate exile from Kenya was as much caused by language as it was by politics. His attempt to establish an oppositional culture, through the Cultural Centre at Limuru, the performance of plays, and the publication of fiction (in particular his novel *Matigari*), were seen by the government as subversive: it reacted violently when the material was issued in Gikuyu. (*Matigari,* which was confiscated by order of the president when it appeared in Gikuyu, is today easily available in Nairobi in its English translation.) The point of Ngugi's stance on language is clear enough (and he has a prison sentence and exile to show for it). The vast majority of the people *are* denied a literature that they can read, or have read to them, because of the political elite's use of an alien tongue. And Ngugi, since residing in the United States, has himself worked with Manthia Diawara and Sembene Ousomene to construct a film on the latter's work in French and English so that it might reach a transatlantic audience. This suggests that there is a more complex issue that needs to be explored.

I have referred to Appiah's approving comment on the "polyglot" Nigerian sculptor. The topic needs to be taken further. Today, the everyday culture of Africa is polyglot, and the sense of what languages these are needs to be explored. A striking feature of at least urban Africa is the number of languages that people have to possess to function at all. Almost everyone in any African city has to have access to at least two languages: the first is the language of home, and the second is whatever lingua franca is necessary to function in the marketplace. The second is typically a European language, though it might also include a third regional language (e.g., Swahili, Hausa, Twi).[16] In these languages, one may or may not be literate in a bookish sense. And even here, as the educational sociologists tell us, we may be functionally literate (able to read street signs, newspaper headlines, and job instructions), culturally literate (able to acquire knowledge about political and cultural norms of a society by reading about them in accepted works of literature and science), and critically literate (able to identify ideological positions of texts and cultural forms to challenge the status quo).[17] People may have any of these literacies in their home language, and less in a lingua franca (or vice versa). In addition to all of these forms of literacy-employing language, there are also the "languages" of the media, the body, the space, the "signs in the street." It may be possible to be "critically" literate without being book literate; and it might be possible to be critically book literate and also be politically impotent. When Appiah appeals to the "changing everyday practices of African life," it is to this concatenation of signs that he appeals.

But how to read *them*? The strategy for reading that is generally adopted normally involves some schematization derived from one or other matrix borrowed from the postcolonial library. This involves many forms. For example, in putting together the exhibition *Africa Explores,* Susan Vogel and her colleagues came up with a fivefold classification to enable them to organize African art: traditional art, new functional art, urban art, international art, and "extinct" art. This neat packaging within the exhibition concealed a curiosity of place: much of the discussion of "traditional" art rests on an examination of Dogon masks from Mali: that of "new functional" art from Nigeria, Sierra Leone, and Ghana; that of "urban" art from Zaire; that of "international" art and "extinct" art randomly from different parts of Africa.

Although there is some heuristic advantage in coming up with some form of classification, it is pertinent to raise the question: In whose interests is this classification made? The answer must surely be the collector. Obviously, this collector is of a tradition different from the one carefully explored by Annie E. Coombes in her detailed study of the British "collecting" of African art in the late nineteenth and early twentieth century and the relationship among imperialism, ethnography, natural history, and the development of the museum.[18] If anything, the Vogel system is a way of trying to transcend that earlier form of classification, and even Vogel's own schema for the earlier exhibition in 1987. In her foreword, Vogel admits that "this book is mainly the work of Western writers who speak as intimate outsiders. There is nothing specifically African about this kind of study; we are aware that the whole exercise is typical of late-twentieth-century Western scholarship. The use of the category 'art' to describe the objects included here—like the category 'museum'—can be defended on grounds of theory and of convenience, but this concept is in no way inherent in all of the African objects under discussion. It is a strictly Western category that we employ here as a useful tool."[19] This disclaimer (even if Mudimbe is given the last word in the catalogue) posits the ongoing problem of creating a discourse that does not have *postcolonial* written all over it. The African artist, crafter, shaman, schoolteacher, hairdresser engaged in their everyday practices operate without knowledge of these categorizations or through them. What takes place in a gallery in New York or Paris is part of a discourse that may trickle down to the seamstress or the teak carver, but chances are that it will do so only if it becomes frozen into the search for particular commodities.

But if the language is not bounded by the museum, where is it? Take two readings, one on the media and another in the languages of everyday negotiation. These have the advantages of being very specific and randomly general. The media is not merely new technology or an opportunity to gain new means of communicating: it is, like every language, processed through power, ideology, and community relations.[20] Some of the explorations of African film, for example, such as Diawara's *African Cinema: Politics and Culture* and Lizbeth Malkmus and Roy Armes's *Arab and African Film Making*, necessarily stress not only the political economy of making films but also the importance of language and community and contrasting narratives. Important as these books are in providing overviews, they barely address the nuances of the negotiating process that places media at the center of both personal and political-economic pressures. African film, in spite of its being based on newer communicative technologies than print, is still, in its African version, less immediate than newspaper communication. African film, because of the processes of funding and distribution, is a minority culture, celebrated through the work of the Fédération Panafricaine des Cinéastes (FEPACI) and the biennial festival at Ougadougou, but otherwise an artform for European and North American film festivals. Most of the Africans who watch films see B movies from the United States, Britain, France, or India, either in their local movie houses or, if they have access, on a television station controlled by the government or owned by an associate of the government.

Newspapers, however, in most parts of Africa, are something different. Although operating under various forms of censorship and government or foreign ownership, their existence is somehow taken as a sacred mandate (because freedom of speech is guaranteed in every constitution? because every country has some commitment to literacy, which is equated with the press?). No country has banned newspapers and magazines altogether, and the idea that "news" should somehow be transmitted in print provides something of an ongoing commitment to a conception of the fifth estate. In his book *I Accuse the Press,* Philip Ochieng, a Kenyan journalist-intellectual living in Africa, at times editor of quite different daily newspapers in Kenya, Uganda, and Tanzania, provides a strategic view of the problems of being a journalist in Africa.[21] This Kenyan *J'Accuse* is ultimately a collective self-accusation. Its importance is that Kenya, in many ways, presents itself as the model of a diversified newspaper industry. Apart from a number of weeklies that come and go, there are three daily newspapers: the *Nation,* the *Times,* and the *Standard.* The first is owned by the Aga Khan, the second by the governing party, the Kenya African National Union (KANU), and the third by the British conglomerate Lonrho. Ochieng worked on two of them either as journalist or in various editorial capacities. In addition, he also worked on the Uganda *Sunday Times* and in Dar es Salaam. As an occasional student, he also studied literature, French, and philosophy in the United States, France, Germany, and Switzerland. It is important to establish Ochieng's credentials partly because he is not well known in the West (he has spent most of his life being a journalist) and partly because of his biographical route. His commitment to being a journalist is as impeccable as that of the best Western journalists and comparable to lawyers, doctors, and academics in Africa who take what they think of as professionalism in the West as their templates. But because he operates in the media, his saga is of relevance to anyone in Africa who wants to work in television, radio, film, theater, or, possibly, the Internet.

Because of his many experiences, Ochieng might be seen as the Great Survivor or Operator: from being a Nyerere socialist to being the coordinator of the propaganda machine for Moi's government. The man who coauthored *The Kenyatta Succession* became the handyman of the successors. This reading, however, would simplify the narrative and the experiences so that they would become meaningless for any thoughtful consideration. For what is written through Ochieng's own narrative is something more powerful. A series of narratives interconnect and then break off from each other. The nomadology of happenstance is compromised by the vocation of being a journalist. Telling a story requires knowing how and where to tell it. The story may change, but the act of telling is all-important. There are different communities for whom one builds up a particular allegiance. Who is to know which communities matter? Ochieng is concerned with the vocation of telling tales in print, in a country where the communicating medium is alien to, perhaps, 90 percent of the population, but important to almost all of the other 10 percent and ultimately to the rest of the world. His particular gift is to describe in detail the ways in which the press in East Africa is run, how important internal and external events are woven together, and how seriously journalists take their vocation. One of his central arguments is that the press is not necessarily freer if it is owned by private enterprise, and that the roots of press corruption are to be found in the inadequate salaries paid to journalists by the owners. Frequently, the government owns newspapers because no one else has the capital to do so, unless, as is the case in Kenya, foreign companies see a political and commercial advantage in having their own mouthpiece. Foreign ownership, however, is no guarantee against government interference. In the late 1970s and early 1980s, the British-owned *Standard* became the mouthpiece of a powerful faction within KANU, led by the Constitutional and Home Affairs Minister Charles Njonjo; the imprisonment of senior editors at the *Nation* was a direct consequence of a campaign waged in the *Standard.* There is no guarantee against such interference in the operations of the press, but journalists, if they are to be honest, must not only acquire the technical skills (which are largely what academic communications departments provide) but must also see their mandate as an educational one. Castigating most journalists and newspapers of printing "trivia," Ochieng has a clear agenda: Journalists must learn their trade in every form of media that is

state is crucial but that it is the notion of civil society that has to be re-thought.[25] Soyinka has gone so far as to argue that the troubles in Rwanda and Burundi would not exist if the populations in that region were to con-struct their own boundaries. These issues will not detain us here. The ap-proach suggested by Hecht and Simone offers an important alternative in situating any questions of culture, building on a growing body of work by independent researchers.[26]

Hecht and Simone provide graphic movements of how Africa dances and how the different specters merge into each other and become real bodies and places. The tactic of simulacrum—of reinventing the art object for those who want the authentic—might be set against the hairdresser's salon or the Sape boutique where the self is reinvented despite whatever poverty stalks around. How different from California, where, as Umberto Eco wrote with august Italian distance, everyone goes to look at the one authentic fake.[27] Quite a lot different, in fact: Africans are faking themselves both for themselves and others. The term *fetish* was constructed by the Portuguese in the sixteenth century to come to terms with the importance placed on objects by West African traders in their contact with the colonials. Its use as an object is derived from its surface properties and was popularized by Marx and has subsequently become a theme in Fredric Jameson and David Harvey's cri-tique of postmodern architecture.[28] Hecht and Simone's analysis suggests that fetish *is* the individual, that, even though the name was given to Africans by Europeans, the naming has been taken up as a playful, yet deeply serious, act. The object has little of the base/superstructure connotations of Marx's fetish, or of the psychoanalytical features of the supplementary nature of fetishism. Both Marx and Freud are concerned with fetish as something that is symptomatic of something else, and therefore not a thing in itself. Fetish is itself a product of two different economic and cultural spaces, hence its appropriation by both Marx and Freud to objectify various transactions. But what if the object itself, this thing we call fetish, becomes itself more than object, is renewable and discardable, is the bearer of stories but itself tells no stories, its surface consciously produced for the surface to laugh *at us* and join in *our* sadness?

A curious cult called Mami Wata (Mother Water) is to be found in many parts of Central, East, and West Africa, and also extends to Brazil and the Caribbean. It has many forms and operates through religious shrines, video stores, computer companies, art galleries (even in New York and Paris), and in hairdressing salons. Mami Wata is usually found in the form of a mermaid. She comes from everywhere and nowhere. When did she originate? Even though some Ghanaian classicists claim she originated in Minoan Crete, it is more likely that she emerged from the head of a slave ship. But she has so many ancestors: the Sirens, Isis, Cleopatra, the Mona Lisa, Shiva, the Virgin Mary, Lady Godiva, the Statue of Liberty, and, more recently, by her own promotion, Madonna. Mami Wata is multicultural, international, and any objects made of her are independent of her power as a moving force. She will make you rich, she will make you poor, but only through objects that are claimed for her. Mami Wata is the ultimate transnational fetish. A painting of her by the Zairean artist Cheri Samba may sell well in Paris, but you will see only the production of a surface. Mami Wata is everything that Freud missed. She is the fetish for the space between land and water, East and West, North and South, black and white. Mami Wata is the name (because she is the occasion) for African cultural theory.

If we think about Mami Wata, several things suggest themselves. This fetish-woman may have her origins in any African myth or none, but she is clearly in her present existence the product of a borderless continent, indeed, of a world without boundaries. Because she is not currency, she cannot be exchanged, yet she is the product of exchange. She symbolizes the commodities that are acquired for use but that are valueless in any long-term sense because there are no repair kits. She is the person as commodity, to be made up, dressed up, painted over, exchanged, disposed of. Because she has no feet, she cannot walk. Because she has no wings, she cannot fly. She is the person who has to be made over constantly to discover who she is. She is the floating signifier.

In her wake swim many others: the trickster, the syncretic cult, the national currencies, the international currencies, French cuisine in Senegal, cross-border shopping, shantytowns, fine clothes, hairstyles, the simulation of old cultural styles. Hecht and Simone quote Ali Mazrui, who commented that Africans had borrowed the wrong things from the West: the profit motive but not the entrepreneurial spirit.[29] They respond: "But this 'shadow, not the substance,' as Mazrui calls it, is not, after all, an obedient mimicry of the West. Rather it can operate as a map, a means of engagement with, and deconstruction of the West, while ambiguating hegemonic control over thought and action. Even by demonstrating overt dependencies on Western economic and cultural practices, Africans covertly shape the tactical practices of self-reliance. Of course, all of this may be nothing but an empty gesture, yet it is the emptiness that gives rise to a greater silence. For centuries, Africans have felt at home with other cultures. . . . But their embrace of one culture rarely excluded the embrace of another and another."[30]

Some years ago, the president of the IMF visited Ghana to check on the progress of structural adjustment. On arriving at the president's castle-home in Accra, he found a helicopter waiting to take him to a location north of Kumasi. Here he met President Rawlings, who, bare-chested, was helping railway workers mend a line. The man from the IMF was asked to join in. Because a TV crew was there, he did. Later, the president asked the workers to join in the conference. They were asked how structural adjustment was working. After saying that it was good to have jobs, they complained about the decline in the social infrastructure: schools, hospitals, the post office, sanitation. All this was relayed live to the TV-viewing public. The man from the IMF agreed to adjust the adjustment.[31] If not all African politicians are as openly mischievous as Rawlings, his political theater is certainly something that any African can appreciate, whether or not they accept structural adjustment.

Decolonizing the Fetish

Hecht and Simone's "micropolitics" operates at every level of African society, and the culture of the bricolage, much more than Benin bronzes that sit on the stairway of the British Museum, is the culture of the everyday. In Achille Mbembe's writings, this culture is considered in detail at the top of the societies and what he refers to as "the banality of power," where he examines the divide between how the political leaders employ the symbols and how the "subject" does. For the powerful, fetish is clearly used "by a regime of domination in seeking to legitimize violent practices."[32] Thus, power is the ultimate fetish, and the play around it is a "zombification" of both the leaders and the led. With a skillful use of theory derived centrally from Bakhtin, but also from Foucault, Certeau, and Bataille, Mbembe locates the fetishization of power in the language of the body, turning "the postcolonial autocrat into an object of representation that feeds on applause, flattery and lies."[33] The people are cowed, but they also "engage in baroque practices which are fundamentally ambiguous, mobile, and 'revisable,' even in instances where there are clear, written, and precise rules."[34] Mbembe's sense of the banality of power is that this masquerade leads nowhere except to the "violent quest for grandeur and prestige" that "makes vulgarity and wrongdoing its main mode of existence."[35]

In his reply to his critics, Mbembe takes up the issue of shared knowledges, and how "dominant and dominated share in the same *episteme.*"[36] The common stock of narratives and counternarratives may derive from the colonial library, but they are made active by "practices of 'disorder' and indiscipline, desertion, disguise, duplication and 'improvisation.'" The large number of "documents" of culture (written materials, visual imagery, music, oral speech) are mute and are "made to speak" by us in terms of "a direct link between lived temporality and the narrative act."[37] *How* we make them speak depends on how we see "power and servitude" operating "as expressive practices."[38] But in what ways the narrative might "transform the general process of decomposition" in Africa, as Mudimbe questions in his critique,[39] is not addressed.

In her response to Mbembe, Judith Butler notes that the term *fetish* is the most problematic of all. "It may be that the state as fetish, derived from the Latin *facera,* is always a fake, a substitute, and that it will be the logic of the fetish, when it poses as origin, to undermine its own originating claims. It was, I think, the psychologist Maud Mannoni who claimed that the structure of fetishism was to claim, 'I know, but still . . .': I know all the reasons not to desire what I desire, but I desire it nonetheless, *or* I know that what I desire is repellant, but I desire it nonetheless."[40] Useful as this is, it is a classic colonialist and neocolonialist reading of the term, skirting around Mbembe's own use. What if, as Mark Wigley has suggested, an alternative reading of fetish is not that of fake, but of a double meaning, "slipping constantly between exemplifying the subordination of the surface and exemplifying its dominance"?[41] In which case, the "desire" that the fetish arouses is not for something else but for the slippage space between itself and its double.

The issue is worth exploring because the colonial library, which invented the term, is now sending it back, through African ventriloquists, to explain what is going on in Africa. Marx, Freud, Durkheim, Mauss, and many others have taken the fetish as a substitute for reality, a token of something else. It easily slides into Baudrillard's simulacrum, the idea of a part of the body being taken for the whole, the inanimate object being taken for the living. And so on. Fetish therefore becomes a metaphor, like many others, to account for another reality. But fetish, though named as such by the Portuguese, is not a metaphor. It is the space within which the individual and nature are united: it is the space (a carving, a painting, a shrine) where the stories of hopes and despairs can coexist. In his "Reprendre," Mudimbe, while talking of contemporary African art, hits the metaphorical nail firmly on its fetishistic head: "[The] popular artists . . . want to transmit a clear message: they claim the virtue of sociological and historical truth; and they try to name and unveil even the unnamable and the taboo. Here technical flaws become marks of originality. The artist appears as the 'undisciplinable' hero, challenging social institutions, including art practices, particularly academic ones. Yet this 'deviant,' who sometimes lacks both a tradition and its modern currents, incarnates clearly the locus of their confrontation. In popular art, the politics of mimesis insert in the 'maternal' territory of the tradition a practice that questions both art and history in the name of the subject. This is work that aims to bring together art, the past, and the community's dreams for a better future."[42]

The problem with the European use of fetish is that it is seen to represent another reality, which was a "source," an origin. Richard Burton and John Hanning Speke thought they had found a "source," and Richard Leakey and his family have established an anthropological industry in Kenya based on the "origins" of mankind. They are the classic colonial fetishists, and *Gorillas in the Mist, Born Free,* and *Out of Africa* are their contemporary mementos. The gun is not a fetish, real as it may seem to be, but a metaphor for someone who has nothing else to do but blast someone else's head off. The American black who comes to view the Slave Castles at Cape Coast is looking for a visible metaphor to dull his or her own pain. The view of pan-Africa as a political thing is surely that which was invented by blacks of the diaspora to create a homogeneous Promised Land.[43] The important fetish is the traveling music of the Rasta Rudie, who turns Ghana or Jamaica or Nigeria into the space of transcontinental hope.[44] In this, the common storytelling becomes part of the music and the music part of the personal image.

If this sense of fetish is valuable, then it operates in precisely the same way as Mami Wata, or Appiah's Many Mansions, or Otabil's biblical text, or Ochieng's newspapers, or, indeed, Mudimbe's library. By living in the slippage between the dominance and the subordination of the surface, a mutation is being created with new languages and new possibilities. It is important that Mbembe has opened up the territory and provided a new strategy for mapping the cultures, but it must be read closely with the other cartographies or else the old metaphors will continue to dominate and prevent the fetish from decolonizing itself.

Notes

The work of which this is an installment was made possible in part by the Social Sciences and Humanities Council of Canada. At least as important was the collegial work with Mwikali Kieti and Ato Sekyi-Otu, without whom none of the contacts, readings, travelings on which this piece is based would have been conceivable. Various colleagues and students added to the fun of being coexplorers in decolonizing of the fetish. The exploration continues.

1   Hear the white world
       horribly weary from its immense efforts
       its stiff joints crack under the hard stars
       hear its blue steel rigidity pierce the mystic flesh
       its deceptive victories tout its defeats
       hear the grandiose alibis of its pitiful stumblings

       Pity for our omniscient and naïve conquerors!
Aime Cesaire, *The Collected Poetry,* trans. with an introduction by Clayton Eastman and Annette Smith (Berkeley, CA, 1983), 69.

2   The quote is from Valentin Y. Mudimbe, *The Idea of Africa* (Bloomington, IN, 1994), 212. Other books by Mudimbe include *The Invention of Africa: Gnosis, Philosophy and the Order of Knowledge* (Bloomington, IN, 1988) and *Parables and Fables* (Madison, WI, 1991). He has also edited a collection of articles on Presence Africaine, *The Surreptitious Speech* (Chicago, 1992).

3   This article appears in Mudimbe's 1992 collection.

4   Mudimbe, *Idea,* 200–201.

5   Kwame Anthony Appiah, *In My Father's House: What Does It Mean to Be an African Today?* (London, 1991). The title of the book has raised some eyebrows about its paternal implications. But the context of that title is clearly explained in the preface: "In my Father's House there are Many Mansions. And if I go I will prepare a place for you. . . ." The paradox of the title is clearly the paradox of Kwame Anthony Appiah's life.

6   Mudimbe, *Idea,* 175.

7   Appiah, *My Father's House,* 223.

8   Ibid., 253–254.

9   Mudimbe, *Idea,* 213.

10   Appiah, *My Father's House,* 254.

11   Homi K. Bhabha, ed., *Nation and Narration* (London, 1990), 4.

12   Mensa Otabil, *Beyond the Rivers of Ethiopia: A Biblical Revelation of God's Purpose for the Black Race* (Accra, 1992). In contrast, Mudimbe writes in *Parables and*

Fables: "adaptation theology . . . establishes an analogical parallel between the missionary performance under colonial rule and the future of Christianity under African initiative. It insists on the necessity of looking into traditional systems of beliefs for unanimous signs or harmonies which might be incorporated into Christianity in order to Africanize it without fundamentally modifying it" (13).

13 "The humility of my abasement, what a glory for man!" Valentin Y Mudimbe, *Entre les eaux* (Paris, 1973), 189.

14 Ngugi wa Thiong'o, *Moving the Centre* (Nairobi, 1993), 41. See also his novel, *Matigari,* trans. Wangugi wa Goro (Nairobi, 1987), which provides an ironic entry to the problems of language, culture, and politics in Africa.

15 See, in particular, Wole Soyinka, *Art, Dialogue and Outrage* (Ibadan, 1988), especially 132–145, for a spirited defence of N'gugi and the importance of Swahili as a lingua franca for Africa.

16 A further complication: In Senegal, probably more people speak a foreign language (French) than anywhere else in Africa. The language was brought in by people who are nominally Catholic. Yet only 10 percent of the population are Catholic; the rest are Muslim. How do the three coexist? Senegal is a *peaceful* country.

17 This summary of forms of literacy is derived from Peter McLaren. See, in particular, *Critical Pedagogy and Predatory Culture* (London, 1994).

18 Annie E. Coombes, *Reinventing Africa: Museums, Material Culture and Popular Imagination* (New Haven, CT, 1994).

19 Susan Vogel, ed., *Africa Explores: 20th Century African Art* (New York, 1991), 10.

20 The pivotal difference between, say, Marshall McLuhan and Walter Benjamin is not so much that the media transforms our means of communicating, and hence of our global sensibilities, but of the auspices under which they become available. The book, for example, was made available in different ways, to different people, over periods of time. How it was made available, and which books were made available, was not simply an issue of technology but of who controlled the production and distribution process.

21 Philip Ochieng, *I Accuse the Press: An Insider's View of the Media and Politics in Africa* (Nairobi, 1991).

22 Ibid., 110.

23 See Michael Taussig, *Shamanism, Colonialism and the Wild Man* (Chicago, 1987), for an elaboration of this.

24 David Hecht and Maliqalim Simone, *Invisible Governance: The Art of African Micropolitics* (Brooklyn, NY, 1994).

25 See, for example, Colin Leys, "Confronting the African Tragedy," *New Left Review* 204 (1994): 33–47.

26 Apart from authors already cited in this article, Hecht and Simone also invoke the work of Eric Hobsbawm and Terence Ranger, *The Invention of Tradition* (Cambridge, UK, 1983); J.-F. Bayart, *The State of Africa: The Politics of the Belly* (New York, 1993); Achille Mbembe, *Afrique Indociles* (Paris, 1988); Paulin J.

Houtondji, *African Philosophy* (London, 1983); and J. MacGaffey, *Entrepreneurs and Parasites: The Struggle for Indigenous Capitalism in Zaire* (Cambridge, UK, 1988); as well as numerous newspaper clippings, anecdotes, and personal observations. Strong theoretical directions are provided by Baudrillard and Derrida.

27 See, in particular, Eco's *Travels in Hyper-reality* (London, 1986), for an elaboration of this theme.

28 Mark Wigley discusses this use of the term *fetish* in the context of architecture in relation to the neo-Marxist uses of fetish in his article, "Theoretical Slippage: The Architecture of the Fetish," in *Fetish,* Vol. 4 of *The Princeton Architectural Journal* (1992): 88–129. The Jameson and Harvey references are to Fredric Jameson's article, "Postmodernism, or the Cultural Logic of Late Capitalism," *New Left Review* 146 (1984): 53–92, and its development by David Harvey. For Harvey, postmodernism is "actually celebrating the activity of masking or covering up, all the fetishisms of locality, place, or social grouping, while denying the kind of meta-theory which can grasp the political-economic processes . . ." (*The Condition of Postmodernity: An Enquiry into the Origin of Cultural Change* [Oxford, 1989], 117). An even more elaborate treatment of fetish, expanding on medical, psychoanalytic, aesthetic, and Marxist uses, is in Emily Apter and William Pietz, eds., *Fetishism and Cultural Discourse* (Ithaca, NY, 1993).

29 Their quote, on p. 106, is from Ali Mazrui, *Cultural Forces in World Politics* (London, 1990).

30 Hecht and Simone, *Invisible Governance,* 107.

31 The story was told to me by Mohammed ben Abdallah, former Minister of Culture in Rawling's government, and professor of Performing Arts at the University of Ghana.

32 Achille Mbembe, "The Banality of Power and the Aesthetics of Vulgarity in the Postcolony," trans. Janet Roitman, *Public Culture* 4, no. 2 (1991): 1–30. This article by Mbembe has appeared in two places. The longer, original piece was first published in *Africa* 62, no. 1 (1992). I am quoting from the slightly shorter version because there was a series of ten responses to Mbembe's article as well as a response from Mbembe.

33 Ibid., 15.

34 Ibid., 23.

35 Ibid., 30.

36 Achille Mbembe, "Prosaics of Servitude and Authoritarian Civilities," trans. Janet Roitman, *Public Culture* 5, no. 1 (1992): 123–145.

37 Ibid., 133–134.

38 Ibid., 144.

39 Valentin Y. Mudimbe, "Save the African Continent," *Public Culture* 5, no. 1 (1992): 61–62.

40 Judith Butler, "Mbembe's Extravagant Power," *Public Culture* 5, no. 1 (1992): 67–74.

41 Wigley, "Theoretical Slippage," 123.

42 Valentin Y. Mudimbe, "Reprendre," in *Africa Explores,* ed. Susan Vogel (New York, 1991), 286.

43 There are many accounts of this phenomenon, but, riding on the backs of Marcus Garvey, W. E. B. Du Bois, George Padmore, Aime Cesaire, Richard Wright, and Edward Blyden, an industry of pan-Africanist rhetoric has been built up, aided and abetted by some Africans: Nkrumah, Sekou Toure, Kenyatta, Senghor. Fanon and C. L. R. James were not of that camp because they knew where it would lead. For an example of the problems that diasporic blacks face in confronting Africa, see Sidney Lemelle and Robin D. G. Kelley, eds., *Imagining Home: Class, Culture and Nationalism in the African Diaspora* (London, 1994). For an attempt to make a connection, see Paul Gilroy, *The Black Atlantic* (London, 1993).

44 For a wonderful rendition of this transmigration, see Neil J. Savishinsky, "Rastafari in the Promised Land: The Spread of Socioreligious Movement among the Youth of Africa," *African Studies Review* 37, no. 3 (1990): 19–50.

The End of Free States:

On Transnationalization of Culture

The literary scholar's excursion into the world of transnational corporation and global capitalism requires explanation, because in the Pacific, the most widely recognized of TNCs have been geographers, economists, and researchers in development studies and business studies. Thus, Mark Taylor's critique of the disciplines that have examined transnational and translocal business in Fiji does not refer to literary studies because either the literary perspective on TNCs isn't recognized as useful and relevant, or other disciplines simply aren't aware of it.[1] In the Pacific, writers and critics have written extensively on colonialism for over two decades, and they have been commenting on several aspects of the transnational phenomenon.

In the West, as Masao Miyoshi points out, the discourse on colonialism has had a brief history, "it was only fifteen years ago—well after the disappearance of administrative colonization from most regions of the world—that the discourse on colonialism entered the mainstream of Western theory and criticism."[2] It needs to be emphasized that in parts of the Pacific, formal colonialism, by Americans and the French, still continues, and that the protracted experience of colonialism hasn't ended yet, nor is it expected to end in the foreseeable future. Although in the Pacific, as in the West, the discourse on colonialism has had a short history, in the third world at large it has a long-standing tradition.

The passions and commitments of "the real world" are therefore present in literary studies, and literary scholars have always examined social issues and the political subtexts of literature. Though the relationship between critical postures and social struggles isn't always apparent, the critic is aware of how culture frames configurations of power. Edward Said, Fredric Jameson, Terry Eagleton, and others have shown how literature is affiliated to its "engagements." Recently, Said in particular has written on "the centrality of imperialist thought in Western culture," and has shown how the relationship between empire and culture could be formulated, recognizing the fact that the imperial vision was "registered and supported by the culture that produced it, then to some extent disguised it, and also was transformed by it."[3] Fredric Jameson, Terry Eagleton, and others also described the relationship between structures of knowledge and forms of oppression. But Jameson, in his essay "Third World Literature in the Era of Multinational Capitalism," approached the subject of transnationals more directly, drawing attention to the connection between TNCs and literature, and to the fact that although there are several postcolonialisms and postcolonial literatures, there is one system, late capitalism, that is "the supreme unifying force of contemporary history."[4] It is because each postcolonialism should be viewed as culturally different that this address is focused on Fiji, a site from which TNCs operate in the Pacific, rather than on the Pacific region as a whole.

The approaches typified by Said and Jameson have had a profound effect on literary studies and on literary scholars engaged in studying postcolonialism. They have been drawn into TNC research because colonialism continues through global capitalism. After the withdrawal of administrative colonialism, the global space created by the empire is filled by TNCs. Thus, even after independence, the bondage of the colonized has remained fixed. In Fiji, this awareness was first expressed not in imaginative literature but in a publication called *Fiji: A Developing Australian Colony.* It is still the most broadly based investigation that includes comments on cultural and political consequences of TNC domination. In 1974, the publication was offered to me in Suva as a secret text of postcolonial subversion. In fact, it is the first scholarly text of resistance, and it is also a noteworthy fact that among its contributors were one graduate student and three undergraduate students of the University of the South Pacific. The publication by Rokotuivuna et al. was an expression of the deeper processes of resistance at work in the region.[5] The regional institution provided the necessary setting for articulating this opposition.

The USP's original architects had designed it as a utilitarian institution to provide training to meet the manpower needs of the region. Its objective was far removed from Cardinal Newman's ideal of the university that would augment "the power of viewing many things at once as one whole, referring them severally to their true place in the universal system, of understanding their respective values, and determining their mutual dependence."[6] The USP started with this imbalance, with the vague hope that in the course of its evolution it might find its equilibrium. That faith is justified, to some extent, by the appearance of the classic publication by Rokotuivuna et al. only five years after the establishment of the university, and also the writing of Pacific-centered histories and the growth of an imaginative literature. Thus, without being aware of it, the USP has become a site of "a culture of resistance" as well as a conservative counterdiscourse, the two recognizable forms of postcoloniality. The USP's positive contribution raises the interesting question of the role of the postcolonial university in counteracting transnationalization of culture.

The notion of a "free state," in its full political and metaphoric senses, is fraught with ironies and paradoxes. Rokotuivuna et al.'s work showed that formal independence meant neither the end of history nor the beginning of a new history. Absolute sovereignty, of course, is always an illusion, and ex-colonies in particular remain attached to the colonial system of dependence. The underlying economic, cultural, and political dependence cast doubt on the very concept of postcoloniality. At the moment of independence in Fiji, as elsewhere, there were not one but two states: the territorial state and the borderless, global interstate. Inevitably, the "free state" freed only small groups of elites. The degree of freedom of others—the landless *vulagi* Indians, "common" Fijians, minorities, the urban and shantytown dwellers—varied from one group to another.

After the crisis of 1987, when, by pursuing openly racist and supremacist policies, the state lost its moral legitimacy, more "stateless" people were created. The events of 1987 also showed how "unfree" a state under the shadow of the military can be. If Satendra Prasad's thesis is correct, that "many seemingly indigenous forces and pressures are in fact conditioned and defined by the global market forces, without appearing as such,"[7] then how autonomous is the "ethnic state" formed by those events? It can be argued that the ethnic state obscures more completely systematic orders of exploitation.

The state is further shackled by the contradictory demands of the provinces and of the chiefly oligarchy. Moreover, a state is not autonomous if it has large debts and unemployment, if the "free enterprise" on which it is based is nonexistent, when its "plantation, agriculture, mining, fisheries, forestry, manufacturing, all have been undertaken by the colonial rulers and transnational corporations. The economic path has been determined by outsiders for outsiders."[8] A state is not self-determining if it is forever embroiled in ethnic tensions, waiting for pandemonium. Thus, a state can be endlessly "unfree," its political freedom controlled by the military, economic life dominated by transnationals, and its governing ability curtailed by internal fragmentation.

Fiji, at the moment of its emergence as a supposedly self-determining state, had a contradictory and fractured polity. The idea of peoplehood did not exist because independence was imposed from above: it wasn't arrived at through dialogue with the people. The same was true of the "rapprochement" of 1970, which had the formula for endless friction. Thus, as Brij Lal observes in his history, "caution, continuity, and continued links with the colonial past rather than fundamental change in new directions would be the hallmark of the postcolonial years."[9] What was born in 1970 wasn't "a young nation" but an example of reconstituted ethnic communities. The larger national space remained "unimagined." In Fiji's context, "nationalism" could have been a positive force in combating the flow of transnational culture. TNCs profit from fascism and chaos, as shown by Chomsky and Herman in their essay, "Why American Business Supports Third World Fascism."[10] Ethnic divisions disunite classes, causing them to be insensitive to their common plight.

There is a connection between narratives and nations. Homi Bhabha has written cogently on this relationship.[11] The absence of larger narratives about Fiji to some extent accounts for the absence of a national sense. At the time of independence, the role of narratives in creating imaginative worlds wasn't realized. Instead, rumors, fantasies, and nostalgia governed the imagination. They still do. A paradoxical phenomenon is the "nostalgia for the present," the Fijian looking back at his or her land and culture that he or she hadn't lost, that he or she fears will be lost through domination by the *vulagi* Indian. The process through which the Fijian culture, though not the Fijian land, is being lost is transnationalization, the domination of Fijian culture by images and symbols transmitted through print, celluloid, and electronic media, and by tourism. Ironically, the *vulagi* Indian's culture is also a postmodern pastiche of unassimilated Fijian rites, for example, kava drinking, pieties and fantasies from Bombay cinema, and thoughts and ideas from Western education. Arjun Appadurai rightly calls for "theories of rootlessness, alienation and psychological distance between individual groups, on the one hand, and fantasies (or nightmares) of electronic propinquity on the other. Here we are close to the central problematic of cultural processes in today's world."[12]

Studies on transnationals have grown since the publication of *Fiji: A Developing Australian Colony,* and investigators, through various routes, have arrived at similar conclusions as Rokotuivuna and others on the impact of transnationals. For instance, James Winkler in his book *Losing Control* makes the following observation after examining the consequence of transnationalization in Fiji and the Pacific: "The Periphery, those nations in the Third World, is tied to the Centre, the industrialised nations, by a web of vested economic interests which have taken root over centuries of colonialism and remain intact today, despite the fact that the Periphery nations have regained their independence in a formal, political sense."[13]

Mark Taylor, an astute analyst, addressing more specific issues—the degree of transnationality and the assimilation of the local into the global through an alliance of transnational and translocal capital—presents an equally bleak scenario for Fiji. The foreign-owned multinationals dominate the economy, changing their form chameleon-like, through mergers and takeovers and relocating branch plants, thus creating the phenomenon of "corporate ephemeralization." Taylor's analysis shows that the TNCs themselves are "peripheralizing," that is, giving the appearance of withdrawing from direct control in the economy, by subcontracting and thereby drawing small local businesses into informal dependent relationships. Peripherization heightens the vulnerability of the local economy because there is no long-term commitment by the foreign-owned multinationals, the managerial and accounting services are provided from the outside, and the subordinate local business has no representation in the boards of directors of the controling company. When the foreign company shifts location, the local counterpart remains poorly prepared to generate employment or export.

I would like to return to literary studies and at this point make the following general remarks: first, that the prolonged experience of colonialism and neocolonialism is giving literary studies a new orientation, that is, greater attention to the context of literature; second, the growing understanding of the interconnectedness of different fields of knowledge is revitalizing the study of literature. Both these remarks are relevant to my argument in this address. Said's recent book, *Culture and Empirialism,* reinforces these observations. "Texts are protean things," writes Said;

> they are tied to circumstances and to politics large and small, they require attention and criticism. No one can take hold of everything, of course, just as no one theory can explain or account for the connection among texts and societies. But reading and writing texts are never neutral activities: there are interests, powers, passions, pleasures entailed no matter how aesthetic or entertaining the work. Media, political economy, mass institutions—in fine, the tracings of secular power and the influence of the state— are part of what we call literature. And just as it is true that we cannot read literature by men without also reading literature by women—so transfigured has been the shape of literature—it is also true that we cannot deal with the literature of the periphery without attending to the literature of metropolitan centres.[14]

I have quoted Said at length because the passage summarizes effectively some of the assumptions in this paper: that literary studies cannot ignore the extratextual framework; that texts express power relations; that no one approach can satisfactorily examine all aspects of a phenomenon; and finally, that it is important to examine the interrelations between literature from the center and literature from the periphery.

Said's broad view is shared by a number of modern/postmodern writers. Arguing against George Orwell's advice that writers should withdraw inside the belly of a whale because the world has become contaminated with politics, "a mass of lies, evasions, folly, hatred and schizophrenia," Salman Rushdie pledges his support for the writer who is in the embattled site of nationalism, racism, and colonialism. For him there is no whale or hiding place, and therefore "we can do what all human beings do instinctively when they realise that the womb has been lost forever—that is, we can make the very devil of a racket."[15] There are many ironies to Rushdie's life and contributions that do not concern us here. What is relevant is the function he has defined of the writer in situations of large-scale oppression, and then his contribution to the novel form, which has never been so widely discussed in the history of the genre—by parliamentarians, lawyers, theologians. In the West, literary critic and literary theorist have never had it so good. The way they are consulted by colleagues in other disciplines and by senators and administrators had made Henry Louis Gates Jr. remark ironically, "the apparent 'relevance' of literary scholars to the actual life of our fellow citizens is quite astonishing."[16]

In this rather long preamble I have tried to explain the literary scholar's involvement in issues concerning transnational corporations. These notes are unavoidably tentative, a pastiche of research on transnationals, description of the movement of critical thought, and survey of the configurations of the problem, rather than a closely argued thesis. The paper doesn't attempt to present a log of pros and cons. The benefits from TNCs—contribution to foreign exchange, improving the balance of payment, worker training, solving unemployment, creating marketing outlets, introducing new technologies, providing competition, diversifying the economy, and so on—have been considered by Castairs and Prasad and Fairbairn and Parry, and other investigators have questioned the size of these gains. I have given culture the main focus in this paper because transnationalization of culture in the Pacific is still inadequately problematized. The main argument has developed from Taylor's article, which begins with a critique of the geographer's preoccupation with space, the economist's tendency to homogenize, and so on. I myself had anticipated the review to broaden into a multifaceted discourse. But Taylor's wasn't that sort of analysis. It is, therefore, an aim of this paper to suggest how that broad discourse might be constructed.

My references to the research on TNCs in the Pacific so far would suggest that the literary scholar was a latecomer to this research. In fact, literary investigation has proceeded toward this inquiry through a different path. The orientation of the early literary research in the 1970s was European representation of the Pacific peoples in Melville, Maugham, Michener, and others. The focus was on the fetishization of the islander, and how fiction was inscribing the Other, and the kind of knowledge and information that was being communicated to the West. Although Conrad didn't write directly about the Pacific, he was considered central to this investigation, and Charles Gould's San Tomé silver mine in *Nostromo* was seen as the great symbol of materialism and corruption. In essence, what was being investigated was a basic form of "orientalism" well before Said had named the phenomenon.

However, Said's great contribution was to define the relationship between culture and imperialism, to illustrate how literature and imperialism fortified each other, to demonstrate how an understanding of the relationship between the two can enrich the reading of texts and expand our knowledge of the imperial practice. And it was Said who drew attention to the famous lines on transnationalization in Conrad's *Nostromo*. Holroyd, the American financier, tells Charles Gould, the British owner of the San Tomé silver mine, "We can sit and watch. Of course some day we will step in. We are bound to. But there is no hurry. Time has got to wait on the greatest country in the whole of God's universe. We shall be giving the word for everything—industry, trade, law, journalism, art, politics, and religion, from Cape Horn clear over to Surith's Sound, and beyond it, too, if anything worth taking hold of turns up at the North Pole. And then we shall have the leisure to take in hand the outlying islands and continents of the earth. We shall run the world's business whether the world likes it or not. The world can't help it—and neither can we, I guess."[17] Conrad's narrative forcefully predicted the route that global finance will take.

Our concern converged on the racial romance and allegory for the following reasons: first, history had already made known the imperial ethnic policy of "divide and rule"; second, the postcolonial elites were already calling race an ineffaceable category; and finally, we saw how European fiction about the Pacific was using race to inscribe difference between people who had contending economic interests.

Thus begins the most infamous of these racial allegories: "Imagine a group of islands blessed by heaven, rich in all things needed to build a good life, plus gold mines and a good climate. Picture a native population carefree, delightful and happy. Add a white government that works overtime to give honest service. Top it all with a democracy that enables dozens of different levels of society—from Oxford graduate to bush dwellers—to have a fine time. That makes a pretty wonderful colony, doesn't it?"[18] The "native," perceived as economically neutral in this narrative, is genial and harmless, and the immigrant Indian unscrupulous and rapacious. The portrayal serves perfectly the imperial ethnic policy; the Pulitzer prize–winning author makes absolute and fixes the ethnic assumptions in an authoritative discourse for the American audience.

How powerfully these ethnocentric assumptions remain intact is exemplified in Daryl Tarte's *Fiji*, the most recent rendering of the same allegory. The issue of intertextuality—how one text reinforces another—is important in imperialism's knowledge formation. Tarte's narrative, described in the blurb as "a novel of James Michener proportions," maintains its dialogic connection with colonial ideology. Tarte's is a postcoup narrative, filled with distorted portraits, the boldest kind of "orientalist" fiction, ending with a strong nostalgia for empire. At the end of the novel, Sir William Heseltine says to Queen Elizabeth:

> "I've just had a signal from Fiji, Your Majesty. Colonel Valu has again assumed power and has stated that Fiji will now become a Republic. Ratu Sir George has resigned."
>
> The Queen set down her pen and took off her glasses. "So, where does that leave us?"
>
> "Well, I suppose, Your Majesty, that such action effectively terminates your reign over those islands."
>
> The Queen was pensive for a few moments.
>
> "Under normal circumstances, yes, you might be quite right, Sir William. But, I wonder, I have been thinking about our rule over Fiji."
>
> Sir William looked puzzled. "What exactly do you mean, Your Majesty?"
>
> "Read the old Deed of Cession, Britain never conquered Fiji. It was ceded to Queen Victoria and her Heirs and Successors by the chiefs of Fiji. There was a personal engagement quite apart from our role as Head of the Commonwealth. It might be said that we are still Tui Viti. It's an interesting situation."
>
> "Yes, Your Majesty, very interesting."[19]

The nostalgia for empire is evident in the novel's closure. Tarte's book is part of a larger phenomenon manifested in the spate of films and publications on Africa and India in the 1980s.

The critical inquiry into the Pacific version of "orientalism," started in the early seventies, is carried on in Sudesh Mishra's recent essays and Robert Nicole's master's thesis. Mishra has centered his investigation on the concept of *vulagism,* the inscribing of the Other in Fijian culture and on racial formations in Fiji.[20] Nicole's conclusion on French writing in the Pacific is relevant to the relationship that is established in this paper between imperialism and knowledge: "the assistance of economic, political, technological, institutional, ideological and other discursive means, the bodies, lands, languages, habitats, economics, politics and sexualities of Pacific islanders have been appropriated, recorded, classified and stored not just in museums, books and libraries but in the minds of Europeans. So much so that the way of seeing the Pacific other has not changed much in the last two centuries. Indeed, from utter fantasy, it has through the discourse, been fossilised and has now virtually acquired 'factual' status . . . 'fiction' plays a central role in the production and dissemination of discourse."[21] One of the main arguments of this paper is that two centuries of this knowledge formation have served perfectly the economic and cultural domination of the Pacific by the transnational empire.

As Said has pointed out, both power and discourse are controlled by the colonizer. However, when the native or local writer writes against the image of race in colonial literature, a counterresponse quickly establishes itself. Thus, when the Indo-Fijian writer objects to the distorted image of Indians in European fiction, he is confronted with the response that "the negative image is not created and spread by Europeans, as many Indians imagine, but by islanders who visit Fiji." And further, "Pacific people tend to suspect businessmen, which is the role in which they saw most Indians."[22] This reaction is not dissimilar to the carefully rehearsed response of TNCs to the questioning of their influence: "it should be said in public that defending free enterprise is in everybody's interest. Therefore, it should be shown, specially in the mass media, that criticism of multinationals is basically criticism of free enterprise, and that behind it are the enemies of the free world, whose view of life is based on Marxism."[23]

At this point I would like to return to the USP and elaborate on its paradoxical role. There is no doubt that the USP has furthered the goal of decolonization, but it has also unwittingly provided opportunities for collusion and complicity with the discourse of exploitation and domination. Its utilitarian policy of meeting manpower needs served, and continues to serve, both the regional governments as well as the transnationals. The TNCs require trained local staff who understand the local culture, who will provide a buffer against nationalistic sentiments and lend legitimacy to their operations. As a conduit of culture, the USP, by raising the educational level, has promoted the cultural penetration of the rich industrialized countries. In the minds of the main elites in the Pacific, "modernization" is equivalent to the assimilation of the lifestyles, ideas, and values of the rich metropolitan center. Because of the prestige attached to Western culture, "modernization" in essence means mimicry: the imitation of the consumption patterns of the metropolitan centers, an orientation away from that which is produced locally.

There is another level of mimicry, a level of internal mimicry, where those with lower income imitate the dominant elites.

The USP's emancipatory role, its contribution to research and publication, has been noted. However, this should be assigned greater prominence. After the publication of Rokotuivuna et al.'s book, the literature on transnationalism expanded with researches on the Colonial Sugar Refining Company (Wadan Narsey), Pacific TNCs (Ganesh Chand), Australian companies in Fiji (Michael Howard and Anand Chand), forestry (Simione Durutalo), commercialization of education (Peni Baba), garment workers (Satendra Prasad), and other contributions. There have also been significant investigations from outside the USP.

Most of these studies, both from the USP and from outside the region, describe who the TNCs are, their activities, and their influences on the economics of the Pacific. The most serious limitation of most of these studies is that, although connections are drawn between economic dependency and cultural dependency, the problem is inadequately conceptualized. In the same way, the "politics" of TNCs is also insufficiently problematized, though investigators are aware of such scandalous stories as the Carroll Report that linked the ruling elites, a local businessman, and overseas consultants working for international business.

The USP was a site where a new cultural and political role for the imagination was realized. The university gave writers employment, and offered them opportunity to work for the region. It was at the USP that Wendt completed his major novel about "god, money and success," and Hau'ofa wrote his own allegorical tales on foreign aid, investments, loans, grants, technical assistance, and government advisers.[24] (The impact of these aspects of TNCs requires closer scrutiny.) At the height of the political crisis in Fiji, Hereniko produced his play *The Monster* at the Laucala campus. And after the curfew was lifted in Suva in 1988, Larry Thomas's play *Just Another Day* was performed at the Playhouse. For the eight hundred people who saw it, the play restored a sense of freedom. A year later his play *The Outcasts,* about the urban poor, criminals, and prostitutes, was performed.

But the literary movement wasn't confined to Suva. With assistance from the USP, writers were producing their works in the regional countries. In Solomon Islands, Celestine Kulagoe and Jully Sipolo were writing impassioned poems on nuclear testing, Japanese fishing, white investors, foreign aid, and development. And Sano Malifa depicted the "empty meeting grounds" outside the Burns Philps store in Apia, the locus of interaction between local craft vendors and tourist fantasy. In Vanuatu, following the example of Kulagoe, Leomala, and Sope, Grace Molissa wrote on colonialism and neocolonialism.

Wilson Ifunoa's poem "Multinational Corporation" requires acknowledgment and quoting in full because it is directly on the subject of this inquiry. The poem is "Dedicated to the victims of economic exploitation."

> Your roots are embedded
> Deep under the soil
> You cling firm to the rocks under the earth
> And no hardness dare withstand your penetrating force
>
> You spring out of the earth
> Like a mushroom appearing overnight
> You spread your arms to all corners of the globe
> To find shelter for your selfish motives
>
> You are a banyan
> That lives on other trees
> You twist your giant roots around me
> And squeeze me by the neck
> Until I have no breath
>
> You eat my flesh to the bones
> You suck my blood to the last pint
> You eat! You suck! You screw![25]

The poem communicates in simple metaphors the awesome power of transnationals. Published in 1977, it anticipates Bishop Bryce's warning to developed countries that they are "unleashing giants" upon small island countries, and that the local leaders "might unwittingly help the big companies to further strengthen their already strong foothold. Some are already co-directors of major companies. These are the same leaders which play an important role in both the life of the church and the community."[26] From a different perspective, Ernst Utrecht appraised the disquieting hold of TNCs:

> Compared with foreign corporate exploitation in the colonial era, exploitation of the local population by TNCs is more rigorous in the present neocolonial period. Previously, local governments had to adopt a serious set of policies to protect the interest of the local population against the opera-

tions of TNCs who, eager to produce huge profits, often disregarded the disastrous consequences of such operations—pollution, deforestation and erosion, food shortages and hunger, displacing of whole village populations, loss of landed property (mostly small plots) and rural employment, impoverishment, starvation wages, urban unemployment (caused by automation and computerisation), forced acculturation, etc. Even reports by conservative international organisations and institutes engaged in social research and social studies have shown that the exploitation of the indigenous population by TNCs is more rigorous, often even more disastrous, than it was in the colonial past.[27]

It is plain that the thrust of the TNCs will not weaken but strengthen. Already the Pacific is being read as the region of contest in the twenty-first century. Winkler explains why the next century is being called "the century of the Pacific":

> In 1980, for the first time in modern history, the value of trade carried in the Pacific exceeded that of the Atlantic. Four of the world's great powers meet in the Pacific: the United States, the Soviet Union, China and Japan. The movement of giant TNCs into seabed and surface mining, forestry and fisheries in the Pacific Islands; the usage made of the ocean for nuclear weapons testing and as a dumping ground for radioactive waste; the militarisation of Japan; American nuclear-armed B52s in Australia; the continuing colonisation of France and the US, are all fundamentally linked to the domination of the region by the great powers and combine to make the Pacific an arena of increasing competition and struggle.[28]

The importance of the Pacific, and not only the rim countries, is likely to increase rather than diminish as the TNCs pursue their quest for "world-wide containment and control, moving away toward the ideal of two economic classes ('local' vs. 'multinational'), one currency, one passport, one market, one government: i.e. global fascism."[29] Winkler recognizes the importance of global militarism and its consequence for the Pacific. The enormous wealth of the transnationals plus their unprecedented ability to control information, gives them the most terrifying military capacity in the world.

In the foregoing overview, I have attempted the following: first, to provide a sketch of studies on transnationals by economists and other experts; second, to trace the progress of postcolonial discourse in imaginative literature; third, to describe the power of TNCs; and fourth, to suggest how the university might be a factor in resisting cultural dislocation.

The survey leads me to make the proposal that in the context of the all-embracing power of TNCs, it is imperative that we develop broad theories and overarching discourses to discuss the economic, political, and cultural control by transnationals of Pacific societies. To achieve this, close collaboration and interaction among disciplines—geography, economics, business and development studies, social anthropology, environmental science, legal studies, and literature—is vitally important. This means joint researches and publications, seminars and conferences, interdisciplinary courses, and more. However, these collaborative enterprises should not preclude rigorous investigation of discrete facets of TNCs.

Much needs to be done in conceptualizing the tangled relationship among economics, culture, and politics in the Pacific. The relationship between ruling elites and management of TNCs, a "sensitive" subject, requires vigorous investigation. And so does the impact of international agencies—the World Bank, International Monetary Fund, Food and Agricultural Organisation, World Health Organisation; and similarly, aid, loans, grants, and so on. The relationship between gender and TNCs in the Pacific context also demands scrutiny.

Up to the present time, the research of economists and others has focused on two aspects of transnational "ideology": the relentless drive to expand and commitment to profit. The third part of that "ideology"—consumerism—hasn't been adequately conceptualized or investigated, except in relation to declining food systems. There are studies on such modes of impact as manufacturing technologies and services, but little on mass media—advertising, television, news agencies, book publishing. A study of the dynamics of consumerism in the Pacific should take into account the images, metaphors, symbols, and fantasies transmitted through print, celluloid, and electronic media, and their effects on cultural and political formations. The question will have to be answered of the impact of commercial movies on small island countries whose potential for creating alternatives is greatly limited, where the local cultures are finding it difficult to hold out against the transnational global culture. It is important to note in conceptualizing consumerism, that transnationalization of culture doesn't simply mean homogenization or leveling of cultures, but also heterogenization, that is, satisfying local group needs through ethnic and multicultural marketing and fulfilling individual cravings by means of diversified goods.

Even though information on activities of transnationals in the Pacific is expanding, we are still far from having complete knowledge and information. For instance, in his study of the Colonial Sugar Refining Company, Wadan Narsey claimed that there was still a lack of information on certain aspects of the company's activities.[30] If the next century will be the Pacific century, it will also be the age of information. And Pacific countries without military might, without vast resources, will have to depend on information as a source of power. The USP is critically situated to negotiate the information needed by Pacific countries.

An inquiry into the relationship between information and imperialism offers a new perspective on domination and resistance. Take the broad context of the British Empire. Even though defenders of imperialism claim that the empire builders did not always know enough about their subjects and their country, and nationalists often charge that "They simply didn't know us," there is a great deal of evidence to show that empires depended on information for their power over vast territories. In the Pacific, we have yet to investigate the role of information in the activities of the Colonial Sugar Refining Company and other TNCs. Information was certainly a crucial factor in the East India Company's ability to centralize authority. As a first step, the Company attracted into its trajectory India's own systems of information-gathering through spies, bazaar writers, bards, professional forgers, soothsayers, astrologers, holy men, pilgrims, pimps, prostitutes, midwives, concubines, itinerant doctors, tribal people, accountants, postmen, and merchant bankers (*banias*) who gave exchange rates as well as political news and reports. The Indian systems of information collection were complemented by the work of linguists, translators, biographers, anthropologists—anyone with orientalist information. And of course fiction writers: Kipling and John Masters. It is not accidental that their fiction is peopled with spies, informers, and imposters.

A study like E. A. Bayley's on empire and information shows that it was the flow of information that made empire possible, and ultimately the improvement in the circulation of information among Indian nationalists that made India's independence movement successful.[31] As Bayley argues, such an examination of "information transactions" adds an important new perspective to discourses on domination and resistance.

If information is the great wealth of the future, then the critical question is:

How can small islands use advanced information and knowledge to reduce cultural and economic dependency? It is precisely here that "information studies" can bring together the researches of sociologists, economists, historians, social anthropologists, and literary scholars and give the governments and peoples of the region the information they require to develop strategies of self-reliance.

To end with "transactions in information" is to articulate a set of heterogeneous, overlapping proposals that could be structured to invent an overarching discourse and theory of information and cultural interaction that will at once be appropriate to the Pacific and be sufficiently historical to be regarded as global. Such a discourse and theory should incorporate strategies for limiting the influence of transnationals on Pacific societies: first, through state legislation, public opinion, appealing to corporate conscience, partnership between capital and labor, mixed companies and cooperatives; second, by supporting those arms of the government that educate and liberate; third, making available the information the local people need to oppose identification between their governments and TNCs; fourth, bringing to light corporate malpractice—law breaking (and, where laws do not exist, flouting the codes of decency) in relation to environmental laws, exchange control, bribery, conflict of interest, dumping substandard products, illegal political contributions, tax evasions, antitrust violations; fifth, opposing antidemocratic, authoritarian trends that favor TNCs; sixth, stressing the primacy of human values over profits, social goals over self-interest; seventh, demonstrating that consumer patterns do not reflect the needs of the people, and persuading them to see the futility of importing "dreams of affluence"; eighth, inventing a pedagogy that makes known that changing the world requires changing ourselves, our bodies, in addition to changing the economy and society; ninth, defining and redefining the national space as a positive force for resistance, and clarifying the ongoing processes of state formation; tenth, contributing to regional and international cooperation in dealing with transnationals; and finally, appropriating the "imaginative geography," seizing it from the colonial cartographer's book, and, as Hau'ofa[32] and Manoa[33] have suggested, turning the periphery into the center so that power doesn't forever flow from the center and wealth from the periphery.

Let me return to the university finally before concluding this paper. The university's foremost responsibility is to hold out against the current trend of remodeling itself as a business organization. At the same time, it should alert society against transferring the norms of commerce to cultural institutions. Academics are aware that problems of society will not disappear by merely investigating them. We also know that a great deal is at stake for them to continue dreaming inside the belly of the whale because, in Rushdie's words, "Outside the whale we can see we are irradiated by history, we are radioactive with history and politics."[33] The least we can do, as the author suggests, is to make a crazy racket.

Let us hope that this celebration at the university inaugurates a new era in which we seek a suitable pedagogy for resisting the rapidly diminishing free zone in our lives in the region and the world at large.

Notes

This essay was first presented as the 25th Anniversary Lecture at the University of the South Pacific, Suva, Fiji, October 1993.

1 Mark Taylor, ed., *Future Imperfect* (Sydney, 1987), 1–13.

2 Masao Miyoshi, "A Borderless World? From Colonialism to Transnationalism and the Decline of the Nation-State," *Critical Inquiry* (summer 1993): 727.

3 Edward Said, *Culture and Imperialism* (New York, 1993), 65.

4 Fredric Jameson, "Third World Literature in the Era of Multinational Capitalism," *Social Text,* no. 5 (fall 1986): 65–87.

5 Amelia Rokotuivuna et al. *Fiji: A Developing Australian colony* (Melbourne, 1973).

6 Henry Newman, "Idea of a University," in *Prose of the Victorian Period,* ed. William E. Bukler (Boston, 1958), 201.

7 Satendra Prasad, "Re-theorising the Post-colonial State: A Case Study of Ethnicity, Industrial Relations and Political Change in Fiji," (Master's thesis, University of New Brunswick, 1992), 182.

8 James Winkler, *Losing Control* (Suva, 1982), 33.

9 Brij Lal, *Broken Waves* (Honolulu, 1992), 215.

10 Noam Chomsky and Edward S. Herman, "Why American Business Supports Third World Fascism," *Business and Society Review* 19, (1993).

11 Homi Bhabha, "Narrating the Nation," in *Nation and Narration,* ed. Homi Bhabha (London, 1990), 1–7.

12 Arjun Appadurai, "Disjuncture and Difference in the Global Cultural Economy," *Public Culture* 2, no. 2 (spring 1990): 3.

13 Winkler, *Losing Control,* 10.

14 Said, *Culture and Imperialism,* 318.

15 Salman Rushdie, *Imaginary Homelands* (London, 1991), 99.

16 Henry Louis Gates Jr., *Loose Canons* (Oxford, 1992), xiii.

17 Joseph Conrad, *Nostromo* (Garden City, NJ, 1925), 77.

18 James Michener, *Return to Paradise* (New York, 1951), 104.

19 Daryl Tarte, *Fiji* (Fairfield, Fiji, 1988), 477.

20 Sudesh Mishra, "Reading Fiji: The Discourse of Vulagism" (paper presented at the Conference on Cultural Pluralism and Theory, University of Melbourne, December 1992).

21 Robert Nicole, "Extending Orientalism to the Pacific" (master's thesis, University of the South Pacific, 1993), 288.

22 Ron Crocombe, "Options for the Pacific Islands' Largest Ethnic Group," in *Pacific Indians,* ed. Ahmed Ali et al. (Suva, 1981), 213.

23 Winkler, *Losing Control,* 71.

24 Albert Wendt, *Sons for the Return Home* (Honolulu, 1973) and *Leaves of the Banyan Tree* (Honolulu, 1979); Epeli Hau'ofa, *Kisses in the Nederends* (Honolulu: 1995) and *Tales of the Tikongs* (Honolulu, 1994).

25 Wilson Ifunaoa, "Multinational Corporation," Dennis Lulei et al., eds. *Twenty-Four Poems of the Solomon Islands* (Honiara, Solomon Islands, 1977), 15.

26 Winkler, *Losing Control,* 1.

27 Ernst Utrecht, ed., *Fiji: Client State of Australia?* (Sydney, 1984), 14.

28 Winkler, *Losing Control,* 23.

29 Ibid., 21.

30 Warden Narsey, "Monopoly Capital, White Racism and Superprofits in Fiji: A Case of the CSR," *Journal of Pacific Studies* 5 (1979): 133.

31 E. A. Bayley, "Knowing the Country: Empire and Information in India," *Modern Asian Studies* 27 (February 1993): 3–43.

32 Epeli Hau'ofa, ed., *A New Oceania* (Suva, 1993).

33 Pio Manoa, "Dreaming Humanities in the Next Decade," unpublished paper, Suva, September 1993.

34 Rushdie, *Imaginary Homelands,* 100.

Is There an Alternative to (Capitalist) Globalization?

The Debate about Modernity in China

As the last remaining socialist country with perhaps the fastest economic growth in the world today, China presents a challenge to critical thinking about globalization. It is imperative that the question of alternatives and other possibilities and potentialities be raised in any attempt at theorizing or conceptualizing the process of globalization. Globalization is generally perceived as the result of the collapse of Soviet-style socialism, as well as the unprecedented expansion of transnational capitalism. While avowedly Eurocentric in its hegemonic formations, globalization also sets up an indispensable structural context for analyzing what happens in the world today. Therefore, globalization must be grasped as a dialectical process: it refers at once to an idea, or an ideology—that is, capitalism disguised as a triumphant, universal globalism—and a concrete historical condition by which various ideas, including capitalism in its present guise, must be measured. China's challenge to globalization can be perceived in both senses, first to global capitalism as an ideology and then to the "new world order," or "world-system," as an accepted reality. China has become increasingly integrated into the global economic system, yet retains its ideological and political self-identity as a third-world, socialist country. Will China offer an alternative?

164

This essay is not intended to argue for such an alternative. Rather, I try to offer an account of the current Chinese debate over alternative modernity, in order to problematize the very assumptions that animate the critical discourses on globalization. In this respect, the Chinese debate, as a concrete case rooted in a particular historical conjuncture, may serve as a critique of the discourse of globalization. I address, very schematically, some major trends involved in the debate, including nationalism, postmodernism, and neohumanism, and a "discursive hybridity" that blends neoconservatism and radicalism. Lately, various forms of nationalist discourse have been on the rise, quickly forming a new cultural dominant. Much of this essay is devoted to this phenomenon, for it seems to represent the locus of a constellation of crucial issues in China's political, ideological, and cultural arenas. Such a cultural reconfiguration centered around nationalism ought to be understood first of all within the context of the search for alternatives to the bankrupt ideological hegemony of the state. Other trends, such as postmodernism and neohumanism, are much weaker responses to, or echoes of, nationalism in its multifarious guises. Postmodernism, and related theoretical discourses such as postcolonialism, seem to be largely eschewed by the intellectual "mainstream," as newly imported Western theoretical shibboleths ill-suited to Chinese situations. The appearance of a politically engaged "hybridity" blending both neoconservative authoritarianism and radical strains reminiscent of Maoism, on the other hand, highlights both the intellectual disorientation and critical potency in the latest struggle to construct an ideological hegemony.

My description and analysis of the Chinese debates will demonstrate that (1) the current Chinese discourse of alternative modernity and globalization is, by its very nature, contradictory and fractured; (2) as a local (Chinese) discourse about global meaning, it articulates both an anxiety over the full-blown absorption of China into the global "world-system" and desires for intervention and resistance; and (3) the centrality of "revolution," not only in the discourse, but also in social and political practices in today's China, has to be recognized and reconsidered within the context of globalization.

How to Map China's Cultural and Geopolitical Imaginary?

First of all, let me briefly characterize the historical conjuncture of China today in its most contradictory aspects. China is experiencing a phenomenal economic growth by adjusting itself to the global market or capitalist world economy. This has given rise to a general consensus, shared by people from very different ideological and political persuasions, that China has abandoned socialism and set itself squarely on the trajectory of capitalism. Its alleged political stalemate (it remains a communist society and has not adopted the Western capitalist political system) and its often dramatized "human rights violations" are usually explained away by the typical "Chineseness" of politics and by a "time lag": the political system has not crumbled simply because Deng Xiaoping and the old generation of revolutionaries have not all lived out their years.[1]

Although the descriptions of China's irreversible assimilation into capitalist economy often sound reductionist and overtly ideological, and predictions of China's political future remain largely speculative and wishful, the question of culture defies any easy characterization. Western commercial popular culture, brought into China by the market in its late phase of world information circuits and exported entertainment, has not been opposed, as one would expect, by the Communist Party. MTV, for example, has been quickly absorbed and adapted into an effective propaganda tool for the Party's policies. American MTV first entered China via Hong Kong satellite channels, which were selectively broadcast over Chinese cable TV in the North in 1992. Then the predominant fad in popular culture was a new wave of Mao nostalgia, exemplified by the cassette album of *Hong Taiyang* (Red sun) series 1 and 2, which reproduced the Cultural Revolution songs eulogizing Mao the Great Helmsman, now set to a rock beat. The album sold over two million copies. In the following year, however, China's pop music scene was turned over to Hong Kong and Taiwanese pop stars. In 1994, disturbed by this trend, Chinese authorities virtually banned Hong Kong and Taiwanese pop concerts on the mainland. They sponsored instead a number of national karaoke contests, which encouraged people to sing revolutionary folk songs or traditional Peking Opera. In other areas such as cinema, overseas critics are now either exuberant or furious about the "orientalist," exotic representations of China's antiquated, folkloric, and superstitious cultural past in the "festival films" of the so-called Fifth Generation directors, like Zhang Yimo's *Raise the Red Lantern* or Chen Kaige's *Farewell My Concubine*. These films echo a national revival of a bygone culture in China, and at the same time grasp and capitalize on the taste of Western audiences (primarily global-savvy yuppies working for transnational corporations). Academic critics both in China and abroad mainly focus on New Cinema's avant-garde, innovative stylistic expressions and overlook the mechanism of a global cultural market by which both the new cinema and academic film criticism are commodified as profitable cultural products.[2] In architecture, along with the massive constructions of buildings and highways across the country, constructions of theme parks have boomed, most of which are reconstructions of the ruined "traditional cultural relics," such as the Yellow Emperor Tomb in Shaanxi, as well as numerous "ethnic minority villages" rebuilt as tourist attractions. These theme parks serve the double purpose of reinforcing nationalist sentiments and transforming local space into a global site for tourism. On the other hand, a mushrooming of postmodern architecture has been quickly transforming the skylines of Beijing and Shanghai into the likes of Tokyo, Hong Kong, and New York. Facing these overwhelming cultural changes, one is bound to ask: Is China culturally already "postmodern," although economically it is still "premodern"?

To say China is culturally "postmodern," before first delineating its cultural and geopolitical conditions, problematizes the concept of postmodernism itself, which is premised on the correlation between advanced capitalist economy and culture. China does not fit into the (Western) postmodern framework neatly. Postmodernity, understood as the cultural logic of late, transnational capitalism, may indeed characterize certain features of China's economically advanced and capitalist neighbors, such as Japan, Hong Kong, and Taiwan. But when describing postmodernity (or postcoloniality) or tracing postmodernism in China, the most obvious (yet the most ignored or deliberately suppressed) problem is China's distinct revolutionary legacy and hegemony, which constitute an alternative, if not post, modernity.[3] We need a "non-Euclidean geometry," as Fredric Jameson puts it, to conceptualize a space where China is situated. "A global or geographical term" is needed, Jameson continues, "for the ways in which chronological nonsynchronicity manifests itself in a spatial and even national form."[4] But the explanatory power of such concepts as *uneven development* or *nonsynchronicity* is limited in delineating China's historical conjuncture, insofar as the globalizing theorization is premised on a Eurocentric and teleological narrative of modernity (and postmodernity), which may ultimately exclude possibilities of historical alternatives and/or alternative histories.

The Chinese, of course, are concerned with the problematic of globalization and modernity (if not postmodernity) and, not surprisingly, with the issue of alternatives. Revolution has been the foremost choice for modern China, and as such, it constitutes a central problematic, along with the need of social reconstruction (in the broadest sense), of China's modernity or alternative modernity, vis-à-vis the modernity of European origin. The latter appears now as universal only through certain historical processes of rationalization. Likewise, formations of an alternative modernity or, better still, of a plurality of modernities (such as Arab modernity, African modernity, or East Asian modernity) are made possible by means of rationalizing the symbolic field, which is inexorably connected with economic and political practices. China's search for an alternative modernity is historically linked with revolution; ideological and political struggle in China has always been explicit and dominant in the symbolic sphere, or the domains of culture. To understand China's modernity, or its alternative modernity, overdetermined by complex and multiple structural relations, the centrality of revolution and political struggle in the field of cultural production must be acknowledged. China's alternative modernity can be best grasped as an ongoing process replete with contradictions: its revolution aiming at constructing socialism in a third-world, unindustrialized economy is alternative to the Western capitalist modernity in political and economic senses, and its emphasis on cultural revolution is also alternative in a cultural sense. But Chinese revolution is an integral part of modernity that is at once fragmentary and unifying, heterogeneous and homogenizing. Its project of modernity is as incomplete as its vision is unfulfilled.[5]

The current Chinese cultural imaginary is dominated by a depoliticizing mood. But such a pervasive political lassitude, as I suggest below, is the result of the ongoing process of political struggle involving various strategies of misrecognition, legitimation, and delegitimation. If the process of globalization is a "global" structural context, then revolution constitutes a "local" context for the Chinese debates about modernity and alternative modernity. One should not lose sight of the complex interplay of these contexts.

Nationalism and Revolutionary Hegemony

Nationalism seems to provide an attractive and viable option for the cultural imaginary of postrevolutionary China within the context of globalization. Nationalism here is not meant as a coherent and well-defined ideology; nor can it be defined as an essentialist concept. Rather, it is understood in the present context as an ensemble of discursive practices, functioning through interaction between historically changing fields of struggle and *habitus* of discrete dispositions, in which ideologies are legitimized and delegitimized. It has been argued that nationalism has a Janus-faced quality, as a modern project that reactivates and transforms the traditional cultural values into the service of new political and ideological hegemony.

To understand precisely what kind of political and ideological identities and hegemony nationalist discourse serves to reinforce, one must, however, differentiate various "modernities." In other words, the monolithic modernity to which world history seems to move has to be problematized. Benedict Anderson, for instance, is mistaken when he claims that nationalism is a discourse of nationhood simply as an "imagined community" invented by Western capitalist modernity, thus implicitly excluding other alternative modernities in which nationalism and nationhood serve revolutionary purposes in opposition to Eurocentric modernity. Anderson is also wrong when, using China as an example, he contends that revolutionaries utilize "official nationalism" as a means of control only when they seize the state power.[6] Although in China today, under the current condition of globalization, nationalist discourse is indeed employed (but never monopolized) by the state as an "official" discourse, throughout Mao's period (before and after the seizure of state power) nationalism had always been a discourse of revolution and resistance, calling for the worldwide support of national liberation.[7]

Chinese modernity, as an "alternative modernity," is first and foremost concerned with the question of revolution, of which national liberation in opposition to imperialist domination is a crucial component. Historically, nationalism in modern China has been a response to the threat of imperialism. It played a crucial role in establishing and legitimizing Chinese Marxism, that is, Maoism, as the ideological hegemony throughout the course of Chinese revolution. Nationalism must, of necessity, reconstruct a "national culture," both as a means of ideological legitimation and a goal of social reconstruction. The goal of national reconstruction is echoed in other colonial countries by figures such as Frantz Fanon, who contends that "a national culture in under-developed countries should take its place at the very heart of the struggle for freedom which these countries are carrying on."[8] At the crucial stage of establishing his Chinese Marxism around the period of the

Sino-Japanese War (1937–1945), Mao recognized the urgent need of incorporating nationalism into the revolutionary hegemony, stating that "we can put Marxism into practice only when it is integrated with the specific characteristics of our nation and acquires a definite national form."[9] In order to establish a new national culture, Mao calls on Chinese Marxists to "sum up critically" Chinese traditional culture "from Confucius to Sun Yat-sen" from the Marxist perspective.[10] Confucianism, as the ideological hegemony of the imperial rulers, is considered the main obstacle for the new revolutionary hegemony and new national culture; hence, in Mao's discourse of new nationalism, it is caricatured as "feudalist junk" and plays the role of villain in China's political and ideological arena. Radical iconoclastic rejection of Confucianism has been an integral part of Mao's new nationalism.

Contrary to the claims that nationalism is a "great failure" or "anomaly" in Marxist theory, Mao effectively erected a Chinese Marxism integrated with nationalism in his project for an alternative modernity.[11] It should be emphasized, however, that Mao is essentially a universalist or "internationalist" in his revolutionary utopian aspirations, whereas nationalism, as a strategy in his revolutionary schema, is always subjugated to Mao's overall vision of the "emancipation of all mankind." The integration of Marxism with nationalism that characterizes Mao's Marxism is conditioned by the historical task of revolution, with its radical reinvention of a "national culture" sundered from Confucian and other traditional values. Although this highly selective and contested "new national culture" may have served Mao's revolutionary strategy of national autonomy and autarky in political, social, and economic realms, especially in the face of imperialist threats and containment, it did not succeed in laying the necessary cultural and ideological foundations for social reconstruction or modernization. It is crucial to note that "modernization" at first did not, contrary to general opinion, occupy a central position in Mao's discourse; it was developed as such only after the Eighth Congress of the Chinese Communist Party (CCP) in 1956, which set the development of productive forces and economic modernization as its central priorities. Mao, however, insisted on the primacy of political struggle in the overall project of modernity (revolution and reconstruction). As a result of complex conflicts of the post-Mao era, modernization has crystallized into an overarching problematic, a vector through which political and ideological struggles have been fought. The antinomy of revolution and modernization has held sway over the cultural imaginary in post-Mao China. Because Deng Xiaoping's reforms have prioritized modernization and economic development without at the same time charting a political and ideological map, culture has become again a major battleground in the volatile and precarious process of reform.

The ideological crisis after the Cultural Revolution (1966–76) was essentially caused by the widening rift between the revolutionary hegemony and economic development that was apparently impeded by the Cultural Revolution itself. Deng Xiaoping's economic reform has intensified the ideological crisis. The pragmatic leadership under Deng's aegis has virtually abandoned Mao's strategy of ceaselessly reenacting, renewing, and reinforcing a revolutionary hegemony to serve social and economic reconstruction. Consequently, contrary to the hope that rapid economic development would reinvigorate socialism as the core of the revolutionary hegemony, socialist ideals and Marxism have fallen victim to economic reform. In China's social consciousness, the ideas of modernization and modernity on the model of the capitalist West, and lately of global capitalism, soon gained prominence. The pro-capitalist discourse of "democracy" and "modernity" clashed head-on with the revolutionary hegemony, which has been severely shaken but has not yet collapsed. The conflicts culminated in the bloody confrontations in Tiananmen Square in June 1989. Yet, the crackdown on the demonstrators only forestalled possible political disorder, but did not settle the ideological crisis. After the collapse of the Soviet bloc, socialism and Marxism in China became further vexed and entangled with the political currents, both domestically and internationally. Wary of any possible political unrest that might result from public ideological debates, Deng Xiaoping issued a ban "for at least three years" on any theoretical discussion of the ideological nature of reform in his new reform directives issued in the spring of 1992. Ironically, questions of socialism and Marxism have become taboo in socialist China under Deng's decree. But China's legacy of revolution and its hegemony remains a central issue to be tackled in its present movement of modernization. Its assertion of nationalism as an ideological substitute for revolutionary hegemony cannot eclipse its historical legacy. When its socialist vision of equality and justice is increasingly replaced by a nationalistic pride, coupled with China's resolute drive to become a central international power, it seems all the more necessary to look back at the genealogy of China's nationalism within the context of revolution.

New Confucianism and "National Learning": New Ideological Bedfellows

In the past decade, as China's revolutionary hegemony lost much of its grip and legitimacy, Confucianism has experienced a dramatic global revival, from North American academia to the Pacific Rim, and finally to its home country, China, not without irony and vengeance. The "feudalist junk" of Confucianism has made a comeback to fill the ideological vacuum caused by the absence of any serious discussion of ideology itself. Lately, the Chinese government has drummed up an endorsement of Confucianism. As part of the celebration of the forty-fifth anniversary of the People's Republic, an international conference on Confucianism was commenced in Beijing on October 5, 1994, as an ideological joint venture by the Chinese government and various official or semi-official organizations from Singapore, South Korea, Japan, Taiwan, the United States, Germany, and elsewhere. Jiang Zemin, Chinese president and the CCP's general secretary, held a much publicized reception of the conference participants. Lee Kuan Yew, former prime minister of Singapore, was named the honorary president of the International Society of Confucianism, and Gu Mu, a former CCP Politburo member and former Chinese vice premier, its president.[12] A month before this conference, the Central Committee of the CCP issued the "Guidelines of Implementing Patriotic Education." "Traditional culture" becomes the core of the curriculum, and it is telling that in this document of some ten thousand words there is only one sentence mentioning Marxism: "We must strengthen the education of Marxist views of nationalism and religion."[13]

Confucianism and "traditional culture" as new symbolic capital in the discourse of nationalism is effective insofar as the struggle for ideological legitimacy remains silent about Chinese revolutionary legacy and ideology, namely, socialism and Marxism. But this is impossible, for it cannot cancel out in one stroke (or by Deng's decree) the whole revolutionary past. It cannot, on the other hand, serve as an indigenous ideology legitimizing a new national autonomy, because contemporary Confucian discourse itself is constituted globally as an integral part of the ideology of capitalist globalization itself. Of course, the more regional East Asian context is obvious, too, which intermediates globalization by its own geocultural and geopolitical formations.[14] Now accepted and sanctioned by the communist leaders as a major component of the new discourse of nationalism, Confucianism itself has been rewritten and reconstituted by the power blocs of a different order. It at once articulates a new power nexus within the context of globalizing capitalism, that spawns local nationalism or fragmentation of the geopolitical imaginary, and that also reflects a radical metamorphosis of nationalism from a discourse of resistance to a discourse of domination.[15] However, when Immanuel Wallerstein speaks of "nationalism as domination," he is primarily concerned with "those more frequent moments when nationalism operates . . . as the nervous tic of capitalism as a world-system."[16] In the case of China, the transition from resistance to domination is a precarious one, contingent upon the suppression of enunciations of a powerful revolutionary legacy that still legitimizes the very domination of that power bloc. Moreover, the current leadership by no means surrenders itself entirely to the capitalist world-system, as shown by the persistence of the slogan, however vacuous and self-contradictory in its content, of "socialism with Chinese characteristics." All this generates profound uneasiness with the Confucian-oriented "official nationalism" both within the Party leadership and in the public sphere. In intellectual circles, a recent topic in vogue is the so-called *guo xue* (national learning), which consciously poses a distance from "official nationalism" and global new Confucianism.

National learning can be construed as a thinly disguised expression of the predicament of the intellectual elites. Entrenched deeply in the post-Tiananmen political apathy, intellectuals are now suddenly overwhelmed by waves of commercialism invading cultural domains, which rapidly relegate them to the social periphery and to irrelevance. National learning thus aims to articulate new subject positions for the intellectual elites by consecrating pure, autonomous scholarship or learning. But it also delivers a more politically and ideologically sophisticated (or more "indeterminate" and "ambivalent") statement of certain ideological positions than the official nationalism conveys.

The advocates of national learning are primarily a group of middle-aged Beijing scholars who were once active in the 1980s debate about culture, known as the Culture Fever. The 1980s debate, as we know, opened up a theoretical space by problematizing the fundamental issues of China's revolutionary hegemony and modernization. But it prematurely ended as a result of the 1989 Tiananmen incident. Those then-young scholars, after a period of silence, now set themselves on a course of recuperating a nonpolitical and nationalist alternative—national learning—while repudiating the 1980s debate as "totalizing" radicalism.

The concept of national learning denotes first and foremost a truly *national* tradition of scholarship, and its second term, *xue* (learning), is a no less important corollary: it signifies *scholarship* as a distinct entity, autonomous from and resistant to nonscholarly, political, and ideological contingencies. In other words, such a move to essentialize scholarship in the humanities, primarily in the realms of literature, history, and philosophy, entails radical debunking of an intellectual tradition in modern China inextricably intertwined with realpolitik, that is, political power struggles as the material condition of social life. It must "rewrite history," to borrow a catchphrase popular in the 1980s debate, to resurrect an alternative national tradition of autonomous scholarship of intellectual inquiry.

National learning posits itself as a neo-(or post-?)hermeneutics reinterpreting modern Chinese intellectual history from a conceptual framework that pits the binary oppositions of the "political-secular/scholarly-transcendental" against "tradition/modernity" as a paradigm in the 1980s debate.[17] A truly modern national learning, according to the current hermeneutics, is concerned not so much with the immediate political, secular, and pragmatic issues, as with nonutilitarian, nonpolitical, and transcendental issues of "truth." Zhang Taiyan (1869–1936), a major intellectual figure who once was closely associated with the late Qing and early republican revolutionary movements, is now extolled as the "self-imposed, unique guardian-god of the Chinese culture (of national classics or national learning) at the moment of national crisis, who in the later years renounced 'secular intervention and utilitarianism' and sought to 'educate scholars and safeguard the national learning in the last ditch.' "[18] But Zhang Taiyan's national learning was primarily concerned with the republican revolution and therefore can hardly be labeled "apolitical." Wang Guowei (1877–1927), who interpreted the classical Chinese novel *The Dream of the Red Chamber* from Schopenhauerian-Nietzschean perspectives and was thus said to inaugurate modern Chinese scholarship by integrating modern Western thinking with Chinese classical tradition has now become the crowning hero of national learning. Chen Yingque (1890–1969), a historian generally regarded as a faithful heir, along with a few others, to Wang Guowei's intellectual legacy, is another modern sage enshrined in the pantheon of national learning. The most significant contribution of Zhang, Wang, Chen, and their like is said to be their unyielding efforts to overcome the political and ideological obstacles to independent, autonomous scholarship.[19]

The overbearing concern to articulate a nonpolitical scholarly autonomy by retrieving a "pure" scholarly tradition from within modern China may explain the relative distance from and silence of the national learning advocates toward new Confucianism. The revival of new Confucianism started in Hong Kong and Taiwan after the triumph of the communist revolution on the mainland, first, in effect, as a "counterrevolutionary" discourse protesting the so-called communist destruction of Chinese traditional culture. Then in the 1970s and 1980s, as I have noted, new Confucianism became popular as a global discourse, thanks to the promotion of some North American academicians who were the former students of Hong Kong and Taiwanese new Confucian masters, as well as to official endorsements from the governments of Taiwan, Singapore, and South Korea. This historical background is too obvious and too recent to conceal.

While national learning favors cultural elitism in the face of the rapidly commercialized popular culture, it has maintained its apolitical academicism. The national learning scholars self-consciously position themselves as the guardians of a national cultural essence and values vis-à-vis social and cultural crisis. Their aim is to reinscribe an ideology of bourgeois liberalism into Chinese national culture by invoking the names and reputations of the older scholars in a quasi-Arnoldian fashion. As Raymond Williams observes of Arnold's "culture-and-anarchy" liberalism, "excellence and humane values on the one hand; discipline and where necessary repression on the other. This, then as now, is a dangerous position: a culmination of the wrong kind of liberalism . . . was a culmination of the most honest kind."[20]

The ideological position of national learning becomes clearer when it characterizes negatively a main aspect of modern Chinese intellectual tradition as "radicalism." The cultural enlightenment projects of the May Fourth movement (1919) and Marxist revolutionary movements are criticized mainly for their "totalistic repudiation of Chinese tradition" and "blind Westernization," old accusations rehashed in an idiom familiar to poststructuralist attacks against "totalization" and "Eurocentrism." But the poststructuralist connotation is by no means what national learning scholars intend to convey. On the contrary, their language is meticulously monitored for its absence of (Western) theoretical jargon. Their discourse is, so to speak, thoroughly "national" and indigenous (although, ironically, these scholars have all recently become prestigious "global scholars," making frequent trips across the world funded by both the Chinese government and the overseas foundations, such as the semi-official Chiang Ching-kuo Cultural Foundation of Taiwan). The all but complete absence of Western theoretical jargon in the discourse of national learning is by no means a scholarly oversight, but a carefully maneuvered symbolic gesture. Moreover, it turns out that its critique of "radicalism" is more ideological and political than theoretical or scholarly. The thrust of this critique is the rejection of revolution and social reconstruction as the central problematics of China's modernity. The 1980s debate about culture is criticized for its "utilitarian preoccupation with modernization," a defect that supposedly underlies intellectual radicalism as such in modern China. The debate, in fact, focused on the tension between modernization and the cultural imperatives of revolutionary hegemony. Now that national learning aims to delegitimize the revolutionary legacy, it cannot but renounce the 1980s debate as "radicalist" and "utilitarian."[21] (The debate, in fact, focused on the tension between modernization and the cultural imperatives of revolutionary hegemony.) "Radicalism" is but a coded term for the revolutionary legacy as the real target, which in the present circumstances can only be labeled euphemistically. National learning's attacks against radicalism can hardly claim political innocence, if it is understood within the context of the recent antirevolutionary wave in China studies in the West.[22]

Nevertheless, in the context of 1990s political culture in China, national learning's position is a "politically correct" one. It is on the one hand in keeping with the CCP's promotion of "traditional and national culture." On the other hand, it represents to the overseas China studies establishments nonpartisan "liberal intellectuals" who can easily become strategic allies for the "peaceful evolution" that will eventually place China on a path of "transition" toward capitalism. Furthermore, national learning's advocacy of a non-socialist, liberal national tradition serves as an effective interface with the ideological network of global corporations, which promotes multicultural alternatives (or fosters illusions of such alternatives) as long as they are allied with, rather than opposed to, capitalism. The national learning group thus faces a fundamental dilemma in identifying their subject position in the current debate. Their elitism may indeed suggest a defiant endeavor to stake out an intellectual realm of self-realization, when they are being ineluctably marginalized in China's social life. But such a defiance is hardly apolitical. By renouncing the 1980s "new enlightenment" movement and espousing national learning, they betray their professed commitment to nonpolitical, purely academic values. In the end, national learning becomes complicit with both the power bloc at home and the ideology of global capitalism abroad. In this sense, national learning and global new Confucianists are ideological bedfellows under the same roof with a nationalism that debunks the revolutionary legacy in the service of global capitalism.

Manufacturing Diversity in a New Cultural Landscape

Although various forms of nationalism constitute a cultural dominant, it can hardly function as an ideological center, imposed from above by the ideological state apparatuses as in Mao's era. The process of ideological decentering reached its summit in the so-called Culture Fever of the late 1980s in the burgeoning public sphere. The scene was, among other things, a carnival imbued with festive, universalist spirit, celebrating liberation, in a Bakhtinian sense, from "the hegemony of a single unitary language."[23] The Tiananmen incident of 1989 disrupted the carnival, but hardly dispelled the universalist aspirations deeply imbedded in the Chinese cultural imaginary. In recent years, universalism has resurfaced in a variety of forms in the cultural arena, not so much to reclaim its disappearing place on the mainland (which is partly due to the diaspora of intellectuals in the wake of Tiananmen incident) as to manufacture a new kind of diversity in the changing cultural landscape of the 1990s. Granted, to label the divergent and often radically different expressions "universalist" is arbitrary, but its arbitrariness may well indicate the extent to which these newer articulations strive to produce an arbitrary and artificial plurality of opinions. It is arbitrary and artificial because this newfangled diversity (or a Chinese-brand "multiculturalism") largely sidesteps the central problematics opened up by the 1980s debate, namely, the revolutionary legacy, and denounces the 1980s political engagement.

Of all the critical discourses in the 1980s debate about culture, arguably the most important was Li Zehou's seminal work encompassing the fields of philosophy, aesthetics, and intellectual and cultural history. Li's wide-ranging intervention, cast primarily in a mode of aesthetic-historical critique, set in motion the process of rethinking the fundamental problematic of revolutionary hegemony and modernization in China. The most important theoretical move that Li made in the 1980s was to reconceive the relationship between Chinese Marxist discourse and Confucian discourse not as antithetical, but as a profoundly complementary and universalist discourse. Li's argument is, simply put, that a constructive Marxist vision of humanity can draw upon Confucian humanism in a "transformative creation" of modernity or alternative modernity.[24]

Chinese culture today is moving on a truly universalizing, or globalizing, course, but surely not in the direction Li Zehou has hoped. Global capitalism has infiltrated China's cultural landscape not only with its commercial mass culture products, but also with its academic, intellectual products, namely, contemporary Western "theory." It is true that imported Western academic theoretical discourse already had a prominence in the 1980s debate about culture, but its function then was radically different from what it does now. In China today, the political and ideological thrust of imported theory is insignificant. Meanwhile, its other symbolic value, namely, its fashionable novelty, a feature already exploited by certain academic elites in the West, now becomes also useful to the self-styled Post–New Era criticism. Postmodernism, for instance, an overtly politically engaged and critical discourse when first introduced to China in the mid-1980s largely through Fredric Jameson's influential lectures at Peking University, now takes up a self-conscious position of manufacturing itself in China as the local variant of a global fashion.[25]

Some postmodernist advocates have gone so far as to claim a nonpolitical, purely academic postmodernist discourse in order to show the compatibility of China with the West in the global academic marketplace.[26] Such a claim is symptomatic of both a desire to become integrated into the global intellectual community dominated by Western hegemony, and a fear that Chinese intellectuals may again be deprived of the freedom to articulate their subject positions. By using postmodernism as a new lingua franca, Chinese intellectuals can partake in global intellectual communications without the intermediary of a powerful existing discourse of the West about China. In this respect, Chinese postmodernism as a critical discourse may serve a political mission in a global context, by threatening to take away some of the exclusive privileges and power of speaking about and for China, vested in the current China studies establishments in the West. It is therefore not surprising that China experts in the West are likely to find Chinese postmodernism offensive.[27]

In China, postmodernist discourse cannot but divulge its confusion in terms of a political agenda. In order to showcase their break with the legacy of the 1980s, some postmodernist or Post–New Era critics now join the chorus of denouncing Li Zehou and others in the debate about culture. The critics of the 1980s are accused of blindly subscribing to the Western Enlightenment discourse of "grand narratives" about "modernity" and "nation-state." Concepts from postcolonial and third-world criticism are also employed by the Post–New Era critics.[28] "Postcoloniality," as we know, suggests in the realm of culture the conditions in formerly colonial societies in which Western culture permeates to such an extent that only a renewed critical self-consciousness or "politics of identity" can expose Western domination and therefore reconstitute their Otherness.

But what the Chinese Post–New Era critics discover in modern Chinese history is that the so-called postcolonial discourse is nothing less than the revolutionary hegemony itself. However, the problematic of revolution subsumes the issues of nation-state and modernization, and is not reducible to postcolonialist championing of nation-building or identity politics. On the other hand, the imported critical vocabulary of postmodernism and postcolonialism may serve as counterhegemonic voices in the current discursive struggles, dismantling the politics and power relationships in various discursive formations and strategies, official or "nonpolitical liberalist." Herein lies the real and significant political potency of Post–New Era criticism, but its critical edge is severely blunted by an ostensible eagerness to partake in the global intellectual fashion.

In contrast to the relative unpopularity of recent imported Western theory, humanism remains a favorite topic of discussion among China's intellectuals in the 1990s. A group of Shanghai-based scholars have recently launched a discussion of "neohumanism" within the context of the current cultural crisis. Like the national learning group in Beijing, these Shanghai scholars set out to attack the legacy of the 1980s as too politically engaged and therefore non-transcendental. But unlike the Beijing School, the neohumanists speak a universalist language calling forth the reawakening of "humanist spirits" in the face of commodity fetishism, which reifies traditional culture and national learning, among other things. The discussion of humanist spirits was carried in *Dushu* (Reading), arguably the most prestigious monthly journal among Chinese intellectuals, published in Beijing in its March to August issues in 1994. Though expressing a desire for resistance to and intervention in globalization, however, the political agenda of the neohumanists is also fractured and self-contradicting. On the one hand, some neohumanists maintain that the subject position of intellectuals in the current circumstances should be a "secular attitude, and [a recognition of the] unique ways by which intellectuals interpret and intervene in the society."[29] There are certain parallels between this position and the strategies of reterritorialization of the Western intellectual Left, in that both moves strive to integrate intellectual, academic, and humanistic pursuits with contemporary social conditions without sacrificing the intellectual's subject position.[30] On the other hand, some neohumanists, echoing the national learning group, assert the "ultimate concern" of values in a metaphysical and religious sense, which is said to be "sequestered" or "concealed" (*zhebi*) by worldly, utilitarian, political, and ideological struggles.[31]

Although the neohumanists are generally ambiguous about the key question of what constitutes "core universal humanist values," some grapple with a "Habermasian strategy of communicative rationality" or Gadamerian hermeneutics to retrieve the humanist values preserved in Confucian tradition as well as in the Western classical canon.[32] It is clear that, without necessarily emulating the recent trends in the West (especially the United States), what the Chinese neohumanists are calling for is in effect a return to "the Great Tradition." The projects of the Chinese neohumanists of the 1990s have some interesting similarities with what the "cultural conservatives" in the United States, such as E. D. Hirsch Jr. and Allan Bloom have done, except that the Chinese case is complicated not only by China's problematic relation to the Western canons, but also by the revolutionary legacy that has practically deconstructed the idea of universal humanist spirits for decades.[33] The neohumanists in China are well aware of both trends and positions of the Western Left and conservative Right, but their assumption of cultural differences often obliterates real, serious political differences that cut across cultural boundaries. Vacillating between a cultural conservatism and a desire for secular intervention, the search for humanist spirits remains a merely chimerical ghost-hunting of no avail. For it cannot rationalize its interventionist claims by denying from the outset the validity of any politically engaged criticism.

"Hybridity" or Critical Alternatives?

But is a politically engaged criticism that directly confronts the ideological deadlocks and that mobilizes radical and oppositional strategies then possible? In an environment of political apathy, the latest controversy in Chinese intellectual circles has centered around a book entitled *Di san zhi yanjing kan*

Zhongguo (Viewing China through a third eye; hereafter *Third Eye*). The book appears as written ostensibly by a German Sinologist named "Dr. Luoyiningger" as the "third eye," and then translated into Chinese by a certain Wang Shan.[34] It can perhaps be better understood as a Chinese version of "hybridity" by forging a space of "in-betweenness" through the counterfeit translation. Its structural similarities to postcolonialist "hybridity" can be further illustrated by its ambivalent hybridization of radicalist claims and political neo-authoritarianism. (It should be noted that I am not suggesting that the author of *Third Eye* is influenced by the postcolonialism of the West. In fact, the text categorically rejects any "Western new theories." The similarities suggested here remain purely formal and structural.) Without losing sight of the contextual differences between *Third Eye* and Anglo-American postcolonial discourse, it may be helpful to see the common fallacy in these professedly politically engaged enunciations that undermines their critical potential or simply renders them serviceable to power blocs of different orders.[35]

Third Eye has attracted widespread attention both domestically and internationally, mainly because it once again brings the central problematic of China's current reform and modernity to the fore. There are at least three aspects to this that merit attention. First, the book forcefully breaks the pervasive political apathy by addressing the most sensitive issues in the current situation in explicit, unequivocally critical language. The feigned German authorship serves to either protect the author or ease the embarrassment of the censorship agency in allowing its publication. The book sharply criticizes the current strategies of the ideological state apparatuses of stubbornly clinging to an outdated, deceptive indoctrination of "communist idealism" and refusing to open up the debates about political and ideological ramifications of the reform.[36] Second, it unmasks some of the most serious and explosive social consequences that the official ideology of reform and modernization has been covering up. On its list of dangerous factors are the massive immigration of peasants that threatens to disrupt the urban-rural symmetry; the self-righteous intellectual elites who choose to ally themselves with the international anticommunist forces; the corrupt bureaucracy; the rapid formation of a new exploitative class and the impoverishment of the increasingly powerless working class, which may trigger serious class confrontations; and the rise of militant nationalism as the potential source of disorder on a global scale.

Third and most significant, the book proposes a critical rethinking of the revolutionary hegemony from the perspective of historical searches for an alternative modernity. It radically reverses the post-Mao pro-modernization attacks on Mao's revolutionary legacy by tracing the positive elements in Mao's theory and practice during his rule, especially the Cultural Revolution. It claims, quite rightly, that "whether or not Mao is correctly evaluated determines the fate of [China's] leadership and society at large in the years to come."[37] For, the book reiterates, Mao's Chinese Marxism has left a significant legacy through over forty years of "education," now deeply embedded in China's social consciousness.[38] It defines Mao's Chinese Marxism as the "key line" of China's alternative modernity: "Mao Zedong represents the key line [of revolution] in China. . . . When Mao's image is damaged, this key line is seriously shaken. In hindsight, it is perhaps the greatest sacrifice that China has sustained in the process of turning away from the Cultural Revolution toward the current Reform. It is because this key line (which is a line of a continuing growth) has a different name: the unique Chinese alternative path of development. . . . China cannot repeat the paths of the East Asian 'Little Tigers,' nor the Japanese, or European ways of modernization, because it is a huge and poor country with a largely illiterate population. Its only correct way is to follow the footsteps of Mao, in order to search for an alternative of its own."[39]

Although it is certainly debatable as to what kind of alternative Mao had in fact created, *Third Eye* unmistakably signals a direction toward rethinking China's modernity by confronting, face to face, the most powerful ideological hegemony that has shaped much of twentieth-century China's cultural imaginary, and that continues to play a decisive role in China's present and future.

However, the book's proposed strategies undercut its very effort of rethinking and reinventing the revolutionary hegemony. For one thing, it argues for a resurrection of Mao's icon or new icons to fill the ideological vacuum, even by appealing to "popular superstition."[40] In the meantime, it advocates the power politics of a select elite, espousing a new authoritarianism in the hands of "the members of an outstanding social class."[41] This is coupled with sharp attacks on the peasantry as a potentially destructive force driven solely by a "get-rich" mentality, as well as on the intellectuals as a politically naïve group who have done a greater disservice to the project of modernity than they can ever admit, in their undiminished zeal for democracy. Such an anti-intellectual and antipeasant position has shocked and appalled a substantial number of Chinese intellectuals, who have yet to recover from the psychological trauma inflicted by the Cultural Revolution and are usually hypersensitive to any move reminiscent of the "great disaster." Indeed, the book's blatant espousal of power politics and autocracy not only belies its manifest goal of seeking rational solutions to China's position within the context of globalization; its latent conservatism and elitism also render its radical strategies politically dangerous. However radical and politically engaged, criticism devoid of a constructive agenda is susceptible to manipulation by radically different power blocs and ideological positions.

Ultimately, globalization itself has to confront this serious issue of concrete political agendas. The discourse of globalization in the West can be seen as a strategy to delegitimize the existing ideological hegemony of global capitalism as well as a means of reinventing, or legitimizing, conceptual and real alternatives to the process of capitalist globalization. However, so far it is far more concerned with the inevitability of capitalist globalization than with any possibility of noncapitalist alternatives. The political agenda of such a discourse, therefore, often remains ambiguous and indeterminate. But as the Chinese cases discussed above demonstrate, very serious political and real consequences will follow from such discursive practice or theoretical debate. Then the question we must ask ourselves is: What are the political agendas of the critical discourse of globalization?

Notes

All translations are mine, unless specified otherwise. This essay was first published in *boundary 2* 23, no. 3 (fall 1996): 193–218.

1   It is crucially relevant here to reflect on the effects of global media and communications that produce the political, ideological, and cultural artifact called "China." Although the cold war caricature of the "Evil Empire," that is, the former Soviet Union, has lost its referent, its vocabulary lingers, and has recently intensified, in the U.S. media representation of China, focusing primarily on the issue of "human rights violations." In contrast to the marginal and negligible influence of critical intellectuals on most domestic and international issues, the U.S. academy plays a critical role in fostering the American public image of China (and of other countries, especially the non-Western and/or the so-called third world). An example is the recent popularity of books disclosing the corruption of Chinese leaders, such as Harrison E. Salisbury, *The New Emperors: China in the Era of Mao and Deng* (New York, 1992); Nicholas Kristoff and Sheryl WuDunn, *China Wakes: The Struggle for the Soul of a Rising Power* (New York,

1994); and Li Zhisui, *The Private Life of Chairman Mao* (New York, 1994). Perry Link, a major China specialist from Princeton, lends his authority to the latest biography of Mao in a lengthy book review in the *Times Literary Supplement,* reiterating an image of Mao as "the freest person in China yet fond of rebellion, refusing to brush his teeth, dependent on barbiturates and sexually insatiable" (*TLS,* 28 October 1994).

2 For the newly booming Chinese film studies, see Nick Browne et al., eds., *New Chinese Cinemas: Forms, Identities, Politics* (Cambridge, UK, 1994); Chris Berry, ed., *Perspectives on Chinese Cinema* (London, 1992); and George Semsel et al., eds., *Film in Contemporary China: Critical Debates, 1979–1989* (New York, 1993).

3 The left cultural criticism has recently begun to pay attention to the area of Asia-Pacific, where China's role becomes increasingly critical. See Rob Wilson and Arif Dirlik, eds., "Asia/Pacific as Space of Cultural Production," special issue of *boundary 2* 21, no. 1 (spring 1994), and Arif Dirlik, ed., *What Is in a Rim?—Critical Perspectives on the Pacific Region Idea* (Boulder, CO, 1993). Discussions of China's current position in Asia-Pacific "cultural production," however, are missing in these volumes.

4 Fredric Jameson, foreword to *Politics, Ideology, and Literary Discourse in Modern China,* ed. Liu Kang and Xiaobing Tang (Durham, NC, 1993), 3.

5 For discussions of modernity see, for instance, Marshall Berman, *All That Is Solid Melts into Air: The Experiences of Modernity* (New York, 1988), and Jürgen Habermas, "Modernity—An Incomplete Project," in *The Anti-Aesthetic—Essays on Postmodern Culture,* ed. Hal Foster (Port Townsend, WA, 1983), 3–15. For more detailed discussions of alternative modernity and Chinese revolution, see Liu Kang, *Aesthetics and Marxism: Chinese Aesthetic Marxists and Their Western Contemporaries* (Durham, NC, forthcoming), and Liu Kang, "The Problematics of Mao and Althusser: Alternative Modernity and Cultural Revolution," *Rethinking Marxism,* 8, no. 3 (1995): 1–26.

6 Benedict Anderson, *Imagined Communities* (London, 1983), 145.

7 For recent works on nationalism, see Ernest Gellner, *Nations and Nationalism* (Oxford, 1983); Anderson, *Imagined Communities;* and Homi Bhabha, ed., *Nation and Narration* (London, 1990). All these works presuppose a unilateral, Eurocentric model of modernity, even though some set out to critique Eurocentrism.

8 Frantz Fanon, *The Wretched of the Earth,* trans. Constance Farrington (Harmondsworth, UK, 1967), 168.

9 Mao Zedong, "The Role of the Chinese Communist Party in the National War" (1938), *Selected Works of Mao Tse-tung,* vol. 2 (Peking, 1967), 209.

10 Ibid.

11 On the issue of "Chinese Marxism," see Arif Dirlik's indispensable works in the field, including, for example, *After the Revolution: Waking to Global Capitalism* (Hanover, NH, 1994), especially chap. 2, "The Marxist Narrative of Development and Chinese Marxism."

12 *Renmin ribao* (People's daily) (overseas ed.), 8 October 1994; 6 October 1994.

13 *Renmin ribao* (People's daily) (overseas ed.), 6 September 1994.

14 The revival of Confucianism or new Confucianism, first starting in Hong Kong and Taiwan, then extending to Singapore, South Korea, and the United States, where it finds perhaps its strongest advocates, such as Tu Wei-ming from Harvard and Yu Ying-shih from Princeton, is intimately related to the so-called East Asian economic miracle and the success of capitalist developments of the so-called East Asian model. This "global Confucianism," as Arif Dirlik puts it, "has been rendered into a prime mover of capitalist development and has also found quite a sympathetic ear among First World ideologues who now look to a Confucian ethic to relieve the crisis of capitalism" ("The Postcolonial Aura: Third World Criticism in the Age of Global Capitalism," *Critical Inquiry* 20 [1994], 341).

15 Anthony Giddens, among others, observes the "rise of local nationalism" in the context of capitalist globalization. See *The Consequences of Modernity* (Cambridge, UK, 1990), especially 63–78.

16 Wallerstein differentiates between "nationalism of resistance" and "nationalism of domination" in *The Politics of the World-Economy: The States, the Movements, and the Civilizations* (Cambridge, UK, 1984), 130.

17 The paradigm of tradition/modernity was promoted by a group of young scholars associated with the journal *Wenhuan: Zhongguo yu shijie* (Culture: China and the world) and the translation project, Twentieth-Century Western Scholarly Classics. Without counting the influence of the same paradigm of modern China studies in the West, the purpose of the Chinese critics of the 1980s was to replace the older opposition of "Western culture/Chinese culture" with "tradition/modernity" in their reinterpretation of modern Chinese cultural and intellectual history. Although they did not purposefully elide and suppress the revolutionary legacy, these critics took the problematic of modernity as their guiding episteme without questioning its historical specificity. See Gan Yang, ed., *Zhongguo dangdai wenhua yishi* (Contemporary Chinese cultural consciousness) (Hong Kong, 1989).

18 Chen Pingyuan, "Qiushi yu zhiyong: Zhang Taiyan sixiang qiao lun" ("Seek truth" and "put to use": Zhang Taiyan's academic thought), *Zhongguo wenhua* (Chinese culture), no. 7 (fall 1992): 148.

19 Liu Mengxi, " 'Wenhua tuo ming' yu Zhongguo xiandai xueshu chuantong" ("Cultural will-passing" and the modern Chinese tradition of scholarship), *Zhongguo wenhua* (Chinese culture), no. 6 (spring 1992): 107.

20 Raymond Williams, *Problems in Materialism and Culture* (London, 1980), 8.

21 Chen Lai, "Ershi shiji wenhua yundong zhong de jijin zhuyi" (Radicalism in twentieth-century cultural movements), *Dong fang* (Orient) 1, no. 1 (1993): 38–44. It is worth noting that Chen Lai, a professor of philosophy at Peking University and a major figure of "national learning," was once an active member of the 1980s hermeneutic group associated with the journal *Culture: China and the World*. See note 17.

22 For a recent controversy on the question of "radicalism," see *Ershi yi shiji* (Twenty-first century), no. 10 (1992) and no. 11 (1992). In these two issues of the Hong Kong journal, Yu Ying-shih, a leading American advocate of neo-Confucianism teaching at Princeton, debates with Chinese historians concerning radicalism in modern Chinese intellectual history. Yu, of course, denounces "radicalism," singling out Marxism specifically, as the true villain in Chinese modernization. See Yu Ying-shih, "Zai lun Zhongguo xiandai sixiang zhong de jijin yu baoshou: Da Jiang Yihua xiansheng" (Further thoughts on radicalism and conservatism in modern Chinese intellectual history: A response to Jiang Yihua), no. 10: 147. In his rebuttal, Jiang Yihua, a Chinese historian, argues that Yu Ying-shih's attack on radicalism "has spawned a new wave of neo-conservatism and anti-radicalism in academic inquiries as well as in political practices" (Jiang Yihua, "Jijin yu baoshou: Yu Yu Yingshi xiansheng shangque" [Radicalism and conservatism: A discussion with Yu Ying-shih], no. 11: 134).

23 Mikhail Bakhtin, *The Dialogic Imagination,* trans. C. Emerson and M. Holquist (Austin, TX, 1981), 371.

24 For discussions of Li Zehou's works in the 1980s, see Liu Kang, "Subjectivity, Marxism, and Culture Theory in China," *Social Text* 31–32 (1992): 114–140.

25 Jameson's China lectures of 1985 were translated and published in Chinese as *Houxiandai zhuyi yu wenhua lilun* (Postmodernism and cultural theory) (Xi'an, 1986). Jameson's lectures are likened by his Chinese introducer to Bertrand Russell's speeches at Peking University in 1921 during the period of early cultural ferment known as the May Fourth Era (ca. 1919–27). "Post–New Era criticism" was coined by Zhang Yiwu to refer to some avant-garde critical discourse that has emerged since 1990, vis-à-vis the cultural and literary criticism of the "New Era" (1979–89). See, for instance, "Houxinshiqi de wenxue piping" (Post–New Era literary criticism: A roundtable discussion of Zhang Yiwu, Wang Ning, and Liu Kang), *Zuojia* (Writer), no. 304 (1994): 71–84.

26 Wang Ning, for instance, proposes that postmodernism may serve as the point at which "a real dialogue with our Western colleagues" can start ("Constructing Postmodernism: The Chinese Case and Its Different Versions," *Canadian Review of Comparative Literature* [March–June 1993]: 60).

27 A case in point is that the present author was involved in a controversy inadvertently three years ago, as I submitted an essay to *Modern China,* criticizing some practices of China studies in the West, drawing on some postmodernist notions. My viewpoints were sharply rejected by several leading American experts of China studies as following blindly the Western new theory while ignoring China's "difference." See "Symposium: Ideology and Theory in the Study of Modern Chinese Literature: Paradigmatic Issues in Chinese Studies, II," *Modern China* 19, no. 1 (1993).

28 The representative works of Post–New Era criticism include Zhang Yiwu, *Zai bianyuan chu zhuisuo: Disan shijie wenhua yu Zhongguo dangdai wenxiu* (Search at the margin: Third-world culture and contemporary Chinese literature); and

Chen Xiaoming, *Wubian de tiaozhan: Zhongguo xianfeng wenxue de houxiandai xin* (Challenges without borders: Postmodernity in Chinese avant-garde literature), both appearing in Xie Mian and Li Yang eds., *Ershi shiji Zhongguo wenxue congshu* (Series of twentieth-century Chinese literature), (Changchun, 1993).

29 This statement is made by Chen Sihe in Chen Sihe et al., "Daotong, xuetong, yu zhengtong—Renwen jingshen xunshi lu zhi san" (Traditions of Dao, learning, and politics—Notes of searches for humanist spirits, pt. 3), *Dushu* 5 (1994): 52.

30 For the strategies of reterritorialization of the Western intellectual Left, see, for instance, Paul Patton, "Marxism and Beyond: Strategies of Reterritorialization," in *Marxism and the Interpretation of Culture*, ed. Cary Nelson and Lawrence Grossberg (Urbana, IL, 1988), 123–139.

31 Gao Ruiquan et al., "Renwen jingshen xunzong—Renwen jingshen xunshi lu zhi er" (Searching the traces of humanist spirits—Notes of searches for humanist spirits, pt. 2), *Dushu* 4 (1994): 73–81.

32 Zhang Rulun argues that to defend the universal values embedded in the Western classics, Habermas and Gadamer are useful to "discard the (historical) content and designate a set of universally acceptable discursive rules." See Zhang Rulun et al., "Renwen jingshen: Shifou keneng he ruhe keneng—Renwen jingshen xunshi lu zhi yi" (Humanist spirits: Whether possible and how—Notes of searches for humanist spirits, pt. 1), *Dushu* 3 (1994): 7.

33 For an incisive analysis of American cultural conservatism, see Ellen Messer-Davidow, "Manufacturing the Attack on Liberalized Higher Education," *Social Text* 36 (1993): 40–80. Also see E. D. Hirsch Jr., *Cultural Literacy: What Every American Needs to Know* (Boston, 1987); and Allan Bloom, *The Closing of the American Mind* (New York, 1987). By drawing parallels between the Chinese and Americans, I do not mean to collapse their vast differences. There is, however, an undeniable and tangible link between intellectual trends in an age of global communication, despite geopolitical differences.

34 "Dr. Luoyiningger [Germany]," *Di san zhi yanjing kan Zhongguo* (Viewing China through a third eye), trans. Wang Shan (Taiyuan, 1994). Soon after the book was published, Wang Meng, renowned writer and ex–Cultural Minister, questioned its authorship by identifying many obvious rhetorical features that betray its forged "foreignness." Wang Meng also strongly criticizes the book's anti-intellectual stance. See Wang Meng, " 'Luoyiningger' yu ta de yanjing" ("Luoyiningger" and his eyes), *Dushu* 9 (1994): 25–31. It was later ascertained by the Hong Kong magazine *Asian Weekly* that the "translator" was the real author. For related information, see *Beijing zhizhun* (Beijing spring) 10 (1994).

35 Homi Bhabha defines postcolonialist hybridity as a "space" "where the construction of a political object that is new, *neither the one nor the Other*, properly alienates our political expectations and changes" in "The Commitment to Theory," *New Formations* 5 (1988): 10–11. Such an ambivalent "in-betweenness," as many critics have noted, only repositions Bhabha and his cohorts to a comfortably esoteric and academic plane, irrelevant to real historical happenings and

events. In the Chinese case of *Third Eye,* however, its relationship to realpolitik is significant. It is said by overseas political commentators to have the backing of top Chinese leaders, including the CCP general secretary and the president of PRC, Jiang Zemin. See the transcription of the Voice of America forum on the book attended by leading Chinese political dissidents Liu Binyan and Su Shaozhi, in the Chinese dissident newspaper published in the United States, *Xinwen ziyou daobao* (Herald of freedom of the press), 14 October 1994.

36 *Third Eye,* 207–228. Also 246: "The rulers often publicize unrealistic slogans of reform to please the public, and these deceptive objectives further stimulate the idealist fervor of the masses in a vicious circle, ultimately causing catastrophic turns to the social reform and transformations."

37 Ibid., 209.

38 Ibid., 259.

39 Ibid., 214.

40 Ibid., 217.

41 Ibid., 246.

III CULTURE
AND THE NATION

Globalization and Culture:

Navigating the Void

Global Capitalism

Somewhat fragile and silvering, Noam Chomsky stands in the footlights, speaking like an angel in profound rage. His unremitting data on capitalism and his indefatigable act of stripping the liberal myth down to its most brutal form is matched by his detached way of calling the bluff of futurist propaganda spinning from the profits of the TNCs that glorify globalization. There is still, among intellectuals and activists, an impassioned backing of Chomsky's analyses. But even as he reveals the Corporate Gulag that destroys through redoubled deceit, and in the name of freedom, sectors of life inimical to the single aim of profit, his loneliness on the world stage deepens.[1]

Current capitalism (that no longer merits the hope that it is the late, or the last, stage of capitalism) can be reduced, despite the rhetoric of liberalization, to hard statistics about slashed wages, massive unemployment and increasing destitution in the heart of the metropolitan North. As for the South, even facts shrivel before the bitter farce played out against its interests. As large parts of its population drop from the purview of the globalists, the "one world" and its media-fed population celebrate, in however schizophrenic a manner, the consumerist utopia.

The terminology of globalism refers unblushingly to an ideology of the market, dictated by the IMF, the World Bank and the G-7 executive, crowned by Gatt; to a global market of which the United States, having "won" the cold war, is the moral conductor. It sets the norm not only for free trade but also (in the same universalizing mode) for human rights, for historical and cultural studies. What is being globalized is therefore American-style capitalism and its implicit worldview.

Edward Said's *Culture and Imperialism* ends on the theme of American domination and delivers its rebuttal in a spirit of sustained opposition to imperial power that newer terminologies like globalization will not be able to pronounce. "There are far too many politicized people on earth today for any nation to readily accept the finality of America's mission to lead the world," Said writes.[2] To that I should like to add, as an inhabitant of the third world (and a little removed from the internecine wars in the American academy about the ontological status of anticolonial histories and the transcription of these onto a condition of postcoloniality), that there is not only "an internationalist counter-articulation" stemming from the resistances in the "underlying world map."[3] This map is in fact the politically alive geography of the South, where ancient ground heaves to change continental relations through economic competition, through the power of anticolonial discourse, through the forceful heterogeneity of cultural practice.

From Where I Speak

A great deal of present postcolonial cultural discourse overextrapolates on the idea of an "underlying world map" and treats it as some sort of a semisurreal terrain with interstitial spaces from within which the colonials/subalterns work out sly strategies of complicity and subversion. Although I do not deny the importance of opening up the too rigid opposition between colonial and postcolonial positions by what one might call the categorical device of hybridity, I should like to recall the more outspoken anticolonial practices of which India holds a fairly honorable legacy.

Until very recently, a judiciously protectionist national economy was a promise and a reality in India. From where I speak there is still ground for debate about the nation-state. With all the calumny it has earned, it may be the only political structure that can protect the people of the third world from the totalitarian system that oligopolies establish—ironically, through the massive state power of the advanced nations. Whether the nation-states of the third world can become, yet again, the site of opposition is now a particularly vexed issue; nor is this the place to go into the possibilities of survival, of national economies and national cultures. Leading Indian Marxists are re-articulating key issues about the nation and the state.[4] From other points of view along the ideological spectrum, there is interrogation underway concerning the ethics of the nation-state in relation to the polity, the people, and communities.[5] Accompanied by a cultural discourse and practice that differs from that of other postcolonial countries, this is worth examining in its own terms and not only as a differential device for theorizing postcoloniality.

Beyond the national there has been a certain kind of utopian commitment to the international in India. There was a revolutionary bias in the definition of internationalism as early as 1920, emblematized by M. N. Roy's exchanges with Lenin at the Second Congress of the Communist International. A social democratic and communist alternative was inscribed within mainstream nationalism from the 1930s. Alongside the anti-imperialist, the antifascist stand during the war signaled by Nehru and foregrounded by the Communist Party of India offered another kind of international solidarity. All this in turn conditioned progressivist cultural and aesthetic categories of modernity, and modernism. Nehru's postindependence internationalism, based on Afro-Asian unity and the nonaligned movement (NAM), not only negotiated the cold war; it transformed itself into the crucial category of the third world pushing internationalism toward a fresh agenda. This was a contestatory postcolonialism, well understood in India though more fully developed in other countries—Cuba, Algeria, Vietnam—fighting a life-and-death war of liberation against Euro-American imperialism at the time.

Given India's sustained struggle for independence and the precise mode of decolonization, its cultural life is alternately conservative and progressive. It is a peculiarly pitched colonial modernity, not derivative in some deducible sense but heavily mediated. The mediations derive from its classical-imperialist past, its civilizational spread, and its strong nationalist movement. Even while Indian nationalism works round the militant motif of *swaraj*, it nevertheless takes the form of a "passive revolution."[6] Independence is gained through Gandhi's uniquely peaceful and intrepid principle of a people's *satyagraha;* but within the terms of a negotiated transfer of power, the sovereign state comes to represent the interests of the Indian ruling classes.

In saying that Indian cultural life is alternately conservative and progressive, I am nevertheless including a reflexivity in the proposition. I am referring to the way nationalist consciousness has been split, supplanted, differentiated, and reconfigured by positions such as that of the *dalit* jurist, Ambedkar, and by that of Gandhi himself, who constitutes *and* deconstructs the "national" via (among other symbols) the oppressed figure of the untouchable. More specifically, key terms like *swadeshi* are discussed within a cultural mise-en-scène that includes among its key players Gandhi and Rabindranath Tagore.[7] One paradigm for national culture can be derived from that seminal exchange. As evidence of Tagore's stand, there is an entire pedagogical system elaborated in the university he builds at Santiniketan, where the national extends into paradoxical realms of the poet's imagination. What is more, Tagore introduces the troubled terrain of the international where he finds himself groping in a manner far more complex than his fuzzy universalist enunciations would indicate. Along with his close yet vexed relationship with the West, he devises an Asian version of internationalism; he communicates with contemporaries in Japan and China; he receives adulation and rebuffs.[8] All of this becomes the more engaging when we sketch the international context of orientalism to include the mystical/futurist tendency of the Russian avant-garde—and thence its radical pull.

It may be useful to elaborate the motif of sovereignty (as it derives from the nationalist discourse) and see it in the richly polyvocal literature of Tagore. He is already, at the start of the century, writing novels both intensely introspective and polemical about the definition of the nation in terms of its people. He links this up with the question of subjectivity (in *Gora,* in the transposed identity of a white man who grows up as a foundling in a Hindu home; in the volatile woman protagonist from a feudal household in *Home and the World*). He steeps these characters in the great vortex of contemporary nationalist history, making them interrogative figures of mixed portent. He prefigures a historically shaped subjectivity with a potential consciousness actually realized in the later narrative of the nation.

To the Tagore lineage may be added the motif of sovereignty worked into an ethnographic allegory in Satyajit Ray's *Apu Trilogy* (1955, 1956, 1959), where the protagonist Apu lends both sublimity and catharsis to the quest of a postindependence nation.[9] This in turn is complemented by filmmakers like Kerala's Adoor Gopalakrishnan who authenticate the desire for sovereignty by keeping it yoked to a modest regionalism, to a modest liberal critique of ideology that devolves to a quiescent personalism (e.g., *Mukhamukham*, 1987, *Kathapurusham*, 1995). This is the kind of cross-referencing between conservative and progressive ideologies that I have been pointing to.

As for the Left, its balance of progressivism is not very different from that of the liberal intellectual stream. I do not deny the modernity it promotes, but the promise of daring new forms that break through the realist conscience is often absent. But daring forms do exist. In Santiniketan itself, a tribal persona with radical affect is assumed by the artist Ramkinkar Baij already in the mid-1930s. He positions his tribals as migrant labor in *Santhal Family* (1937) in the compound of Kala Bhavan at Santiniketan. From the next decade onward, the history of the Bengal IPTA (Indian People's Theatre Association) testifies to major theatric achievements, like *Nabanna*. From the heart of this vortex the revolutionary filmmaker Ritwik Ghatak brings to bear the left movement as witness to moments of advance and regression in modern Indian history. His last film, *Jukti Takko Ar Gappo* (1974), becomes an occasion for him to reflect, autobiographically, on the interposed meanings of revolutionary practice in art and politics. Not surprisingly, the mode is tragic.[10] During the same period, the radical feminist writer from Bengal, Mahasweta Devi, devises the role of a surrogate mother in monumental proportions, stretching the gendered subject to allegorical attenuation and thus to the ends of historical narrative. As Gayatri Spivak says, Mahasweta Devi offers to the young Naxalites of the time a "history imagined into fiction."[11]

We may continue with the radicals of subsequent generations, who favor a dialectic of the modern with the primitive/subaltern and seek to elicit from it a politics of the local—as against the national—community. Certainly in the valorized mode of contemporary ethnography, the local is a place of knowledge; the local in India often signifies tribal, vernacular authenticity. The local is also the site for politically honed sets of choices at a given place and time. Both the peasant and the proletariat must take the local as immanent ground for a politics of revolt, a concept that was used to the bitter end in Mao's Cultural Revolution and was matched in India through the 1960s and '70s as a ground for militant action by the Naxalites. This created a radical nihilist poetics that marked the ground of Indian art but often shortened the life of the protagonists. Witness the case of two Kerala artists of exceptional talent: filmmaker John Abraham and sculptor K. P. Krishnakumar, both of whom died prematurely in the 1980s, signaling the desperation—economic, existential, political—of producing art in our times.

A linkage of the local and the national communities is sustained by today's interventionist documentary filmmakers like Anand Patwardhan who are functioning in the face of a partially communalized society—*communal* being the term coined in India for sectarian and increasingly fundamentalist religious communities. Wounded but still fairly democratic, the polity of contemporary India is a worthy audience; to them Patwardhan addresses his trilogy on the *unmaking* of secular India in the past ten years, culminating in the 1994 documentary, *Father, Son and the Holy War.* Here religious fundamentalism is seen as the pathetic discourse of virility. Resistance is shown building up in the everyday life of the women who appear in the film as the lean survivors of an unholy war raging in the streets of urban India.

The preceding examples show why Fredric Jameson's formulation about the national allegory being the preeminent paradigm for third-world literature continues to be valid.[12] This view of the national can be complemented by James Clifford's reformulation of the local in terms of ethnographic allegories—the narrative means for a grassroots recuperation of lost identities.[13] In both cases the allegorical breaks up the paradigmatic nature of the *cause:* in the first case it questions the immanent condition of culture taken as some irrepressible truth offering; in the second case it splits the symbolic homogeneity of the people (from whom a whole series of organic metaphors is drawn) into its differentiated parts. There may be good reason to break the metaphoric mode suitable to a romantic version of culture/people/nation and thus avoid heavy condensation of these terms. There is a pending hermeneutic task to work out a mode of displacement and exegesis; to go beyond the historicist argument and into an ethical imaginary—an ethics that does not become constraining law or institutional decree. As Edward Said puts it, "One may speak of secular space, and of humanely constructed and independent histories that are fundamentally knowable, although not through grand theory or systematic totalization. . . . I have been saying that human experience is finely textured, dense and accessible enough *not* to need extra-historical or extra-worldly agencies to illuminate or explain it. I am talking about a way of regarding the world as amenable to investigation and interrogation. . . ."[14]

Taking the cue from wide-ranging Indian literature produced since the middle of the nineteenth century, we can claim a tradition of the modern that inscribes within its very narrative the aspirations of a secular nation.

The Postcolonial/Postmodern Entanglement

Is there in the third world today a historical commitment to national self-hood and collective cultural praxis? Or is it a pragmatic undertaking, an interpretive process, a sorting out of the representational dilemmas of post-coloniality? At one level of discourse this question devolves to a rather simple political preference. Without going into detail, I should like to position myself, as I hope I have already indicated, in favor of a conflictual rather than a negotiating stand on the question of postcolonial culture.[15]

Speaking for the artist, however, one has to reckon with modes of operation that are both transgressive and negotiating and therefore naturally eclectic. K. G. Subramanyan, one of India's most distinguished artists with a nationalist-Santiniketan background, has argued, at a pedagogical level, for an unabashed eclecticism. His own work, along with that of Bhupen Kha-khar and Gulammohammed Sheikh, offers a lively hybridization: subtly inflected, noncontestatory but subversive.[16] As a consequence of the histor-ical determinants coloniality imposes, one can see codes still available to the postcolonial artist in staggering variety. These offer strategic choices and benign practice ranging from the high to the low, from the center to the periphery, from the local to the global. The postcolonial artist may be seen navigating the void between these seductively posed polarities, sustaining a romance by turning exoticized otherness into social realignments.

Consider in this context what Homi Bhabha is theorizing. "Driven by the subaltern history of the margins of modernity," he wishes to "rename the postmodern from the position of the postcolonial."[17] And to thus assert alterity through a valorizing of the other, who is now so demonstrably the speaking subject.

Bhabha's politics of cultural difference favors the short maneuver and the subtle negotiation. There is also the longer navigational pull—to borders, frontiers, horizons, which are all deferred to postpolitics and pitched beyond the fin de siècle present:

Our existence today is marked by a tenebrous sense of survival, living on the borderline of the "present," for which there seems to be no proper name other than the current and controversial shiftiness of the prefix "post."[18]

And further:

> The present can no longer be envisaged as a break or a bonding with the past and the future, no longer a synchronic presence: our proximate self-presence, our public image, comes to be revealed for its discontinuities, its inequalities, its minorities. Unlike the dead hand of history that tells the beads of sequential time like a rosary, seeking to establish serial, causal connections, we are now confronted with what Walter Benjamin describes as the blasting of a monadic moment from the homogenous course of history, "establishing a conception of the present as the 'time of now.' "[19]

Walter Benjamin's melancholy metaphors of exile, taken over by Raymond Williams and Edward Said, become leitmotifs for the twentieth century, markers for the modern consciousness. Infused with their own generational anguish of the diaspora, we can track through them modernity's émigré soul and the political opponent's exile. We can also extrapolate therefrom the postcolonial condition of refugee labor developing into a new kind of peripheral identity. But to go from the tragic life of a Benjamin, from the interventionism of Williams and of Said, to Homi Bhabha's discursive moves on otherness, this is a detour. A celebration of migrancy as exile, of vagrancy as diaspora: what shall we make of that?

His politics is ratified, Bhabha would no doubt claim, from his engagement with Frantz Fanon.[20] Here is, however, the paradox. Bhabha actually denies the relevance of the old politics of anticolonialism; he turns it into a discursive radicalism that says: "There is no longer an influential separatist emphasis on simply elaborating an anti-imperialist or black-nationalist tradition 'in itself.' There is an attempt to interrupt the Western discourse of modernity through these displacing, interrogative subaltern or postslavery narratives and the critical theoretical perspectives they engender."[21] Having virtually buried the struggle, he still elicits support from Fanon and goes on to speak about unbelonging, black resistance, the lure of community, and gun-running politics—as in Nadine Gordimer's *My Son's Father.* There is a kind of spiral Homi Bhabha constructs around otherness, giving it an abstracted political dynamic. Skimming metropolitan manifestations of multiculturalism, he then plunges into the hallucinatory consciousness of the black murdering mother in Toni Morrison's *Beloved.* He matches this with Fanon's interrogations of deformed ontologies in the colonial process of othering.

"The power of the postcolonial translation of modernity rests in its *performative, deformative* structure," Bhabha says.[22] At his best, there is with Bhabha the foregrounding of subjectivity, the extraction of it from the margins of the metropolis through a series of masquerading tactics. In an emphatically postsocialist narrative mode, this performative flair is all. Bhabha supplements it with a concentration on the subjects' inwardness, stillness, and negative praxis—the narcissistic, deformative othering of self. This is to stand in for the dispossessed of the world. Bhabha's literary examples allow for the privilege of belonging to finally disintegrate, for a self-transgression to take place. There is a preference for a psychic subversion of any given notion of identity: a preference for a surrealist (and therefore anticapitalist?), liberal/libertarian (therefore anarchist?) mode.

If one disentangles the postcolonial and the postmodern, Bhabha leaves one with a discursive as against an insurgent subjectivity.[23] In fact, the Bhabha legacy functions best in the cosmopolitan world of the "twice-born," the immigrant intelligentsia from the third world lodged within the first world, whose identity is ambivalent, restless, interrogative—though hardly in this age diasporic. Indeed, Bhabha's position is strengthened and enlivened by Salman Rushdie's sharp-witted self-parody of the immigrant identity. *The Satanic Verses,* Rushdie writes, "rejoices in mongrelisation and fears the absolutism of the Pure."[24]

Given the flawed self-image Rushdie provides, and the theatrics of the indeterminate soul in his virtuoso fiction, the virtuoso discourse of Bhabha about the tactical maneuvers of postcoloniality becomes the more ironically valid. But this is also where the problem lies. Thus mythologized, the material tends to become serviceable for ethnographic investigation, extravagant fiction, or, in a less friendly register, for ideological maneuvers by vested interests in the globalization project.

This is a floating intelligentsia to supplant a rooted intelligentsia; the discourse of postmodernity puts to rout the notion of the "organic intellectual." Once again continents and nations recede into native habitations, and we have interpreters and translators decoding cultures across the globe. Paradoxically, if hybridity is the survivor's credo in the age of globalization, global culture, under the chasing speed of radical representation, emits a great buzz on *identity.* It also produces an extraordinary communications syndrome, except that in the absence of any sense of projected equality, communications can too often be an empty signal. This is what might be called the simulacrum of cultural identity, where theories of representation and the rhetoric about the ineluctable otherness of identity press urgently. But it is only a *play* of choice, not a test of praxis.

In the all-round navigation of the shoreless horizon, there is a surfeit of semantics about displacement; we are always "somebody's other," always dodging the mockery of co-option.[25] The real choices, about community versus the communal, about ethnic vulnerability and neoreligious fundamentalisms—choices that are national vexations turning into tragedies—remain blurred in the exile's imagination.

Consider in this light what chaos was stirred within the Asian communities in relation to the Rushdie problematic.[26] Religious and nonreligious members reacted with a defensive rage to the ideological provocation *The Satanic Verses* was seen to pose. Whether the secularists were ranged with the white intellectuals or with the fundamentalists, they lost the opportunity to wrest the terms of the debate from the hands of the Western liberal intelligentsia. They surrendered the right to discuss the matter of self-representation at the cutting edge of "blasphemy"—to discuss, for instance, whether or not an allegorization of painful moments in a people's history leads to a new reflexivity; whether a relentless parodying of grand moments in a national charade of representations leads to a sharpening of real difference; and whether this difference involves, besides fictive characters, embattled collectivities that elude the politics of exile. These were some of the questions worthy of Rushdie's audacity.

"However, the third world liberal intelligentsia—in some sense, citizens of the world, out of synch everywhere—have to pay its cost in their daily lives," says Alok Rai, speaking from the entrenched position of a third-world intellectual. Rai enfolds these issues in defense of Rushdie but significantly via the intransigent Fanon:

> As Frantz Fanon was to discover, for all his keen sense of himself as a unique individual, he was ineluctably burdened with the experience of his people: "I was responsible at the same time for my body, for my race, for my ancestors." . . . Quite apart from the comprehensive material damage, one carries the coded inscription of the unequal colonial relationship in the deepest recesses of one's being. Thus, Fanon was an eloquent analyst of

the twists and turns of the dialectic of the post-colonial consciousness, in which betrayal and inauthenticity are a constant danger, and appear in bewildering and unsettling disguises.[27]

There are societies that have undergone a long period of decolonization and developed beyond the terms of hybridity a sustained postcolonial vision that has, along with concrete manifestations, the ability to theorize on societal conditions. These societies have devised, moreover, styles of historical praxis and futures beyond postcoloniality. This may be kept in view to arrive at a more dialectically worked-out politics than a perennially in-between position allows.

Let us concede that it is the privilege of those who live their lives within the format of a national culture to resist globalization, as against the privilege of those who live more global lives to seek its emancipatory features. Let us concede that it is pointless setting up a symmetrical hierarchy of belonging and unbelonging that works like a seesaw. Even conceding this, my disagreement with the exile rhetoric of Bhabha, and even Rushdie, is predictably that I want the location of self and culture to be less shifty, less a matter of continual displacement of categories one to another. In Bhabha's view, "The contingent and the liminal become the times and the spaces for the historical representation of the subjects of cultural difference in a postcolonial criticism."[28] I would argue for a greater holding power of the historical paradigm where differences are recognized to have real and material consequences, where agency is not ghost-driven nor collapsed into a series of metonymically disposed identities that are but fragments spinning their way to entropy.

"[T]he *post-* in postcolonial, like the *post-* in postmodern, is the *post-* of the space-clearing gesture," says Kwame Anthony Appiah,[29] and claiming greater location and agency for the African artist, he goes on to elaborate:

> Sura Suleri has written recently, in *Meatless Days,* of being treated as an "otherness machine"—and of being heartily sick of it. Perhaps the predicament of the postcolonial intellectual is simply that as intellectuals—a category instituted in black Africa by colonialism—we are, indeed, always at the risk of becoming otherness machines, with the manufacture of alterity as our principle role. . . . This is especially true when postcolonial meets postmodern. . . . The role that Africa, like the rest of the Third World, plays for Euro-American postmodernism—like its better-documented sig-

nificance for modernist art—must be distinguished from the role post-modernism might play in the Third World. . . .

For all the while, in Africa's cultures, there are those who will not see themselves as Others. Despite the overwhelming reality of economic decline; despite unimaginable poverty; despite wars, malnutrition, disease, and political instability, African cultural productivity grows apace: popular literatures, oral narrative and poetry, dance, drama, music and visual art all thrive.[30]

Clearing Space

Global culture could be a less suspicious enterprise if it became clearer what the culture is that equates with marketism and how it can be critiqued. Can global culture still be critiqued in terms Adorno used, such as culture industry, or as the ideology of mass culture within capitalism?[31] To this there is already an ample "answer" provided from the same context by Fredric Jameson.[32] Writing about the peculiar dilemma of cultural reification within the citadel of the modern itself, he places consumerism on the cusp of the modern and the postmodern, and he offers ideological safeguards in the wake of the historical and systemic changes underway. He does this through a generous yet relentless exercise of critical reason that leaves little scope for nostalgia but that helps check the despair about the market from evolving into ritual maneuvers and mean survival. Thus, he saves cultural praxis from moving into reverse gear, crushing in the process what remains of the emancipatory imagination. With Jameson, as always, critical reason and cultural praxis are pegged together to form a utopian discourse—but whether that discourse, given its historical antecedents, tends to exclude the third world remains a difficult question. Does the third world so designated, as a place of aggregative self-representation and collective nemesis, become a revised, anthropologically dictated narrative that excels in revenge histories about otherness but lacks the initiative on historical reflexivity for envisaging a future? It is one of my intentions to contend in the subsequent argument that the pros and cons of this very problematic make up the critical path toward selfhood, authorship, and avant-garde practice among third-world artists.

As regards the global culture industry, there is now a recycling argument attached to first- and third-world relations. Globalization, which has a great deal to do with selling commodities, including units of the culture industry (exemplified by how hard the United States fights for the export advantage of Hollywood and the American TV networks), comes with the theory that people around the globe negotiate at every turn and recycle/refunctionalize the foreign inputs anyway, to arrive at a hybrid fecundity.

Hybridity for Bhabha, let us remember, is the historical effect of colonialism, and it is to be used as a discursive device to decode the condition of postcolonialism. There is, along with this, a more functional form of hybridity. Therefore, a distinction has to be maintained between hybridity as a long-term cultural process involving materials, language, and difficult choices of discourse; hybridity as practice leading to a certain virtuosity learned against the risk of extinction in colonized cultures; and hybridity as a matter primarily of quick ingenuity required to ride current market demands, where an indigenous form and artisanal life adapts itself to the national-global market in whatsoever manner is most readily available. Néstor García Canclini's trenchant argument along this track holds good for the survival, in Mexico, of indigenous traditions.[33] They survive in their plurality by means that have a good deal to do with urbanism, innovation, and a simultaneously closed and open identitarian politics of the postmodern age when the artifact has a new exchange value and prospers as a sign for reified communities in the globalized market. This can also serve as a success story for Indian crafts and for the evolving forms of popular art that capture the national and international imagination, not least the great Indian film industry.

We can go on from here to very briefly designate the more lively aspects of global culture as it transforms indigenous and national cultural formations. There have been cultural scenarios set up (as, for example, in Mexico and other Latin American societies) to prise open superposed cultures in an appropriate masquerade of representations. There are formal recodings of cultures, altering the terms devised in the great metropolis of the Western world (as happened in Japan after the Second World War). There have been probings by historically deprived identities of a radically reconstituted otherness (as, for example, among the black vanguard in literature, in art, in performance). There are fantasies of plenitude proffered as resumed orientalist desire in contemporary Chinese films. And there is, finally, the reflexive option set up by each one of these intertwined possibilities that contribute to establishing a utopian realm of the other that is best reclaimed *by* that other. This is proved by the avant-garde now sweeping through the South, including Asia.

In India, at present, the national formation is disintegrating. There is an uncomfortable relationship between the public and the private, the state and commerce, the national and the global. With the new links between the Indian and the global markets, international ramifications are surfacing across the board in the culture industry (in the electronic media, film, advertising, and art), and this cannot but have a certain emancipatory result—even if in the form of unbottled genii and quick innovation. Moreover, globalization allows for the first time a freedom from the national/collective/communitarian straitjacket; freedom also from the heavily paternalistic patronage system of the state. It allows freedom from a rigid anti-imperialist position in which postcolonial artists find themselves locked; and the freedom to include in postcolonial realities other discourses of opposition such as those of gender and the minorities—discourses that question the ethics of the nation-state itself.

It is possible, then, that in India, as in various parts of Asia—Thailand, Indonesia, Hong Kong, Korea, the Philippines, China—the positively post-colonial avant-garde in film and in art will come now: a reflexivity posed as some form or other of countermodernity made possible by the changed norms of cultural hospitality in the postmodern age. The initiative to hold international film festivals and biennials with a third-world, Southern, or regional focus is but a symptom of more substantial change in the actual political conditions building up to a breakthrough in the contemporary arts. With the older institutional structure built up during the nationalist or revolutionary phase in flux, with the *not so hospitable* economic realities of the postmodern age, the naked expropriation of the South by the trade and labor laws of the North, and with growing disparities mocking the unity of the nation itself, a new battleground for cultural action opens up. If it seems that this avant-garde will be a postmodern affair, it will not be without a serious challenge to the *terms* of that phenomenon precisely where these become baldly global.[34]

The local-global, a geopolitical proposition, can be turned into a spatial metaphor for what I call navigating the void. The natives' (by now) multiple passages beyond involve a progressively more precise signaling procedure on each shore and threshold: a performative or even properly theatric gesture that marks these as a series of *disjunctures*. This is propitious ground for the emergence of a historical avant-garde. Let me take a quick example from India. If there is a sudden spate of installation art in India (raising the questions: Why so late? Why now?), we have to look first to the appearance of the art market for an answer. Installation is an art of *presence* in the field of the object; it is a form of the deconstructed object where it invokes the dynamics of presence but in an unhomely, indeterminate setting. I choose the work of three Indian artists to make the point. The first is a female act of passion staged (in Bombay, 1993) by Nalini Malani and Alaknanda Samarth. It is an installation/performance of Heiner Muller's *Medea,* the barbarian princess who murders her children to avenge her exile, her betrayal, her redundancy in the superior civilization. The second is an installation that gives evidence of public murder; this is Vivan Sundaram's *Memorial* (Delhi, 1993), a ceremonially laid out site to bury the victim of communal carnage from the 1993 Bombay riots—the documentary image of the sacrificed Muslim providing by its presence the mise-en-scène for national mourning. Third, N. N. Rimzon's *Man with Tools* (Delhi, 1994) provides a recuperative symbol for self-sufficiency, his commitment to the ethics and poetry of use objects producing an icon out of the dedicated body of labor.

These examples propose intrepid stands in the tragic mode: one from a feminist position offers a kind of ecological nemesis on man's greed; another constructs a renewed space for political affect where historical anchoring is marked as different from national belonging; and the third attempts a transposition of the hieretic into the human: the humble figure adorned with a ground-halo of tools from a poor smithy becomes the icon with an aura. Contrapuntally, these works are proposing a utopianism precisely on the ground of the national and the regional, securing these as sites for political battle. With allegories of home and journey, departures and death, work and apotheosis, a subjective quest becomes a politically measured space for transcendence. It also involves a strategic doubling of identity where no authority holds.

Thus, when we speak on behalf of postcolonial countermodernity, we should be speaking not just about identity—which can appear from the vantage point of postmodernism as a reflection of dead realisms and of an unreconstructed reality. We should be speaking about psychic and formal sublimation as one finds in the avant-garde heritage of surrealism, for example, where the quest for selfhood combines with libertarian freedoms. We should also be speaking of a practice based on the epiphanies of language understood not only as a grammatical proposition but also as something that springs from purposeful intransigence and lost utopias. We should be speaking about the structure of potential consciousness (after Lukacs), from a "blasting of a monadic moment" (after Benjamin), both of which are still able to render the historical experientially—one on a sustained diachronic scale, the other as a hermeneutic revelation.

The modern is charged with the energy of revolutionary struggle; it is replete with the memory of "native" transgressions. Today it is the secular cultures of the postcolonial era that are premised on a countering impulse. It is this heritage that is to be carried over into the present postmodern to evolve a more definite commitment to praxis. This will incur perhaps a dispersal of the regimental movement of the Euro-American avant-garde into more differentiated moments that we can now begin to see as radical interventions in the ideologically regressive one-world system.

Indian Avant-Garde Filmmaker: Kumar Shahani

There are artists in the third world who would globalize themselves but cannot because of their utopian sense of the international, and also because of their relationship with their own cultural tradition and its hermeneutic potential that does not fit into the conventions of mainstream internationalism. I have in mind the case of a contemporary Indian filmmaker, Kumar Shahani.[35]

What Shahani does is actually to demonstrate the terms of conversion between an older universalist concept of the international and globalization. He grounds himself in the Enlightenment notion of a theory/practice dialectic; he offers the possibility of aesthetic abstraction based on a rational discourse on the world, but matches it with obscure metaphors and willing surrender before the imaginary. And lest it turn narcissistic, he delivers this imaginary into the great symbolic realm that is the compassionate pedagogy of the epic.

In *Maya Darpan* (1972), *Tarang* (1984), and *Kasba* (1990), the theme is at the first level pedagogical: industrialization and the emancipation of women; capitalist development as part of a historical process toward socialism; the desired breaking up of the feudal family, and of the nation, into class categories. He builds up a national allegory—but not to confirm the nation. It is a framing device for an analysis of class; from an altogether different point of view, it is a space for the location of artistic traditions that have a civilizational spread and therefore extend the nationalist discourse. As Shahani puts it:

Perhaps the failure of India to re-constitute itself as a nation is an oppor-
tune indication for the world to see that the era of nationalism, founded
upon the exclusively Western European experience of the last few centuries cannot serve as a model of self-determination any longer anywhere
in the world, not even for the emerging sub-nationalities. I imagine that
the future of civilization demands an extension and inclusion of the civil
society to the other, rather than the divisive exclusions that the ano-
mic processes have set in motion through ethnic, linguistic, and other
fundamentalisms.[36]

If the national is broken up, so for that matter is the male collective of the
working class: both are disciplinary concepts and in their later, more abstracted phases often authoritarian. They are broken up through futurist
projections into states of plenitude, among other devices through the sheer
beauty of image, the excess of which allows imagist cinema to signal a surplus
attraction and break open hermetic constructs. Shahani's own brief is precisely to *not* let the one subsume the other: to not privilege the symbolic over
the imaginary, or vice versa. He keeps hold of the "real" through demonstrating a condition of concrete immanence in the actual work. This is done by a
materialist semiology, if one might call it that: first, by a systematic signification of the sensuous in the structure of the film; second, by the image turning
itself inside out through chosen contra-conventions of cinematic narration.
In *Maya Darpan,* the woman protagonist barely escapes; there is a didactic
closure tolling the literal end of the feudal family. In *Tarang,* which is like a
chronicle foretold, the exploitative male protagonist slips into a position of
mythologically sanctioned defeat and exposes himself.

As Shahani moves in *Tarang* from the national allegorical to the epic, he
introduces a subtheme of male sacrifice, its outer parameters based on the
Urvashi myth. He completes the dismantling of male authority, not only by a
Brechtian style of didactic inversion between subject and object (master and
slave) but also by the subtle axe of irony as in Chekhov, on whose story ("In
the Gully") his third feature film, *Kasba,* is based. In *Kasba,* a dignified
exit from the petty deceits of provincial life is prompted by the gentle self-
evacuation of the girl protagonist. A nonidentificatory mode with disposses-
sion as a key word is used whereby Shahani, taking the cue from Chekhov,
invests the film with an almost mystical melancholy.

Shahani's forthcoming film is based on Rabindranath Tagore's novella,

Smita Patil and Amol
Palekar in Kumar
Shahani's *Tarang,* 1984.

Char Adhyaya, where the subject, dedicated to the cause of the nation and of
the collective good, is bound for betrayal. After the ascetic logic of history is
spent in the way of death, the lost subject "realizes" the higher dynamic of
love as the very premise of subjectivity and therefore of responsible action.
The Tagore novella is the last of the trilogy (preceded by novels I have already
mentioned: *Gora* and *Home and the World*) in which he examines the ideology of passion in its many aspects. Shahani's adaptation will be driven by his
own interrogation of ideological constructs, by his pursuit of a more compassionate form of agency that he would like to designate as the subject in
history.

Such issues as these are often "resolved" by Shahani through the female
presence that always takes the shape of a dual persona of nurture and death,
an actual duo that combines to make an elegiac figure of disinterested desire.
It is in that metaphysical moment of self-naughting that a dialectical move
into the third alternative is made. Shahani uses this dialectic to arrive at the
figure of the "true beloved," a hypothetical figure who embodies the erotics of
pain and resurrects herself in the uncharted space of transfigured knowledge.

In *Khayal Gatha* (1988) and *Bhavantarana* (1991), two films based on classical Indian art forms (the first based on the musical mode of north India called
khayal and the second, shorter film, on the person of the great *odissi* dancer

Navjot Hansra and Shatrughan Sinha in Kumar Shahani's *Kasba,* 1990.

Guru Kelucharan Mahapatra), Indian aesthetics, usually offered as a rhapsodic means for deliverance, is treated through cinematic iconography and narration to metaphoric effect. There is an extreme condensation of art forms in their continuum through the centuries. At the same time, there is introduced a displacement of one art form into another, so that each of these becomes part of the metonymic chain that reconfigures Indian poetics as a vastly imbricated, and structurally replete, system that is still fully alive.

Khayal Gatha is consciously about excess, further complicated by an involute form-within-form structure. It makes each of the traditions of art, from Indian music to painting to film itself, dovetail to constitute a great *formal* riddle. (On the question of formalism, one may mention that *Khayal Gatha* is followed by *Kasba,* a succession that suggests an ironic retake on modernist formalism, specifically its fixation with consistency and semantic opacity. For *Kasba* is once again about transparence and translatability. From Russian story to Indian film, it is about economy in the literal and formal cinematic sense, to which the economy of self in the renunciate mode is tendentiously added.)

The context for these condensed interpretations of traditions is a narrative space where there is also a sublimation of material cultural history to a pure

Manohar Singh in Kumar Shahani's *Kasba,* 1990.

cinematic time of now. This is an undeclared avant-garde gesture where traditions are disengaged from the national past (and so turned into a critique of that kind of appropriative configuration), but where the cinematic text, as in *Khayal Gatha,* proves the limits of translatability before the foreign viewer and thereby obstructs the way to any easy process of internationalist assimilation. This then puts the question of the national, or a larger category such as civilization, once again into the discussion.

Through these series of films, there is a conversion of pleasure into excess, then into greed, then into instructive pedagogies about true plenitude and redemption. The inner core of compassion is probably the universalizing principle that Shahani gains from the Indian civilizational matrix. He has learned to complement Marxist rationality with the Buddhist double paradigm of logic and compassion from the imbricated discourse of the anthropologist and historian D. D. Kosambi, Shahani's Marxist mentor.

We talked earlier about the problems of self-othering. What does Shahani do with the question, persistent in third-world art practices, of the artist as ethnographer? Compared with those of Satyajit Ray and his other more intimate mentor, the filmmaker Ritwik Ghatak, Shahani's solutions are confounding. He allows, for example, a bold exoticization of his subject; he allows otherness to inhabit the cinematic space with full romantic allusion; he

Rajat Kapur in Kumar Shahani's
Khayal Gatha, 1988.

elicits the longing from within national cultures and gives them a civilizational aura of desire; he even baits the question of orientalism that has been
revived by the postmoderns in the era of globalization.

   And it is on this basis that he tackles the subject of reification. He will redo
Hollywood material in the form of an allegory that simultaneously deals with
the actual material process of modernization. He will deal with the predatory
instinct of capital; with the flowering of traditions; with mortality played out
in the epic versions of the female personae. He will deal with the displacement of meaning from sacred to profane and back so as to precipitate the
inevitability of a secular culture.

   Shahani, I propose, seeks his own globalization but in such a way as to
make it impossible. The globalization he seeks has to do with the commodity
form: to make film and the subject of the film and cinematic narration and
the image it offers vulnerable to this fetish obsession. And the prime case for
this paradoxical desire for globalization rests with his unproduced scripts,
which make a parallel argument to those that have been realized. I take only
one of these projects: a film on the history of *cotton,* which speaks simultaneously about material production, commodity exchange, and democracy.

Navjot Hansra in
Kumar Shahani's
Khayal Gatha,
1988.

Here his being Indian becomes a real challenge, for the projected scenario
stakes India's place in world civilization through manufacture and trade. This
he then transforms into a universal poetics of production—even as there is
proof today of the most vicious tariff systems coming into global operation to
destroy these productive capacities:

> The Soviet Union collapses. The USA begins to make final thrusts to
> control *all audio visual* production through a market-directed production
> process. Even the earlier "collaborators" of capitalist design, like Zanussi,
> protest and are aghast at the complacency of their American colleagues.
>
> Against this background, the GATT negotiations: the gradual subtle
> shifts of production, distribution etc. which make for a nearly complete
> take-over of European cinema. . . .
>
> Yet, there are people who seem to want one to try and move out of the
> increasing marginalisation in a uni-polar world which has reduced Ber-
> tolucci to a slick craftsman and Straub into an eccentric. But we still have
> to find ways of striking out—through institutions and individuals whose
> voices may be heard above the din of the market-place, with the kind of
> material and spiritual resources that such initiatives need.[37]

It cannot be a coincidence that each of the unproduced scripts of Shahani
is a global venture in terms of span, sponsorship, and finance. His odyssey, or

that of his scripts, in search of producers and finance makes up an allegorical tale on its own. He raises both ideological and accounting fears in the conservative and still powerful cultural bureaucracy of India, and he embarrasses foreign agencies with an approach premised on his right to abstract through and beyond his nationality—reconfiguring even the set matrix of Indian civilization. He believes he has a right to deploy an Enlightenment ethics via a materialist/Marxist worldview, to release and critique the image through psychoanalytic procedures. That all this can be done by an Indian filmmaker through a symbolic structure that does not name itself according to any national tradition is a challenge that the potential producers cannot meet. He fails, in other words, to convince Indian and foreign funding agencies alike that an Indian filmmaker can engage with the historical avant-garde.

Why he will *not* be globalized is of further interest. The critique and reflexivity within his films of the very phenomena he aesthetically presents is the obvious reason. The other reason is that he still codes his narration within a modernist method; he still makes his subject matter esoteric, and to that extent the postmodern stylistics, to which his form of presentation seems to belong, refuse to unpack their signifying motives according to rule. The "political unconscious" in Shahani's works offers a contrary aesthetic time and again.

Finally, there is another reason Shahani will not be globalized: he insists on *secularizing* traditions, the ones he handles being the ones that have been touched by technology and seen through the sophisticated lens. Having done that, he constantly produces the kind of metonymies that require inverse forms of reading. Turning what has been made technologically available into coded relays of archaic/classical forms once again, he creates an elliptical relationship between techne and meaning.

Secularizing tradition also means that the key to the hermeneutic is not, ironically enough, in the hands of the occidental viewer enthralled by oriental tradition or the mystique of ethnography. Nor is it in the hands of an authentic Indian seeking immanent truth. It is in the hands of the one who will allow the metaphysic of the universal discourse to abide while being able to differentiate the modal points within the historical; to elicit, in consequence, not universal culture but a universal meaning out of the widely varying cultures of the world in the more advanced anthropological sense of the term *culture*. We are then back to a utopian promise that does away with solipsism of present-day aesthetics through a negative dialectic. Adorno's words recall this best:

In an intellectual hierarchy which constantly makes everyone answerable, unanswerability alone can call hierarchy by its name. The circulation sphere, whose stigmata is borne by intellectual outriders, opens a last refuge to the mind it barters away, at the very moment when refuge no longer exists. He who offers for sale something unique that no one wants to buy, represents, even against his will, freedom from exchange.[38]

Notes

This essay also appears in *Third Text* 39 (1997): 21–38 and in my *When Was Modernism? Essays on Contemporary Cultural Practice in India* (Tulika, Delhi, 1998).

1   This image refers to Chomsky's keynote speech on 11 November 1994, at the conference on which this volume is based.
2   Edward Said, *Culture and Imperialism* (London, 1994), 348.
3   Ibid., 377.
4   Marxist economist Prabhat Patnaik argues today that the liberalization program in India should be cautiously paced out rather than opposed altogether. The old agenda of economic nationalism, he says, was worked out at a time when an international economy worth the name did not exist; initiated in Latin America during the Depression, the subsequent ideological variations on that theme have been based on the actual experience and intellectual developments of the 1930s. "Other developing countries like India adopted such strategy, properly speaking, only after independence when the consolidation of the international economy had not progressed far and when the process of internationalization of capital in our sense was still in its infancy." He admits that the programme of economic nationalism is unsustainable; but he also argues that "the 'marketist' response, which has the backing of leading capitalist powers and agencies like the Fund and the Bank, and has internal support within a section of the capitalists (seeing in 'globalization' a means of expansion, even as rentiers), and in a section of affluent middle classes (seeing in it a means of access to new commodities), is likely to be detrimental to the working masses, not only transitionally but over a protracted period. A neo-mercantilist strategy is not easily replicated nor as workable in the context of world recession, nor necessarily desirable in the context of India's extant democratic structures. Is it possible then for an economy like India to evolve a response of its own?" Prabhat Patnaik, "International Capital and National Economic Policy: A Critique of India's Economic Reforms," *Economic & Political Weekly*, 29, no. 12 (19 March 1994): 686, 688. See also Prabhat Patnaik, *Whatever Happened to Imperialism and Other Essays* (Delhi, 1995).
5   Partha Chatterjee's continuing interrogation of the nation-state in relation to the polity finds recent elaboration in his *Nation and Its Fragments: Colonial and Postcolonial Histories* (Princeton, NJ, 1993).

Anthropologist Veena Das writes, "The emergence of communities as political actors in their own right is related in India to changes in the nature of political democracy. We know that the anticolonial struggles, as embodied in several local, regional, and national-level movements in the late-nineteenth and early twentieth centuries, were about the sharing of power. Yet by the end of the twentieth century the nature of representative democracy has itself been put into question, for it has become clear that even when power is exercised in the name of representation it tends to become absolute, and 'to speak in the name of the society it devours' (Tourraine, 1992, p. 131)." She continues: "It is this political context of the state's assertion and arrogation of authority which explains why so many social scientists have raised powerful voices in support of 'tradition,' and why they have expressed the hope that alternative visions of life may be available in the form of traditional ways of life, of which diverse communities are the embodiment." Veena Das, *Critical Events: An Anthropological Perspective on Contemporary India* (Delhi, 1995), 14.

6 For an elaboration of this Gramscian concept in the Indian context, see Partha Chatterjee, *Nationalist Thought and the Colonial World: A Derivative Discourse?* (Delhi, 1988), 131–166.

7 For the Gandhi-Tagore debate, see R. K. Prabhu and Ravinder Kelkar, eds., *Truth Called Them Differently* (Ahmedabad, 1961). For a recent interpretation of the significance of this debate, see Suresh Sharma, "Swaraj and the Quest for Freedom—Rabindranath Tagore's Critique of Gandhi's Non-Cooperation," *Thesis Eleven,* no. 39 (1994): 93–104.

8 For a brief evaluation of Tagore's international engagement, see Tan Chung, "The Rabindranath Thunder of Oriental Dawn: A Sino-Indian Perspective of Tagore," and Swapan Mazumdar, "The East-West Colloquy: Tagore's Understanding of the West," in *Rabindranath Tagore and the Challenges of Today,* ed. Bhudeb Chaudhuri and K. G. Subramanyan (Shimla, 1988), 265–285, 294–306 respectively.

9 For an elaboration of this argument, see Geeta Kapur, "Cultural Creativity in the First Decade: The Example of Satyajit Ray," *Journal of Arts & Ideas,* no. 23 (1993): 17–49.

10 See Ashish Rajadhyaksha, *Ritwik Ghatak: A Return to the Epic* (Bombay, 1982), and Ashish Rajadyaksha and Paul Willemen, eds., *The Encyclopedia of Indian Cinema* (London, 1994), 95–96. For a further exposition on his last film, see my "Articulating the Self into History: Ritwik Ghatak's *Jukti Takko Ar Gappo,*" in *Questions of Third Cinema,* ed. Jim Pines and Paul Willemen (London, 1989), 179–194.

11 Gayatri Chakravorty Spivak, "A Literary Representation of the Subaltern: A Woman's Text from the Third World," in *In Other Worlds: Essays in Cultural Politics* (New York, 1987), 243.

12 Fredric Jameson, "Third World Literature in the Era of Multinational Capitalism," *Social Text,* no. 15 (1986). This should be read in the context of the now

famous reply by Aijaz Ahmad, "Jameson's Rhetoric of Otherness and the National Allegory," *Social Text,* no. 16 (1987).

13 James Clifford, "On Ethnographic Allegory," in *Writing Culture: The Poetics and Politics of Ethnography,* ed. James Clifford and George E. Marcus (Berkeley, 1986).

14 Said, *Culture and Imperialism,* 377.

15 For a passionate polemic with Homi Bhabha on the continuing validity of the anticolonial struggle as against the more elusive track of postcolonial discourse, see Benita Parry, "Signs of Our Times: A Discussion of Homi Bhabha's *The Location of Culture,*" *Third Text,* nos. 28–29 (1994): 5–24.

16 K. G. Subramanyan, *The Creative Circuit* (Calcutta, 1992), 24–52. For a contextualization of Subramanyan's eclectic art practice, see Geeta Kapur, *K. G. Subramanyan* (Delhi, 1987).

17 Homi K. Bhabha, *The Location of Culture* (London, 1994), 175.

18 Ibid., 3.

19 Ibid., 4.

20 Homi Bhabha, "Remembering Fanon: Self, Psyche, and the Colonial Condition," in *Remaking History,* ed. Barbara Kruger and Phil Mariani (Seattle, 1989), 131–148.

21 Bhabha, *The Location of Culture,* 241.

22 Ibid.

23 Parry, "Signs of Our Times," 13.

24 Quoted in Alok Rai, "Black Skin, Black Masks," *Economic and Political Weekly* 27, no. 39 (26 September 1992): 2103.

25 For a sustained polemic on the travails of otherness, see Rustam Bharucha, "Somebody's Other," *Third Text,* no. 26 (1995).

26 See the special issue "Beyond the Rushdie Affair," *Third Text,* no. 11 (1990).

27 Rai, "Black Skin, Black Masks," 2100.

28 Bhabha, *The Location of Culture,* 179.

29 K. A. Appiah, "Is the Post- in Postmodernism the Post- in Postcolonial?," *Critical Inquiry,* no. 17 (1991): 348.

30 Ibid., 356.

31 Theodor Adorno and Mark Horkheimer, *Dialectic of Enlightenment* (London, 1979), 120–167.

32 Fredric Jameson, *Postmodernism, or, The Cultural Logic of Late Capitalism* (London, 1991), 317.

33 Néstor García Canclini, "Memory and Innovation in the Theory of Art," *The South Atlantic Quarterly* 92, no. 3 (1993): 423–443.

34 For a discussion on the conditions for a historical avant-garde that not only accommodates but derives from the conditions of radical disjuncture in the three worlds alike, see Paul Willemen, "An Avant-Garde for the 90s," in *Looks and Frictions: Essays in Cultural Studies and Film Theory* (Bloomington, IN, 1994), 141–161.

35 Born in India in 1940, Kumar Shahani graduated from the Film and Television

Institute of India in 1966, where he had been a student of Ritwik Ghatak. He went to France for the advanced study of cinema and spent the tumultuous years 1967–68 in Paris. Here, he gained the experience of an apprenticeship with Robert Bresson while the latter was shooting *Une Femme Douce* (1969). Back in India, Shahani became famous with his first feature film, *Maya Darpan* (1972), following which his major films, *Tarang* (1984), *Khayal Gatha* (1988), *Kasba* (1990), and *Bhavantarana* (1991) have won awards and have been exhibited in a range of mainstream and avant-garde film festivals all over the world. Problems of commercial release make showings of his films rare. He has been designated a difficult filmmaker, intellectual and ideological in ways that make him controversial and at the same time seminal in the Indian cultural context. A forthcoming film, based on a Tagore novella, *Char Adhyaya,* is being supplemented with a whole series of unproduced films: these include scripts in various stages of completion on the psychoanalyst W. R. Bion; on the Indo-European woman painter, Amrita Sher-Gil (1913–41); on Tolstoi's *Anna Karenina;* and on the world history of the production of cotton.

A theoretician of cinema, Kumar Shahani has written and published extensively. For a selection of his essays, see "Dossier: Kumar Shahani," *Framework,* nos. 30/31 (1986). For further information, see Rajadhyaksha and Willemen, eds., *Encyclopedia of Indian Cinema,* 197–198.

36 Kumar Shahani, unpublished letter to the historian Ravinder Kumar (Bombay, September 1994).
37 Kumar Shahani, unpublished letter to the author (Bombay, 14 October 1994).
38 Theodor Adorno, *Minima Moralia* (London, 1974), 60.

Nations and Literatures

in the Age of Globalization

Some Theoretical Questions and Practical Agendas

Nations and literatures exist in the plural. That is commonsense enough. But how much use is this common sense? It certainly serves to challenge some familiar notions, such as of nationhood as an immutable essence or at least a readily definable social unit; or of Literature (with a capital *L*) no less definite and unchanging in its distinction from what is not Literature. But things that exist in the plural must have existence in the singular as well, at least conceptually. The vexing questions What is a nation? and What is literature? remain unresolved.

I have no intention of offering nor ability to offer a definitive answer to either of these questions. Rather, as a participant in what in South Korea is known as the national literature movement, I should like to give some reasons for our embracing such ambiguous notions as *the nation* and *literature,* even combining the two in the term *national literature*—an operation that perhaps renders the venture doubly suspect.

But first, some elaboration on common sense may help. Nations are plural not merely because they are by definition not the whole of humanity, but

218

because in the form in which we find them around us they are the product of the modern age, of what Immanuel Wallerstein calls its "inter-state system," that is, a system comprising many states and *hence* nations. The *hence* deserves emphasis on this particular view, for Wallerstein's point is that "in almost every case statehood preceded nationhood, and not the other way around, despite a widespread myth to the contrary."[1] Of course, the different and sometimes overlapping roles of premodern, modern, colonial, and post-colonial states in nation-forming remain to be clarified, and also the reactive impacts of nationhood upon statehood once "a nation" has been formed; and in Korea we can even boast of an additional complication in the existence of a divided state, as part of what I have elsewhere called the "division system" on the Korean peninsula.[2] Amidst all this confusion two things appear relatively clear. First, the nation-state as an ideal form of combining nationhood with statehood—a combination that at one time perhaps did produce, in a few European nations, something closest in the modern world to the Greek polis—no longer enjoys the same authority in the current age of globalization. But second, nations and nation-states (or remnants thereof) will continue to be a material presence, and nationhood a going concern, so long as the interstate system is a necessary feature of the modern world-system, however globalized. No effective action then, whether to adapt oneself to this modernity or to abolish it and arrive at a genuine postmodernity, will be possible without coming to terms in some manner with the reality of nations and nationhood.

As for literature, its plurality is obvious not only because a work of literature is always composed in a particular tongue or set of tongues, but, besides a common language, there are other factors that define a particular body of works as belonging to a common "literature." If you add that all these factors are changeable both in themselves and in their mutual combinations, and that a given work could belong to more than one tradition (as in the obvious case of a contemporary American work belonging at once to "American literature," to "English literature" in the wider sense of literature in the English language, and possibly also to a cosmopolitan "postmodernist" culture), then it becomes all the clearer how impossible it is to speak of Literature as such.

True, the challenge does not stop short at Literature with a capital *L*, as may be witnessed in the proclaimed "death of the author," the deconstructionist and cultural-materialist critiques of the very concept of literature, and the widespread preference of the term *text* over *work*. Nor do I believe such theoretic challenges to be unrelated to the fact of globalization. For one thing, it is the radical modification and even breakdown of national literary traditions through globalization as such and through global dominance of capital that have problematized the concept of "literature," for literatures in the modern world have existed preeminently as national literatures—of certain European nation-states, to be explicit—though always with a wider European (and later Euro-American) dimension as well. The same process of globalization, however, creates among latecomers to the world-system both a desire to emulate the national-literary endeavors of the earlier models, and a related need to preserve or revivify their own ethnic/regional heritage. The former aim may be more specious than real; the latter, quite possibly, more a felt need than a viable prospect. But what if a particular combination of the two elements should converge with the needs of those very model nations whose own finest traditions are being swept away by the globalizing tide?

It is this practical question rather than the merits of the concerned theories as such, on which I wish to concentrate. Not that I find such theories devoid of interest or even of urgent challenge. But the fact remains that certain texts that have the word as their predominant medium are bound to pass for "literature" in one sense or another, and that a judgment as to their being superior or inferior by one standard or another is ineradicable, though not necessarily conscious, in any actual reading of such texts. It is also a fact that, for many Koreans at least, a dignified life by any definition appears impossible without the creative continuation of what is best in our past, much of it available only in literature or letters, and yet the possibility of a near-total obliteration of this heritage appears by no means a mere flight of fancy. Nor do we feel more than momentarily beguiled by the suggestion that it is mere elitism or obscurantism to discriminate between, say, Shakespeare and any given "cultural production" of contemporary consumerist culture and to identify the former as a "superior work." Learning to read Shakespeare is onerous enough, and his use in the cause of cultural imperialism demands constant watchfulness; for all that, we do not wish—indeed cannot afford—to do without the emancipatory potentials we may find in him, or in Goethe or Tolstoy, for that matter. Given these facts, the more urgent task, if we are serious in speaking about the challenges of the global age and alive to the real dangers to human civilization inherent in that process, would be the production and the sorting out of those texts most relevant to these challenges, and the identification (and promotion) of those standards of judgment most conducive to an effective response. Literatures as actual works, and "literature" as a guiding notion rather than a mystic entity, seem to me indispensable for this purpose.

It is, moreover, a strategic folly to neglect the field of literature in any struggle to contain the invasion of global consumerist culture. The well-known language barrier, and the amount of specific local knowledge required even for infiltration through translation, make it a most difficult terrain for that culture to penetrate, unless one makes things easy for the invaders by being prematurely cowed by all the talk about the obsolescence of literature in the microelectronic age.

I have already indicated that I am speaking as a practitioner and participant in an ongoing literary movement that has espoused the notion of "national literature." I shall come back later to some of its agenda though without having time to give a detailed history or even a quick survey of its productions. But I hope the foregoing remarks have shown that our espousal of that notion does not wholly derive from backwardness or total ignorance of recent intellectual discourse in the West. In view of the features of the present age adumbrated above, "national literature" obviously leads one to an uncertain and even treacherous terrain, but a terrain away from which no meaningful effort can be made in the endeavor to deal adequately with the problems of the age, and upon which for certain nations in a given conjuncture the main effort should be concentrated. Korean national literature and its proponents may not have lived up to their own agenda, but the agenda itself represents a deliberate, and I believe thoughtful, response to the challenges of the global age.

"World Literature" in the Age of Globalization

In one sense, globalization started with the onset of capitalist modernity—perhaps as early as the sixteenth century, when the capitalist world-economy established itself in a northwest European portion of the globe and began its relentless expansion over the earth. At any rate, by the late nineteenth century, East Asia and virtually all other regions had been incorporated in it. By the late twentieth, the claims of the Soviet bloc to being a separate world-system have been decisively shattered. And perhaps one may speak of globalization in a strict sense only in this present era of full modernity (sometimes named postmodernity).

Yet, one may do well to remind oneself that the birth of national literatures, or literatures in the respective vernaculars that come to be cherished by—or at least in the name of—"the entire nation" rather than a particular region or province, would itself be one of the first consequences of the globalizing age (in a wider sense). Of course, there is nothing like a neat picture. In some cases, the production of such literature—for example, the work of Dante in Italy or Chaucer in England—predate the sixteenth century. But these occur precisely in areas where indigenous developments, including those in literature, provided the chief motor force in the transition to modernity. Conversely, when a people's entry to the capitalist world-system is more or less enforced through outside pressure, the formation of a national literature would tend to lag behind the beginning of "the modern period" in general history and to take on the character of a self-conscious endeavor—as in the case of Korea obviously, but to some extent also in countries like Germany and Russia.

But further progress in globalization brings on the need for and the possibility of a "world literature." After the famous passage in *The Communist Manifesto* where Marx describes the relentless revolutionizing of the whole relations of society by the bourgeoisie and the endless expansion of the world market, he goes on to remark the new spiritual needs created thereby, including the need for a "world literature":

> In place of the old wants, satisfied by the productions of the country, we find new wants, requiring for their satisfaction the products of distant lands and climes. In place of the old local and national seclusion and self-sufficiency, we have intercourse in every direction, universal interdependence of nations. And as in material, so also in intellectual production. The intellectual creations of individual nations become common property. National one-sidedness and narrow-mindedness become more and more impossible, and from the numerous national and local literatures, there arises a world literature.[3]

Marx is neither the earliest nor the best-known proponent of the idea of world literature (*Weltliteratur*). That honor surely goes to Goethe, who promoted the idea in a series of pronouncements in early 1827, probably coining the term as well. Less often remembered is the fact that what Goethe meant by the term (as Fredric Jameson pointed out some years ago)[4] was not so much a bringing together of the great literary classics of the world, but rather a networking among intellectuals of various lands (chiefly of Europe, naturally) through reading of one another's work and shared knowledge of the important journals as well as through personal contact. That is, something much more like what in our day would be called a transnational *movement* for world literature.

Associating the old Goethe—famed for his "Olympian" detachment—with a world literature movement may sound improbable, but less so if we recall that in his youth he had been engaged in a German national literature movement of his own and that his detachment resulted in large part from his disaffection with the later, narrowly nationalistic version of that movement represented by the Romantics. At any rate, the thrust of his meaning is clear in the message to the international gathering of natural scientists—not poets or critics—in Berlin in 1827, urging them to work for the development of a world literature.[5] A better-known and equally pregnant passage occurs in his *Conversations with Eckermann,* in the entry for 31 January 1827:

> I am more and more convinced, [he tells Eckermann,] that poetry is the universal possession of mankind, revealing itself everywhere and at all times in hundreds and hundreds of men. One makes it a little better than another, and swims on the surface a little longer than another—that is all. . . . [N]obody need think very much of himself because he has written a good poem.
>
> But, really, we Germans are very likely to fall too easily into this pedantic conceit, when we do not look beyond the narrow circle that surrounds us. I therefore look about me in foreign nations, and advise everyone to do the same. National literature is now rather an unmeaning term; the epoch of world literature is at hand, and everyone must strive to hasten its approach. But, while we thus value what is foreign, we must not bind ourselves to some particular thing, and regard it as a model.[6]

By this time, Goethe has already produced classics of German literature and felt no false modesty about it, and was, of course, familiar with other great works in a number of tongues. The conception of world literature as something "at hand," therefore, implies a new *kind* of literature, not necessarily greater than the existing classics but more adequate to the evolving needs of the modern man, for whom "[n]ational one-sidedness and narrow-mindedness become more and more impossible"; it is also something whose approach must be hastened by conscious effort. I find it noteworthy, too, that the crucial remark in Goethe is, on the one hand, prefaced by a warning against mystifications of poetic or literary talent and, on the other, followed by a clear assumption of the reality of one's own national—as against "foreign"—literature. World literature, for all its nomination in the singular, consists of a plurality of literatures and a great variety and multiplicity of literary productions.

If Goethe's notion of *Weltliteratur* proves on closer view a good deal more Marxian than is commonly thought, Marx shows himself, both in the above quotation and in his other pronouncements on literature, a faithful inheritor of the classical German culture and of the Goethean conception of world literature as a multiplicity of particular literatures. But what should we think of this Goethean-Marxian project (if I may so name it) in the present age? What signs do we see of its realization at a time when the material process analyzed in *The Communist Manifesto* has gone to lengths probably unimagined by Marx himself?

Perhaps the one transnational, large-scale movement consciously to espouse that project was Socialist Realism of the former Communist countries. That particular version is now virtually in tatters—and deservedly so, not merely because far too much repression of art and literature was carried out in its name but, more important, because it tried to ignore the reality foreseen by Goethe and explicitly emphasized by Marx, namely, the globalization of the world market and the corresponding transformation of intellectual production.

But what has come to reign after the collapse of Socialist Realism, especially in the advanced capitalist nations of the West, shows little resemblance to the Goethean-Marxian project. To be sure, the hegemonic culture of the day—often called postmodernist, though with little agreement as to the exact meaning of the term—is global enough. But in my view, this culture represents a suppression and disintegration, rather than the "hastening" or "arising," of a world literature. Indeed, many of its famed theorists are hostile to the very notion of literature, while among its actual products what the Pakistani writer Tariq Ali calls "market realism" seems to drive out the kind of critical and creative engagement with reality valued equally by Goethe and

Marx. "There is a growing tendency," writes Ali (regarding today's literary scene in the West),

> to uniformity of thought and style. Trivia reigns supreme and literature becomes a branch of the entertainment industry. Instead of "socialist realism," we have "market realism." The difference being that it is a self-imposed straitjacket. "Market realist" literature needs to be resisted every bit as strongly as the old "socialist realism." It demands literature that is treated as a fetishized commodity, self-contained and self-referential. The upmarket commodity fosters a surrogate religion, while downmarket kitsch prevails. But such is the velocity at which commodities circulate that soon all such boundaries are broken down. Instead of indicting the arrogance and corruption of power and wealth it fawns before the media magnates.[7]

If "world literature" and literature as such are threatened by this particular version of globalization, so would be national literatures a fortiori. Not only "national one-sidedness and narrow-mindedness," but any distinctly national traditions even within the larger life of a world literature must be condemned in this rush toward "uniformity of thought and style." For the vaunted diversity of postmodernism amounts in reality only to what "the cultural logic of late capitalism" allows and to some extent demands. If this is so—if both world literature and national literatures are among the objects to melt into air as a consequence of capitalist globalization—then those attached to the idea of the former should look upon the proponents of the latter with more sympathy than suspicion, indeed, even with an active sense of solidarity.

Of course, the theoretical merits of the Goethean-Marxian project remain to be argued, and I do not believe that they can be argued without serious questioning of some of the fundamental assumptions about literature, nationhood, the non-European world, and many other topics held by Goethe and Marx, whether in common or each in his own way. But here again I should limit myself to what I consider the larger question: How much can globalizing humanity afford to lose of the literary (and other cultural) inheritance behind that project for a world literature, and what kind of life, if any, would globalized humanity enjoy in the event of total collapse of that project? We in the movement for a Korean national literature, at any rate, having always aimed at joining the ranks of world literature, now find an additional justification for our endeavors in discovering those ranks in such disarray that contributions by a movement like ours seem essential to the very survival of world literature.

Relevance of South Korea's National Literature Movement

Let me now address some aspects of South Korea's national literature movement that may qualify it for making those contributions.

When the notion of a national literature first emerged in the waning days of the Chosun dynasty (1392–1910), it was no doubt a direct response to the impact of the opening of the kingdom to the modern world-economy in 1876, and mainly took the form of trying to duplicate the achievements of European national bourgeoisies. Yet even then, rival currents were to be found in the resistance offered in the name of Confucian universalism—not of Oriental exceptionalism, which is a different matter—and in the insufficiently articulated but impressively mobilized popular struggle for an alternative modernity represented by the Tonghak Peasants' War of 1894. Under Japanese colonial rule (1910–45) the discourse of modern nationhood and of regaining national sovereignty comes to predominate, whether the emphasis falls on bourgeois or proletarian patriotism. But here again, it is a gross simplification to find in this anticolonial nationalism a mere duplicate or variant of certain models provided by Western precursors, for, as Partha Chatterjee has argued, "The most powerful as well as the most creative results of the nationalist imagination in Asia and Africa are posited not on an identity but rather on a difference with the 'modular' forms of the national society propagated by the modern West."[8]

True, the gaining of formal independence usually results in a national state that turns into a most unquestioning participant in the interstate system, and in the virtual dissipation of the anticolonial potential for difference. But in Korea, the liberation from Japanese rule was quickly followed by the division of the country along the 38th parallel and then, after the devastating war of 1950–53, by a slightly revised Armistice Line, producing two state structures of patently contrasting ideologies and institutions but also interlocked, as I believe and have argued, within a single "division system" that, in its turn, constitutes a subsystem of the larger world-system. The distinctive mark of the national literature movement of our generation, therefore, has been its

preoccupation with this particular "national question"[9]: the national division that is certainly a legacy of colonial rule and even more a direct product
of neocolonial intervention, yet that has taken on a systemic nature of its
own with self-reproducing antidemocratic structures on both sides of the
dividing line.

A national literature that seeks to engage with this specific national predicament could hardly be nationalistic in any obvious sense. In fact, the situation entails an inevitable deconstruction of any simplistic conception of "the
nation"—or "class," for that matter, although class analysis itself becomes
indispensable if one is to make sense of that mechanism of self-reproduction.
The "nation" in this instance happens to be a nation divided into two "societies" and belonging to two different states, hence possibly on the way to
becoming two nations. "Class" also becomes problematic because the very
term *Korean working class,* for example, would hardly make sense: South or
North would first have to be specified and, if reunification of some kind is the
practical aim, one must also take into account the relation of that particular
class (or segment of a class) with its counterpart on the other half of the
peninsula, as well as with various other social classes and strata within its own
half. Add to this the fact that the division system is but a *sub*system of the
capitalist world-system, whose sexist and racist, as well as capitalist, nature I
can only note in passing; then due attention to the workings of the latter and
the consequent forging of transnational alliances to fight its global ravages
become an integral part of the "national" agenda.

In South Korea, too, the quickening pace of globalization since the geopolitical changes of 1989, and all the more so with the launching of the World
Trade Organization regime, has worked to amplify those voices dismissing
national literature as an outmoded idea. But in one aspect, at least, the same
globalization has worked both to foreground and strengthen the latter's central agenda: the recent U.S.–North Korea settlement in Geneva will finally
bring the end of the cold war to the Korean peninsula, too, and remove a
major prop, though no more than one, for its division system. We must thus
see in the current globalization both a threat and an opportunity: threat,
whether in the name of "international competitiveness" or "global culture,"
to what limited autonomy and democracy we may now enjoy, but an opening
for the needed effort to work across, as well as within, national and quasi-
national (i.e., intra-Korean) borders for a more democratic and egalitarian

world. If a genuine overcoming of the division system does come to pass—that is, a reunification with meaningful popular input, leading to an innovative state structure responsive to the real needs of the population in the globalizing age rather than to any preconceived notion of the nation-state—then it will represent a crucial reordering of the world-system itself, perhaps even a decisive step in its transformation into a better system.

I am not saying that actual literary productions of today's Korea have quite risen to this challenge. A different way of putting it would be to admit that other and worse futures for the division system retain their probabilities: either an indefinite prolongation of the division, though in a somewhat ameliorated state, leaving the Korean people a victim both to its pair of undemocratic states and to manipulative and exploitative foreign powers; or a unilateral annexation on South Korean capitalist terms, resulting in the emergence of virulent Korean nationalism (greatly strengthening its sexism as well) or the disastrous collapse of the Korean economy, or both. Either prospect is too dismal for any self-respecting people not to seek a genuine alternative—particularly for those working in the field of literature.

At this point, it is worth recalling that not only national literatures but also world literature find themselves threatened by the global age; that today, global capital and its cosmopolitan cultural market, rather than "national one-sidedness and narrow-mindedness," represent the chief danger. I believe the same goes for the sphere of political action. Various ethnic, national, and racial prejudices do present a threat to a peaceful and democratic world, but in the final analysis, they work in accordance with, and within the limits of, a global system of accumulation and attendant exploitation. The ultimate need is surely for "an internationalist politics of citizenship," as Etienne Balibar argues,[10] but the practical success of such a politics would depend on the wisdom and creativity with which each individual or group in question manages to combine the various dimensions from the most individual and local to the fully global. And in this range of activities, the national dimension—as a particular type of an intermediate and not overly fragmented "regional" dimension—still remains essential, both in literature and other fields. Those of us working for a Korean national literature believe that we are engaged precisely in this creative experiment for a praxis adequate to the global age, and for the preservation and enhancement of world literature as well.

Notes

1 Etienne Balibar and Immanuel Wallerstein, *Race, Nation, Class* (London, 1991),
   81.
2 Paik Nak-chung, "South Korea: Unification and the Democratic Challenge,"
   New Left Review 197 (January–February 1993): 67–84.
3 Karl Marx and Friedrich Engels, *The Communist Manifesto* (Harmondsworth,
   UK, 1967), 84.
4 Fredric Jameson, "The State of the Subject, pt. 3," *Critical Quarterly* (winter
   1987): 16–25.
5 Cf. editor's afterword in Horst Günther, ed., *Goethe: Schriften zur Weltliteratur*
   (Frankfurt am Main, 1987), 337–338.
6 Goethe, *Conversations with Eckermann,* trans. John Oxenford (Berkeley, CA,
   1984), 133.
7 Tariq Ali, "Literature and Market Realism," *New Left Review* 199 (May–June
   1993): 144.
8 Partha Chatterjee, *The Nation and Its Fragments* (Princeton, NJ, 1993), 5.
9 See my "The Idea of a Korean National Literature Then and Now," *positions: east
   asia critiques* 1, no. 3 (1993): 553–580.
10 Balibar and Wallerstein, *Race, Nation, Class,* 64.

Media in a Capitalist Culture

From Local Activism to Global Media

I have spent most of the past fourteen years using video and film as a means of community organizing and as a tool for social change. Prior to that, in the mid-sixties, I worked as an activist and a community organizer. In the late 1970s, I was an EXPERT: Senior Training Specialist for the Action Agency, which oversaw the Peace Corps and VISTA (Volunteers in Service to America). In earlier times, I did my work while only receiving money as a welfare mother. One way or another, I have always managed to do what I thought was important and still stay alive.

In 1982, I was on a trip across the country as part of an organizing effort marking the Second UN Special Session on Disarmament. I was a member of a group of people leaving from California in a kind of touring demonstration. We stopped at all the nuclear facilities (test sites, research laboratories, enrichment sites, mining and manufacturing sites) on the way to New York City. Academy Award–winning filmmaker Haskell Wexler traveled with us to

I am deeply grateful to Shelton Waldrep, without whose generous assistance this paper would not have been completed.

230

make a film about our activities. This experience made me realize the potential that film has for activism, and I decided to become involved in it myself.

I had spent many years going into towns of five hundred or a thousand people—as well as cities like Detroit and Chicago—bringing stories from one to the next of how one community group beat redlining in Duluth, Minnesota, or how someone won another issue in another place, so that tactics could be shared and repeated. The idea that film and video could take these stories of hopeful and positive experiences to those with similar struggles was a very inspiring concept. After a decade in the business, I am definitely worn out by the process, but I am still inspired by the impact we have had.

In 1984, Davis Kasper and I founded The Empowerment Project, a media resource center that serves hundreds of independent video producers and filmmakers each year. We occasionally make videos and films ourselves; we have made three films on global issues that have received international releases. The last one, *The Panama Deception,* won the Academy Award for Best Feature Documentary of 1992. We have had much more success in bringing this story to people in countries around the world as a result of winning this award. The experience of traveling with the film worldwide has, however, been an eye-opening one. I have gone to festivals in Argentina, Panama, Mexico, Cuba, Canada, and in Europe, where I always see the names of major U.S. films splashed across billboards and subway stations. Having lived in Los Angeles, where I had been accustomed to seeing all of these advertising images, I found it odd to walk through the streets of Argentina and see the same image for a film placed with a different language. I began to get a firsthand look at the dominance that this type of international monopoly of the media, centered in the United States and generated in Hollywood, has had over other countries.

The impact that Hollywood has on filmmakers in the countries where I have traveled is really quite amazing. For instance, the highest award-winning filmmakers in Mexico, those who have won awards in Mexico that are similar or identical to the Academy Awards in the United States, cannot find theaters in Mexico to release their films. Even though they are the top filmmakers in the country—and their films, in Spanish, do not require subtitles—they cannot find theaters. It is much too profitable for the theaters to continue to take films from Hollywood. This fact has a grave impact on independent filmmaking. If people are not able to distribute their films, eventually they are not able to make their films. This has been, to a great degree, what has happened already in Latin America. Directors in these countries are still making excellent films, but they are certainly not able to produce anything near what they are capable of because of the financial dominance that the Hollywood industry has over their countries. Even though we might try to fight that same influence in the United States by attempting to release an independent film, it is a nightmarish experience. Theaters and video stores in this country are the only places where you can still release independent and uncensored media products. Television is just much more monopolized and content-controlled. To really saturate the country with any new information is almost impossible, unless you own a network or a national cable network. Just as private theaters and independently run video stores are the only places where you can find pornography, they are the only places where you can find alternative political positions because they are, as yet, not fully censored.

In the United States, the relationship between theater chains and Hollywood studios is closer than many people might think. For example, at one point, *The Panama Deception* ran in a theater multiplex on one of seven screens. Our film brought in more money than any of the other films running there: Whoopi Goldberg's *Sister Act, 1492,* and other big-budget Hollywood films. And yet, at the end of what we thought was an open run, where the theater continues to show the film as long as the grosses are good, Warner Brothers or another studio called the theater and said, "We need a screen," and our movie was the one that got bounced because it was an independent film. We may not make another film for several years, but Warner Brothers is going to have another ready in two weeks, and another after that. When you read in the local paper "Coming to theaters soon," you can believe it, no matter what it has to shove out, and no matter how lucrative the film it is replacing. For me, these pressures, which must be honored by the theaters, destroy not only our ability in the United States really to coordinate a film's release in any significant way, but inhibit as well independent filmmakers similar to us around the world.

The issue is one of censorship. I always tell audiences that the United States does have perhaps the freest press in the world, but it is free to the highest bidder and we know who those bidders are. For example, David Jones, the former chair of the Joint Chiefs of Staff, and William Smith, the ex–U.S. Attorney General, sit on the board of General Electric, which owns NBC. Meanwhile, Henry Kissinger and the former secretary of defense, Harold Brown, help run CBS. The issue for me is not a free press, but, instead, an independent and courageous one. We need such media outlets, and our lack of them is one of the most serious threats to our attempt to have a participatory democracy. To look at how our democracy works in its present form, I will use *The Panama Deception* and other of our Empowerment Project films as an example.

Destination Nicaragua; COVERUP: Behind the Iran Contra Affair; and The Panama Deception: Three Case Studies

In 1988 Panama had an election. In advance of the election, Panamanians were getting the news on a daily basis from the United States through the Southern Command. The U.S. military's largest aggregation of weapons and personnel outside of the continental United States, the Southern Command operates a television broadcast station in Panama. U.S. news shows, such as *Nightline,* and other U.S. programming are beamed over this network. For two years, the Panamanians had been hearing on these broadcasts how evil their present government was and how devastated their country had become. As the election drew near in 1988, the problem, as reported by the U.S. media, was that people should expect widespread violence and fraud in the election.

Partly as a result of constantly hearing U.S. misinformation from what is supposedly the freest press in the world, the people who tabulated the votes at the end of the election day did not take them to the election commission. Instead, they were told to take them to a Catholic church because there was the threat of widespread fraud and violence, and that if the pollsters tried to take the ballots to the commission itself they would be stolen by Noriega's thugs. Not all of this was false. Ultimately, what happened was that people reacted to the rumors and 20 percent of the tabulations of the votes went out of the legal chain of command. The national assembly then called the election invalid, and as a result of that and other U.S. interference, the Organization of American States refused to recognize the election. At this point, Noriega was appointed indefinitely as a kind of Supreme Leader, a state of emergency was declared, and new elections were intended to be held. People actually broke the law, in part, on the basis of rumors that were begun by a U.S. news organization.

One day, you turn on the television set, as we did, and George Bush announces that he has sent 26,000 troops to arrest one person in Panama. You know that something must be terribly wrong: either we have the most incompetent military in the world, which is not the case, or there is really another agenda at work. We attempted to explore the latter.

We decided that we wanted both to do research and tape interviews in Panama and in the States to see if we could discover what the real agenda was. For starters, our names were left out of the press pool. Independent producers are rarely allowed the privilege of being set down in the middle of a war, and even the representatives of the major media who did go were held for a day and a half on U.S. military bases before being allowed to see for themselves what was happening. Yet, this was only the beginning of the censorship we were to encounter.

We did not make it to Panamanian ground when the invasion began, but we still wanted to produce the film. Our problem was raising the necessary money. The film cost us $300,000, and it took two years to make. It cost us more than it should, although $300,000 is considered inexpensive for a documentary of this length. We began to try to raise funds within days of the invasion. It is difficult to raise funds in the United States because a large majority of the progressive foundations and grassroots donors find a lot of other equally important issues to subsidize, issues that do not put them into a position to expose the U.S. government directly. Rhino, a video label in the United States, gave us our first major funding, a $40,000 advance. The largest amount, $75,000, came from Channel Four in the United Kingdom. I think our next film will have advance money from probably three or four countries as well—countries who have bought our films in the past and have some confidence in our track record.

Still, we did receive a small amount of domestic money: $20,000 from the J. Roderick McArthur Foundation, $10,000 apiece from the National Council of Churches and from the Grateful Dead through the Rex Foundation, $3,000 from the Veteran's Foundation, and so on. We have never received funding for our films from larger foundations such as the National Endowment for the Arts (NEA), although the NEA is in our credits because we received $15,000 from the American Film Institute, which participates in regranting NEA money. The NEA has turned us down for every film, as has the State Arts Council, state and national humanities councils, all possible government options, the Corporation for Public Broadcasting (CPB), public television, and all U.S. television stations that we have ever approached individually. Fundraising is an enormous obstacle for a film that effectively challenges the public's preconceived image of reality.

Nonetheless, we gathered enough money to go ahead with the film. We have our own editing equipment, but we had to rent a camera. We knew that we had to have an insurance certificate to rent a camera from a commercial rental house, so we borrowed one from a friend. For our first film, *Destination Nicaragua,* there was no insurance company in the United States that would give us insurance for a Betacam to take to the war zone. The insurance policy had to be bid out on the floor of Lloyd's of London. National television networks have cameras; if they lose one, they buy another. They are free to take a camera almost anywhere. Because of this freedom, it is always their images and perceptions we see in the mainstream media. What I am trying to demonstrate is that for people who make controversial films, there are many tedious economic obstacles that add up and that prevent independent films from getting made.

There is also the issue of people being threatened, especially those who act as sources for us in the countries where we shoot. These countries are ones in which the United States has "restored democracy," and they are the most dangerous places in which I have ever made films. We interviewed people whose faces we blacked out. We interviewed people with whom we met clandestinely in Panama and with whom we had to stay in touch up to the final day of editing to see whether or not we could or could not include their footage. People were often in the process of going back underground because the U.S.-installed government of Panama was after them: a warrant had gone out for them. Then, things would cool off and people would be above ground for a while. These people's words and opinions could endanger them, and we always respected their fears. People with whom we worked directly usually paid the highest price, and this fact is a very difficult one for us. The truth is that when we come into a country, we are going to be able to leave that country, whereas the people who help us, who stay behind because they live there, continue to be in danger.

There is always the issue of responsibility. Before the film was completed, our cameraman died, as did our primary researcher. The partner of our production coordinator in Panama died the last day of the shoot. Chu Chu Martinez, one of the wisest and most respected leaders in Panama and with whom we worked, died during the postproduction period. Unfortunately, when people died while performing certain tasks for us, aside from sorrow, it caused us great concern in other ways as well. But we have never had the luxury—emotionally, financially, or logistically—to stop our work to investigate thoroughly these deaths. We did not have the money in the bank to go to Panama with a forensic doctor and an investigator to do the research to find the evidence to prove that a murder had taken place—if in fact it had. Even if we had the time and money to do the investigation, we did not know if we could come up with the physical evidence. And if we could find the evidence and could prove it, we did not know that anyone would really care. There were already plenty of deaths during the invasion that seemed to arouse little concern. A few more would hardly be front-page news. Each time someone died we made the decision to move forward with the film because it was the only task at which we believed we could succeed. I firmly believe, however, that each time we walked away, it took a chunk out of our sense of humanity.

There was also a problem for us in Panama because some of the people working with us felt that our approach to Manuel Noriega was too critical. One of our advance researchers came from a politically active family—the perfect person to escort us around the country and set up interviews—but after the second day of shooting he became uncomfortable with the questions we were asking. He abruptly left the shoot. Nonetheless, our greatest source of help was from people who came out of the twenty-one-year history of the Torrijos and Noriega era, even though these were sometimes the same people who were deeply concerned that we might do a big anti-Noriega piece, which of course the international press had already done.

Threats to our safety in Panama were also a huge problem. These threats came primarily from two sources. One was the Southern Command, whose representatives regularly stopped us on the streets and would walk up to a uniformed Panamanian that I was interviewing, grab him by the shirt, pull him out of the frame, and say to him, "You don't want to be doing this interview." Second, we were threatened by the private guards of the president and vice presidents who had been installed by the U.S. government: Endara, Calderon, and Ford, respectively. Each man had up to a hundred escorts, nonregimental and not in uniform. The guards wore wide-bottomed pants to conceal guns in each of their low-cut boots, and they wore large shirts that hung out over their pants because they had guns tucked into their belts. They would panic, pull a gun out, and then put it away. These people were the most serious threat to us because they were undisciplined.

The most painful part of filming in Panama, for me, was seeing the poorest of the people in Panama, who had suffered the most from the invasion. It took us six months from the day of the invasion to raise the money to get to

Panama with our equipment. By the time we were there, people had been taken advantage of and had told their story many times. Yet, the U.S. press was still saying that the Panamanians were happy that we had invaded their country. *U.S. News & World Report* had a spurious piece on the refugee center that I later visited, where, as can be seen on the film, 2,650 people lived in an airplane hanger. *U.S. News* portrayed the rapid creation of the center as a marvelous job by the U.S. forces, reporting hardly a word about the suffering of the refugees.

Because the Panamanians had lost faith in journalists, and because many of the people in the sovereignty movement were dead or underground, the people left on the streets were not well organized. Of all the Latin American countries that I have been to, none has adopted as colonized a mentality as Panama's. In Panama, people would come up to us with photos inside their coats and show us three or four that they had taken during the first three days of the invasion. They wanted a lot of money for them and they wanted it right then, on the spot, not the next day and not at a later meeting. If we did not have the money and did not buy the photos, it was okay with them, they would find someone else to sell them to. All these people were able to hope for was that the $35 or $50 would buy their family security for another month. The idea of these pictures ever getting out into the world and making a difference to Panama was outside of most people's sensibilities, which was really difficult for me to understand. This situation was unlike anything I had experienced before in Central or South America. People were so poor in some areas that our equipment and everything we had with us were targets for theft. Paul Troughten, one of our volunteer assistants, was brutally mugged on the street and had to return to the United States because of his injuries only twenty-four hours after arriving in Panama. During the shoot, we always hid the footage after we shot it, and we took many other security precautions as well.

Getting the footage back into the United States was yet another problem. As a rule, we split the video tapes among three or four people returning separately to the States. If someone was returning with a lot of footage at once, that person was given a letter from a congressman or congresswoman who had been supporting us; addressed to customs officials, the letter said, "If you want to stop this woman, you stop her, but don't separate her from her footage. Call my office, and I'll have one of my assistants waiting for your call at such and such a time when her plane comes in." The letter was on official congressional stationery with an embossed seal. Without these kinds of safe-guards, footage does not always make it into the country. While Haskell Wexler was doing his film *Latino* (1985) in Nicaragua in 1984, at the same time we were shooting *Destination Nicaragua*, he had film taken by customs that, when finally returned, was blank.

Once we got the tape into the United States, we dubbed all of the footage and made VHS copies, like home videos, which we kept in our offices during postproduction. The original footage was stored in vaults in Hollywood postproduction houses that also store video for major television shows. Even-tually, we brought all of the film together to do the on-line edit. This time is particularly vulnerable for us: we have spent a lot of other people's money, abandoned the rest of our daily lives for this project, and the culmination of these risks and sacrifices hinges on the irreplaceable footage we have acquired. At this point, we take turns sleeping with and guarding the footage twenty-four hours a day, remaining in the office, sometimes for several months, to make our project less convenient for sabotage.

After coming back to the United States, having shot what we had, there were still documents that we needed. We were fortunate to have established a strong working relationship with the Center for Defense Information and, particularly, with the National Security Archive, which has done a wonderful job pursuing Freedom of Information Act (FOIA) requests resulting in the release of thousands of previously classified materials. The Archive maintains a vast number of documents and exemplifies the cooperation that is essential to independent research and media.

The Pentagon shot between 600 and 650 hours of footage during the invasion. Through the FOIA, the Pentagon has released only 50 hours. We pressed for access to the rest, and we were denied these requests on the basis that it would endanger national security. When we continued to press them until the final days of the edit, almost two years later, their response was that the footage had been of no particular value and had been recorded over. But I do not believe that this is true. The invasion of Panama was the first time a number of weapons systems were tested out in the "arena" (as the Pentagon likes to call the battlefield, in their sportsmanlike language of war), and we know that arms builders and the Pentagon rely on that footage to analyze the performance of new weapons. Even Congress has been unable to see the footage. In many ways, we do not know what happened in Panama, and what our film does as much as anything is to open up a lot of questions; we present evidence, but still leave some questions unanswered.

Our next challenge was getting the simplest kind of additional footage from the major networks. We figured that to make this film we had to bring people up to speed on the history between the United States and Panama, so we included footage of President Carter signing the Carter-Torrijos Treaty, the death of Torrijos, the rise of Noriega, and the Iran-Contra scandal. The footage, from ABC and Vis News, costs $150 per second. NBC is much cheaper, so we did most of our work with them, but it still cost $45 per second. This meant tens of thousands of dollars we had to raise for the most common, innocuous historical footage. Footage that is over twenty or thirty years old we can get from the National Archives for free, but anything else is still under copyright.

When the networks make a film, they buy footage from each other. At the end of the year, when they add up how much they owe, the totals cancel each other out and nobody owes anybody anything. But an independent must come up with the real cash. This is another important economic factor that limits our ability to make politically challenging films.

Some of the best footage our research identified clearly demonstrated how the news media manipulated the public to accept, anticipate, and support the invasion of Panama (a technique that reached new heights preceding and during the Persian Gulf war). We have clips in our film of Dan Rather during the evening news juxtaposed with footage illuminating the reality of events in Washington and Panama. The process that one must go through to obtain clips of network "talent" (as they call their news people) was difficult in itself. You must submit your script for their approval, and, if you receive it, their price is still astronomically high because it includes their "talent." According to copyright law, however, you can use copyrighted material from the media without permission and without payment if you are using it to critique the media itself. In other words, you cannot use the piece of footage to tell the story, but you can use the footage to critique the way they told the story. So it is perfectly legal for you to have the footage in the film and to claim "fair use." The problem comes in getting the networks to release the footage; they are not required to do so. This catch-22 makes it difficult to critique television news in this country by using their footage. We were able to acquire footage through several lucky breaks that I am not at liberty to discuss; our standard

explanation is that three of our producers have parents who have been recording the news for the last thirty years.

Eventually our work came down to doing the final on-line edit that meets
broadcast standards. We could actually do most of this editing in our own
facility, but there were certain things that we could not do at that time,
certain technology that we simply did not have. We were able to find large
edit houses that made generous donations that, interestingly enough, sometimes ended up costing us more money. The sound studio time was donated
by George Lucas's Skywalker Sound, but the sound equipment there was a 32-
track digital system. Their specifications for our source materials were very
detailed, so preparing our materials to take advantage of this offer cost us far
more than we had anticipated. Likewise, some of the people who offered to
prepare materials for free in order to develop their own skills on very sophisticated equipment made errors that caused us to lose entire days already
slated for us at Skywalker. In the end, Skywalker Sound ran short on the time
they could continue to donate as major paying clients came under time-line
crunches of their own. Ultimately, our final sound mix was more rushed than
was advisable. We may have made some errors in accepting some of these
contributions; I think we got in over our heads. But the smaller 24-track
studios often are not in a financial position to donate time.

For the first six months during the release of the film, although I traveled
with it from city to city, I was never able to watch it. You never see a film from
start to finish when you are working on it. You just work on pieces of it a little
at a time. I did not sit through the whole thing for close to a year because I
would leave in tears. I would watch a section, and I would not be able to stand
it because I knew that there was a whole soundtrack that never got mixed in
because we ran out of time and money. There were also images that we had
intended to change but had to leave as they were. After spending two years of
our lives making a film, and having gone through everything we endured, we
would like to think the film would be what we had planned it to be, so it is a
little painful at first to accept the imperfections.

When we finally finished *The Panama Deception* and it won an Academy
Award, we went to potential television buyers in Europe and around the
world. Constantly we heard, "We already did Panama." Why? Because PBS's
Frontline did a piece called "War and Peace in Panama" and there were
numerable *McNeil/Lehrer Reports* on the topic. None of these reports discussed the four reasons given by the Bush administration for the invasion.

The shows never really touched any of the important information about the media and the U.S. government's purposeful manipulation of public opinion, both within the United States and internationally. But how many television hours is Germany or France supposed to spend on a small war in which they were not even involved? The fact that networks produce programming quickly and get it out into the marketplace first means that they can consume the only time allotted for the subject, thereby burying the real issues. In effect, this is damage control for the government. *Frontline,* for instance, uses a very good distributor for whom we have a great deal of respect, Charles Shurhoff Associates—an aggressive and highly successful distributor throughout the world. *Frontline,* with the help of the duped taxpayers' contributions, creates a steady stream of programming on current affairs that is widely distributed. Their productions, in effect, censor the marketplace by always filling the available time slots with seemingly critical journalistic explorations of an issue before anyone else has the opportunity to complete and distribute anything really powerful, anything that probes the real heart of the matter, naming names and having the courage to place blame when necessary. *Frontline* appears to be controversial, but it often produces no more than an inoffensive whitewash of the issue, thereby posing no threat to PBS's corporate sponsors or the U.S. government, its primary sponsor. I see this as a real problem.

In other countries, theatrical releases are less feasible than television broadcasts. We have sold our film to about twenty-five other countries for broadcast, and the selling usually involves going to a festival, showing the film, getting a lot of press, and creating a buzz about the film. A distributor comes forward after realizing that there is an audience for the film. You really have to go to each country and prove that the people are interested in the issues in the film, so that the gatekeepers, the people who are in control of the venues, can see that a broadcast is feasible. At this point, buyers get involved.

Television in the United States is much more painful. None of our movies has been broadcast nationally by PBS. The real scandal is what PBS does at the national level, beginning with their *POV* series, a show thrown like a bone to the progressive community. To defend their decision not to show our film, they basically smeared it. How else can they defend not showing an Academy Award–winning documentary broadcast in twenty-five countries that has received fabulous reviews in all the major papers in the country, and has been shown in a hundred cities and cinemas? I have a letter, from our buddy Jennifer Lawson, executive vice president of National Programming, PBS, which says, "*The Panama Deception* covers an important topic, but does not meet our standards for fairness. In our view, some of the assertions about the intent of U.S. policy and the conduct of U.S. troops are not adequately substantiated." The only people who were the primary leads for us, in terms of our assertion of U.S. foreign policy in Panama, were people like Maxwell Thurman, the four-star general who led the invasion. He was the first person (who obviously had not been debriefed) to say that the purpose of the invasion was to destroy the Panamanian defense forces (a purpose never stated by the Bush administration). Pete Williams, a Pentagon spokesperson, backed up that assertion in an interview, saying that it was the "essence of the operation." We did not even put Williams's comments in because we felt they would be repetitious, that we would be hitting the public over the head. Perhaps we forgot that the public includes television programmers.

What PBS means by dismissing some of the film's testimony in their statement "the conduct of U.S. troops [is] not adequately substantiated" is that poor, black, often non-English-speaking victims on the ground cannot compare to Dan Rather in terms of knowing what really happened in Panama. PBS's stance is racist and classist. The letter goes on to say that "PBS has already extensively reported on U.S. relations with Noriega, the invasion of Panama and the conditions in post-invasion Panama." But the coverage included two *Frontline* documentaries, *The Noriega Connection* (as if he was the issue) and *War and Peace in Panama*. The second film analyzed the logistics of the invasion: Did they have good maps, was it planned well, did more people die than was anticipated? The film begins by ticking off the four official reasons given for the invasion as if these reasons were the truth. The whole point of our film was to expose the fact that the reasons given by the president had nothing to do with the invasion.

If something is not shown on PBS, the progressives, or at least the liberals, in the United States think the film must not be valid. They think it must be some kind of conspiracy film. The public has an enormous amount of respect for PBS's official position, which I think is particularly damaging. I know people who have done *Frontline* pieces. These films are a contribution, but they pull back and do not give us the final names or show the faces. I say: Show the faces, name the names, and take us all the way to the end.

Two things happen when PBS rejects a film. First, their rejection is released to the press. Independent stations, who otherwise might feel courageous and show the film, get nervous when PBS says a film does not meet their fairness standards. Who is the program manager in Sioux City, Iowa, to say he or she knows better than the corporate heads of PBS? If he or she should choose to broadcast our film, would he or she not in fact be considered possibly irresponsible, and if the program manager and the station are sued, how could they defend themselves when the national office of PBS has already made it clear that the film is not acceptable as journalism? PBS's power to disrupt our ability to distribute our films for broadcast is substantial. I know that every now and then there is a fight to save PBS, and I can tell you to count me out. My feelings are not merely sour grapes; I would rather see the money that goes to PBS go to the CPB or the NEA. Let these organizations fund films, and let these films compete for broadcast on a level playing field.

The only channel that originally would show our film was Cinemax. Now the Independent Film Channel is showing it as well. Do you know who showed the most challenging piece on the J.F.K. assassination, by Nigel Turner from the U.K.? Arts and Entertainment. HBO, Discovery, and other national cable stations are doing cutting-edge, risky programming. I believe that individual PBS stations that actually serve their constituents will survive. KQED, the PBS affiliate in San Francisco, broadcast *The Panama Deception* shortly after our theater run in California. This station showed our previous film, COVERUP: *Behind the Iran Contra Affair*, as well. It was good to have a prestigious station show the new film before the national PBS office could smear it. This situation allows a bit of a defense, especially since the viewers' reactions are always phenomenally supportive. WGBH in Boston, KBDI in Denver, and WNYC in New York were the next affiliates to take the leap. These stations are major public affairs programmers, and their decision to broadcast *The Panama Deception* in its entirety has had a strong effect on smaller, more hesitant stations who would like to show it. Similarly, viewer response supports our belief that the public is hungry for deeper investigations of controversial affairs. A small station, KCSM in San Mateo, California, aired *The Panama Deception* and received an unsolicited $100,000 donation from a contributor impressed by their courage. This demonstrates the support that exists for this type of programming.

I would like to address some solutions I see for enhancing independent filmmakers' aims to share ideas worldwide by distributing films to theaters, video stores, and television. Our method for releasing films to theaters across the country is one of the primary ways we break the government/corporate stranglehold on information. When we go from town to town releasing the film in theaters in coordination with local community groups already in-volved in the issues most relevant to the film, a whole series of events takes place. Community groups do a tremendous amount of advertising and PR in newsletters, on the radio, and in newspapers. They function as publicists. Their position in the community is elevated by being associated with a high-profile opening night. They get a portion of the opening-night proceeds and also get copies of all of the donation checks written throughout the film's release so that they can maintain contact with these donors. This process helps to build their organization and their ability to make change. As a result of our release, literally hundreds of people in each town will write letters, speak up on talk radio, and take a wide variety of actions to create positive change in our world. In addition, the experience provides local activists with valuable training. We have produced a manual called *Taking It to the Theaters,* which provides blow-by-blow instructions for this kind of social activist release. When we leave each town, the activists carry on without us, often for weeks, while the film continues to play at the theater. The problem is that when we come back two years later and want to open in a former location, the people we trained are not there anymore, and we have to start from scratch.

I am convinced that we have to explain to major foundations that the millions of dollars they sink into producing independent films is lost if they are not also going to create an environment in which people can release these films. The movement is just wasting money, breaking hearts, and burning out well-meaning people. There needs to be a support system for independent producers to prepare for and coordinate distribution of films and videos. Most filmmakers are not natural-born distributors, and yet, many are left with no choice but to distribute their film or video by themselves. I would like to see something like a retreat where filmmakers could go to work with skilled people to prepare a strategy, develop promotional materials, book theaters, and launch the organizing campaign to fill the theaters and get the information out. If such an environment existed, and was funded, a number of good films could be chosen each year to take advantage of the process, thereby guaranteeing a good release and guaranteeing community groups and independent theaters around the country a constant source of important films for organizing. There would be a standing army of people in each community ready to come to the theaters to see the new film. We are not talking about getting people to come to a church basement or a conference, but to a theater with a marquee, preceded by a review in the paper and interviews on the radio.

There also needs to be a revolving fund for ads: a certain amount of money put in by a foundation to be loaned out to assist in releasing films. The money would then be recouped from film profits, so that filmmakers would not have to do everything in the most uneconomical way. We have never been able to do a mass run of posters, for example, which could be done much more economically if a thousand were done at one time. Finally, we need to consider underwriting an agent or distributor to put time into each film. What often happens even with good distributors who agree to take on politically controversial films is that they usually spend more energy, resources, and time on their more commercial films, which have a greater likelihood of bringing in more money. The films that make money are the ones that grab the attention of the distributor, and we have to find a way to more effectively compete. If we believe that there is an audience out there—and I am convinced there is—then we have to find a way to launch an ongoing series of films.

As for video, we need to have a fund so that we can provide something called a "buy-back guarantee." This means, for example, that when my video manufacturer, Rhino Home Video, offers our video to big distributors who warehouse the tape region by region, the distributors will buy five hundred copies because Rhino can say they will buy back any tapes that the distributors cannot sell. This is how all videotapes are distributed except social and political documentaries because few manufacturers have enough faith in the marketability of these films to back them with money. But if a video does sell, as all of ours have, the manufacturer does not lose money, it makes money. We are disappointed that we have not been able to convince foundations to put together a pool of money to guarantee these videos enough financial backing so that they will have the opportunity to find a market. Independent distributors need to develop relationships with stores and chains around the country who will agree to take a certain number of controversial videos. People would then begin to know that they could go to these stores to get the film. Blockbuster carries such films, for instance, and a lot of other stores could be encouraged to do likewise. In terms of television, we must start focusing, as I have said, away from public television, and put money into other kinds of options and develop relationships with A&E, HBO, The Learning Channel, TBS, Cinemax, the Independent Film Channel, the new Sundance Channel, and others if we want people to keep making controversial films and if we want to really exploit these films to their fullest.

There is a terrific need, in my opinion, to support independent media and independent analysis and news reporting and to continue to work with people around the world and within our own "third world" here in the United States. We need to support ourselves, our sisters, and our brothers in recording our own history and creating images of ourselves and the world that we can share with each other. It is time to take action.

Masao Miyoshi

"Globalization," Culture, and the University

In March 1996, a UAW walkout was settled at two GM brake factories in Dayton, Ohio. The strike was important because its outcome was expected to suggest whether General Motors—and by implication, any corporation— could further transfer the manufacturing sites to any part of the world that offered lower prices, or labor could successfully resist such attempts. The settlement was hailed by some as the workers' victory, though many were skeptical.[1] It was a sort of victory for labor, especially when compared with another UAW walkout at Caterpillar, Inc., in Peoria, Illinois, that ended after eighteen months in November 1995 in complete defeat; at least the union received a modest pay hike for the Dayton GM workers, though failing to resolve the issues of outsourcing. The UAW contracts with all three U.S. auto manufacturers—GM, Ford, and Chrysler—are going to expire in mid-September 1996. And whether the union can do anything to stop or even slow down the pace of outsourcing without jeopardizing the future of the auto industry and workers in the United States is a grave enough question that concerns everyone interested in economy. What I would like to discuss in this paper is, first, the conditions of the so-called globalized economy as an outgrowth, or continuation, of colonialism; second, its effects on local culture;

and finally, the position the university occupies in today's world economy. Here I mean not only the conditions of the United States, but refer to other parts of the world as well. In this sense, it is an exploratory, some people might well call it a "totalizing" or even "oversimplified," argument; but that is a risk we might be willing to take for some glimpse of where we are in this extremely confusing world. Detailed qualifications and variants can be supplied in a different context.

"Globalization"

The term *globalization* is nearly as abused as *postcoloniality*. If globalization means that the world is a seamless unity in which everyone equally participates in the economy, obviously globalization has not taken place. We do not live in an integrated economy, nor are we likely to in the foreseeable future. Similarly, if globalization means merely that parts of the world are interconnected, then there is nothing new about this so-called globalization: it began centuries ago, as Columbus sailed across the Atlantic, if not earlier. The only novelty is in the degrees of expansion in the trade and transfer of capital, labor, production, consumption, information, and technology, which might be enormous enough to amount to a qualitative change.

Capitalism has always been international, and thus there are a number of analysts who deny the current idea of globalization altogether. Let me briefly mention just two cautious arguments on the subject among a great many. One is in an article by two British economists, Paul Hirst and Grahame Thompson.[2] They begin by defining the exact meaning of the word globalization by constructing an ideal model of global economy and then comparing it to current tendencies in international economy. The model is characterized by several features of a theoretically transnationalized economy. First, transnational corporations are totally unattached to any nation-state. They point out, quite correctly, that there are very few real TNCs, most of the huge corporations being "multinational" corporations, meaning having their headquarters in one country while operating semi-independently in many other countries—for example, General Motors, Honda, Coca Cola, Nestlé, and by now practically all other major, and many minor, corporations. Hirst and Thompson do not discuss, however, how "multinationalism" relates to "transnationalism." Is one likely to evolve into the other, or is transnationalism to be precluded by immutable nationhood? Second, they argue that international trade is regional rather than global. By this they mean that the intra-OECD trade (Organization of Economic Cooperation and Development: the E.U., U.S., and Japan) amounts to 80 percent of world trade. This, too, is correct, except that no one disputes that wealth is inequitably distributed, and so in dollar figures, the North-South trade is obviously far smaller than the North-North trade. But this does not prove much. Globalization never meant global equality (in fact, its exact opposite is true: the gap between rich and poor is growing greater as time passes, and that is precisely where this globalization discourse vitally connects with colonialism discourse). That is, the economic contributions of poorer countries and regions are bound to be small in absolute quantities and values, while at the same time these economies affect the economic and social structure of both themselves and industrialized countries by offering potential sites for outsourcing. Thus, the relative size in value terms of regional versus global trade means very little in discussing globalization. Third, Hirst and Thompson argue that international trading is a minor portion of the total economic activities of most countries except the European Union members. The figures they give are 25–30 percent for European economies, and 10–15 percent for the United States and Japan. Wrong: the total trade/GDP ratios are: Canada 46 percent; Japan 21 percent; U.S., 20–25 percent; and some NIES (newly industrialized economies), especially Taiwan, South Korea, Singapore, and Hong Kong, are even more active in global trade—Taiwan, 77 percent, and South Korea, 62 percent, for instance.[3] Finally, they believe that the two most successful economies, Germany and Japan, are successful because they are "nationalistic." I think they are wrong again: first of all, I am not in the least sure that these two economies are so successful on their own; and to the extent, for example, that the Japanese economy has been stagnant and unsuccessful for the past several years after the real estate bubble burst, the reason most often offered for the failure is the excessive intervention by Japan's national bureaucracy that strangles the corporations with outmoded rules and regulations. If these two economists want to argue that globalization, complete integration, has yet to take place, of course they are right. It has not happened. But, if they want to say that regionally integrated economies (the triadic European Union, Nafta, and the East Asia Co-Prosperity Sphere) are the future of the world economy, then I believe they are misreading the present and future of the world economy.

I prefer David Harvey's careful position offered in chapter 11 of *The Condi-*

tions of Postmodernity, entitled "Flexible Accumulation—Solid Transformation or Temporary Fix?" To briefly summarize the chapter in this well-known book, it offers three views regarding the recent developments in the world economy. The first is the globalists' (as represented here by Michael J. Piore and Charles F. Sabel), which sees a transformation that is so radical that in every dimension of social and political life "none of the old ways of thinking and doing apply any more." The contrasting "conservative" position (taken by Anna Pollert, David Gordon, and R. Andrew Sayer) is that "there is nothing new in the capitalist search for increased flexibility or locational advantage," and that there is no solid evidence for any radical change in the way of capitalism—somewhat like Hirst and Thompson's position, discussed earlier. Against these two, Harvey takes a middle ground: he sees a transition from Fordism to flexible accumulation, a mix of "highly efficient Fordist production (often nuanced by flexible technology and output)" in the United States, Japan, or South Korea, and more traditional production systems in other regions. Such a situation has changed "the nature and composition of the global working class," as have "the conditions of consciousness formation and political action. Unionization and traditional 'left politics' become very hard to sustain." "Gender relations have similarly become much more complicated . . . as resort to a female labor force has become much more widespread. By the same token, the social basis for ideologies of entrepreneurialism, paternalism, and privatism has increased."[4]

I believe these three positions more or less suggest the range of views of world economy as it is being transnationalized at an extremely uneven pace in various regions of the planet. It is "global" if we mean the plan and capability of market and labor penetration by industrialized economies. We need to recognize, as does Harvey, that industrial development is extremely uneven, and many parts of the world merely serve the benefits of industrial capital that is more and more restricted to fewer and fewer people. We will come back to this situation of ongoing economic colonialism later, but before that, I want to briefly trace the transition from colonialism to transnational corporatism around wwii.

Neocolonialism

As was often repeated, 85 percent of the earth's land surface was under the subjection or domination by the colonial powers around the turn of the century, and colonialism remained the dominant geopolitical pattern until 1945. At the end of the war, the world hegemony shifted from Britain to the United States. At this conjunction, it is important to remember the domestic economy of the new hegemon preceding WWII. F.D.R.'s New Deal, initiated in 1932, had not been able to erase the effects of the Depression. During the years between 1931 and 1940, the U.S. unemployment rate remained in two digits straight, reaching nearly 25 percent in 1933. Similarly, the GNP fell in 1931 by as much as 14.7 percent. Roosevelt's concern with the wars in Europe and the Far East was due—this, too, has been often pointed out—as much to an economic need of the United States as to the transgressions of Germany and Japan. After 1940, the U.S. GNP shot up at once: during the war years, the GNP increase rate was in two digits for three straight years, and the unemployment rate sank to the historical low of 1.9 percent in 1943 and 1.2 percent in 1944.[5] It would be odd indeed if American leaders hadn't learned the invaluable benefits of war from these figures.

The war ended in a complete triumph of the United States, with nearly every other industrial nation reduced to rubble. Britain and France were clearly unable to maintain their overextended colonies after 1945. Germany and Japan were completely vanquished. (Japan's industrial production in 1945, for instance, stood at 10 percent of the normal prewar level, and in 1946 it was only 30 percent of its 1934–36 output.)[6] And the Soviet Union, which lost 20 million citizens and almost all of its major cities, was also near total exhaustion. Victory, however, is no guarantee of lasting economic prosperity, and peace is indeed a suspect condition for capitalism. With its huge wartime industrial expansion, the United States was faced with a crisis of overproduction. Men returned from war, flooding the labor market. Women who had taken their place during the war had to go home. Thus, the U.S. GNP was stagnant in 1945 and fell in 1946, and strikes were rampant. The frightening specter of a repeat depression loomed before the Truman policymakers. Here, let me quote a statement by George Kennan in February 1948: "we have about 50 percent of the world's wealth, but only 6.3 percent of its population. . . . In this situation, we . . . [must] devise a pattern of relationship which will permit us to maintain this position of disparity without positive detriment to our national security. To do so, we will have to dispense with all sentimentality and day-dreaming. . . . We should cease to talk about vague and—for the Far East—unreal objectives such as human rights, the raising of the living standards, and democratization. The day is not far off when we are going to have to deal in straight power concepts."[7] This statement is more fascinating than his famous Soviet containment piece, known as the "X" article, published in the July 1947 issue of *Foreign Affairs* (or National Security Council Paper 68, authored by Paul Nitze). An internal paper to be kept top-secret for many years, it was one of the rare candid statements about U.S. policy concerning the postwar economy. Furthermore, the statement cannot be dismissed as an expression of postwar uncertainties under circumstances totally different from ours. When the papers were declassified and published in 1983, Kennan in the foreword not only cautioned against such a hindsight reading, but also insisted that "some of the positions of principle taken in these papers were of so fundamental a nature that they will not have lost their relevance, and possibly even their validity, for another generation and another age."[8]

Wars, even small ones, are often helpful to capitalism. The slump in the economy was picked up by U.S. interventions in Greece and Turkey as well as by the Marshall Plan in Europe, and then by the Korean War. No one knows how the war started in North Korea. Bruce Cumings ends his two-volume *Origins of the Korean War* by asserting that it is futile to try to pinpoint the origins. Elsewhere, he agrees with Kennan in the general assessment of the cold war as having started in 1918 with the Bolshevik dissolution of the Constitutional Assembly.[9] (Noam Chomsky might trace it back to Columbus's landing in North America in 1492.)[10] Anyway, the Korean War brought great benefits to the U.S. economy and to the Japanese. When the Peace Treaty was concluded with North Korea in 1953, the U.S. anticommunist efforts were at once redirected to South Vietnam in the form of economic aid to the French government.

The cold war was concurrent with the liberation and independence of many former colonies in Africa, Asia, the Middle East, the Far East, the Caribbean, and the rest, leaving out only a few places. In fact, it is by now unavoidable to think of the cold war as part of a larger Anglo-American policy of third-world, or global, containment. That is, as the West's administrative colonialism in third-world nations waned, the imperial hegemon made sure that these less industrialized, newly independent countries remain economically and industrially dependent. The Soviet Union, in this view, is not the archenemy threatening the security of Western capitalism, but just another third-world nation, bloated with a military system but hardly anything else. The "evil empire," so seen, is an invention of the imaginative policymakers in

Washington and London—although the Soviet Union cannot be entirely exonerated from the charge of playing the role of the polar superpower.

During the 1950s and '6os, this containment policy proved a great success. With the national security system firmly in place, the Department of Defense—as Seymour Melman pointed out—functioned as an industrial planning agency, expending more than the combined net profits of all U.S. corporations every single year from 1951 to 1990.[11] And it served to boost the U.S. economic engine quite well. The growth of the U.S. economy was steady since the Korean War despite several recessions. The war in Vietnam was also a success story for the growth of the national economy, although there was an enormous social cost, of course. The opposition to the war nearly split the country. Corporations such as GM, GE, and Dow Chemical were often targets of fierce protest and denunciation, and labor demands for higher wages were also rising. It is thus no accident that huge corporations began to transfer their productions abroad in the 1960s and '70s, although there were other compelling reasons as well—such as increasing competition from Germany, Japan, and other industrial nations. This is the time transnational corporatism can be said to have commenced.

Before moving on to discuss the growth of TNCs, I would like to raise a question that still remains a bit of mystery to me—that is, why did the United States allow Japan to grow into the economic power that it is now: the U.S. economy is $6 trillion, and Japan's economy stands at $4 trillion; trailing far behind are Germany at $2 trillion, France and Italy at $1 trillion, and Britain at $900 billion. The usual explanation is that the United States needed to keep Japan on its side in the cold war divide, but it is unsatisfying in several ways. An ally need not, should not, be a competitor, especially when it is a dependent client state. (Japan is, after all, still under U.S. occupation even now.) And if the United States has been consistently determined to contain the third-world nations in the line of Kennan's statement, Japan's growth is indeed a puzzle. Did the United States miscalculate? Did Japan somehow outwit the United States?

Perhaps the United States did underestimate Japan's ability for recovery; what can Japan, after all, a mere Asian backward country, do? We can see this in the division of Korea. Why didn't the United States instead split Japan into two halves, one for the Soviets and the other for the United States, as it did Germany, another aggressor? That would have been a more reasonable decision. Possibly, the United States was indifferent to Korea and did not fear Japan as it did Germany. But a more likely reason might be that national economy no longer mattered much, as U.S. corporate leaders saw it, by the time Japan really emerged as a super economic power around 1980. Increasingly, what needed to be protected was the corporate interest as a whole: not the interest of particular nations or particular corporations of Nation A or Nation B, but simply the interests of all capitalist enterprises that ultimately lead to the enrichment of the financial and industrial capital of any place, any nationality. In such a development, the form of governance known as nation-state is steadily losing its appeal and function. Of course, one does note that Japan is still largely insular, jealously guarding its "national economy." But that is because conservatives in the Japanese government and business are not sufficiently informed, just as their U.S. counterparts are not, although some of its corporate managers are keenly alert to TNC developments. There is wide agreement among the business leaders of both countries that sooner or later, the Japanese will come around to join this global capitalist alliance.

Transnational Corporatism

Transnational corporatism became earnest during the 1980s under Margaret Thatcher in Britain and Presidents Reagan and Bush in the United States. After the collapse of the Soviet Union, the triumphant capitalist West became desirable, fearless, and unrestrained. Capitalism meant nothing short of transnationalism, and all the earlier apologies for economic adventurism and opportunism were felt to be unnecessary and irrelevant.

Earlier, the merits and demerits of privatization were seriously discussed; now privatization is accepted as a given, even a fait accompli in most sectors of industrialized countries. Instead of previous disagreements regarding public responsibility, especially the role of the government, unanimity now prevails among all politicians about the inefficiency and waste of "big government." The federal deficit suddenly has become an urgent issue everywhere. And entrepreneurship is an unrivaled virtue for practically everyone. That means, in a world no longer on the brink of a nuclear holocaust, that few public expenditures—except those for defense—are recognized as legitimate. Profit and production are now the universal goals, and nothing is ignored in the striving to maximize personal and private gains.

To cut labor costs, corporations as well as public offices seek to downsize their operations. The reduction of employees in the 1990s is unprecedented in several aspects. First, the scale of layoffs is immense. The *New York Times* in March 1996 ran the most massive series of articles since the Pentagon Papers in 1971, which lasted for seven days and well over twenty full pages, on "The Downsizing of America." The articles, later published as a 356-page book,[12] may not say much as a whole, the *New York Times* being the *New York Times,* a liberal-conservative mainstream paper. The sheer length of it, however, underscores the prominence the *Times* has given to the phenomenon. It points out, at any rate, as do many other publications in recent years, that more than 43 million jobs, or one-third of all the jobs in the United States today, have been extinguished since 1979. After a layoff, many workers find new jobs, but most of them (65 percent) either work at a lower pay, part time, or are self-employed, and 24 percent remain unemployed or out of the labor force altogether; 72 percent of the entire population admit that they or someone close to them has been affected by a layoff.[13]

The second peculiarity of the current downsizing is that it has nothing to do with the negative performance of the corporations. Rather the opposite: the more downsized, the greater dividends and executive pay. Caterpillar, Inc., of Illinois—which I mentioned earlier—lost $400 million in 1991 but gained nearly $1 billion in 1994, and that was precisely the year when the company discovered that they needed no union workers.[14] Every time a company announces a huge layoff, its stock rises to signal the approval of Wall Street. Thus, the day Sears announced the reduction of employees by 50,000 jobs, its stock jumped nearly 4 percent; when Xerox decided to eliminate 10,000 jobs, its stock surged 7 percent. Over ten years Chase Manhattan Bank reduced its workforce by 28 percent, while its assets rose by 38 percent.[15] Throughout such turmoil, some workers do survive—mostly those who are better educated. But they are often reported to be seriously depressed with a sense of guilt and insecurity. The impact of corporate downsizing began to be intensely and extensively discussed in 1995, and that was the year Wall Street had the greatest gain in history. On March 8, 1996, the Dow dropped by 171 points, the largest decline since 1991, and its reason was by now a familiar one: a rise in employment figures was announced that very morning.[16]

Third, those who lose jobs entirely are mostly high school graduates or dropouts, but even survivors lose in this bracket: the average hourly wage of American production workers in manufacturing has gone down since 1972 from $13.21 to $12.06 after adjusting for inflation.[17] Capitalism is always inequitable in the distribution of wealth, but however big the gap between rich and poor, until recent years American society always grew richer in absolute terms in every segment of society. Indeed, even the poorest 20 percent grew richer, however minuscule the increase. Since 1973 or thereabout, however, this stable feature changed for the first time in history. Now the poorest are getting poorer in absolute terms, while the rich are getting a disproportionate share of the increase: "those changes mean that American society is divided in a way that it has never been before."[18]

In all this, the fourth and most bizarre new feature is the disproportion in wages. We were told around 1990 that the gap in wages between corporate CEOs and line workers was around 60 to 1. A grotesque enough figure, but Kevin Phillips, a Republican economist, upped that figure to 130–140 to 1 in 1993. The Caterpillar president's salary zoomed to $4.07 million, up 53 percent from the year before, when the union surrendered.[19] Although the discrepancy of incomes across class lines was always huge in the United States (despite Tocqueville's observations), this drove *Newsweek,* Washington's establishment weekly, to a screaming rage. It printed "Corporate Killers" in huge letters with the CEOs' pictures, names, and the number of jobs they eliminated on the cover, and their salaries in the article itself under the title "The Hitmen." The CEO of AT&T: 40,000 layoffs (and still 100,000 more expected in the coming five years, atop the 250,000 cut since the Bell system breakup in 1984,[20] his salary, $3.4 million; the CEO of Chemical/Chase: 12,000 layoffs, $2.5 million; GM: 74,000 layoffs, $1 million: and so on.[21] These figures of course do not include their options and bonuses (*Newsweek* knows manners), which are far bigger—like $200 million for the chairman of Walt Disney, $127 million for the CEO of Hospital Corporation of America, and $67.6 million for the CEO of Primerico in 1992. This connection between downsizing and the rise in stock and CEO pay is grotesque for most people, but the administration in Washington seems unconcerned. Only after Pat Buchanan's bigoted populism made it impossible to remain silent did Senator Kennedy, Congressman Gephardt, and Labor Secretary Robert Reich suggest some congressional measures to restrict downsizing and outsourcing. But Buchanan's popularity declined rapidly and the Democrats' concern, too, quickly evaporated. President Clinton called it merely a matter of corporate ethics. In his speech at Xavier University in Cincinnati on March 23, 1996, obviously feeling queasy even about this vacuous statement, he reaffirmed that "the most fundamental responsibility for any business is to make a profit."[22]

Downsizing is certainly not limited to the unskilled. The skilled are the next target.[23] The Pew Health Professions Commission forecasts a surplus of 100,000 to 150,000 physicians and 200,000 to 300,000 nurses by the end of the century. Only about 1,000 Ph.D.s are produced in mathematics in the United States, and half of them are foreigners. But unemployment among mathematicians is reported to be over 10 percent.[24] In the spring of 1996, the University of Rochester decided to eliminate the Department of Mathematics—together with Linguistics, Chemical Engineering, and Comparative Literature. The March–April 1996 issue of *Lingua Franca* reports that of the fifteen Ph.D.s produced by the Yale English Department, only two received ladder-rank appointments.[25]

I might add that downsizing began, as I have already suggested, with replacing unionized and expensive American employees with cheap overseas workers unprotected by civil rights, human rights, environmental concerns, and feminist consciousness. We all know by now the case of Nike shoes. Nike manufactures all of its shoes outside the United States. The production is subcontracted mostly to Korean entrepreneurs, over whom Nike until recently claimed no responsibility. The subcontractors operate their factories in Indonesia, Thailand, and China. The young women who work in Indonesia all day long sewing these shoes get $1.35 a day (actually, the Indonesian minimum wage was raised by 29 percent in 1994 because of the pressure from American NGOs, thus the Nike workers now receive as much as $1.80 a day, presumably), and the contractors charge $6.50 a pair to Nike, which in turn sells them in the United States for $50 to $100. The entire Indonesian operation that employs 30,000 women cost Nike less than what it pays Michael Jordan for his endorsement of the brand, some $20 million.[26] What we have not seen yet in this episode is Nike's possible downsizing of the headquarters operation in Oregon, where a host of white-collar workers now design the shoes and oversee its sales campaign. The middle-rank managers are next in line—to be replaced with eager and bright beginners who cost less and can be hired on reduced benefit arrangements, if not by automation, or both.[27] TNCs and MNCs are readily capable of ignoring borders and creating areas of poverty in any place, either in Oregon or in Jakarta. And when the Indonesian labor demands become too exorbitant, the Nike operation might move again, this time to China, the Philippines, Vietnam, to the sweatshops in Los Angeles, California, or New York City (where the workers are as coercible and unprotected),[28] or even to the inside of state prisons and penitentiaries, where literal slave labor is being carried on with the approval and support of the taxpayers of the United States.[29]

Some economists believe that outsourcing is not nearly as devastating a factor in the disappearance of jobs as automation. With the phenomenal advance in electronic technology, a vast amount of manufacturing work has already been replaced by robotics in the industrial areas. The exact consequences of such a development are not predictable, of course. But Japan, which fears the pollution of its mythical pure blood by imported aliens, has made great strides in the development of cybernetic reengineering. And the radical reduction of labor in the production process seems inevitable anywhere else.[30]

The economy is complex and unpredictable. It never stands still and changes are constant. Downsizing may slow down or be replaced by some other strategy. The spring 1996 media outbursts against the corporate practice soon quieted down. The press began to publish articles extolling the wisdom of avoiding drastic personnel reductions. Then the news of economic recovery reappeared, emphasizing companies creating new jobs and hiring back employees. Unemployment fell, the labor force grew, and the average worker's pay rose. All this, however, does not mean that the long-term prospect has changed. There may have been a rise in employment, but the press does not specify in which categories; the pay average may have risen, too, but nothing is said about in which income brackets. In fact, the news of downsizing still keeps appearing, and there are no signs of structural change in the "globalized" economy.

Culture in the TNC World

I have so far mainly concentrated on one aspect of the transnational corporate structure as the continuation of exploitation and colonialism, domestic and overseas. Now I would like to move on to the conditions of culture in the TNC structure.

When Matthew Arnold constructed the idea of "culture," borrowed from the Germans in the mid-nineteenth century, it was a joke for the Radicals of the time like Frederick Harrison, who called it "fiddlestick and sauerkraut."[31]

Arnold himself expressed enjoyment of the banter in *Friendship's Garland*. Actually, culture was a dead-serious matter from the beginning for Arnold. His enlightenment ideology of "Hellenism," that is, secular, liberal, and canonic intellectualism, is an apologia for the state—as he defines it in no uncertain terms in the conclusion of *Culture and Anarchy*: "the very framework and exterior order of the State, whoever may administer the State, is sacred; and culture is the most resolute enemy of anarchy."[32] Culture was to serve as an agency for law and order.

As it goes through adjustments in the hand of Pater, Eliot, Trilling, and many others in the Anglo-American mainstream humanities, "culture" becomes the program for modern centralism and authoritarianism. Arnold's "sweetness and light" is intellectual modernism consisting in high arts and poetry, criticism and consciousness, the enabling stuff for the imaginary community, which Benedict Anderson mistakenly calls "imagined community." So considered, Anglo-American culture, or even general modern culture, was bound to be statist, not to say nationalist. Transnational corporatism is a process of decomposing the state; and along with it, of economicization of culture. With all the urgency and energy to maximize corporate and private gains, it converts most social and political activities into economy, and culture into a commercial program. Arts and architecture are absorbed into business; music, theater, and film into entertainment and/or entertainment cum speculation. History and geography, in fact all "differences," are treated seriously by economic leaders only as a part of tourism, often packaged in museums, restaurants, and theme parks. Thus, all cultural productions are susceptible to TNC appropriation as profitable commodities. If there is an identifiable style in TNC culture, it is "universal" consumerism that spreads beyond the boundaries of the first world into the second and third, providing that they have leftover money to spend. Consumerism offers a powerful allurement for homogenization. Thus, there is always a theoretical possibility that regional cultures everywhere may be obliterated before long. The Hollywood film's global hegemony is indisputable by now, but what's remarkable about it is the near total quantification of its qualities: either a film is a blockbuster or not, whether it has made $100 million in the first week or not, and little else finally matters. Quantitative measurement is spreading in the print media: a contract recently has been drawn for three "techno-thrillers" by Tom Clancy for $60 million, for five books by Danielle Steel for $60 million, and for four novels by Stephen King for $40 million.[33] We seem to hear less and less about serious novels. This market practice expands further into other areas. We know from the examples of rock, rap, break dancing, and graffiti art that even protest and resistance arts are easily made profitable and compromised.

However determinedly critical and disinterested, high culture as defined by Arnold and his modernist successors is especially vulnerable to incorporation into elite consumerism. Once the nation-state as a supposed communal space disintegrates, high culture is doomed to fall under the sway of wealth and snobbery, celebrity and profit. To take just one random example, in the summer of 1996 the Philadelphia Museum of Art held one of the most comprehensive exhibitions of Cezanne's work jointly organized with the Réunion des Musées Nationaux/Musée d'Orsay in Paris and the Tate Gallery in London. That it had commercial sponsors such as Advanta ("an innovative financial services company") and U.S. Air is nothing unusual. Nor is the transnational joint organization. Nor is the text of the ad that selects the artist's early, sensational mixed-race *Abduction* as its opening illustration. What is new, however, is that the exhibition took out a special advertising section of ten pages in *Business Week,* and that its informational page lists "participating hotels" with their rates, ranging from $149 to $275. (The price of admission, too, is coordinated to these upscale hotel recommendations: $12.50 for adults, $9.50 for seniors, students, and children five out of six open days a week.)[34] The campaign was a great success. At midseason, the show was reportedly "just about sold out." Even more startling, however, was the response of New York City. Fearful of losing valuable summer visitors to Philadelphia, its three major museums, the Metropolitan, MOMA, and the American Museum of Natural History (featuring, respectively, Winslow Homer, Picasso, and dinosaurs), placed their joint newspaper advertisements in Philadelphia, Boston, and Baltimore. The ad headline read: "A Blockbuster on Every Block."[35] Cezanne and Picasso are now a commodity securely tied to tourism as well as to art dealers. This does not mean, of course, that all museumgoers are consumers, but it should be admitted that the corporate buyout of high culture is rapidly changing the nature and role of art as criticism.

Still, all hope is not lost. Culture as a people's way of life, counterculture rather than official culture, emerges and reemerges in these moments before the TNCs' appropriation of them. True, the TNC is alert and quick, and the life of counterculture is getting briefer. And yet, people do continue to live and try to survive, and as they manage to survive, they still produce texts and objects interpreting the meaning of social relations while giving hope and courage—without surrendering at once to mindless consumerism. In these moments of hesitation and resistance, people carve out a space free from transnational corporatism and a site for further reflection and criticism.

The University

Early in the year 1995–96, the Department of Literature at the University of California, San Diego, received a letter from the new dean of the humanities. The letter was specifically addressed to various institutional issues in bald quantitative terms—with no reference whatever to substantial intellectual or pedagogic matters. Over several paragraphs, the dean traced the ups and downs of course enrollment, the faculty-student ratio, and the number of majors in the department. He was also concerned with the ranking of the department by the National Research Council. A unique research department of "literature" as a whole, not of any specific national literature, the UCSD department has no comparable institution. And the NRC proceeded to compare its subsections to the departments of other universities as if the small sections were full-scale departments. Thus, UCSD's 18-member section of "Literatures in English" was compared to the 60-member Berkeley English Department, and was ranked No. 37 as against Berkeley's No. 1. The dean asked for explanations, accepting such figures and numbers and ignoring the differences in the organizational rationale or research performance. As a member of the department, I found the document to be unusually unsubtle in its blunt arithmetic and its implied policy to quantify university education. I had not heard of such a memo that was so unself-conscious about its corporate management style either at San Diego, Berkeley, Chicago, or any other university where I had taught. I started composing my response to the dean, but just before mailing out the letter, I called my friends and colleagues at NYU, Princeton, Duke, Syracuse, Hawaii, Chicago, UCLA, UC Irvine, and other schools to make sure that my reaction to this administrative memo was not completely off. To my amazement, all those I talked with in the humanities, without exception, told me that they had received similar letters from their administrators. Many said that their deans had been writing them about the faculty-student ratio for years, and they were surprised that I had never been exposed to a quantified assessment. If there was anything exceptional in this, it was not the dean's rhetoric and performance, but my own naïveté and ignorance. The one story that struck me most was a case at an Ivy League university where a course with a low enrollment (although above the required minimum) was discouraged from being offered again by the department. A course with a large enrollment, on the other hand, was encouraged without any scrutiny of its contents. (One of the latter courses was called something like "Faith in Life" or "Life and Truth," its syllabus sounding like a New Age manual, little expected from an institution with an international reputation.) Number, and number alone, counts increasingly in our universities.

Ever since the university was established as a modern institution around 1800, it has been repeatedly defined and redefined as to its relationship to society. And yet from Fichte and von Humboldt, through Newman and Arnold or even Thornton Veblen, the university was thought of as a part of national culture, national history, national identity, and national governance. The construction and maintenance of the coherent nation-state was at the core of its agenda.

The turmoil in the 1960s clearly marked a new phase in the history of the university. *The Uses of the University,* written in 1963 by Clark Kerr, the president of the University of California, was both a cause and an effect of such a transformation. His "multiversity" was the first candid manifesto for the abandonment of the presumed integrity of the university as an interpretive agency of the general public, if not of the "universal." It was now reconceived as a service station for social segments, the most—or only—important of which were the state apparatus (the cold war was very much on then) and corporations. The reaction to the book, among other things, led to a student rebellion, the free speech movement at Berkeley, but President Kerr's idea of the "multiversity" also signaled the beginning of the university as accountable not to the public as a whole (what the nation is supposed to be), but to multiple forces in society that are in control of the state more directly than its citizens at large. It ought to be recalled here that the supposed unity of the nation-state was visibly unraveling in the 1960s. A great number of universities were engulfed in often violent strifes not only in the United States, but also in Africa, Europe, Central and South America, East and Southeast Asia, and the Middle East. The word that represented the protesting students' mood of the decade was *relevance.* They applied the test of relevance as the principal tool of criticism and deconstruction to the prevailing ideas and assumptions. In the United States, the civil rights movement opened the 1960s, and toward the end of the decade the university reform and antiwar protest movements converged with ethnic minority issues, giving rise to ethnic, feminist, and popular culture studies as alternative curricula. They were further broadened throughout the 1970s into the general problem of canonicity. From then on, the vanguard in the humanities was split mainly into two camps, affecting aspects of social sciences as well: one centered around discursive theories following French poststructuralist criticisms; the other, more historical and materialist, on Marx and the Frankfurt School theorists.

The traditionalists were, as always, very audible, but they were in the mainstream, clearly outside the vanguard of scholars and students. Thus, some subjects were discussed with refreshing vigor from poststructuralist, Marxist, and other perspectives. Modernity and postmodernity, neocolonialism, multiculturalism, cultural studies, bio-environmentalism, identity politics (that is, gay/lesbian studies, queer theories, and feminist and ethnic studies)—these all marked departures from nineteenth-century traditionalism, and they generally crossed disciplinary borders. These topics were what should have been included in the object of learning a long time ago, and as such, the development deserved full support from everyone who wished to be truly universalist. And by now—decades later—the alternative curricula are in the ascent, pushing aside conventional culture-based aesthetic criticism.

Such developments in higher education, however, are far from liberationist. First, the logic of nation-state—its history and apologia—that has at times served to protect academia from wholesale absorption by the corporate system has radically declined in the postwar transnational corporate integration. Connection and relation, definition and emphasis are increasingly being sought internationally across state borders not only in business but also in the pursuit of social science and the humanities, not to say natural sciences. Second, whatever remained in support of the coherence of a nation-state during the cold war lost its rationale and efficacy at its demise in 1989. Global corporate operations now subordinate state functions, and in the name of competition, productivity, and freedom, public space is being markedly reduced. And the university that was at times capable of independent criticism of corporate and state policies is increasingly less concerned with maintaining such a neutral position. The function of the university is being transformed from state apologetics to industrial management—not a fundamental or abrupt change perhaps, but still an unmistakably radical reduction of its public and critical role. Third, the introduction of new disciplines and perspectives such as multiculturalism, ethnic studies, cultural studies, postcolonial studies, and gender studies was an academic response to the postwar reconfigurations of the prevailing social and economic conditions that were Eurocentric, patriarchic, and hegemonic. As part of the effort to redefine equity and justice, the emerging academic programs were needed and salutary, as already mentioned. It is, at the same time, important to remember that such reforms hardly constituted a challenge to corporate domination, as many of their proponents seem convinced. There is a large area of agreement between corporate needs (labor control, market expansion, denationalization, privatization, entrepreneurism, and transnationalization) and such cross-border studies. "Multiculturalism [together with other emergent studies] is a phenomenon with a silent partner: the broad and radical change now taking place within world capitalism."[36]

To return to the University of California, San Diego, Robert C. Dynes, vice-chancellor for Academic Affairs, was designated to assume the recently vacated chancellorship in April 1996. Dynes proposed seven goals for UCSD on the occasion. Of these, two objectives were concerned with the students, one with the faculty, one with the campus community, one with the regional community, and two with partnerships between the university and business "locally, nationally, and internationally."[37] He may well be proud of having had an unusual corporate background for a professor of physics (he moved in 1991 from "AT&T Bell Laboratories, one of the nation's preeminent corporate research organizations," as he announced), and his emphasis on the active collaboration between research institutions and the business community may indeed be justified. It is a little surprising, however, that an academic administrator of considerable status and influence is seemingly oblivious to the essential need of university research to safeguard its integrity and independence from corporate demands. In fact, he says nothing in the speech about the humanities or even social sciences, on which the responsibility of articulating criticism and assessment of corporate activities and state conducts might well fall, should there be occasions.

A few weeks later, the newly appointed president of the University of California, Richard C. Atkinson (whom Dynes replaced in San Diego), made public his vision for the university. He reiterates the importance of technology for "increased productivity, higher living standards, and faster economic growth." Atkinson knows that some may think of this as dangerous, "raising the specter that universities will abandon their pursuit of fundamental knowledge in favor of short-term research with a quick payoff." But he dismisses such fears in the next sentence, calling industry's growing interest in university research "more an opportunity than a threat." Thus, the partnerships of universities with industry are the key to successful economies of the twenty-first century. We have learned "a great deal about safeguarding the freedom to publish research findings, avoiding possible conflicts of interest and in general protecting the university's *academic atmosphere* and the free rein that faculty and students have to pursue what is *of interest to them*" (my italics). Possible—or, some might say, actual—contradictions and adversarial relations between university and business are brushed aside by ignoring the whole range of thorny issues such as uneven distribution of wealth, profit maximization, unemployment and downsizing, environmental destruction, corporate greed, and countless other vital questions. President Atkinson, too, avoids terms like *intellectual, humanities,* or even *tradition,* preferring *knowledge* and *technology.*[38] What is fascinating about this remark is not that the brief essay is extreme or radical—though it indeed is if placed in the context of the academic discourse of Veblen, Barzun, or even Kerr—but that President Atkinson remains wholly self-assured and matter-of-fact throughout. In fact, unlike the stormy responses *The Uses of the University* raised a generation ago, this op-ed essay did not stir a single scholar or critic to rebut or even discuss. The appropriation of the university by industry is now complete.

Inside the university, on the other hand, uncertainty prevails. There is a widespread feeling, to begin with, that the current institutional departmentalization of knowledge is quite inadequate; in fact, the supposed disciplinary borders that function as the academic rationale for organization are visibly blurring everywhere. There is very little that can be agreed on as to what should constitute the substance being taught. In most English departments, for example, courses involving writers and theorists, regardless of their nationalities, languages, or even disciplines, are being offered with little self-consciousness—from Bakhtin to Bataille, from Derrida to Habermas, from Irigaray to Devi, from Foucault to Lévi-Strauss, from Lacan to Lyotard. University presses no longer know how to classify their publications (thus the recent emergence of inclusively topical "series"), and the same is true of bookstores. Discussions and controversies continue: disciplines, area studies, cultural studies, identity politics—even such large and general categories are being fought over with fervor inside academia.

To return to my dean's and apparently countless other letters written in recent years by academic administrators, what we are witnessing here is the principle of corporate economy in control of universities. Courses are being canceled whether they teach basic mathematic theories, or the Achebe-Ngugi controversy about the use of language, or the South American testimonials, or Derrida's dependence on the ghost, or the power of hybridity, or fifteenth-century English poetry unless enough students enroll. Conversely, if a good many students are interested, any vacuous course can be taught. Of course, departments and schools could always coerce students by requiring courses. But university education without a substantial guarantee for job placement will not remain an unchallengeable authority forever. The students' reluctance and resistance can grow. There are signs that the number of applicants for admission to college is on the decline.[39] Besides, agreement as to which courses to require is getting harder and harder to reach among the faculty. The division and fragmentation diagnosed by Clark Kerr in the early 1960s are now quite conspicuous on every campus.[40]

A few years ago, people in the humanities were excitedly talking about the vanishing subject matter. Now it is the disappearance of the students, the changing nature of the university, and the disappearance of faculty positions that we are obsessed with. The late Bill Readings's excellent book *The University in Ruins* (1996) discusses with great insight the history of the university from its Enlightenment inception to its twentieth-century demise. His diagnosis of the university outside the nation-state structure, which he calls "the university of excellence," traces in greater detail the outline I have sketched out here.[41] He means by the term "excellence for the sake of excellence" the skill in trade, any trade—with no direction, except an aggregate of market demands. Readings's prognosis for the university of dissensus is, however, finally not clearly distinguishable as an operational alternative from Gerald Graff's idea of the university and faculty as mediator/facilitator—the university where students are encouraged to disagree and argue—with the faculty as an open-minded witness, though covertly assuming an ultimate consensus, like a talk-show host.

Outside academia—in union halls, neighborhood meetings, NGO programs, and alternative activist groups—resistance, opposition, and struggle are unavoidable daily routines for survival, but they are quietly dismissed from academic discourse as insignificant, ineffective, and outmoded, if not wholly delusional. In its condemnation of the master narratives, academic discourse refines and complicates the ideas of gender and ethnic identities to such an extent that class conflicts are conveniently pushed aside. What is not seen does not exist. One's own identity, on the other hand, is private property to be guarded from all others. Minority discourse is often no longer a step toward the establishment of social equality, but a claim to monopoly rights. Among competing groups—especially between the dominant and the dominated—hybridity, accommodation, and pragmatism are aggressively promoted as if they were the only viable strategies in the postmodern reality of the capitalist world. History as a combative process is advertized to be over, and conflicts and contradictions are declared to be already resolved. In fact, the university classroom as a talk show that promises to entertain rather than discuss seems to be more and more the typical undergraduate expectation. Students also want to have been, but not be, in the classroom. It is a sadly vacuous place that has little to offer except for licensing and professionalism— Readings's "excellence" plus diversion—without the substance of profession. Once professors presumably professed; they are now merely professionals, entrepreneurs, careerists, and opportunists, as in the corporate world. We may be in a far worse situation than we like to imagine—unless we seriously tackle what we should think, teach, and do.

The *New York Times* of March 27, 1996, published an editorial on the news of City University of New York's having cut its budget by $97 million. The chancellor as a result declared a state of financial emergency, which means a legal authority to suspend tenure. Which in turn means that Anne Reynolds, the chancellor, can decide what to teach, what not to teach, who can teach, and who cannot teach. Higher education is now up to the administrators. And sooner or later, research, too, will be up to the administrators. Of course, we know that the administrators are merely in the service of the managers of society and the economy, who exercise their supreme authority vested in the transnational corporate world.

When do we begin to fight back? And how do we—the workers in Dayton, Ohio, and those of us in the university—form an alliance?

Notes

1 Donald W. Nauss, "Little Apparently Accomplished with Costly GM Strike," *Los Angeles Times,* 23 March 1996, quotes Harley Shaiken as saying that the UAW "triumphed" in Dayton.

2 Paul Hirst and Grahame Thompson, "The Problem of 'Globalization': International Economic Relations, National Economic Management and the Formation of Trading Blocs," *Economy and Society* 21, no. 4 (November 1992): 357–395.

3 U.S. Department of Labor, Bureau of Labor Statistics, *Productivity and Economy: A Chart Book, 1985* (Washington, DC, 1986).

4 David Harvey, *The Conditions of Postmodernity: An Enquiry into the Origins of Cultural Change* (Oxford, 1989), 190–192. In a more recent unpublished paper, "Globalization in Question," presented in February 1996 at the University of California, San Diego, Harvey again raises the question, "has there been a qualitative transformation wrought on the basis of these quantitative shifts?" and replies, "My own answer is a very qualified 'yes' to that question immediately accompanied by the assertion that there has not been any fundamental revolution in the mode of production and its associated social relations and that if there is any real qualitative trend it is towards the reassertion of early nineteenth[-century] capitalist values coupled with a twenty-first century penchant for pulling everyone (and everything that can be exchanged) into the orbit of capital while rendering large segments of the world's population permanently redundant in relation to the basic dynamics of capital accumulation" (15).

5 U.S. Department of Commerce, Bureau of the Census, *Historical Statistics of the United States: Colonial Times to 1970*, vol. 1 (White Plains, NY, 1989), 135, 226–227.

6 Mikiso Hane, *Modern Japan: A Historical Survey* (Boulder, CO, 1986), 341.

7 U.S. Department of State, *State Department Policy Planning Study 23*, 24 February 1948.

8 U.S. Department of State, Policy Planning Staff, *The State Department Policy Planning Staff Papers* (New York, 1983), 1:viii. I learned of this document through a conversation with Noam Chomsky many years ago. Since then I have quoted it several times and am again reproducing it here—only because I consider Kennan's pronouncement crucial for the understanding of U.S. postwar policy.

9 Cumings made these remarks in a discussion at a workshop I organized at the University of California, San Diego, in 1995. George Kennan, *Russia Leaves the War* (Princeton, NJ, 1956), 352–363.

10 Noam Chomsky, *Year 501: The Conquest Continues* (Boston, 1993).

11 Seymour Melman, "Military State Capitalism," *The Nation*, 20 May 1991, 649, 664–668.

12 The New York Times, *The Downsizing of America* (New York, 1996).

13 John Cassidy's rebuttal, "All Worked Up: Is Downsizing Really News or Is It Just Business as Usual?" (*New Yorker*, 22 April 1996, 51–55), faults the *New York Times* and other publications for distorting the statistics of current layoffs and unemployment. Cassidy attributes downsizing to capitalism's inevitable aspect of "creative destruction." But his actual complaint is limited to the *Times*'s not consulting the 1996 *Displaced Workers Survey (D.W.S.)* by the Department of Labor, which is not published as of this writing. The survey, according to Cassidy, might

present a different picture: "all suggest that there has been little change in overall job stability" (53). Having made the statement, however, Cassidy proceeds to concede that displaced workers have to take a pay cut, that more educated workers are now losing their jobs, and that "the intensification of global capitalism has been undermining the living standards and the prospects of the unskilled." "But," Cassidy goes on, "contrary to common belief, people who lost their jobs in 1993 suffered no more than those laid off in 1983." Cassidy may prove right, but in the absence of the *Displaced Workers* statistics, I cannot agree or disagree. One thing that occurs to me, though, is that Cassidy, too, might have waited for the publication of the Labor Department report if he is serious in complaining that the *New York Times* should have waited.

14 There is an excellent report covering the Caterpillar strike in the *Los Angeles Times*. The five-part series began on May 14, 1995, and this series, too, was published later in book form.

15 Louis Uchitelle and N. R. Kleinfield, "On the Battlefield of Business, Millions of Casualties," *New York Times*, 3 March 1996 (later included in *The Undersizing of America* as the first chapter, "The Price of Jobs Lost").

16 Kenneth N. Gilpin, "Market Takes Steepest Drop since '91," *New York Times*, 9 March 1996.

17 Barry Bearak, "After a Long Tug of War, Labor Slips," *Los Angeles Times*, 14 May 1996.

18 Benjamin Schwartz, "Reflections on Inequality: The Promise of American Life," *World Policy Journal* (winter 1995–96): 38.

19 Louis Uchitelle, "1995 Was Good for Companies, and Better for a Lot of C.E.O.'s," *New York Times*, 29 March 1996.

20 Catherine Arnst, "The Bloodletting at AT&T is Just the Beginning," *Business Week*, 15 January 1996.

21 Allan Sloan, "The Hit Men," *Newsweek*, 26 February 1996.

22 Todd S. Purdum, "Clinton, in Ohio, Asks Industry to Share with Their Workers," *New York Times*, 24 March 1996.

23 See Simon Head, "The New Ruthless Economy," *The New York Review of Books* 43, no. 4 (29 February 1996): 47–52.

24 Daniel S. Greenberg, "Well-Educated—and Unemployed," *San Diego Union-Tribune*, 6 December 1995.

25 Emily Eakin, "Walking the Line," *Lingua Franca* (March–April 1996): 52–60.

26 The Nike case has been often reported (see, for example, Richard J. Barnet and John Cavanagh's *Global Dreams: Imperial Corporations and the New World Order* [New York, 1994], 325–328). See also John Cavanagh and Robin Broad, "Global Reach: Workers Fight the Multinationals," *The Nation*, 18 March 1996, 21–24, and Bob Herbert, "Trampled Dreams," *New York Times*, 12 July 1996.

27 Barry Bearak, "Getting Cut Off by AT&T," *Los Angeles Times*, 18 February 1996.

28 "A 1989 report by the General Accounting Office found that some two-thirds of the 7,000 garment shops in New York City were sweatshops. Last year, a Labor

Dept. spot check of 69 garment shops in Southern California found a stunning 93% had health and safety violations" (Susan Chandler, "Look Who's Sweating Now," *Business Week,* 16 October 1995). See also Marc Cooper, "Class War: Silicon Valley: Disposable Workers in the New Economy," *The Nation,* 27 May 1996, 11–16.

29   Christian Parenti, "Making Prison Pay," *The Nation,* 29 January 1996, 11–14.

30   Jeremy Rifkin's *The End of Work: The Decline of the Global Labor Force and the Dawn of the Post-Market Era* (New York, 1995) is, I believe, finally wrong both in its diagnosis and recommendation, but contains interesting and important information along the way.

31   Frederick Harrison, "Culture: A Dialogue," *The Choice of Books and Other Literary Pieces* (London, 1886), 103.

32   Matthew Arnold, *Culture and Anarchy,* ed. J. Dover Wilson (London, 1960), 204.

33   Mark Miller and Katrine Ames, "A League of Her Own," *Newsweek,* 22 July 1996.

34   *Business Week,* 22 April 1996. I have not systematically examined other periodicals. It's entirely possible that the advertisements were placed elsewhere as well.

35   Glenn Collins, "Advertising: Manhattan Museums Combine Resources for Newspaper Campaign," *New York Times,* 19 July 1996.

36   David Rieff, "Multiculturalism's Silent Partner: It's the New Globalized Consumer Economy, Stupid." *Harper's,* August 1993, 62.

37   Official Notices, no. 573, dated April 11, 1996. The remarks were delivered at a news conference on April 9.

38   "High Stakes for Knowledge," *Los Angeles Times,* 28 April 1996, op-ed page.

39   See Commission on National Investment in Higher Education, for the Council for Aid to Education, *Investing in American Higher Education: An Argument for Restructuring,* 5 January 1995.

40   Clark Kerr, *The Uses of the University,* 3rd ed. (Cambridge, MA, 1982), 101.

41   Although Bill Readings and I are not specifically in debt to each other, I would like to acknowledge—with deep grief—that toward the end of his brief life, we shared days discussing these issues and were planning to work together on university projects. *The University in Ruins* was published posthumously by Harvard University Press.

IV CONSUMERISM

AND IDEOLOGY

Dollarization, Fragmentation, and God

As a young medical student, born and brought up in a colony, like many other people in my country, Egypt, I quickly learned to make the link between politics, economics, culture, and religion. Educated in an English school, I discovered that my English teachers looked down on us. We learned Rudyard Kipling by heart, praised the glories of the British Empire, followed the adventures of Kim in India, imbibed the culture of British supremacy, and sang carols on Christmas night.

At the medical school in university, when students demonstrated against occupation by British troops it was the Moslem Brothers who beat them up, using iron chains and long curved knives, and it was the governments supported by the king that shot at them or locked them up.

When I graduated in 1946, the hospital wards taught me how poverty and health are linked. I needed only another step to know that poverty had something to do with colonial rule, with the king who supported it, with class and race, with what was called imperialism at the time, with cotton prices falling on the market, with the seizure of land by foreign banks. These things were common talk in family gatherings, expressed in a simple, colorful language without frills. They were the facts of everyday life. We did not need to read books to make the links: they were there for us to see and grasp. And every time we made a link, someone told us it was time to stop, someone in authority whom we did not like: a ruler or a father, a policeman or a teacher, a landowner, a *maulana* (religious leader or teacher), a Jesuit, or a God.

And if we went on making these links, they locked us up.

For me, therefore, coming from this background, cultural studies and globalization open up a vast horizon, one of global links in a world where things are changing quickly. It is a chance to learn and probe how the economics, the politics, the culture, the philosophical thought of our days connect or disconnect, harmonize or contradict.

Of course, I will not even try to deal with all of that. I just want to raise a few points to discuss under the title of my talk, "Dollarization, Fragmentation, and God." Because I come from Egypt, my vantage point will be that of someone looking at the globe from the part we now call South, rather than "third world" or something else.

A New Economic Order: Gazing North at the Global Few

Never before in the history of the world has there been such a concentration and centralization of capital in so few nations and in the hands of so few people. The countries that form the Group of Seven, with their 800 million inhabitants, control more technological, economic, informatics, and military power than the rest of the approximately 430 billion who live in Asia, Africa, Eastern Europe, and Latin America.

Five hundred multinational corporations account for 80 percent of world trade and 75 percent of investment. Half of all the multinational corporations are based in the United States, Germany, Japan, and Switzerland. The OECD (Organization for Economic Cooperation and Development) group of countries contributes 80 percent of world production.

This concentration of capital corresponds to the character of the new technological revolution. Here the cycle of accumulation depends less and less on the intensive use of natural resources, labor, or even productive capital and more and more on the accumulation of technology based on the intensive use of knowledge. The concentration and centralization of technological knowledge is more intense and monopolistic than other forms of capital and only increases the gap between the rich and the poor and especially between the "North" and the "South."

This accumulation of technology can function in different ways:

1. *A growing dematerialization of production:* Over the past twenty years, the Japanese production process has reduced by a third the amount of raw materials used per product. Since 1980, the annual reduction has been 3 percent, that is, sixfold over the period 1965 to 1976.

This dematerialization, among other factors, has resulted in a tendency toward lower real prices for thirty-three principal raw materials. Price deterioration is even more pronounced in recent years.

Dematerialization of production combined with automation of productive processes means that labor loses value both in the North and the South; that is, people are losing their value or are no longer needed. The South, which depends more on labor and raw materials, suffers most.

2. *Market manipulation* and speculation based on informatics, telecommunication, and rapid movement works to the advantage of the biggest and richest.

3. *The revolution in telecommunications, transport, and informatics* has produced management innovations facilitating mergers of capital. Private business is incorporated more and more in a way dependent on centralized capital. National business, state or private, is increasingly marginalized and more and more isolated from the functioning of the domestic market and the survival of the impoverished majority.

Dollarization or Global Poverty?
Glancing South at the Multitude

1. *Plunder* is a word we associate with the mercantile period, with the Spanish Armada, the buccaneers, the British East India Company, Queen Elizabeth (the first, of course), the slave trade, the Ottoman Turks, and others. Today it is known under other names: aid, free trade, loans, speculation, and even development.

The result of all these is that from 1980 to 1990, the net financial transfers from the South to the North were equal to about ten Marshall Plans. About $180 billion were transfers from the third world to commercial banks in the West during the period of 1984 to 1990.

2. What the World Bank calls *structural adjustment* is a potential economic genocide. The dollarization of prices in the South means raising these prices to world levels equal to those prevalent in the United States and Europe. However, average earnings in the South are seventy times lower than in the North. A retail salesman in the North receives a wage that is forty times more than a factory worker in Egypt. The salary of a medical doctor in Egypt starts at the equivalent of $40 a month.

3. International trade is plunder of the majority of people, especially in the South. A pair of Nike shoes are sold in the United States for about U.S. $80. A woman worker in the Nike factory in Indonesia receives for the labor 12¢ in every pair. Roasted coffee retails at more than $10 a kilogram in the market of developing countries, yet the international price of green coffee is U.S. $1 per kilogram. The farmer in the third world will receive approximately 25–50¢ per kilogram. Nonproducers in the third world will receive 50–75¢ in the form of profits and commercial margins associated with transportation, storage, processing, and export of the coffee. From its retail price of U.S. $10, U.S. $9 will be appropriated by international merchants, distributors, wholesalers, and retailers in the OECD countries. The surplus appropriated at this phase, essentially by nonproducers, is more than twenty times the farm-gate price. Only a fraction of the farmers' 25–50¢ actually enters his pocket for the work put in. Rent must be paid, agricultural loans must be reimbursed, farm inputs must be paid, and so forth.

Similar patterns of price formation exist with regard to most primary commodities produced in the South.

A Global Culture for a Global Market

To expand the world market, to globalize it, to maintain the New Economic Order, the multinational corporations use economic power and control politics and the armed forces. But this is not so easy. People will always resist being exploited, resist injustice, struggle for their freedom, their needs, security, a better life, peace.

However, it becomes easier if they can be convinced to do what the masters of the global economy want them to do. This is where the issue of culture comes in. Culture can serve in different ways to help the global economy reach out all over the world and expand its markets to the most distant regions. Culture can also serve to reduce or destroy or prevent or divide or outflank the resistance of people who do not like what is happening to them, or have their doubts about it, or want to think. Culture can be like cocaine, which is going global these days: from Kali in Colombia to Texas, to Madrid, to the Italian mafiosi in southern Italy, to Moscow, Burma, and Thailand, a worldwide network uses the methods and the cover of big business, with a total trade of $5 billion a year, midway between oil and the arms trade.

At the disposal of global culture today are powerful means that function across the whole world: the media, which, like the economy, have made it one world, a bipolar North/South world. If genetic engineering gives scientists the possibility of programming embryos before children are born, children, youth, and adults are now being programmed after they are born in the culture they imbibe mainly through the media, but also in the family, in school, at the university, and elsewhere. Is this an exaggeration? an excessively gloomy picture of the world?

To expand the global market, increase the number of consumers, make sure that they buy what is sold, develop needs that conform to what is produced, and develop the fever of consumerism, culture must play a role in developing certain values, patterns of behavior, visions of what is happiness and success in the world, attitudes toward sex and love. Culture must model a global consumer.

In some ways, I was a "conservative radical." I went to jail, but I always dressed in a classical, subdued way. When my son started wearing blue jeans and New Balance shoes, I shivered with horror. He's going to become like some of those crazy kids abroad, the disco generation, I thought! Until the age of twenty-five he adamantly refused to smoke. Now he smokes two packs of Marlboroughs a day (the ones that the macho cowboy smokes). That does not prevent him from being a talented film director. But in the third-world, films, TV and other media have increased the percentage of smokers. I saw half-starved kids in a marketplace in Mali buying single imported Benson & Hedge's cigarettes and smoking.

But worse was still to come. Something happened that to me seemed impossible at one time, more difficult than adhering to a left-wing movement. At the age of seventy-one, I have taken to wearing blue jeans and Nike shoes. I listen to rock and reggae and sometimes rap. I like to go to discos and I sometimes have other cravings, which so far I have successfully fought! And I know these things have crept into our lives through the media, through TV, films, radio, advertisements, newspapers, and even novels, music, and poetry. It's a culture and it's reaching out, becoming global.

In my village, I have a friend. He is a peasant and we are very close. He lives in a big mud hut, and the animals (buffalo, sheep, cows, and donkeys) live in the house with him. Altogether, in the household, with the wife and children of his brother, his uncle, the mother, and his own family, there are thirty people. He wears a long *galabeya* (robe), works in the fields for long hours, and eats food cooked in the mud oven.

But when he married, he rode around the village in a hired Peugeot car with his bride. She wore a white wedding dress, her face was made up like a film star, her hair curled at the hairdresser's of the provincial town, her finger and toe nails manicured and polished, and her body bathed with special soap and perfumed. At the marriage ceremony, they had a wedding cake, which she cut with her husband's hand over hers. Very different from the customary rural marriage ceremony of his father. And all this change in the notion of beauty, of femininity, of celebration, of happiness, of prestige, of progress happened to my peasant friend and his bride in one generation.

The culprit, or the benevolent agent, depending on how you see it, was television.

In the past years, television has been the subject of numerous studies. In France, such studies have shown that before the age of twelve a child will have been exposed to an average of 100,000 TV advertisements. Through these TV advertisements, the young boy or girl will have assimilated a whole set of values and behavioral patterns, of which he or she is not aware, of course. They become a part of his or her psychological (emotional and mental) makeup. Linked to these values are the norms and ways in which we see good and evil, beauty and ugliness, justice and injustice, truth and falseness, and which are being propagated at the same time. In other words, the fundamental values that form our aesthetic and moral vision of things are being inculcated, even hammered home, at this early stage, and they remain almost unchanged throughout life.

The commercial media no longer worry about the truthfulness or falsity of what they portray. Their role is to sell: beauty products, for example, to propagate the "beauty myth" and a "beauty culture" for both females and males alike and ensure that it reaches the farthest corners of the earth, including my village in the Delta of the Nile. Many of these beauty products are harmful to the health, can cause allergic disorders or skin infections or even worse. They cost money, work on the sex drives, and transform women and men, but especially women, into sex objects. They hide the real person, the natural beauty, the processes of time, the stages of life, and instill false values about who we are, can be, or should become.

Advertisements do not depend on verifiable information or even rational thinking. They depend for their effect on images, colors, smart technical production, associations, and hidden drives. For them, attracting the opposite sex or social success or professional achievement and promotion or happiness do not depend on truthfulness or hard work or character, but rather on seduction, having a powerful car, buying things or people.

Another important area is the culture of violence, about which much has been said. And violence is linked to the sale of arms, to crime, to armies, to war. The United States maintains the most powerful military force in the world even after the end of the cold war and has a military budget of U.S. $300 billion. Perhaps it now needs this military force and expenditure to buttress its failing economy against dynamic rivals like Germany and Japan. But who pays the price here and in the rest of the world? That's also where the media comes in. The United States produces two-thirds of all the media images in the world. The media culture of the United States is an integral part of global culture, global power, and the global economy. And so the United States struggled hard to lift subsidies and tariffs on media production at the Gatt conference in Uruguay.

But to have an army, people must be prepared to kill. And killing is related to arms and to crime, organized or otherwise. Also to the trade in arms.

To kill, one has to learn at an early age, or at least that's the best way. If you are brought up to be human and kind, the chances are that you will not kill later on unless under very exceptional circumstances.

The cartoons shown to children in the United States are one example of how you can develop a culture of violence with all it implies. A child in the United States is exposed on the average to 41 killings or violent acts for every hour of cartoon viewing. *U.S. News & World Report,* in its issue dated 12 July 1993, published the results of a study undertaken by the American Psychological Association. In this report, it was calculated that, on the average, an American child will watch television for three hours each day. By seventh grade, he or she will have seen 8,000 murders or killings and 100,000 acts of violence. Children who are exposed to this flood of violent images unload the nervous charge in bad dreams and nightmares or are inflicted with one degree or another of "anxiety." But at one stage or the other, there is no way of discharging the "nervous tension" except by violent games and imitation, that is, passing to action.

What applies to TV cartoons is even truer for video games. An American adolescent, by the age of eighteen, will have killed around 40,000 opponents or enemies merely by pressing a finger on an electronic button, and without a single tremor of guilt. This is how these games instill the habit, the culture that kills, the attitude of scorn for the value of human life in the mental and moral makeup of young men and women. They breed crime by making the viewing of crime an ordinary, everyday, acceptable occurrence, which even increases the excitement and the pleasure. And little by little, the dose, the threshold has to be raised.

These electronic games depend on creating an imaginary world, an imaginary "heroism" where the hero is endowed with exceptional capabilities. These capabilities are exercised by the "players" merely by touching a number of buttons. But when the game is over, the child or the adolescent returns to the real world, in which he or she has lost those extraordinary powers and feels small. Thus is created a distorted personality unable to live in the "real world," a personality that yearns for the other world, so that it can continue to exercise the capabilities it has lost, continue to carry out acts of great prowess (killings) and feel satisfied with itself. For without this world of killing, he or she no longer exists.

Thus the media produce and reproduce the culture of consumption, of violence and sex to ensure that the global economic powers, the multinational corporations can promote a global market for themselves and protect it. And when everything is being bought or sold everyday and at all times in this vast supermarket, including culture, art, science, and thought, prostitution can become a way of life, for everything is priced. The search for the immediate need, the fleeting pleasure, the quick enjoyment, the commodity to buy, excess, pornography, drugs keeps this global economy rolling, for to stop is suicide.

Fragmentation, God, and Other Things

Restoring Old Fortifications

The end of World War II and the advent of the nuclear age spelled the end of the empire for Britain and of the colonial stage of imperialism. The result was the emergence of a new imperialism and a new colonialism, of the accompanying globalization of both markets and intervention as well as cultural control through technological outreach.

In my part of the world, Britain has been replaced by the United States, with Britain, France, Germany, and Japan as lesser partners. So for me, the term *postcolonial* conceals the real situation, like many other words used in global politics and global culture. I prefer the word *neocolonialism* because it describes the essential reality of our situation. And when we speak of the New World Order and of globalization I remember the Gulf war, in which Egypt participated in exchange for the $7 billion paid to the government by the Bush administration and retrieved within a period of fifteen months by the United States through the lopsided trade imbalance.

The period after the Second World War was a period of hope for many people. There were those who believed in socialism and thought it was being built in the Soviet Union and Eastern Europe and in part of Asia. There were those who believed in democracy and freedom and thought we were on the way to achieve them. There were the nations of Asia, Africa, and Latin America moving more rapidly than before to independence. Today, most of these hopes have collapsed under the assault of a global transnational imperialism.

The loss of hope, the failure of movements that represented the chance of a better future or were portrayed as leading to a better future, the deception, the difficulties of the economic situation, the attack launched by a global system on what people may perceive as their interests, their identity, their history, their culture, their nation, has evoked a reaction. In the absence of perceived perspectives for the future, people often fall back on what they know, cling to the familiar, the reassuring, the things that made them what they are, the things of the past, not the future. Rather than a change forward, the reaction is backward to the closed family, the closed community, the race or ethnic group, the religion. Back to what is identity. Instead of being open, we close up like an oyster, break off, fight tooth and nail with one another, become divided. And the worse the situation, the greater the rivalry and the more cruel the fighting. In the face of the global assault, instead of uniting as human beings we build up destructive barriers and fortifications, attitudes that divide us, political and cultural movements that take us backward and separate us. We revive all the old ways of thinking, the norms, the values of intolerance and discrimination. We delink, disconnect, and think in terms of rigidity and fragmentation.

For many of us, these are the roots of communal, ethnic, racial, and religious conflicts and confrontations, the essence and the message of such movements.

It is a protest movement, a movement of peoples protesting by going backward rather than forward. And like any protest movement, it can be used by economic and political groups, by those who lead the power game, utilize the hopes, the passions, the despair of people for their own purposes.

This is the source of the religious revival, the return to God, of fundamentalism in the Arab region, in India, in the United States, and in many other places, the source of the religious movement back to dogmatism, intolerance, and dehumanization rather than toward a progressive liberalization of religious teachings. It is a political and cultural movement that merits extensive study because of its repercussions, but that so far does not seem to have excited the interest of scholars in the arts and literature, in the humanities, or in gender studies. What is true of fundamentalism is also true of the ethnic and racial revivals in different parts of the world, especially Eastern Europe.

Two Faces of the Same Coin

If we look at the world scene today, we can observe a movement from above for economic concentration and centralization, for unification, a unification that is to the advantage of the few, the very few, at the expense of the many, coupled with a progressive marginalization and pauperization of many people in the North but mainly in the South.

In the political arena, the scene is different in some ways. Processes of political unification are taking place in Europe and Asia; the United States is unified and is expanding its economic borders to Canada and Mexico through Nafta, but this unification is taking place at the top. At the bottom, in Eastern Europe and the former Soviet Union, there is increasing disunity. This is also the case for many parts of the South such as Africa, the Arab region, and, to a lesser extent, Latin America. Eastern Europe is on its way to becoming a part of the South economically, politically, and culturally.

In the cultural field, the process is similar to that in the political field. The spread of global culture is the necessary corollary of a global economy and a global market, but there is also an opposite movement leading to increasing cultural division and fragmentation, which is related to an increase in ethnic, racial, communal, and religious conflict.

The movement toward a global culture might seem to be contradicted by the other movement toward cultural division, fragmentation, and strife. My contention is that there is no real contradiction. These are two faces of the same coin. To unify power, economic or cultural, at the top, in the hands of the few, it is necessary to fragment power at the bottom. "Divide and rule" is the old adage. To break down resistance, a monopoly on culture is necessary. A peoples' culture, which would cross over borders between people, which is human and universal despite differences, unifying in diversity, seeking what is common despite individual, communal, national, cultural, class, racial, or gender identity, signifies the possibility of resisting global economic and cultural hegemony. To maintain the global economy and the global culture, unification must exist at the top among the few, the very few. It must not take place at the bottom among the many, the very many. People must remain divided, confused, fragmented. They can think, but only in the way that the global powers want them to think. The global economy, the global culture, must exercise an undivided rule. And if people think, they must think in a way that will keep them from finding out what they have in common. The other must remain the other, at most to be gazed at, exhibited, studied, and also help me to feel superior, enjoy myself, be amused, be interested, experience the thrill of knowing. But never, never must the "other" become a part of myself.

The Arab Islamic fundamentalist movements seem to be in conflict with the North. Yes, there are skirmishes going on. It happens in all families, even between the United States and France, Japan, or Germany. But not over the fundamentals. Not over the development of the global economy. The Arab fundamentalists, with their banks, their companies, their trade, their arms, with business headquarters in Geneva, Luxembourg, Frankfurt, the Bahamas, are part of the global economic system. The Gulf countries, especially Saudi Arabia, are the buttress for fundamentalist movements with their petrodollars and their reactionary religious stance. They helped in Afghanistan. They opposed every secular, liberal, democratic, patriotic movement in the Arab world. And throughout, they have been supported first by Britain, then by the United States. They propagate a culture that believes in fate, in obedience, in not questioning, in believing that happiness or unhappiness, wealth or poverty are apportioned by Allah, and so people should accept whatever lot is theirs. What better ally does the global economy want? And if they come to power in Algeria or in Egypt after a period of adjustment, just as before, all will be well.

The anti-West peoples' religious protest movement is one thing. The leading forces behind it are another. They use this protest movement for their ends; to come to power, to grow in strength, they instigate religious strife. And the global powers use them: the British at one time against the national movement, the United States later on, with Sadat, who unleashed them against the opposition until, as a true democrat, he decided in September 1981 that the best policy was to throw everyone in jail. Or Sheikh Omar Abdel Rahman, whose two sons fought in Afghanistan and who is now safely in jail here in the States away from the clutches of Mubarak's police.

Cultural Studies: How and to What End?

The title of our session is "Cultural Studies and Globalization." I have tended to reverse the emphasis and deal with the title as though it were "Globalization and Cultural Studies." This is a reflection of my background, of my involvement in oppositional politics for a long time.

Culture is interwoven with the economic and the political throughout. And for me it remains meaningless, unexplainable, unless placed in its economic and political context and unless linked to the struggles of our life, whether in the North or the South. I am incapable of understanding cultural processes and the role culture plays if I do not locate it in the power struggle, in the movement of gender and class, rulers and people. Linking culture to economics is one of the merits of our conference, and I am hoping that the tone will be set in this direction by the speakers in the first session, entitled "Globalization and Culture." If so, I may be reiterating some of what has already been said. This may, however, help to reinforce certain points. Universities all over the world have been notoriously prone to deal with cultural studies and with the humanities in general in isolation from their political and economic context and from what is commonly called *practice*.

When speaking of cultural, multicultural, or intercultural studies, in the academy or in conferences, the practice has so far always been that intellectuals, scholars, experts, and others from the North are looking at the culture of groups, communities, races, or nations in countries of the South. In this process, there may be some representatives from the South who have been chosen to join in these studies or who are émigrés working in various institutions, or both. Sometimes the study or the conference will deal with communities or groups or races living in the North but whose situation is similar in many ways to the inhabitants of the South. So far I have not heard of things happening the opposite way round, that is, people from the South undertaking to study or hold a conference about people in the North.

Of course, this is a result of the power relations prevailing in the system, and there are tens of reasons for which such an exercise would appear unreasonable or impossible. But this is something people in culture and cultural studies should think of. The awareness of this unequal situation might cause them to wonder whether the new terms now in vogue, such as multicultural or intercultural studies, can be separated from the larger history of orientalism. Recent cultural theory has been trying to deal with the other/I dichotomy on a different plane, to find ways out of this dilemma in the representations of other cultures, but the questions related to this rethinking remain largely in the realm of politics, and culture per se finds them difficult to negotiate.

With the rise of cultural studies in American institutions and in some other parts of the academic world in Germany, France, and Switzerland, can we say that the aim is to "dissolve" the subjected other, or will it be only another stage of a continuing neocolonialist project? How can scholars and theoreticians and theory avoid falling into the trap of serving the Northern drive toward an even more consolidated global hegemony?

Perhaps cultural, multicultural, and intercultural studies need to identify themselves more clearly. If they do, what could be the result? What is the path or the paths that could make cultural studies prove a greater concern with and solidarity for people and their cultures in the South? How can we transfer knowledge and technology to those working in the area of culture in the South without appropriating them to the power system and power culture in the North?

The globalization forces are homogenizing other indigenous cultures everywhere. In villages that continue to be deprived of the basic necessities of life it is possible to see Star TV, MTV, Zee TV, cable TV, and blue movies. The cultural invasion by consumerism is becoming pervasive, creating a severe conflict between what is desirable and what is available. The invasion by images is critical. For the first time in the history of countries like ours we are watching the homogenization of Western or Northern culture into a consolidated, alluring image of the other, of a liberal, capitalist, materially and sexually enticing market, of a world where comparison with our life can only force us to look up to it in reverence.

What can multicultural studies carried out in the North by institutions or scholars or academicians in the North do to critically appraise the image created and that we know is quite false?

When speaking of the other, the two poles involved in cultural studies are usually North and South. Yet the other for us in the South is not necessarily in the North. The other for me, an Egyptian, can be someone else: an Algerian, a Jordanian, or a Yemenite from Hadramaut. Religious, ethnic, and racial strife are increasing the gap and reinforcing barriers between people in many parts of the world. The "other" is therefore not only a matter related to North and South, but also to North and North and to South and South. What we might call intracultural studies can therefore be useful in bridging the dichotomy of a bipolar world, of coming closer to a global world not from above, but from below, a global world in which people understand one another through joint ventures of study, work, and research rather than a hegemonic pyramidal world where culture is decided and globalized in the boardrooms of multinational media companies and other institutions.

The Orient or the South has served as a source of self-definition to the West or the North for over four centuries. The mechanism used throughout has been the same: taking the societies, the cultures, the ways of life in Asia, Africa, and Latin America out of context so that they appear irreal, strange, foreign, with no history. Distancing them as much as you can. And this still happens on a wide scale today. I have attended African art festivals in the North that were exhibitions of disparate samples brought to entertain and delight without any reference to the societies, the problems, the miseries they represent and the factors behind all this, including relations with the North. Books that are translated are a glaring example of this tendency to choose the "exotic" and the "strange." French publishing houses are past masters at this art, aided and abetted unfortunately by North African Arabs or Africans living in France. The modern novel produced in the South, especially if it deals with the problems of our age, with the reality behind relations between North and South, with gender and class, is not considered suitable for cultural consumption in the North. The area of translation should be exposed to serious and systematic cultural studies in conferences, in academia, and in scholastic research. I think I read somewhere a saying that went, "Tell me whom you translate and I will tell you who you are."

Films are of particular importance, especially video filming. The modern means of technology have created enormous possibilities of outreach for the multinational corporations and the diffusion of what we are now calling a global culture. We all know that the bulk of production in films and above all in video goes into "trash," replete with sexism, violence, racism, and class prejudice. On airplane flights I have seen video films about Arabs that people, including myself, have protested to no avail. To protest too much on a plane can be interpreted as a breach of security.

However, at the same time, the new media technology has also opened up wide vistas to small groups and even individuals. In countries of the South, even the production of feature-length films is relatively inexpensive. In Egypt, the maximum today would reach about U.S.$300,000. My son directed a short feature film called *Bride of the Nile* for a production cost of U.S.$12,000. It lasts twenty minutes and won six prizes at international film festivals in Spain, France, England, Canada, and elsewhere, and this was only his second directing experience. The possibilities opened up in the cultural field by film, and above all by video, are enormous. People in the institutions, academia, media, and so on just have to think about it, find a little money— and little it really is—and depend on their own and other people's good will. North-South cooperation and groups can do wonderful work and achieve results in the production of video and cinema films. Problems exist. But perhaps the main problem is that we have not been oriented to think in that way, to build up the knowledge and expertise of people everywhere and depend on it instead of appropriating it for the benefit of a system to which we belong even though we might not always agree with it.

Here in the States, there are groups of young people working like that and broadcasting their work on public TV. The difficulties are great, but they have started. The countries of the South are fertile ground for this kind of work and at very low cost.

The practice of interculturalism has not yet separated itself from the neo-colonial obsession with materials and techniques from the so-called third world, which draw on our traditional disciplines rather than on the progress that many people in the South have made despite tremendous obstacles. Instead of allowing these people to represent themselves, Peter Brook, for example, appropriates the *Mahabarata* to make an essentialized "poetical history of mankind" and play into the hands of global culturalism, which now needs to accommodate a distorted multiculturalism and to carry postmodernism as far along the road as it can go. Multiculturalism and other postmodern trends often appropriate the culture of the "others" instead of allowing them to speak for themselves. It is like the multiparty system imposed on countries of the South by the World Bank as a condition for "aid" and which has become a parody of democracy, a chess game, a speaking façade that hides the fact that behind it are the global powers pulling the strings with the help of their friends.

Multiculturalism, unless contextualized, politicized, practicalized, and aimed really at creating a humanized and diversified global culture, cannot resist the hegemony of global culture tailored to the global market of Bill Gates, the Sultan of Brunei, and other members of the global clan. It can only be another facet of postmodernism. And postmodernism provides a super-market culture geared to everything and nothing in particular except maintaining the global economy, because it refuses to contextualize itself, refuses common goals for humanity, refuses an emancipatory movement built on solidarity between people, deconstructs without constructing, fragments. It finds allies in multiculturalism, interculturalism, and subaltern culturalism because they often have a Foucauldian bent that denies a common, universal, human thread on which resistance can be built even if it helps us to break down into more detail, to widen our sights, to take more and more in. It is, as Jameson has written, the culture bred by late capitalism, by the global era in which we live.

In this immensely rich and controversial issue linked to multiculturalism and interculturalism, which ostensibly resist the global culture but which, to my mind, can play and have played an intellectual role in consolidating it, arises the issue of emigration.

In the era in which we live, emigration and emigrants exist almost everywhere. However, most emigrants have moved from the South to the North, usually in search of better opportunities. Some of them are working in academia, in culture, in science, or in the media, and quite a number have become prominent or even eminent contributors to the fields in which they work.

It is natural that those emigrants who are involved in literature, the arts, the humanities, in writing and culture should become attracted to the areas of multicultural and intercultural thought. They represent more than one culture, or at least a dual culture. They reflect this dual culture and are better equipped to navigate between the two cultures absorbed by them. The mutual fertilization by two cultures can be an asset, give insights into the two poles of North and South, permit comparison. They have at their disposal all the accumulated knowledge provided by technology and its means, the discipline, the training, the frame of mind that motivate research and understanding. They are therefore well equipped to deal with multicultural thought and studies.

I have benefited a lot from some of them, although sometimes I have sweated hard to understand parts of what they write and at certain times have even failed to grasp what was being said. One of the problems of academic language is that it is a language of its own, which outside people cannot understand. It is the problem of cultural work divorced from life. Nevertheless, some of the writings published in the area of multicultural studies have been probing and deep.

This is very important. Studies of this kind can help to bridge the gap between people in the South and people in the North. They can bring the cultures of the South closer to the North, combat the ill effects of orientalist tendencies and their offspring. They can bring the cultures of the North to the attention and understanding of the South in a different way. They can do a lot to dispel the misconceptions, the ugly images that people in the North and the South have of one another, and contribute to build up solidarity and resistance to the developments engineered by power groups. They can help in setting up intercultural studies based on multicultural groups with equal rights.

However, if the studies undertaken by them do not avoid the pitfalls common in this kind of work, émigré scholars and intellectuals may become intermediaries who help the North to appropriate the culture of the South, instead of letting the "others" in the South speak for themselves.

The problem with representation is that it is very difficult to represent even oneself, let alone others. Technology and knowledge can help. But there remains the everyday struggle, the failures, the successes, the suffering, the misery, the joy, the involvement, the passion. And there has been a tendency by émigrés in the field of cultural and political thought sometimes to think and declare that they can represent people in the South better than the people themselves can do it, because of the sophistication, the means, the knowledge at their disposal. When I was a young militant in the Left I thought I could express the ideas and thoughts and needs of peasants and working-class people better than they could themselves. After all, I could read and write, and very often they could not. I read foreign books in English and French, Marx and Engels, Bertrand Russell, Foucault, and Jung, and all that. I knew the history of Egypt, of the Arab countries, had read about India and China and the British Empire. And I was a medical doctor, disciplined to think and diagnose. Sometimes these people just shouted out something, or sat there silent, their eyes straying to this and that.

Then, as the years went by, I discovered that what we thought we knew was very different from reality, from the facts. Because we had forgotten something very important: practice, life. As the Egyptian proverb says, "He who has his hand in the fire is not like he who has his hand in water."

I am not trying to defend ignorance, my own or anyone else's. I am just saying that ignorance is of different kinds. In the fields of culture and politics, the social sciences, and the humanities, it is very difficult to represent, to speak for the other. And if people involved in multicultural and intercultural studies do that, they will be serving the ends of global power and global culture.

With things as they are, it is very difficult to disengage from the logic of the system that holds sway in cultural studies. Cultural studies cannot be separated from the struggle of people everywhere for justice, freedom, and peace. All those who are troubled by the consequences of a global culture that distorts and destroys the potentialities of human beings are partners in this struggle.

Leslie Sklair

Social Movements and Global Capitalism

This paper begins with some ground-clearing work, namely, a brief and selective review of recent contributions to the literatures on "social movements" and "globalization." The central argument is that, although capitalism is increasingly organized on a global basis, effective opposition to capitalist practices tends to be manifest locally.

The traditional response of the labor movement to global capitalism has been to try to forge links among workers' organizations internationally. As is being argued increasingly by those of all anticapitalist persuasions, this strategy, despite some notable successes, has generally failed. Most of the debate has focused on whether this is due to some sea change in workers' consciousness or is more of an organizational question. The argument here is that a key issue is the globalization of capitalism in the economic, political, and culture-ideology spheres and that important theoretical and substantive questions for social movements research are the extent to which the characteristic institutional expressions of this globalization—transnational corporations, transnational capitalist classes, and the culture-ideology of consumerism—can be resisted locally. The *local* is defined in terms of subglobal communities that can be meaningfully represented through collective action. The *global* and the *local,* in this context, are not exclusively geographical terms but have organizational and representational dimensions.

Theory and Research on Social Movements

Social movements, under a variety of labels, have always been of interest to sociologists. The literature, unsurprisingly, is enormous, and it is significant that "social movements research," which used to be rather marginal, is now being drawn into the center of social theory, particularly under the rubric of New Social Movements (NSM). For example, two recent books by Eder and Ray, in rather different ways, convincingly argue this position in terms of a "new politics of class" and "critical theory," respectively.[1] The argument that, even when they are not apparently interested in seizing state power, NSM can still be as sociologically interesting as, say, revolutionary movements, has in some ways liberated the study of them.

The idea of NSM has proved extremely useful both methodologically and ideologically. Methodologically, it points to the unmistakable novelty of the practices (for example, the use of credit card donations and the media for mobilization) and the appeal of some of the most prominent social movements of recent decades, notably the women's and environmental movements. Ideologically, NSM theory and research also provide ammunition for those who proclaim that the working class as a revolutionary force organized through the labor (and/or trade union) movement is finally dead. From the publication of Herbert Marcuse's *One-Dimensional Man* in 1964 to the project of Touraine,[2] and before and after, this thesis has had many adherents. Whether from Marcuse's impressionistic eloquence or from Touraine's empirical research-based analysis, the central idea is the same: the working class cannot hope to defeat national or global capitalism and, even more seriously, NSM "weaken working class consciousness and erode its self-confidence, rather than providing new sources of energy for it."[3]

Three recent books, far removed geographically, rather different in substance, but not so far removed theoretically, take up these issues fruitfully. Each in its own way illuminates the issue of the relationship of the NSM and the labor movement in very concrete terms and connects this with the opposition between what can be identified as "organization" models and "disruption" models of social movements and resistances to capitalism.

Gail Omvedt's *Reinventing Revolution: New Social Movements and the So-*

cialist Tradition in India is a major study that points out that the notable Indian social movements since the 1970s have not been traditional Marxist class ones, but movements of women, low castes, peasants, farmers, tribals, ethnics. None of them, Omvedt argues, has effected much change, but they have tended to be movements of groups either ignored or exploited by traditional Marxism or exploited in new ways (for example, environmentally).[4] So, although Marxism has traditionally been a historical materialism of the proletariat, what is needed, she argues, is a historical materialism of all oppressed groups and their varying forms of oppression. With an impressive degree of clarity, Omvedt attempts this for the anticaste, women's, farmers', and environmental movements in India and argues that NSM are best defined as movements that redefine spheres of exploitation (especially economic exploitation) that are not properly addressed by traditional Marxism, thus the choice of the four NSM at the center of her book. Conflicts between toilers and those who directly employ them play a relatively small role in Indian NSM, and, although wage struggles are not central, more important are encroachments on state or landlord lands and peasant struggles for community control, job reservation for anticaste groups, women's struggles against male property rights, and higher prices for farmers. These struggles and the disruptions they produce are directed as much against state agencies as against capitalists. The inescapable conclusion of this analysis is that Marxism definitely needs to be rethought and the idea of revolution needs to be reinvented. Central to this rethinking and reinvention is that NSM are not necessarily aiming to seize state power but use many tactics to achieve many shorter-term ends. Indeed, this argument can be expanded to suggest that the actual revolutionary consequences of such movements can far exceed the rhetorical revolutionary utterances of most movements dedicated to seizing state power.

Verity Burgmann's *Power and Protest: Movements for Change in Australian Society* is a study of five key NSM in Australia: the black (Aborigine), women's, lesbian and gay, peace, and green movements.[5] Despite the large differences (only two of the movements overlap), there are some surprising parallels with Omvedt's book. Burgmann argues that NSM tend to represent the better-off among the disadvantaged, and that NSM frequently lose control of the ways their demands are conceded. As all these movements take place in capitalist societies, albeit of different types, class relations mediate what is possible. "It is for this reason that the support of the labour movement, with its ability seriously to contest the power relations based on class, offers the best potential means for more substantial gains to be achieved by the movements for change."[6] But the labor movement has to change too, and modified for the Indian case, this is also Omvedt's conclusion. The problem is how to forge links of solidarity among people as workers and as more or less oppressed in other social spheres. Research such as that reported in Hayter and Harvey on the relationships between workers at Cowley in Oxford and local community groups shows exactly how difficult this can be.[7]

The title of Brecher and Costello's contribution to this debate, *Building Bridges: The Emerging Grassroots Coalition of Labor and Community,* at least names the question.[8] The new social alliance, they argue, is unheralded nationally in the United States because it is being built at the grass roots, where the mass media have little interest. "These coalitions have generally been created without the dominance of a single unifying organization, program, or leader. Rather they have been constructed by active efforts of mutual outreach—by 'bridge-building.'"[9] Most surprising is the participation of unionists, evidence of some breakdown in the traditional separation of labor from social movements. The array of projects and movements described in this collection is certainly impressive, though it is difficult to work through the very disparate causes that lie behind these social movements in order to see the forest for the trees.

The evidence arrayed in these books, and others like them, suggest that NSM theory needs to rethink the dichotomy between *labor movement* and *new social movement.* This is necessary because insufficient attention has been paid to two factors, namely, the organizational question and the changing nature of global capitalism, the globalization question. For the first of these, Piven and Cloward propose an uncompromising proposition.[10] Fundamentally, they argue that the success of a movement depends not on its organizational prowess but on its ability to disrupt, so collective defiance is the key to social movements. The reason why movements fail is to be found in the capacity of the authorities to divert their disruptive force into normal politics, usually with the collaboration of the movement organizers.[11] This is, of course, not an entirely novel thesis. At least since Michels's *Political Parties* (first published in 1911), the idea that the workers' leaders would be likely to subordinate revolutionary goals to bureaucratic means has been a commonplace. Acknowledging the difficulty of retaining revolutionary goals within a capitalist or a Stalinist communist society while actually improving the lot of those whose interests the movement is intended to serve might soften some of the moral outrage felt about such leaders, but it does little to solve the problem of the successes and failures of social movements. Burgmann puts this in an oblique but significant way: "The relative purity and incorruptibility of the leaders of new social movements attests not to their moral superiority but to their relative powerlessness. . . . You cannot sell out if you have nothing to sell. . . . The corruptibility of the labour movement is evidence of its real political power, for good or evil."[12] And, when NSM are seen to have power, they too can sell out.

Although their approach has been criticized on a variety of grounds (for example, by Castells),[13] Piven and Cloward have elaborated a theoretically coherent and empirically researchable set of theses on this very problem. So we can see how the militants of the workers' movements, the civil rights movement, and the National (and local) Welfare Rights Organization (whom Piven and Cloward so evocatively document) each in their own ways tried, succeeded, or failed to establish different connections in their struggles against "the system." Touraine, in his influential studies of the workers' movement, and Piven and Cloward make one essentially similar point, which might be seen as a defining moment for the problem of social movements in its totality. Piven and Cloward write: "*people cannot defy institutions to which they have no access, and to which they make no contribution*";[14] Touraine and his colleagues write: "As well as finding increasing difficulty in self-definition, the working class actor is also finding it increasingly hard to identify his [*sic*] adversary."[15] On the surface, these *appear* to be opposing rather than similar points: Piven and Cloward arguing that people cannot defy institutions that exclude them, Touraine arguing that workers no longer know who to oppose. But they are, in reality, mirror images of the same dilemma, which can be identified as the local and the global. The dilemma is that the only chance that people in social movements have to succeed is by disrupting the local agencies they come into direct contact with in their daily lives rather than the more global institutions whose interests these agencies are serving directly or, more often, indirectly, while workers are often confused about who (which representation of capital) to oppose when their interests (conditions of labor, livelihoods) are threatened. Increasingly, as capitalism globalizes, subordinate groups find difficulty in identifying their adversaries.[16]

Now neither Touraine nor Piven and Cloward say anything like this; neither mentions local-global issues. The implication in their works is that labor and other types of social movements are national, not global.[17] There have been few, if any, examples of successful movements against the global capitalist system, which is not very surprising. As Tilly and others have argued, most social movements have developed in relation to the nation-state. If we are, indeed, entering a phase of global capitalism, we might expect this to change. The next section outlines one conception of globalization with a view to clarifying how global capitalism works, and to begin to construct the argument that, although contemporary capitalism is organized globally, it can be resisted only locally.

Global System Theory

Globalization is a relatively new idea in sociology, though in other disciplines, such as international business studies and international relations, it has been common for some time. The central feature of the idea of globalization is that many contemporary problems cannot be adequately studied at the level of nation-states, that is, in terms of *international* relations, but need to be theorized in terms of *global* (*transnational*) processes, beyond the level of the nation-state. Globalization researchers have focused on two new phenomena that have become significant in the last few decades: (1) qualitative and quantitative changes in the transnational corporations (TNCs) through processes such as the globalization of capital and production, and (2) transformations in the technological base and subsequent global scope of the mass media. For these reasons, it is increasingly important to analyze the world economy and society *globally* as well as nationally. There are several different competing models of globalization theory and research, for example, the world-system, global culture, globalization of space-time, globo-local, and world society approaches.[18] Here I shall focus on my own contribution, global system theory.

Global system theory is based on the concept of transnational practices, practices that cross state boundaries but do not necessarily originate with state agencies or actors. Analytically, they operate in three spheres: the economic, the political, and the cultural-ideological. The whole is what I mean by "the global system." The global system, at the end of the twentieth century, is not synonymous with global capitalism, but the dominant forces of global capitalism are the dominant forces in the global system. The building blocks of the theory are the *transnational corporation,* the characteristic institutional form of economic transnational practices, a still-evolving *trans-national capitalist class* in the political sphere, and, in the culture-ideology sphere, the *culture-ideology of consumerism*.[19]

In the economic sphere, the global capitalist system offers a limited place to the wage-earning masses in most countries. The workers, the direct producers of goods and services, have occupational choices that are generally free within the range offered by the class structures in national capitalisms. The inclusion of the subordinate classes in the political sphere is very partial. To put it bluntly, the global capitalist system has very little need of the subordinate classes in this sphere. In parliamentary democracies the parties must be able to mobilize the masses to vote every so often, but in most countries voting is not compulsory and mass political participation is usually discouraged. In nondemocratic capitalist polities even these minimal conditions are absent.

The culture-ideology sphere is, however, entirely different. Here, the aim of global capitalists is total inclusion of all classes, and especially the subordinate classes insofar as the bourgeoisie can be considered already included. The cultural-ideological project of global capitalism is to persuade people to consume above their "biological needs" in order to perpetuate the accumulation of capital for private profit; in other words, to ensure that the global capitalist system goes on forever. The culture-ideology of consumerism proclaims, literally, that the meaning of life is to be found in the things that we possess. To consume, therefore, is to be fully alive, and to remain fully alive we must continuously consume. The notions of men and women as economic or political beings are discarded by global capitalism—quite logically, as the system does not even pretend to satisfy everyone in the economic or political spheres. People are primarily consumers. The point of economic activity for "ordinary members" of the global capitalist system is to provide the resources for consumption, and the point of political activity is to ensure that the conditions for consuming are maintained.

Pro-capitalist global system movements are, therefore, those that support the transnational corporations, serve the interests of the transnational capitalist class, and promote the culture-ideology of consumerism.[20] Anticapitalist global system movements, consequently, are those that challenge the TNCs in the economic sphere, oppose the transnational capitalist class and its local affiliates in the political sphere, and promote cultures and ideologies antagonistic to capitalist consumerism. In the next section, the argument is advanced that movements working in all three spheres for the global capitalist system are very successful both at the global and the local levels, although movements working against global capitalism have been singularly unsuccessful globally, though their prospects of challenging global capitalism locally and making this count globally, globalizing disruptions, seem more realistic.[21]

Disrupting the TNCs

The characteristic institutional focus of transnational economic practices is the transnational corporation. Therefore, challenging global capitalism in the economic sphere involves disrupting the TNCs' capacity to accumulate profits at the expense of their workforces, their consumers, and the communities that are affected by their activities. These are the truly global contexts of the TNCs, the places where their raw materials come from, where these raw materials are processed, the places through which they are transported, where the components are made and assembled, and where the final consumer goods are manufactured, sold, used, and eventually disposed of. As is well known, an important part of economic globalization today is the increasing dispersal of the manufacturing process into many discrete phases carried out in many different places.[22] Being no longer so dependent on the production of one factory and one workforce gives capital a distinct advantage, particularly against the strike weapon, which once gave tremendous negative power to the working class. Global production chains can be disrupted by strategically planned stoppages, but this generally acts more as an irritation than as a real weapon of labor against capital. By the nature of the case, the international division of labor builds flexibility into the system so that not only can capital migrate anywhere in the world to find the cheapest source of labor but also few workforces can any longer decisively "hold capital to ransom" by withdrawing their labor. At the level of the production process, as many have argued, globalizing capital has all but defeated labor. In this respect, at least, the global organization of the TNCs will invariably be too powerful for the local organization of labor.

But what of the global organization of labor? The traditional response of the labor movement to global capitalist hegemony has been to try to forge international links among workers in different countries. This strategy, despite some notable successes, has generally failed, and it is not difficult to understand why it has failed.[23] Where the TNCs have been disrupted to the extent that their hegemony has been weakened and even where, in some cases, they have been forced to change their ways and compensate those who have grievances against them, it has usually been due to local campaigns of disruption and counterinformation against TNC malpractices that have attracted worldwide publicity. There are sufficient cases (the Distillers' Company thalidomide tragedy, Union Carbide's Bhopal disaster, various oil companies' environmental catastrophes, ongoing campaigns against Nestlé's infant formula, logging companies, etc.) to suggest that such single-issue social movements do have genuine disruptive effects in curbing the worst excesses of profiteering TNCs. Omvedt argues this starkly: "Bhopal was the major disaster that revealed for the whole world the murderous nature of the multinational companies and of the capitalist 'development' that was the major ideological base of postindependence third world regimes."[24] The knowledge that workers, citizens, churches, and other concerned groups all around the world are monitoring their activities clearly encourages some TNCs to act more responsibly than they otherwise might be doing. The fact that it takes constant monitoring and public exposure of wrongdoing to force some corporations to act responsibly helps transform local disruptions of TNC activities into global challenges to capitalist hegemony.[25]

Disrupting the Transnational Capitalist Class

The transnational capitalist class (TCC) is transnational in the double sense that its members have global rather than or in addition to local perspectives, and it typically contains people from many countries who operate internationally as a normal part of their working lives. The TCC can be conceptualized in terms of the following four fractions:

1. TNC executives and their local affiliates
2. Globalizing state bureaucrats
3. Globalizing politicians and professionals
4. Consumerist elites (merchants, media)

This class sees its mission as organizing the conditions under which its interests and the interests of the system can be furthered in the global and local contexts. The concept of the TCC implies that there is one central *transnational* capitalist class that makes systemwide decisions, and that it connects with the TCC in each locality, region, and country. Although the four fractions are distinguishable analytic categories with different functions for the global capitalist system, the people in them often move from one category to another (sometimes described as the "revolving door" between government and business).

Each of the four fractions of the TCC tends to be represented, to a greater or lesser extent, in movements and campaigns on behalf of the interests of the global capitalist system. TNC executives and their affiliates typically organize themselves into local, national, international, and global trade and industry associations all over the world. Chambers of Commerce, Lions, Kiwanis, and similar organizations are also prime sites for the study of how TNC executives and their local affiliates work "in the community" on behalf of the capitalist global project. The political activities of "civil servants" provide ample evidence of the role of *globalizing state bureaucrats* in pro-capitalist movements all around the world, notably in many countries officially hostile to global capitalism in previous decades. This is not to say that all bureaucrats in all governments are entirely and wholeheartedly in favor of the global capitalist project—far from it. Indeed, this conception of the global system theorizes the transition from a capitalism that is circumscribed by national interests to one in which globalizing bureaucrats and politicians in national governments increasingly begin to see their interests best served by a more open adherence to the practices of global capitalism and in more open alliance with the TNCs. Substantial lobbying efforts by governments on behalf of regional trade agreements, for example, are particularly important markers of this transition.

The role of globalizing *politicians and professionals* is also illustrated by the case of regional trade agreements. Globalizing politicians either simply line up behind their governments in the voting lobbies or, sometimes, take more active parts in promoting such initiatives. The PR people and professional lobbyists, business and trade consultants of all shapes and sizes, legal personnel, and others flock to the global capitalist banner. It can be argued that such people will sing any tune they are paid to sing, and this is, largely, true. But it cannot be denied that the big money tends to be largely behind one tune. That is why it is such an important test case for the argument about the TCC. On many issues, big (transnational) business sings many tunes, but on "free trade" the fundamental interests of global capitalism are clear and relatively single-minded. To this extent, the TCC all over the world is united.

Consumerist elites (merchants and media) are frequently active in social movements for global capitalism. Most merchants and media, unsurprisingly, back global capitalism with more or less enthusiasm. The major retailing chains naturally support every move that looks likely to increase mass markets anywhere in the world. The mass media, although giving some space and time to oppositional arguments, generally present the viewpoints of the TCC in prime-time, general news presentations, features, and editorial matter. The mass media extend and deepen the "global reach" of the TCC.[26]

Apart from communist and revolutionary socialist parties and movements dedicated to the seizure of state power, there is a long and varied history of social movements against the capitalist class. Representatives of big business have rarely been popular, even among those who work for them. Piott, in his informative study of popular resistance to the rise of Big Business in the U.S. Midwest in the decades around the turn of the twentieth century, usefully labels it "the anti-monopoly persuasion."[27] For the antimonopolists of the late nineteenth century, banks, land, and railroad trusts represented a new antidemocratic America, symbolizing outside interests threatening local communities. In his analysis of the St. Louis streetcar strike of 1900, Piott comments: "The strike developed a cross-class sense of community consciousness. . . . People in roles as consumers, housewives, workers, taxpayers, citizens, and merchants united against the streetcar monopoly."[28] Similar antimonopoly movements against the beef trusts and Standard Oil led to a nationwide movement against the "robber barons."[29] The "antimonopoly persuasion" still exists, but with the decisive difference that it now has to combat a genuinely global adversary whose capacities, mobility, and flexibility are unprecedented in human history.[30]

Disrupting Consumerism

It is now almost commonplace to label contemporary society, East or West, North or South, rich or poor, "consumerist." Nothing and no one seems immune from commodification, commercialization, being bought and sold.[31] Ordinary so-called countercultures are regularly incorporated into the consumer culture and pose little threat. Indeed, by offering both real and illusory variety and choice, they are a source of great strength to the global capitalist system and of personal enrichment for those able to enjoy the abundance of cultural forms undeniably available. The celebrations of the twentieth anniversary of the student revolts of the 1960s became media events and were relentlessly commercially exploited, with the willing and presumably lucrative participation of many of those who had then been (and still are) dedicated to the overthrow of the capitalist system. Consumerist appropriations of the bicentennial of the French and American Revolutions are other interesting examples. We shall have to wait for the year 2017 to see what the culture-ideology of consumerism makes of the Bolshevik Revolution!

The only countercultures that do present threats to global capitalist consumerism at present, now that Stalinist communism is thoroughly discredited and has lost most of its institutional supports, are religious (particularly Islamic) fundamentalism and environmental movements.[32] Religious fundamentalism, with a few isolated exceptions, does not challenge consumerism on a global scale. Environmental movements, in some forms, could certainly challenge the culture-ideology of consumerism, but evidence from the Earth Summit in Rio in 1992 suggests that at least some of its main representatives appear to be in the process of being incorporated, and those that refuse incorporation are being marginalized. The "greening of the corporation," in both its genuine and its false manifestations, is well under way, but it is the corporations, not the "Greens," who are firmly in control of the process.[33]

The logic of this argument is clearly underconsumptionist. Capitalists in the twentieth century have the capacity to produce consumer goods in historically unprecedented quantities and varieties, but capitalist relations of production tend to inhibit the level of consumption of these goods by the masses on a global scale. The cycles of boom and slump are periods of high consumer spending followed by overproduction of goods, which causes business failures, unemployment, a drop in consumer spending, and, thus, underconsumption. Not wishing to become embroiled in the technicalities of this debate, I shall simply note that the point of the concept of the "culture-ideology of consumerism" is precisely that, under capitalism, the masses cannot be relied upon to keep buying, obviously when they have neither spare cash nor access to credit, and less obviously when they do have spare cash and access to credit. The creation of a culture-ideology of consumerism, therefore, is bound up with the self-imposed necessity that capitalism must be ever-expanding on a global scale. This expansion crucially depends on selling more and more goods and services to people whose "basic needs" (a somewhat ideological term) have already been comfortably met as well as to those whose "basic needs" are unmet.[34]

This suggests that the culture-ideology of consumerism may serve different functions for different social groups and even for different societies. Clearly, the culture-ideology of consumerism is superfluous to explain why people who are hungry or cold eat or clothe themselves, whereas it does help to explain snacking or "grazing" on food and drinks that are demonstrably unhealthy and why people go into debt to buy many sets of clothes, expensive cars, and so on. Even more challenging is the enigma of why poor people, in poor and rich countries, apparently defy economic rationality by purchasing relatively expensive global brands in order to forge some sense of identity with what we can only call, in a rather crude sense, "symbols of modernity" (or even "symbols of postmodernity").

The implications of the spread of the culture-ideology of consumerism and the economic and political institutions on which it is built, from its heart-lands in the first world and the other places where tiny privileged minorities have adopted it, to the rest of the world, is a social change of truly global significance. To understand fully what has been happening in the "neo-liberalizing" West, let alone Eastern Europe and China in recent years, my contention is that it is important to theorize about the culture-ideology of consumerism, its role in confusing the issue of the satisfaction of basic needs, and the difficulty of mobilizing against global capitalism on the basis of anticonsumerist ideology.[35] Any attack on capitalist consumerism is an attack to the very center of global capitalism. In the context of environmental movements, some nervous members of transnational capitalist classes around the world are quite correct when they label consumer movement activists (particularly those propagating green ideology) "subversive."[36]

One example of an anticonsumerist social movement, small in scale but large in potential significance, is the Seikatsu Club in Japan, based on the idea of consumer self-sufficiency through cooperatives.[37] This is a consumers' cooperative that started out in a small way in 1965 by organizing collective purchases of milk to offset price increases imposed by the few companies that dominated the market. As of March 1992, the Club had over 200,000 members in thousands of small local units making purchases of over 66 billion yen (about U.S.$700 million) annually, a political network with representatives on local city councils, twenty-seven workers collectives (mostly small food businesses), investments in suppliers' enterprises, and a Social Movement Research Center. One telling statistic is that, whereas the volume of waste per day in the average Tokyo household is 560 grams, in Seikatsu households it is only 210 grams. Every three years an intensive review of all purchases is carried out to distinguish between real needs and what the Club calls pseudo-needs that are foisted on consumers by those interested only in profits. Therefore, "co-operative purchase is a way to deny the capitalistic system of consumption."[38] Although possibly the best organized and the most ideologically coherent of such movements, there are many others all over the world.

Some may consider this a rather "sublime" example of a social movement against capitalist consumerism, so let me briefly allude to the "ridiculous," namely, reclaiming the shopping mall as public space! In his absorbing study of the "Magic of the Mall," Goss points out that shopping is the second most important leisure-time activity in the United States (after watching TV, and much of TV promotes shopping anyway): "Shopping has become the dominant mode of contemporary public life."[39] Although this is true at present only for parts of the first world and perhaps some privileged elites elsewhere, the rest of world appears to be following rapidly. The study of shopping malls, therefore, is important.

The idea of the mall signals a third, public, space after home and work/school in which to see and be seen. Malls are not just places to buy and sell but are increasingly taking on other functions (for example, educational, cultural, child care) but very much oriented to the middle classes. They aim to provide safe, secure environments for "normal" consumers, but are reluctant to provide genuine public services like drinking fountains, public toilets, telephones, and so on where deviants or nonshoppers can congregate. Goss reports that the average length of time spent in shopping center trips in the United States has increased from 20 minutes in 1960 to nearly three hours in the 1990s, no doubt facilitated by the omnipresent grazing opportunities in the fast-food outlets. Art and museums are now being brought into the mall directly: the first U.S. National Endowment for the Arts grant to a private corporation went for art projects in malls.

Having established the centrality of the mall in the United States and, by implication, the future of the world, Goss poses the interesting question: How can the mall be reclaimed for the people? He suggests that citizens could:

1. Expose commodity fetishism, and force advertisers and retailers to become more honest

2. Resist the economic and spatial logic of malls by helping community groups struggle against redevelopment

3. Open up the mall as a genuine public space
4. Organize tactical occupations of spaces
5. Subvert the systems of signification.

Goss is clearly ambivalent about consumerism and about malls, and he is not alone. The merit of his approach is that it hints of the possibility of an opposition to capitalist consumerism that does not entail hair shirts and a life totally bereft of all the consumer goods that make life "better" for ordinary people today all over the world. Those who are guilty about their excessive consumerism are more likely to be so because of environmental reasons than because they believe that their consumption patterns somehow subvert or destroy meaning in their lives. Victory in the struggle for a decent standard of living (that changes over time) clearly does not have a simple connection to resistance to capitalist consumerism.

Conclusions

The burden of my argument has been that, although capitalism increasingly organizes globally, the resistances to global capitalism can be effective only where they can disrupt its smooth running (accumulation of private profits) locally and can find ways of globalizing these disruptions. No social movement appears even remotely likely to overthrow the three fundamental institutional supports of global capitalism that have been identified, namely, the TNCs, the TCC, and the culture-ideology of consumerism. Nevertheless, in each of these spheres there are resistances expressed by social movements. The TNCs, if we are to believe their own propaganda, are continually beset by opposition, boycott, legal challenge, and moral outrage from the consumers of their products and by disruptions from their workers. The TCC often finds itself opposed by vocal coalitions when it tries to impose its will in new ways. There are many ways to be ambivalent about the culture-ideology of consumerism, some of which the green movement has successfully exploited. In an informative compendium, Ekins describes the winners of the Right Livelihoods Awards from 1980 to 1990 (known to some as a sort of "alternative Nobel prize") and their social movements, some very well known (such as the Sarvodaya Shramadama movement in Sri Lanka), some much less well known (like the Six S Association/NAAM movement in Burkina Faso), all trying to escape from the domination of the global capitalist system and experiment with alternative ways of living.[40] The irony is that so many of these social movements actually rely on funding from foreign agencies to grow.

Opposing capitalism locally, from households, communities, and cities, all the way up to the level of the nation-state, has always been practically difficult but, at least, organizationally and ideologically manageable. In most capitalist societies, social movements for what has come to be known as social democracy have united those who are hostile to capitalism, those who struggle to alleviate the worst consequences of capitalism, and those who simply want to ensure that capitalism works with more social efficiency than the so-called free market allows. This has inevitably meant that anticapitalists (principally socialists) of many kinds have seen no alternative to using capitalist practices to achieve anticapitalist ends, whether locally or nationally. The implication of the foregoing argument is that the transition from social democracy to democratic socialism is one that can only be achieved through social movements that target global capitalism through its three main institutional supports: the TNCs, the TCC, and the culture-ideology of consumerism.[41] These three supports manifest themselves both globally and locally, but they can be effectively challenged only locally by those who are prepared to disrupt their antisocial practices.

The issue of democracy is central to the practice and the prospects of social movements against capitalism, local and global. The rule of law, freedom of association and expression, and freely contested elections, as minimum conditions and however imperfectly sustained, are as necessary in the long run for mass market–based global consumerist capitalism as they are for alternative social systems.[42] As markets for many types of consumer goods become saturated in the first world, TNCs have been visibly expanding their activities to the new second[43] and third worlds. This shift has contradictory effects: it gives the institutions of global capitalism previously unimagined actual and potential powers to extend and target their global reach, and at the same time it makes these institutions peculiarly vulnerable to challenge and disruptions on a global scale.

To conclude where I started off: to be effective, social movements against global capitalism will need to find new forms that do not reproduce the failures of Piven and Cloward's "poor people's movements" but rather reproduce their successes.[44] This will mean disrupting capitalism locally and finding ways of globalizing these disruptions, while seizing the opportunities to transform it that democracy provides.

Notes

This is a slightly revised version of an article originally published in *Sociology* 29, no. 3 (August 1995): 495–512.

1 Klaus Eder, *The New Politics of Class: Social Movements and Cultural Dynamics in Advanced Societies* (London, 1993); Larry J. Ray, *Rethinking Critical Theory: Emancipation in the Age of Global Social Movements* (London, 1993).

2 Alain Touraine, *The Voice and the Eye: An Analysis of Social Movements,* trans. Alan Duff (Cambridge, 1981), and Alain Touraine, et al., *The Workers' Movement,* trans. Ian Patterson (Cambridge, UK, 1987).

3 Touraine et al., *Workers' Movement,* 224. Eder, *New Politics,* also engages with these issues and proposes a solution based on the discourse of modernity and "culture" as the missing link between class and social movements. Although this type of analysis does not seem to me to solve any of the problems identified in this paper, his *New Politics of Class* is certainly an impressive piece of work.

4 Gail Omvedt, *Reinventing Revolution: New Social Movements and the Socialist Tradition in India* (Armonk, NY, 1993).

5 Verity Burgmann, *Power and Protest: Movements for Change in Australian Society* (St. Leonards, NSW, 1993).

6 Ibid., 263.

7 Teresa Hayter and David Harvey, eds., *The Factory and the City: The Story of the Cowley Automobile Workers in Oxford* (London, 1993).

8 Jeremy Brecher and Tim Costello, *Building Bridges: The Emerging Grassroots Coalition of Labor and Community* (New York, 1990).

9 Ibid., 9.

10 Frances Fox Piven and Richard A. Cloward, *Poor People's Movements: Why They Succeed, How They Fail* (New York, 1979).

11 See, in particular, the discussion of the 1968 model agreement between the Commonwealth of Pennsylvania and the Philadelphia Welfare Rights Organization, in ibid., 327ff and chap. 5 passim. There are many other examples of this in the three books just mentioned. This crosscuts the distinction between actor approaches to social movements organizations and structural approaches to social movements, elaborated by Alan Scott, *Ideology and the New Social Movements* (London, 1990).

12 Burgmann, *Power and Protest,* 264.

13 Manuel Castells, *The City and the Grassroots: A Cross-Cultural Theory of Urban Social Movements* (Berkeley, CA, 1983).

14 Piven and Coward, *Poor People's Movements,* 23; italics in the original.

15 Touraine, *The Voice,* 109.

16 Robert J. S. Ross and Kent C. Trachte, *Global Capitalism: The New Leviathan* (Albany, NY, 1990), chap. 7. Although they do not frame their argument in exactly these terms, they demonstrate this in the case of the Detroit automobile industry.

17 Marta Fuentes and Andre Gundar Frank, "Ten Theses on Social Movement," *World Development* 17 (1989): 188 make the point that NSM could be transnational, that is, nonnational, people-to-people movements. However, as I argue elsewhere in the context of transnational environmental movements ("Global Sociology and Global Environmental Change," in *Social Theory and the Global Environment,* ed. Michael Redclift and Ted Benton [London, 1994]), these tend to be quite bureaucratic organizations liable to all the problems globally that Piven and Cloward identify nationally. Similar arguments have been made over the attempts to globalize the international labor and women's movements. Ray's attempt (*Rethinking*) to apply the insights of critical theory to global social movements is also of interest here.

18 The main sources for these approaches (Wallerstein, Giddens, Harvey, etc.) are well summarized and discussed in Tony McGrew, "A Global Society," in *Modernity and Its Futures* (Cambridge, UK, 1992). For my own rather different attempt to survey the globalization literature, see Leslie Sklair, "Globalization: New Approaches to Social Change," in *Contemporary Sociology,* ed. Steve Taylor (London, 1998).

19 For a fuller elaboration of this framework, see in general Leslie Sklair, *Sociology of the Global System* (London, 1995); on the global environmental system and the transnational capitalist class, see Sklair, "Global Sociology" and my contribution to Leslie Sklair, ed., *Capitalism and Development* (London, 1994). Although the argument that national capitals are becoming increasingly "disorganized" certainly has some merit, my contention is that, globally, capitalism does have distinctive systemic features.

20 As Ross and Trachte point out in their important contribution to the literature on global capitalism, "one does not require a pact with a party with which one has no potential conflict of interest" (*Global Capitalism,* 275 n. 10).

21 There are very few direct attempts to study social movements in genuinely global, as opposed to international, perspective. One of these, a collection edited by Burke, starts off promisingly in the introductory chapter by Burke and Walter Goldfrank: "One of the aims of the present volume is to demonstrate . . . the utility of incorporating a global dimension into the study of social movements" (Edmund Burke III, ed., *Global Crises and Social Movements: Artisans, Peasants, Populists, and the World Economy* [Boulder, CO, 1988], 1). However, the individual chapters, excellent as some of them are, rarely see the necessity for distinguishing between the "global" and the "international," central to a global analysis. Another problem is that most of the chapters are concerned with cases before the 1960s, the time when a new concept and practice of globalization begins to

emerge (see Ross and Trachte, *Global Capitalism*, and Sklair, *Sociology of the Global System*).

22 For examples, see the chapters in part 2 of Sklair, *Capitalism and Development.*

23 Robin Cohen, *The New Helots: Migrants in the International Division of Labor* (Aldershot, UK, 1987). "The Coca Cola case in Guatemala [the dismissal and intimidation of trade unionists in a bottling plant] is one of the few cases where unions have actually disrupted production or distribution out of solidarity with workers in another country" (personal communication, Paul Garver, IUF, Geneva, March 1994).

24 Omvedt, *Reinventing Revolution,* 149.

25 For details and references on the Nestlé case, see Sklair, *Sociology of the Global System,* chap. 5. There are many good sources for such campaigns and the social movements they give rise to, for example, the magazines *Multinational Monitor* (Washington, DC) and *The Ethical Consumer* (Manchester, UK).

26 The allusion here is, of course, to Richard B. Barnet and Ronald M. Muller's influential book (New York, 1974) under this title which, though dated, is still one of the most powerful indictments of the largely unfettered power of the transnational corporations. It is, however, important to point out that global reach does not imply that everyone who is reached (consumers, audiences, etc.) necessarily accepts the message, or that the message itself is necessarily uniform for all those who receive it. This is a central issue in media studies that needs incorporating into globalization research.

27 Steven L. Piott, *The Anti-Monopoly Persuasion: Popular Resistance to the Rise of Big Business in the Midwest* (Westport, CT, 1985).

28 Ibid., 70.

29 Those interested in the political influence of sociologists might care to look at Piott's discussion of the first National Attorneys General Conference in 1907, which discussed the shifting emphasis from fining to jailing trust magnates, under the influence of E. A. Ross's *Sin and Society: An Analysis of Latter-day Iniquity* (Boston, 1907).

30 In a most informative book about antibusiness pressure groups in Australia, Bob Browning turns this argument on its head and claims that it is the Left that is organized in a global "network" (*The Network: A Guide to Anti-Business Pressure Groups* [Victoria, Australia, 1990]). This belief, of course, is not confined to Australia. See, for example, the discussion of business propaganda in North America, where it is argued that since the 1970s, U.S. business has been mobilized "to reverse a dramatic decline in public confidence in big business which is blamed on the media" (Peter Dreier, "Capitalists *vs.* the Media: An Analysis of an Ideological Mobilization among Business Leaders," *Media, Culture and Society* 4 [1982]: 111). I have developed this argument in Leslie Sklair, "Social Movements of Global Capitalism: The Transnational Capitalist Class in Action," *Review of International Political Economy* 4 (1997): 514–538.

31 Anyone who has the slightest doubt about this proposition is invited to consult

Alan Durning's lively, instructive, and critical account of the extent of capitalist consumerism, *How Much Is Enough* (London, 1992). See also Alan Warde, ed., "The Sociology of Consumption," *Sociology* 24 (1990). For an interesting comment on "The Consumption of the Rich" in India, see Omvedt, *Reinventing Revolution,* 141–144.

32 Ray, *Rethinking,* chaps. 6 and 7; Burgmann, *Power and Protest;* Eder, *New Politics;* Omvedt, *Reinventing Revolution.*

33 Sklair, "Global Society and Global Environmental Change."

34 The argument that the workers in the United States (and to some extent in other countries) trade extra leisure time for more money to sustain even higher levels of consumption is very strong. See Benjamin Kline Hunnicutt, *Work without End: Abandoning Shorter Hours for the Right Work* (Philadelphia, 1988), and Juliet B. Schor, *The Overworked American: The Unexpected Decline of Leisure* (New York, 1991), for somewhat different interpretations of this fundamental thesis.

35 The often strained relations between the green and the labor movements illustrate this problem well. An interesting, though short-lived Australian case is the "green-ban campaign," when the New South Wales Builders Labourers' Federation reduced urban blight and overdevelopment between 1970 and 1974 (Burgmann, *Power and Protest,* 192–195). Eder, *New Politics,* argues that environmental (or nature-society) social movements are replacing the labor movement as *the* new social movement.

36 The attempts by the transnational capitalist class, through TNCs and official agencies, to incorporate the green/environmentalist movement is both a fascinating research topic and a central political issue for our time, and not just in the rich first world. See Omvedt, *Reinventing Revolution,* and Sklair, *Sociology of the Global System.* The contrast in the descriptions of the Australian Conservation Foundation in Browning, *Network* (pt. 5), as a dangerous leftist organization, and Burgmann, *Power and Protest* (205–207), as respectable and tax-deductible, is both instructive and ironic.

37 See Seikatsu Club Consumers' Co-operative, *Co-operative Action Based on "Han"* (Tokyo, 1992). I am grateful to Shuei Hiratsuka of Seikatsu Club and to the IOCU office in Penang for valuable materials on these initiatives. See also the discussion in Peter Ekins, *A New World Order: Grassroots Movements for Global Change* (London, 1992), 131–134.

38 Seikatsu, *Co-operative,* 21. Paradoxically, the Seikatsu Club was inspired by the Rochdale pioneers in England, the forerunners of the cooperative movement, which has become highly consumerist in its own way. For example, its associated Cooperative Bank issues one affiliated credit card that donates a percentage of all purchases to the British Labour Party and others that donate to chosen local and global charities.

39 Jon Goss, "The 'Magic of the Mall': An Analysis of Form, Function, and Meaning in the Contemporary Retail Built Environment," *Annals of the Association of American Geographers* 83 (1993): 18–47.

40 Ekins, *New World Order;* Ponna Wignaraja, ed., *New Social Movements in the South: Empowering the People* (London, 1993).

41 Sklair, *Sociology of the Global System,* chap. 9.

42 I say, "in the long run." In the short term, as the Chinese example suggests, a self-styled communist regime can ignore demands for democratization and push forward consumerist market reforms. For a wide-ranging selection of well-informed essays on the 1989 Chinese people's movement, see Tony Saich, ed., *The Chinese People's Movement: Perspectives on Spring 1989* (Armonk, NY, 1990).

43 I use the term *new second world* to signify that although the old second world is surely gone, the countries of Eastern Europe and the former Soviet Union are neither first nor third world, and the effects of the old second world on them will continue to be important for the foreseeable future. We can, of course, dispense with the three-worlds formulation altogether, but if we do, we lose something important in our efforts to understand the global system. For some of the consequences for consumerism in Eastern Europe, see Andras Hernadi, ed., *Consumption and Development: Economic, Social and Technical Aspects* (Budapest, 1992).

44 Piven and Cloward, *Poor People's Movements.*

Joan Martinez-Alier

"Environmental Justice" (Local and Global)

Environmental Impacts and Social Movements

The relationship between economic growth and environmental impacts is much debated by ecological economists. Does economic growth lead to environmental improvement or to deterioration? Environmental movements signal the conflicts between the economy and the environment, that is, the "second contradiction" of capitalism.[1] But which environmental movements? Local or global? In rich countries or in poor countries? Reliance on environmental movements (whether in rich or in poor countries) might seem misplaced because they are mostly local, whereas environmental problems such as global warming or loss of biodiversity are *apparently* beyond the reach or comprehension of local environmental movements.

This paper looks for the links between the local and the global in the distributional conflicts over the ecological conditions of livelihood and production. As defined by Frank Beckenbach, Martin O'Connor, and me, *ecological distribution* refers to the social, spatial, and temporal asymmetries or inequalities in the use by humans of traded or nontraded environmental resources and services, that is, in the depletion of natural resources (including the loss of biodiversity), and in the burdens of pollution. *Political ecology* refers to the study of such ecological distribution conflicts.[2] As examples: (1) an unequal distribution of land and pressure of agricultural exports on limited land resources may cause land degradation by peasants pushed to mountain slopes;[3] (2) there is increasing discussion on "ecologically unequal exchange" and also on "biopiracy"; (3) work has been done on the environmental space really occupied by industrial economies (both for procuring resources and for disposal of emissions);[4] and (4) we Europeans pay nothing for the environmental space we are using to dispose of our emissions of CO_2. In this case, Europeans act as if we owned a sizable chunk of the planet outside Europe. The value of "externalities" depends on the allocation of property rights on the environment and on the distribution of income. Almost nobody is yet complaining or trying to charge us a fee, but the occupation of an *environmental space* larger than one's own territory gives rise to an *ecological debt* with spatial and temporal dimensions.[5]

The 1993 Friends of the Earth's report on the Netherlands, using appropriate assumptions, showed that the Netherlands takes up an environmental space that is about fifteen times larger than its own territory.[6] Another indicator is the human appropriation of net primary production, which, if calculated for different regions and countries of the world, would show how some of them live beyond their own biomass production and some of them are still much below their own production and therefore allow more space for other species.[7] In an urban context, Rees and Wackernagel have developed the notion of the *ecological footprint* (implicit already in the "organic" urban planning of Patrick Geddes and Lewis Mumford).[8] Another good idea is the contrast between "ecosystem people" and "ecological trespassers."[9] If increasing wealth means (despite efforts at increasing efficiency in resource use) more use of undervalued natural resources from other territories, and also an increased production of residues, then there is an increasing ecological debt (which is admittedly difficult to quantify in money terms). Such ecological debt is not only toward future generations; it is also toward the members of our own generation who are using little environmental space.[10] It also includes a historical element, on account of the past occupation of environmental space.

Certainly, a strict thesis of global ecological limits would reduce economic growth to a zero-sum game, and this may lead (in the rich North) not so much to feelings of guilt over the burden of the ecological debt as, on the contrary, to an aggressive reaction (e.g., the colonial war against Iraq in 1991, or the present emphasis in NATO toward the Southern Flank, rich in oil and gas). Fortunately, there are no strict global ecological limits because there is some scope for "dematerialization" and "de-energization" without a decrease in living standards. However, in the meantime, while courageous calls are heard for a "factor 4" or even a "factor 10" reduction in energy and materials throughput in the rich economies, the ecological debt, which arises from excessive use of environmental space, is piling up.

Postmaterialist Values?

There has been a discussion if the relations between wealth and environmental impact, in terms of the so-called inverted-U relationship.[11] This relationship applies to sulphur dioxide. Emissions per head increase in the early stages of industrialization and then decrease as filters are installed in metal smelters or power stations, or by changes in fuel (from lignites to gas). If one defines improvement in "environmental quality" by the decrease in emissions of sulphur dioxide, then rich industrialized countries are improving environmental quality. However, there is no evidence yet of a general relative delinking, much less of an absolute delinking (as there exists for SO_2 emissions) between growth of the economy and environmental impact.[12]

Nevertheless, that wealth provides the means to correct environmental damage and that wealthy people are environmentally more conscious because they can afford to care about quality-of-life issues are widely held beliefs. To many environmentalists and ecologists from the South, such beliefs provoke outrage, even when the speaker himself, Finance Minister of India Dr. Manmohan Singh, comes from the South. Singh justified programs of trade and market liberalization on the grounds that they would generate resources for cleaning up the environment.[13]

Let me ask now, Which are the reasons for the growth of environmentalism: the actions taken, or the concerns expressed over the state of the environment due to human action? Some authors believe that the growth of environmentalism in rich countries is explained mainly by a post-1968 shift to "postmaterialist" cultural values. This optimistic position, which takes "dematerialization" for granted, is known as Inglehart's postmaterialist thesis. I do not agree with it, or rather, it seems to me that it only accounts for one variety of environmentalism. Inglehart accepts that in the affluent countries there is worry about the deterioration of some environmental indicators, and about the increasing part of GNP that must be spent on "protective," "defensive," "corrective," or "mitigatory" expenditures against environmental damage (as shown by Leipert); nevertheless, quite apart from "objective" environmental impacts and costs, Inglehart's thesis is that the cultural shift toward "subjective" postmaterialist values is making some societies more sensitive toward environmental issues.[14] Indeed, mainstream environmental and resource economists in the United States[15] had proposed that the demand for environmental amenities increases with income, and that, implicitly, the poor are "too poor to be green."

In trying to disentangle the sources of support for environmentalism in various countries, Inglehart describes the environment of the Netherlands as relatively "pristine," a surprising assessment because this is a country with a population density of four hundred persons per square kilometer and, roughly speaking, nearly as many cows, pigs, and cars as humans. This misrepresentation allows him to attribute Dutch environmentalism mostly to "postmaterialism." The Scandinavian countries are also classified by Inglehart as relatively "pristine" environments.[16] They are certainly less populated than the Netherlands. Scandinavian environmentalism is attributed by Inglehart mostly to "postmaterialism" with no regard to the following facts: their economies are partly based on extraction of natural resources; one of them (Sweden) has an excessive number of nuclear power stations relative to its population; they have been subject to radiation from Chernobyl; and they have been subject to acidification from external sources. There are then as many material reasons to become environmentalist in Scandinavia as in the Netherlands or in Germany. There are even more reasons to become environmentalist in poor countries or in poor regions whose environmental space is being used to the benefit of the rich.

Varieties of Environmentalism

As we have seen, the postmaterialist thesis explains environmental movements in rich countries by the fact that economic distribution conflicts are no longer so acute. This leads to a generational shift toward new values, which include an increasing appreciation for environmental amenities because of the declining marginal utility of abundant, easily obtained material commodities. Inglehart's thesis can be criticized if we take the position that economic growth goes together with environmental degradation. Hence, in rich countries there exists a materialist environmentalism against dangerous or annoying "effluents of affluence."[17] The postmaterialist thesis has also been criticized because it is easy (through opinion polls) to find evidence for a strong interest in the environment also in poor countries.[18] There is indeed evidence for the "environmentalism of the poor" not only in opinion polls but in many social conflicts in history and at present.[19] Sometimes such conflicts are identified as environmental by the actors themselves; at other times, such conflicts have been expressed in nonenvironmental idioms— thus, *seringueiros* in Acre in the late 1980s were members of a union, had some links to Christian local movements inspired by "liberation theology," and became known as environmentalists, perhaps to their own surprise.

In poor countries, environmentalism is sometimes supposed to have been imported and organized by the postmaterial environmentalism of the North, inspired by people with incomes high enough to allow them to worry about postmaterial quality-of-life issues rather than about livelihood and survival. Hugo Blanco, a former peasant leader in Peru, wrote in 1991:

> At first sight, environmentalists or conservationists are nice, slightly crazy guys whose main purpose in life is to prevent the disappearance of blue whales or pandas. The common people have more important things to think about, for instance how to get their daily bread. Sometimes they are taken to be not so crazy but rather smart guys who, in the guise of protecting endangered species, have formed so-called NGOs to get juicy sums of dollars from abroad. . . . Such views are sometimes true. However, there are in Peru a very large number of people who are environmentalists. Of course, if I tell such people, you are ecologists, they might reply, "ecologist your mother," or words to that effect. Let us see, however. Isn't the village of Bambamarca truly environmentalist, which has time and again fought valiantly against the pollution of its water from mining? Are not the city of Ilo and the surrounding villages which are being polluted by the Southern Peru Copper Corporation truly environmentalist? Is not the village of Tambo Grande in Piura environmentalist, when it rises like a closed fist and is ready to die in order to prevent strip-mining in its valley? Also, the people of the Mantaro Valley who saw their little sheep die, because of the smoke and waste from La Oroya smelter. And the population of Amazonia, who are totally environmentalist, and die defending their forests against depredation. Also the poor people of Lima are environmentalists, when they complain against the pollution of water on the beaches.[20]

I have direct knowledge of similar cases in some other countries. For instance, in Ecuador, Peru's northern neighbor, are they not environmentalists—the poor and indigenous population of Zámbiza—living around the valley in northeastern Quito, where more than 1 million kilograms of domestic waste are dumped every day, who unsuccessfully ask that this dumping ground be closed? And the population of Salango, on the coast, who complain against the pollution from a fishmeal factory, as in many other places on the Pacific Coast of Chile (Talcahuano) and Peru (Chimbote)? Have they not been ecologists, the peasants of Salinas in Bolívar province, who, without the support of their own communal authorities, nevertheless prevented mining by Rio Tinto in their territory? And the Amazonian population who complain against oil spills? And the poor, black population of Esmeraldas province on the coast, mainly women, who are in the forefront of the defense of the mangroves against the shrimp industry, as in so many other places in the world?

And to the south of Peru, in Chile, were they not truly ecologists, the poor urban inhabitants in Santiago, who complained and complained until the waste dump of Lo Errázuriz was closed? Were they not environmentalists or ecologists, despite their ignorance of such terminology, the Huilliche communities of Compu and Güequetrumao in Chiloe island, who confronted the forest firm Golden Spring in a case similar to so many others in southern Chile and elsewhere? And the population of Paipote, who complain against sulphur dioxide emissions from copper smelting, risking their own sources of employment? And the farmers of Huasco, some poor, some not so poor, their olive trees damaged by emissions of iron particles from the pellets factory in their valley?

Perhaps the best known instances of environmentalism of the poor are Chico Mendes and the *seringueiros,* the Chipko movement, the movement against the Narmada dams, and now the Ogoni struggle against Shell. But there are many more. In the Brazilian Amazonia, Acevedo and Castro describe the trouble that fell upon an ethnic group of the Trombetas River, reminiscent of *quilombos* of ex-slaves, which from the mid-1970s tried to fight back against hydroelectricity and bauxite mining from Brazilian and foreign companies (which threatened to destroy the waterfall Cachoeira Porteira, a sacred place to them).[21] This group confronted IBAMA, the Brazilian environmental agency which designated the territory occupied by these *negros do Trombetas* a "biological reserve" to the benefit of mining corpora-

Table 1   Some Varieties of Environmentalism

	Materialist	Nonmaterialist
In affluent countries	Reaction against the increased impact of the "effluents of affluence," e.g., the environmental justice movement in the U.S., the antinuclear movement	Cultural shift to postmaterial quality-of-life values and increased appreciation for natural amenities because of declining marginal utility of abundant, easily obtained material commodities[1]
In poor countries	The "environmentalism of the poor," i.e., the defense of livelihood and communal access to natural resources, threatened by the state or the market	Biocentric religions (as distinct from "Western" anthropocentric religions)[2]
	Reaction against environmental degradation caused by unequal exchange, poverty, population growth Social ecofeminism[4]	Essentialist ecofeminism.[3]

1. Ronald Inglehart, *The Silent Revolution: Changing Values and Political Styles* (Princeton, NJ, 1977).
2. Lynn White, "The Historical Roots of Our Ecological Crisis," *Science* 155 (1967): 1203–1207.
3. See Vandana Shiva, *Staying Alive: Women, Ecology and Development* (London, 1989).
4. Bina Agarwal, "The Gender and Environment Debate: Lessons from India," *Feminist Studies* 18 (1992).

tions. In the region around Santarem, a conflict exists between *ribeirinho* fishermen, who fish in the *varzea* lakes that the Amazon leaves behind in the period of low waters, from July to December, and industrial fishermen, called *geleiros* (ice-men). Attempts are being made to legally institute a system of communal management of the lakes, to the benefit of local people and for conservation of the resource.[22] The movement in defense of the babassu palm in Maranhao and neighboring states, in the Brazilian Northeast, based mainly on women, the *quebradeiras de coco,* is also becoming well known.[23] Tens of thousands of people are involved, over a wide area. Women who make a living or complement their meager income by collecting and breaking the coconuts and selling the oil-rich seed want to preserve the palm trees against the landowners. A further instance all over Brazil is the movements of *atingi-*

dos pelas barragens, similar to other movements against big dams throughout the world.[24]

One could travel around the world collecting cases of "environmentalism of the poor." What an enjoyable research journey that would be! In between journeys, research on works of fiction could be done, if *fiction* is the word.[25] Table 1 classifies the varieties (and theories) of environmentalism. One criterion is the material/nonmaterial dimension. Another criterion is the environmentalism of affluence versus the environmentalism of survival; the environmentalism of enhanced quality of life versus the environmentalism of livelihood.[26] Some situations cross the boundaries of the boxes of Table 1. For instance, there are fights in poor countries against toxic waste (imported or locally produced), and there are fights in affluent countries (Canada, New Zealand, the United States) by native peoples to enforce territorial rights to protect access to their own natural resources or to protect themselves against waste dumping.[27] Also, the defense of communities against state or market sometimes rests in part on religious values, as in the belief in *pachamama* in the Andes. And, certainly, there are cases that do not fit at all into the idea of an "environmentalism of the poor"—for instance, the Amazonian *garimpeiros* who look for gold and pollute rivers with mercury. Notice that the global-versus-local dimension is still absent from Table 1; it will be discussed in the final section of this paper.

Ecological Distribution Conflicts: The Global and the Local

Although (after Bhopal) there is some debate ("internationalization of the internalization of externalities") produced by transnational corporations, environmental movements are usually local movements, whereas many environmental problems are global in scope. What are the connections, if any, between environmental problems that are perceived as global (such as the increased concentration of carbon dioxide in the atmosphere, or the loss of biodiversity) and local environmental movements? For instance, the lack of action in the North to prevent emissions of carbon dioxide (the main greenhouse gas) that exceed the Earth's ability to absorb carbon dioxide through new vegetation or in the oceans is accelerating the debate on the ecological debt. The discussion on joint implementation, that is, paying for reforestation projects in the South to offset excessive carbon dioxide emissions in the North, will animate a generalized claim in the South of property rights on the absorptive capacity of the Earth, perhaps in terms proportional to population.[28] There is also an Alliance for Climate, between COICA (an umbrella group for indigenous peoples in Amazonia) and many European cities, whose authorities pay at least lip service to the cause of CO_2 reduction. Indigenous peoples oppose deforestation; northern environmentalists may complain against deforestation only if they set an example for CO_2 reductions. The global discussion on carbon dioxide is made locally relevant by linking it to campaigns in favor of poor people and good public transport and against urban planning in the service of the motor car—an issue even more relevant in Bangkok or Mexico City than in, say, Bologna. The use of global ideas in the service of local or national social and environmental aims is also present in debates on ecological trespassing, the ecological debt, ecologically unequal exchange, and biopiracy. There have been complaints against foreign bioprospecting firms that buy genetic resources and indigenous knowledge cheaply.[29] In agriculture there is now a worldwide movement of self-conscious peasant agroecology that is not at all a postmodern fad but a route toward an alternative modernity based on the defense of agricultural biodiversity and sensible agronomic practices.[30] Global environmental ideas are used for, and supported by, local struggles. As an answer to the attempts through the Gatt negotiations to enforce intellectual property rights on "improved" seeds, when nothing has ever been paid for traditional seeds and traditional knowledge (despite FAO's support for so-called farmers' rights), there were strong movements of protest in India. In fact, an "agricultural exception" against Gatt would make more sense than the "cultural exception" demanded by some French and other European filmmakers against the free entry of Hollywood products. For instance, the opposition to Nafta in Mexico could combine Mexican oil nationalism (as Cárdenas of the 1930s) and the defense of *milpa* agriculture, by pointing out that Nafta means the intensification of ecological dumping. Cheap exports of oil from Mexico to the United States (at prices that certainly do not internalize local and global externalities) will be exchanged for imports of maize at cheap prices. Such imports will destroy the agriculture of southern Mexico despite the fact that maize agriculture in the United States is more wasteful of fossil fuel energy and biologically more fragile than in Mexico. Hence Victor Toledo's wishful expression after the Chiapas uprising: *un neozapatismo ecológico*.

The term *toxic imperialism* has been used for struggles against the export of toxic waste. Such struggles could easily link up with the environmental justice

Table 2   Ecological Distribution Conflicts and Related Resistance Movements

Term	Definition	Main source (to my knowledge)
Environmental racism (U.S.)	Dumping of toxic waste in locations inhabited by African Americans, Latinos, Native Americans	Robert Bullard, *Confronting Environmental Racism: Voices from the Grassroots* (Boston, 1993)
Environmental justice	Movement against environmental racism	Bullard, 1993
Environmental blackmail	Either you accept LULU (locally unacceptable land use), or you stay without jobs	Bullard, 1993
Toxic imperialism	Dumping of toxic waste in poorer countries	Greenpeace, ca. 1989
Ecologically unequal exchange	Importing products from poor regions or countries, at prices that do not take account of exhaustion or of local externalities	
Raubwirtschaft	Ecologically unequal exchange, plunder economy	Raumoulin, 1984
Ecological dumping	Selling at prices that do not take account of exhaustion or externalities; takes place from North to South (agricultural exports from Europe or U.S.), and from South to North	
Internationalization of the internalization of externalities	Law suits against TNCs (Union Carbide, Texaco, Dow Chemical) in their country of origin, claiming damages for externalities caused in poor countries	
Ecological debt	Claiming damages from rich countries on account of *past* excessive emissions (e.g., of CO_2) or plundering of natural resources	IEP Chile, 1992; Azar, 1994; Borrero, 1993

Table 2   *Continued*

Term	Definition	Main source (to my knowledge)
Transboundary pollution	Applied mainly to SO_2 crossing borders in Europe and producing acid rain	
National fishing rights	Attempts to stop open access depredation by imposing (since the 1940s in Peru, Ecuador, Chile) exclusive fishing areas (200 miles and beyond, as in Canada, for straddling stocks)	
Environmental space	The geographical space really occupied by an economy, taking into account imports of natural resources and disposal of emissions; empirical work has been done	Friends of the Earth, Netherlands, 1993
Ecological trespassers vs. ecosystem people	Applied to India, but could be applied to the world: the contrast between people living on their own resources and people living on the resources of other territories and peoples	M. Gadgil and R. Guha, *Ecology and Equity: The Use and Abuse of Nature in Contemporary India* (New York, 1995)
Ecological footprint, or appropriated carrying capacity	The ecological impact of regions or large cities on the outside space; empirical work has been done	William Rees and Mathis Wackernagel, "Ecological Footprints and Appropriated Carrying Capacity," in *Investing in Natural Capital*, ed. A. M. Jansson et al. (Covelo, CA, 1994)
Biopiracy	The appropriation of genetic resources ("wild" or agricultural) without adequate payment or recognition of peasant or indigenous knowledge and	Pat Mooney, RAFI, ca. 1993

Table 2   *Continued*

Term	Definition	Main source (to my knowledge)
Biopiracy (*cont.*)	ownership over them (including the extreme case of the Human Genome project)	
Workers' struggles for occupational health and safety	Actions (in the framework of collective bargaining or outside it) to prevent damages to workers in mines, plantations, or factories	
Urban struggles for clean water, green spaces, etc.	Actions (outside the market) to improve environmental conditions of livelihood or to gain access to recreational amenities in urban context	Castells, 1983
Indigenous environmentalism	Use of territorial rights and ethnic resistance against external use of resources (e.g., Crees against Hydro Quebec)	Geddicks, 1993
Social ecofeminism, environmental feminism	The environmental activism of women, motivated by their social situation; the idiom of such struggles is not necessarily that of feminism and/or environmentalism	Bina Agarwal, "The Gender and Environment Debate: Lessons from India," *Feminist Studies* 18 (1992)
Environmentalism of the poor	Social conflicts with an ecological content (today and in history), of the poor against the (relatively) rich, not only but mainly in rural contexts	Ramachandra Guha, *The Unquiet Woods* (Delhi, 1989)

movement in the United States. There are other cases in which the local is connected to the global in a generalized movement of resistance. Thus, Oil-Watch unites local environmental groups in tropical countries threatened by the oil industry, from Mexico, Ecuador, and Peru to Nigeria, Indonesia, and Timor.[31]

In lieu of a conclusion, I offer Table 2, listing the names and definitions of some ecological distribution conflicts and the related resistance movements, both domestic and international. This list remains to be developed.

Notes

1 Enrique Leff, *Ecología y Capital* (Mexico City, 1986); Enrique Leff, *Green Production* (New York, 1994); James O'Connor, "Introduction," *Capitalism, Nature Socialism* 1 (1988).

2 As used by anthropologists and geographers already for some time. A. Schnaiberg, N. Watts, and K. Zimmerman, eds., *Distributional Conflicts in Environmental Resource Policy* (Aldershot, UK, 1986); Marianne Schmink and Charles Wood, "The Political Ecology of Amazonia," in *Lands at Risk in the Third World,* ed. Peter D. Little and Michael M. Horowitz (Boulder, CO, 1987), 38–57.

3 Susan Stonich, *I Am Destroying the Land!: The Political Ecology of Poverty and Environment Destruction in Honduras* (Boulder, CO, 1993).

4 See the reports by Wuppertal Institute, *Towards Sustainable Europe* (1995), and *Zukunftsfähiges Deutschland* (1995).

5 Christian Azar and J. Holmberg, "Defining the Generational Environment Debt," *Ecological Economics* 14 (1995): 7–20; José Borrero, *La deuda ecológica* (Cali, 1994); M. L. Robleto and Wilfredo Marcelo, *Deuda ecológica* (Santiago de Chile, 1992).

6 Maria Buitenkamp, Henk Venner, and Teo Wams, eds., *Action Plan: Sustainable Netherlands* (Amsterdam, 1993). On the concept of environmental space, see also the references in J. B. Opschoor, "Ecospace and the Fall and Rise of Throughput Intensity," *Ecological Economics* 15 (November 1995): 137–140.

7 Peter Vitousek, Paul Ehrlich, Anne Ehrlich, and Pamela Matson, "Human Appropriation of the Products of Photosynthesis," *Bioscience* 34 (1986): 368–373.

8 William Rees and Mathis Wackernagel, "Ecological Footprints and Appropriated Carrying Capacity," in *Investing in Natural Capital: The Ecological Economics Approach to Sustainability,* ed. A. M. Jansson et al. (Covelo, CA, 1994).

9 M. Gadgil and R. Guha, *Ecology and Equity: The Use and Abuse of Nature in Contemporary India* (New York, 1995). Gadgil and Guha's focus is on India, but their work could be applied to the world.

10 Azar and Holmberg, "Defining"; Anil Agarwal and Sunita Narain, *Global Warming in an Unequal World: A Case of Environmental Colonialism* (Delhi, 1991).

11 Kenneth Arrow et al., "Economic Growth, Carrying Capacity, and the Environment," *Ecological Economics* 15 (1995): 91–95; Opschoor, "Ecospace"; Thomas M. Selden and Daqing Song, "Environmental Quality and Development: Is There a Kuznets Curve for Air Pollution Emissions," *Journal of Environment, Economics, & Management* 27 (1994): 147–162.

12 S. M. De Bruyn and J. B. Opschoor, "Is the Economy Ecologizing?" Tinbergen Institute, working paper 94-65 (Amsterdam, 1994): 27; Opschoor, "Ecospace." Moreover, although some indicators might improve, other indicators deteriorate, and we would need to know which relative weights to give to them to assess overall environmental impact. Thus, MIPS might improve while HANPP (Vitousek et al., "Human Appropriation") or the "energy cost of obtaining energy" deteriorates. Incommensurability of values and multicriteria evaluation in ecological macroeconomics is discussed in Martinez-Alier, Munda and O'Neill, "Weak Comparability of Values as a Foundation for Ecological Economics," *Ecological Economics* (1998).

13 Manmohan Singh, "Economics and the Environment," Foundation Day Address, Society for the Promotion of Wastelands (New Delhi, 1991).

14 Ronald Inglehart, "Public Support for Environmental Protection: Objective Problems and Subjective Values in 43 Societies," *Political Science & Politics* (1995): 57–71; Ronald Inglehart, *The Silent Revolution: Changing Values and Political Styles* (Princeton, NJ, 1977); Christian Leipert, *Die heimlichen Kosten des Fortschritts* (Frankfurt, 1989).

15 At least since H. J. Barnett and Chandler Morse, *Scarcity and Growth* (Baltimore, 1963), and John Krutilla, "Conservation Reconsidered," *American Economic Review,* 57, no. 4 (1967).

16 Inglehart, "Public Support," 61.

17 For example, the environmental justice movement in the United States. See Robert Bullard, *Confronting Environmental Racism: Voices from the Grassroots* (Boston, 1993); Jim Schwab, *Deeper Shades of Green: The Rise of Blue-Collar and Minority Environmentalism in America* (San Francisco, 1994); Andrew Szasz, *Eco-Populism: Toxic Waste and the Movement for Environmental Justice* (Minneapolis, 1994).

18 Steven R. Brechin and Willet Kempton, "Global Environmentalism: A Challenge to the Postmaterialism Thesis?," *Social Science Quarterly* 75 (June 1994): 245–269.

19 Ramachandra Guha, *The Unquiet Woods* (Delhi, 1989); J. Martinez Alier, "Ecology and the Poor: A Neglected Issue in Latin American History," *Journal of Latin American Studies* 23 (1991).

20 Article in *La Republica* (Lima), 6 April 1991. The words *ecologist* (not in the sense of scientist but of social activist) and *environmentalist* are used interchangeably.

21 Rosa Acevedo and Edna Castro, *Negros do Trombetas: Guardaes de Matos e Rios* (Belem, 1993).

22 D. McGrath et al., "Fisheries and the Evolution of Resource Management in the Lower Amazon Floodplain," *Human Ecology* 21 (1993).

23 Alfredo Wagner Almeida, *Carajas: A Guerra dos Mapas* (Belem, 1995); Anthony Anderson et al., *The Subsidy from Nature: Palm Forests, Peasantry, and Development on an Amazon Frontier* (New York, 1991); Peter May, *Palmeiras em Chamas, Transformaçào Agrária e Justica Social na Zona do Babaçu* (Sáo Luís, 1990).

24 Sonia Barbosa Magalhaês, "As grandes hidroeléctricas e as populaçôs camponesas," in *A Amazônia e a crisi da modernizaçâo,* ed. Maria Angela d'Incao and Isolda Maliel da Silveira (Belém, 1994), 447–456; Claudia Jobb Schmitt, "A Luta dos Atingidos pelas Barragens do Rio Uruguai," in *Conflitos sócio-ambientais no Brasil,* vol. 1 (Rio de Janeiro, 1995), 71–85; Mauricio Waldman, *Ecologia e lutas sociais no Brasil* (Sáo Paulo, 1992).

25 Back to Peru: In the Peru of *Todas las Sangres* ("A mixture of all bloods") of José María Arguedas, were they not environmentalists, the poor neighbors of the village of San Pedro de Lahuaymarca, who, in alliance with the Indians of the community, complained so strongly against the mining firm Wisther and Bozart, which placed its tailings in their maize fields of La Esperanza, that they burned their own village church and killed the engineer of this mine?

26 J. Martinez Alier and Eric Hershberg, "Environmentalism and the Poor," *Items SSRC* 46 (March 1992).

27 Women's environmentalism sometimes has been explained in terms of a non-materialist, essentialist identification with nature. I give as an example Vandana Shiva, *Staying Alive: Women, Ecology and Development* (London, 1989). The same author has published work along more social, materialist lines. Excellent attempts at overcoming the social/essentialist tension in ecofeminism are in V. Kuletz's interview with Barbara Holland-Cunz (1992), in Ariel Salleh's chapter in O'Connor, *Sustainable Capitalism,* and in Bina Agarwal, "The Gender and Environment Debate: Lessons from India," *Feminist Studies* 18 (1992).

28 Agarwal and Narain, *Global Warming.*

29 For a case study of Shaman Pharmaceuticals in Ecuador, see Victoria Reyes, "El valor de la sangre de drago," *Ecologia Politica* 11 (1996).

30 J. Martinez Alier, "The Merchandising of Biodiversity," *Etnoecologia* 3 (1994).

31 See *Tegantai,* the newsletter in English and Spanish of this network, published by Acción Ecológica, Quito ⟨oilwatch@acecol.ecx.ec⟩. The deaths of Ken Saro-Wiwa and other Ogoni people, in their struggle against Shell and the dictatorship in Nigeria, were deaths foretold in *Tegantai.*

David Harvey

What's Green and

Makes the Environment Go Round?

Socialism and Environmental Politics

How to ground a socialist approach to environmental-ecological politics has proven, for a variety of reasons, a peculiarly difficult problem in the history of the Left. In part, this has to do with the way in which the socialist-Marxist movement inherited from capitalism a strongly productivist ethic and a broadly instrumental approach to a supposedly distinct natural world and sought a transformation of social relations on the basis of a further liberation of the productive forces. From this perspective it has proven hard to wean Marxism away from a rather hubristic view of the domination of nature thesis that has, in recent years, come in for strong criticism.[1] In addition, Marxism has shared with much of bourgeois social science a general abhorrence of the idea that "nature" can control, determine, or even limit any kind of human endeavor. But in so doing it has either avoided any foundational view of nature or resorted to a rather too simplistic rhetoric about "the humanization of nature" backed by a dialectical and historical materialism that somehow absorbed the problem by appeal to a set of epistemological/ontological principles. So, although there have been numerous principled writings in the

Marxist tradition on the question of nature, beginning with Engels's *The Dialectics of Nature* and continuing through works by Schmidt, Smith, and Grundmann, the armory of Marxism/socialism to counter the rhetoric and politics of a rising tide of ecological movements has not been well stocked. The resurrection of certain figures within the Marxist/socialist tradition (such as William Morris and Raymond Williams) who exhibited considerable sensitivity to the ecological-environmental issue has only gone some way to compensate for the lack.[2]

As a consequence, the response within the Left to rising ecological concerns has been either to reject environmental/ecological politics as a bourgeois diversion (as, indeed, much of it patently is) or to make partial concessions to environmental/ecological rhetoric and try to rebuild Marxism/socialism on rather different theoretical and practical foundations from those traditionally chosen as a grounding for working-class politics. And in some formulations a noble attempt has been made to do both, though not, I believe, with particularly felicitous results.

Consider, for example, a book by John Bellamy Foster, published with all the Marxist credibility of the Monthly Review Press, entitled *The Vulnerable Planet: A Short Economic History of the Environment.*[3] It is a book that strongly argues that "the crisis of the earth is not a crisis of *nature* but of *society.*" It goes on to discuss how accumulation for accumulation's sake in the West and production for production's sake in what was the communist world have had devastating effects upon the world's environment since World War II, setting the stage for a contemporary condition of planetary ecological crisis. There is much that is persuasive and telling in the account, but there are two central failings.

First, the postulation of a planetary ecological crisis, the very idea that the planet is somehow "vulnerable" to human action or that we can actually destroy the earth, repeats in negative form the hubristic claims of those who aspire to planetary domination. The subtext is that the earth is somehow fragile and that we need to become caring managers or caring physicians to nurse it back from sickness into health. This leads to Foster's extraordinary conclusion that "the conscious and collective organization of the entire planet in the common interest of humanity and the earth has become a necessity if we are to prevent the irreparable despoliation of the earth by forces of institutionalized greed." Against this, it is crucial to understand that it is materially impossible for us to destroy the planet Earth, that the worst we can do is to engage in material transformations of our environment so as to make life less rather than more comfortable for our own species, while recognizing that what we do also does have ramifications (both positive and negative) for other living species.[4] It is vital, furthermore, to disaggregate "the environmental issue" into a tangible set of problems that exist at quite different scales, varying from the global issues of ozone, climate warming, and biodiversity to regional problems of soil depletion, desertification, and deforestation to the more localized questions of water quality, breathable air, and radon in the basement. Politically, the millenarial proclamation that the end of the world is nigh has had a dubious history at best and hardly appears as the best possible basis for left politics. It becomes very vulnerable to the arguments long advanced by Simon and now by Easterbrook, that conditions of life (as measured, for example, by life expectancy) are better now than they have ever been and that the doomsday scenario of the environmentalists is far-fetched and improbable.[5] Furthermore, as Foster's conclusion all too clearly indicates, there is nothing in the argument that cannot be made (as I shall show below) broadly compatible with a segment of corporate capital's concerns to rationalize planetary management of the world's global resources in the name of ecological modernization. But then this is precisely what happens when the class content of the whole environmental-ecological argument gets subordinated to a millenarial vision of a planetary ecological crisis.

The second failing (which connects powerfully to the first) lies in the specification and interpretation of four ecological laws (largely drawn from Barry Commoner, whose dedication to progressive left and ecological issues has been long-standing).[6] They are: "(1) everything is connected to everything else, (2) everything must go somewhere, (3) nature knows best, and (4) nothing comes from nothing."[7] The first is an important truism that has very little meaning without recognizing that some things are more connected than others. It is precisely the task of ecological analysis to try and identify unintended consequences (both short and long term, positive and negative) and to indicate what the major effects of actions are. Without such understandings there is little that can be said for or against specific forms of environmental modification on the basis of this law. The second law properly indicates that there is no solution to active pollution problems except to move them around (a version of Engels's comment on how the bourgeoisie handles its housing problem). The fourth law properly points out the cautionary principle (based on the laws of thermodynamics) that energy in usable form for human beings can indeed be depleted (though never destroyed). The third law is where the real problem lies. For to say "nature knows best" is to presume that nature can "know" something.[8] This principle then dissolves either into the (once more hubristic) idea that we are somehow in a privileged position to know what nature knows or into the conservative view that our environmental transformations should be as limited as possible (the "tread lightly on the surface of the Earth" injunction favored by many ecologists). Foster thus accepts uncritically Commoner's argument that "any major man-made change in a natural system is likely to be detrimental to that system." To which I would want to reply "I hope so," leaving open the question as to whether the changes are favorable or detrimental to social or other forms of life and what meaning such changes might have for social relations, life chances of individuals and other species, and the like.

Foster uses these laws to arrive at a thorough and convincing condemnation of capitalism: the market, not nature, knows best; the only connection that matters is the cash nexus; it doesn't matter where something goes as long as it doesn't reenter the circuit of capital; and goods in nature are a free gift. All of this is reasonably true and Foster does a good job of explaining how destructive the consequences can be. But the difficulties begin when these same ecological laws are applied to socialism. For myself, I hope it would be true that socialists, rather than nature, will know best. Indeed, the only persuasive reason for joining the socialist (as opposed to the fascist, libertarian, corporate capitalist, planetary management) cause is precisely that we know best how to engage in environmental/ecological transformations in such a way as to realize long-term socialist goals of feeding the hungry, clothing the poor, providing reasonable life-chances for all, and opening up paths toward the liberation of diverse human creativities.

These sorts of difficulties with Foster's analysis are endemic to much of the environmental/ecological movement. Conventional wisdom in ecological circles indeed stresses, for example, that everything relates to everything else. The inference, and hence the political implication, is that we should be more sensitive and less hubristic in our use and appropriation of other elements of and processes in the natural world. Yet there is something odd and lopsided in this rhetoric. For although it claims that everything relates to everything else, it does so in a way that excludes a large segment of the practical ecosystem in which we live. In particular, it excludes the ecosystemic character of human activity in favor of a curious separation, inconsistent with its own biocentric vision, of human activity. If, after all, biocentric thinking is correct, then the boundary between human activity and ecosystem must be collapsed, and this means not only that ecological processes have to be incorporated into our understandings of social life; it also means that flows of money and of commodities and the transformative actions of human beings (in the building of intricate ways of urban living, for example) have to be understood as fundamentally ecological processes.

The politics of this are transparent. Taylor notes:

> The more established environmental organizations do fight issues of survival, and they use the survival theme to get the support of their members, but these are survival issues as they pertain to endangered species, national parks and preserves, threatened landscapes. . . . These survival debates are not linked to rural and urban poverty and quality of life issues. If it is discovered that birds have lost their nesting sites, then environmentalists go to great expense and lengths to erect nesting boxes and find alternative breeding sites for them; when whales are stranded, enormous sums are spent to provide them food and shelter; when forests are threatened large numbers of people are mobilized to prevent damage; but we have yet to see an environmental group champion the cause of homelessness in humans or joblessness as issues on which it will spend vast resources. It is a strange paradox that a movement which exhorts the harmonious coexistence of people and nature, and worries about the continued survival of nature (particularly loss of habitat problems), somehow forgets about the survival of humans (especially those who have lost their "habitats" and "food sources").[9]

But beyond that, there is the vital analytic point that much of what happens in the environment today is not only highly dependent upon capitalist behaviors, institutions, activities, and power structures, but its very "sustainability" (to use that much abused contemporary buzzword) depends upon keeping those capitalistic activities going.

Put bluntly, there are very few if any ecosystems in the world today that do not bear the marks of continuous human action, and the continuity of that action is essential to their maintenance. If global capitalism collapsed tomorrow, there would be a dramatically stressful period of ecological adaptation as dams and irrigation ditches deteriorated, as fertilizer inputs diminished, as urban and agrarian systems collapsed. It is, then, flows of money that make the contemporary environment what it is, and any interruption in those money and commodity flows will potentially have ecological consequences just as catastrophic as the history of the development of those flows has had since World War II.

To put things this way is not to argue for continuation of the capitalist system of environmental transformation, but to recognize that the task of socialism is to think through the duality of ecological-social transformations as part of a far more coherent project than has hitherto been the case. That, too, may sound hubristic, but we simply have no option except to think of our environmental transformations not in terms of some fixed term called "nature" (with all of its supposedly pristine qualities contaminated by human action), but in terms of the radically different environments that have been created under several centuries of capitalism. To paraphrase Marx, we can collectively hope to produce our own environmental history, but only under environmental conditions that have been handed down to us. And these environments have been created by capital circulation, the extraction of surplus values, monetized exchange, and the circulation of commodities. Therefore, the circulation of money is a prime ecological variable, and the continued circulation of money is essential if the material qualities of the environment are to be maintained. On this point, at least, the Brundtland Report was both clear and correct.[10]

Money, Politics, Environment, and Saccard's Dream

If, in the history of capitalism, it has very much been capital circulation that has made the environment go round, then there is no way to avoid the consequences of money valuations of environmental assets and profit-driven transformations of environmental conditions. The complex dialectic in which we make ourselves by transforming the world gets reduced in a strongly monetized economy into a rather simple one-track affair, even allowing for the ways in which aesthetic judgments, romantic reactions, nature tourism, vegetarianism, animal rights movements, and monetized protections of nature through wilderness and habitat preservation surround the daily crass commercialism of our use of nature and give it a veneer of accountability and respectability.

It is not fashionable these days, of course, to evoke triumphalist attitudes to nature. But I think it important to understand that this is what we do, whether we care to acknowledge it or not, whenever we let loose the circulation of capital upon the land. Here is how Saccard, Zola's antihero in his novel *Money*, sees the issue as he builds his Universal Bank to finance innumerable projects for the transformation of the Levant:

> "Look here," cried Saccard . . . "you will behold a complete resurrection over all those depopulated plains, those deserted passes, which our railways will traverse—yes! fields will be cleared, roads and canals built, new cities will spring from the soil, life will return as it returns to a sick body, when we stimulate the system by injecting new blood into exhausted veins. Yes! money will work these miracles. . . .[11]

As the geographer Isaiah Bowman once put it, "man can move mountains, but first he must launch a bond issue."[12] Zola's language here is instructive, however; the circulation of money is assimilated to the idea of the circulation of the blood and the biological/sexual metaphor is then put to work so strongly that it seems less and less to be metaphoric than expressive of a deep continuity:

> "You must understand that speculation, gambling, is the central mechanism, the heart itself, of a vast affair like ours. Yes, it attracts blood, takes it from every source in little streamlets, collects it, sends it back in rivers in all directions, and establishes an enormous circulation of money, which is the very life of great enterprises. . . .
>
> "Speculation—why, it is the one inducement that we have to live; it is the eternal desire that compels us to live and struggle. Without speculation, my dear friend, there would be no business of any kind. . . . It is the same as in love. In love as in speculation there is much filth; in love also, people think only of their own gratification; yet without love there would be no life, and the world would come to an end."[13]

Saccard's vision, his love of life, seduces all around him, including the cautious Mme Caroline, whose brother has the engineering expertise to make the projects work and whose participation in Saccard's schemes will eventually lead him to financial ruin. But even Mme Caroline, who knows the Levant well, is struck by how unharmonious is the present state of the land with human desires and potentialities:

she became angry, and asked if it was allowable that men should thus spoil the work of nature, a land so blest, of such exquisite beauty, where all climates were to be found—the glowing plains, the temperate mountainsides, the perpetual snows of lofty peaks. And her love of life, her ever-buoyant hopefulness, filled her with enthusiasm at the idea of the all-powerful magic wand with which science and speculation could strike this old sleeping soil and suddenly reawaken it. . . . And it was just this that she saw rising again—the forward, irresistible march, the social impulse towards the greatest possible sum of happiness, the need of action, of going ahead, without knowing exactly whither . . . and amid it all there was the globe turned upside down by the ant-swarm rebuilding its abode, its work never ending, fresh sources of enjoyment ever being discovered, man's power increasing ten-fold, the earth belonging to him more and more every day. Money, aiding science, yielded progress.[14]

Filth, growth, evil, goodness, all become mixed in Mme Caroline's mind:

Money was the dung-heap that nurtured the growth of tomorrow's humanity. Without speculation there could be no vibrant and fruitful undertakings any more than there could be children without lust. It took this excess of passion, all this contemptibly wasted and lost life to ensure the continuation of life. . . . Money, the poisoner and destroyer, was becoming the seed-bed for all forms of social growth. It was the manure needed to sustain the great public works whose execution was bringing the peoples of the globe together and pacifying the earth. . . . Everything that was good came out of that which was evil.[15]

But what is also so significant in Zola's story is the transformation/contestation in the field of social relations, the struggle for power and authority, that parallels the struggle for the transformation of the qualities of material (physical and biotic) environments. The creative destruction wrought upon the land is inseparable from the creative destruction of social relations as traditional wealth, seduced by the sheer sexual energy of Saccard's speculative schemes, loses its means of livelihood to the stock-exchange wolves and the "bloodless jew," Gundermann (transparently based on the money power of the Rothschilds).

The circulation of money capital not only makes the environment go round, but it simultaneously makes social relations in such a way as to bring back the golden rule that environmental transformations are always transformations of social relations. But that golden rule has yet another, even more insidious manifestation. One path toward consolidation of a particular set of social relations is to undertake an ecological project that requires the reproduction of those social relations in order to sustain it. Worster doubtless exaggerates in his flamboyant projection onto the American West of Wittfogel's thesis on the relation between large-scale irrigation schemes and despotic forms of government, but his basic argument is surely correct.[16] Once the original proposals for a communitarian, decentralized, "bio-regional," river-basin-confined settlement system for the American West, drawn up by the geologist John Wesley Powell at the end of the nineteenth century, were rejected by a Congress dominated by large-scale corporate interests (Powell being thoroughly villified in the process), those interests sought to assure their own reproduction through construction of dams, mega–water projects of all sorts and vast transformations of the western ecosystem. Sustaining such a grandiose ecological project came to depend crucially upon the creation and maintenance of centralized state powers and certain class relations (the formation and perpetuation, for example, of large-scale agribusiness and an oppressed landless agrarian proletariat). The consequent subversion of the Jeffersonian dream of agrarian democracy has ever since created intense contradictions in the body politic of states like California (Polanski's film *Chinatown* tells exactly such a tale). But another implication follows: contradictions in the social relations (in Worster's case of class, but gender, religion, etc. can also be just as significant) entail social contradictions on the land and *within* ecosystemic projects themselves. Not only do the rich occupy privileged niches in the habitat while the poor tend to work and live in the more toxic or hazardous zones (see below), but the very design of the transformed ecosystem is redolent of its social relations. Conversely, projects set up in supposedly pure ecological terms—the so-called green revolution, for example— have all manner of distributive and social consequences (in the green revolution case, the concentration of land holdings in a few hands and the creation of a landless agrarian proletariat).

Created ecosystems tend to both instantiate and reflect, therefore, the social processes and systems that gave rise to them, though they do not do so in noncontradictory (i.e., *stable*) ways. This simple principle ought to weigh much more heavily than it does upon all angles of the environmental-ecological debate. It is a principle that Lewontin argues has been forgotten as much in biology as in social science: "We cannot regard evolution as the 'solution' by species of some predetermined environmental 'problems' because it is the life activities of the species themselves that determine both the problems and solutions simultaneously. . . . Organisms within their individual lifetimes and in the course of their evolution as a species do not *adapt* to environments; they *construct* them. They are not simply *objects* of the laws of nature, altering themselves to the inevitable, but active *subjects* transforming nature according to its laws."[17] But this then implies that we cannot somehow abandon in a relatively costless way the immense existing ecosystemic structures of, say, contemporary capitalism in order to "get back to nature." The constructed ecosystems we have inherited cannot be allowed to deteriorate or collapse without courting ecological disaster not only for the social order that produced them, but for all species and forms that have become dependent on them. But herein lies a key difficulty: the proper management of already constituted environments (and in this I include their long-term socialistic or ecological transformation into something completely different) may require transitional political institutions, hierarchies of power relations and systems of governance that could well be anathema to both ecologists and socialists alike. This is so because, in a fundamental sense, there is in the final analysis nothing *unnatural* about New York City, Los Angeles, or the New Jersey Turnpike, and sustaining such created ecosystems even in transition entails an inevitable compromise with the forms of social organization and social relations that produced them. If it is money that has made these environments go round, then we have no option except to sustain the money flows or find some substitute that has the same effect.

The intertwinings of social and ecological projects in daily practices as well as in the realms of ideology, representations, aesthetics, and the like are such as to make every social (including literary and artistic) project a project about nature, environment, and ecosystem, and vice versa. Such a proposition should not, surely, be too hard for those working in the historical materialist tradition to swallow. Marx argued, after all, that we can discover who and what we are (our species potential, even) only through transforming the world around us, and in so doing he put the dialectics of social and ecological change at the center of all human history. But is there some way to create a general enough language to capture that dialectical evolutionary movement?

Ecological Modernization

The thesis of "ecological modernization" has periodically emerged as one way to structure thinking about the dialectics of social and ecological change. In the United States it became popular during the Progressive era (when the name of Pinchot dominated discussions) and reemerged during the 1930s in the soil conservation movement and within institutions like the National Resources Planning Board.[18] In recent years, there are signs of its adoption/ co-optation by both environmental pressure groups and certain institutionalized configurations of political-economic power.

Ecological modernization depends upon and promotes a belief that economic activity systematically produces environmental harm (disruptions of "nature") and that society should therefore adopt a proactive stance with respect to environmental regulation and ecological controls.[19] Prevention is regarded as preferable to cure. This means that the more typical ad hoc, fragmented, and bureaucratic approach to environmental regulation should be replaced by a far more systematic set of policies, institutional arrangements, and regulatory practices. The future, it is argued, cannot be expected to look after itself, and some sorts of calculations are necessary to configure what would be a good strategy for sustainable economic growth and economic development in the long run. The key word in this formulation is *sustainability*. And even though there are multiple definitions of what this might mean (and all sorts of rhetorical devices deployed by opponents to make the term meaningless or render it harmless—no one, after all, can be in favor of "unsustainability"), the concept nevertheless lies at the heart of the politics of ecological modernization.

The thesis is justified in a variety of ways. The irreversibility problem is emphasized, not only with respect to biodiversity but also with respect to the elimination of whole habitats, permanent resource depletion, desertification, deforestation, and the like. High orders of environmental *risk* are emphasized, coupled with a rising recognition that unintended ecological consequences of human activity can be far-reaching, long-lasting, and potentially damaging. There has also been a growing recognition that ad hoc and afterthe-fact practices can produce unbalanced and ineffective results.

The role of scientists in promoting ecological modernization has been important.[20] It was science that revealed global problems (acid rain, global warming, and ozone holes) demanding wide-ranging collective action beyond nation-state borders, thereby posing a challenge (legal, institutional, and cultural) to the closed bureaucratic rationality of the nation-state. And some individual scientists pushed the knowledge of ecological systems and interrelatedness to the point where the unintended consequences of human activities could be seen to be far more widespread, irreversible, and potentially serious than had previously been recognized. This kind of science provided crucial support to many environmental pressure groups, many of whom initially viewed scientific rationality with skepticism and distrust, given their roots in the "romantic" and aesthetic traditions of, say, Wordsworth and Thoreau. The thesis of ecological modernization has now become deeply entrenched within many segments of the environmental movement. The effects, as we shall see, have been somewhat contradictory. On the one hand, ecological modernization provides a common discursive basis for a contested rapprochement between them and dominant forms of political-economic power. But on the other, it presumes a certain kind of rationality that lessens the force of moral arguments and exposes much of the environmental movement to the dangers of political co-optation.

The general persuasiveness of the ecological modernization thesis rests, however, on a refusal to see the supposed trade-off between environmental concerns and economic growth in zero-sum terms. What are known as "win-win" examples of ecological control are increasingly emphasized. Given the power of money, it is vital to show that ecological modernization can be profitable. Environmental care, it is argued, often contributes to efficiency (through more efficient fuel use, for example), improved productivity and lower costs (through soil conservation practices, for example), and long-term preservation of the resource base for capital accumulation. If, furthermore, pollution is merely being moved around (from air to water to land), then aggregate efficiency is being impaired in the long run if, as is increasingly the case, there are fewer and fewer empty "sinks" within which pollutants can costlessly be absorbed. And if, to take the parallel case of supposedly "natural" resources, depletion is occurring too fast to allow for smooth market adjustment and measured technological change, then costly disruptions to economic growth may be in the wind. To some degree, the search for "win-win" solutions has also been prompted by environmental litigation, environmental impact legislation, and, in some sectors, such as those directly associated with occupational and consumer safety and health, by extraordinarily high compensation awards for injured parties (as, for example, with the case of asbestos liability that drove firms and some insurers—a group of celebrated "names" of Lloyds of London—into bankruptcy). The costliness of recent clean-up efforts—the "superfund" experience in the United States to clean up hazardous waste sites being perhaps the best example—has also pushed many to take a new look at prevention.

Environmental equity (distributive justice) plays a role in ecological modernization arguments. This is in part due to the inroads made by the environmental justice movement and various other movements around the world expressive of what Martinez-Alier calls "the environmentalism of the poor."[21] But leaving these aside, cooperation is required to gain support for proactive environmental initiatives so that the question of environmental justice has to be integrated into the search for long-term sustainability, partly as a pragmatic adaptation to the internationalism of several key contemporary ecological issues: sovereign nation-states, including those that are poor, have to agree to a certain regulatory environment on, for example, carbon emissions and CFC use, and, furthermore, enforce its provisions. So some sort of configuration has to be envisaged in which ecological modernization contributes both to growth and global distributive justice simultaneously. This was a central proposition in the Brundtland Report, for example.[22] How, and if, that can be done is at the heart of deeply contentious debates. There are also signs of a discursive shift, perhaps fashioned as a response to the contentiousness of the distributive justice issue, in which economic *development* (improvement in human capacities and conditions) is seen as quite distinctive from economic *growth* (the increase in output of goods and services). If governments can be persuaded to take the former path, then the competitive challenge to the hegemony of the advanced capitalist powers with respect to capital accumulation through economic growth will be lessened.

One side-consequence is that environmental management is no longer seen to be the exclusive province of governments or the nation-state. The nation-state, although clearly still important, should be supplemented by strong international organizations as well as local governments. The general import of the Rio conference, for example, was to give far greater powers to international organizations (such as the World Bank and the United Nations Environmental Program) and to set up local government mandates for environmental quality. Many layers of government operating at many different scales should be implicated as partners in the search for better paths of environmental management. This move to construct some sort of hierarchy of powers tacitly recognizes the diverse scales at which environmental issues can arise. Although very little of this has actually been worked out in practice, a discursive shift away from the nation-state toward some sort of recognition of the scalar layering of environmental issues can certainly be detected. A wide range of forces in civil society (nongovernmental organizations, pressure groups, community agents) can then become involved. The debate over "values" becomes much more explicit, preparing the ground for a veritable industry of philosophical reflection devoted to "environmental ethics." And much more open and democratic as well as wide-ranging discussions of environmental issues become possible. It is precisely at this interface that the fine line between incorporation and open contestation again and again gets crossed and recrossed, with legal, scientific, and economic discourses, institutions, and practices becoming deeply implicated.

In portraying the general characteristics of the ecological modernization thesis in this systematic way, I am exaggerating its coherence. The raggedness of the environmental-ecological debate over the past twenty years defies any such simple characterization. But the debate in the public realm has been much more open to ecological modernization arguments than was previously the case. And as often happens with a public discourse in formation, all sorts of interventions and openings have occurred, through which quite a bit of radicalization has been achieved. Some radical environmental groups have been partially drawn to the ecological modernization thesis, sometimes as a tactic because it provides convenient and more generally persuasive public arguments with which to pursue other objectives, but sometimes as a matter of deeper conviction, viewing it as the only way to move a deeply entrenched capitalism toward ecological sanity and a modicum of global justice. Socialists, for their part, could take to the argument as a way of combining traditional commitments to growth and equity with rational planning under socialized control. Commoner's *Making Peace with the Planet* and Leff's *Green Production: Toward an Environmental Rationality* can be read, for example, as left-wing versions of this thesis. I shall come back to this particular line of thinking by way of conclusion.

But the discourse would not have the purchase it evidently has had without a significant tranche of support from the heartland of contemporary political-economic power. The rising tide of affluence in the advanced capitalist countries after World War II increased middle-class interest in environmental qualities and amenities and "nature" tourism and deepened concerns about environmental dangers to health. Although this lent an indelible bourgeois aesthetic and politics to much of the environmental movement, it nevertheless pushed environmental issues onto the political agenda where they could not easily be controlled as a mere adjunct of bourgeois fashion. The health connection, as Hays points out, became particularly salient and peculiarly open-ended in relation to environmental concerns in the United States after 1950 or so.[23] Systematic environmental concern for everything from landscape despoliation, heritage and wilderness preservation, control of air and water quality, exposure to toxins, waste disposal, regulation of consumer products, and the like became much easier to voice given middle-class acceptance of such issues as fundamental to its own qualities of life. *The Limits to Growth* (published in 1972), which in many respects was a powerful warning shot to say that the standard view was inadequate, was supported by the Club of Rome (an influential group of bankers and industrialists), and the Brundtland Report of 1987, which consolidated the ecological modernization discourse in important ways, bringing the question of "sustainability" to the fore, was an effort supported by many government officials, industrialists, financiers, and scientists.[24] And since that time, major world institutions, such as the World Bank, which previously paid no attention whatsoever to environmental issues, some corporations (IBM and even Monsanto), and powerful establishment politicians, like Margaret Thatcher and Al Gore, have been converted to some version of the ecological modernization thesis. Even *The Economist* now sees fit to celebrate "a budding romance between greens and business" in an article entitled "How to Make Lots of Money, and Save the Planet Too."[25]

There is a more sinister side to the argument, however. The severe recession of 1973–75, the subsequent slowdown in economic growth and rise of widespread structural unemployment, made an appeal to some notion of natural limits to growth more attractive. Scapegoating natural limits rather than the internal contradictions of capitalism is a well-tried tactic. When faced with a crisis, said Marx of Ricardo, the latter "takes refuge in organic chemistry."[26] This way of thinking put particular blame on population growth, again and again raising the specter of Malthus, thereby reducing much of the ecological-environmental problem to a simple population problem. This reactionary political approach was paralleled in *The Limits to Growth* and the Brundtland Report by concerns for natural limits to capital accumulation (and, hence, for employment possibilities and rising standards of affluence worldwide). The rhetoric of "sustainable development" could then be attached to the ideal of a growth economy that had to respect natural limits. Demands for higher wages or more rapid economic growth in poorer parts of the world were countered by appeal to certain immutable laws of nature, thus diverting attention from the far more mutable laws of entrenched class and imperialist privilege. The supposed sheer physical inability of the planet to support global populations with aspirations to the living standard of Sweden or Switzerland became an important political argument.

The evident failures of capitalist modernization in many developing countries also made the rhetoric of ecological modernization more attractive. The World Bank, for example, took to blaming the governments of Africa for the failure of its own development projects there and then sought to decentralize the process of development to see if indigenous methods led by indigenous peoples, with women cast in a much more central role, could work so as to pay off the accumulating debts built up precisely through World Bank–imposed Western-style development.

Finally, many corporations, IBM, for instance, saw a great deal of profit to be had from superior environmental technologies and stricter global environmental regulation. For the advanced capitalist nations, struggling to remain competitive, the imposition of strong environmental regulations demanding high-technology solutions promised not only a competitive advantage to their own industries but also a strong export market for the more environmentally friendly technology they had developed (the environmental cleanup in Eastern Europe has proven particularly lucrative). If only a small fragment of corporate capital thought this way, it was nevertheless a significant dissident voice arguing for ecological modernization from within a powerful segment of the bourgeoisie. Global environmental management "for the good of the planet" and to maintain "the health" of planet Earth could also be conveniently used to make claims on behalf of major governments and corporations for their exclusive and technologically advanced management of all the world's resources. So although a good deal of corporate capture of the ecological modernization rhetoric (particularly via "green consumerism") can be found, there are also positive reasons for some segments of corporate capital to align themselves with a movement that emphasized certain kinds of technological change coupled with highly centralized global environmental management practices.[27]

As a discourse, ecological modernization internalizes conflict. It has a radical edge, paying serious attention to environmental-ecological issues and most particularly to the accumulation of scientific evidence of environmental impacts, without necessarily challenging the capitalist economic system head-on. It is reformist in its objectives rather than revolutionary and poses no deeply uncomfortable questions to the perpetuation of capital accumulation, though it does imply strict regulation of private property rights. Such a discourse can rather too easily be corrupted into yet another discursive representation of dominant forms of economic power. It can be appropriated by multinational corporations to legitimize a global grab to manage all of the world's resources. Indeed, it is not impossible to imagine a world in which big industry (certain segments), big governments (including the World Bank), and establishment, high-tech big science can get to dominate the world even more than they currently do in the name of "sustainability," ecological modernization, and appropriate global management of the supposedly fragile health of planet Earth. This is precisely the shift that Sachs fears: "As governments, business and international agencies raise the banner of global ecology, environmentalism changes its face. In part, ecology—understood as the philosophy of a social movement—is about to transform itself from a knowledge of opposition to a knowledge of domination. . . . In the process, environmentalism . . . becomes sanitized of its radical content and reshaped as expert neutral knowledge, until it can be wedded to the dominating world view."[28]

Are there class forces at work to prevent such a reshaping?

Environmental Justice and the Defense of the Poor

In the United States, the movement for environmental justice and against environmental racism has become a significant political force.[29] It is a political movement that has been long in gestation, owing its most recent reincarnation to two particular incidents. First, the celebrated case of Love Canal in 1977, when houses built on top of an infilled canal in Buffalo, New York, found their basements full of noxious liquids with serious health effects on resident children.[30] This led to the formation of a Citizen's Clearing House for Hazardous Waste, which, according to Taylor, now works with over 7,000 community and grassroots groups nationwide.[31] The second arose out of the 1982 protests in Warren County, North Carolina, when a mostly African American community was selected as the site for burial of soil contaminated with PCBs. The vigor of the protests (multiple arrests of well-known civil rights figures) and the involvement of a wide range of organizations focused attention on what soon came to be known as environmental racism. In 1991, a very dispersed and highly localized movement came together around the First National People of Color Environmental Leadership Summit held in Washington, D.C. There it adopted a manifesto defining environmental justice in no fewer than seventeen different clauses. I select just a few:

Environmental justice:

Affirms the sacredness of Mother Earth, ecological unity and the interdependence of all species, and the right to be free from ecological destruction.

Mandates the right to ethical, balanced and responsible uses of land and renewable resources in the interest of a sustainable planet for humans and other living things.

Demands the cessation of the production of all toxins, hazardous wastes, and radioactive materials, and that all past and current producers be held strictly accountable to the people for detoxification and the containment at the point of production.

Affirms the need for urban and rural ecological policies to clean up and rebuild our cities and rural areas in balance with nature, honoring the cultural integrity of all our communities, and providing fair access for all to the full range of resources.

Opposes the destructive operations of multi-national corporations . . . military occupation, repression and exploitation of lands, peoples and cultures, and other life forms.

Requires that we, as individuals, make personal and consumer choices to consume as little of Mother Earth's resources and to produce as little waste as possible; and make the conscious decision to challenge and reprioritize our lifestyles to insure the health of the natural world for present and future generations.[32]

The environmental justice movement advances a discourse radically at odds with that of ecological modernization, and it has proven far less amenable to corporate or governmental co-optation. Five issues in its history stand out:

1. Inequalities in protection against environmental hazards have been felt in very tangible ways in enough instances, such as Love Canal, to make com-

pensation for and elimination of such inequalities a pressing material (largely health) issue for many. Putting the inequalities at the top of the environmental agenda directly challenges hegemonic environmental discourses.

2. "Expert" and "professional" discourses have frequently been mobilized by dominant forms of political-economic power to either deny, question, or diminish what were either known or strongly felt to be serious health effects deriving from unequal exposure. The resultant climate of suspicion toward expert and professional discourses (and the form of rationality they frequently espouse) underlies the search for an alternative rationality (even, if necessary, "irrationality") with which to approach environmental hazards. Although science, medicine, economics, and the law may remain important ingredients within the discourse of environmental justice, they are not therefore ever permitted to frame the arguments in toto.

3. The adoption of biocentric discourses that focus on the fate of "nature" rather than of humans on the part of many environmental groups (albeit modified by incorporation of theses of ecological modernization) has prompted a reaction. The environmental justice movement puts the survival of people in general, and of the poor and marginalized in particular, at the center of its concerns. And in focusing on the environmental issues that have the greatest impacts upon the poor and the already dispossessed, it links back into an extraordinarily rich tradition of concerns with occupational safety and health in the workplace and local environmental qualities in the impoverished segments of a rapidly urbanizing society.[33]

4. The marginalized, disempowered, and racially marked positions of many of those most affected, together with the strong involvement of women as dominant carers for the children who have suffered most from, for example, the consequences of lead paint poisoning or leukemia, have forced otherwise disempowered individuals to seek empowerment outside of prevailing institutions. The coupling of the search for empowerment and personal self-respect on the one hand with environmentalist goals on the other means that the movement for environmental justice twins ecological with social justice goals in quite unique ways. In so doing, the movement opens itself to distinctive positionalities from which injustice can differentially be measured. As Krauss observes:

women's protests have different beginning places, and their analyses of environmental justice are mediated by issues of class and race. For white blue-collar women, the critique of the corporate state and the realization of a more genuine democracy are central to a vision of environmental justice. . . . For women of color, it is the link between race and environment, rather than between class and environment, that characterizes definitions of environmental justice. African American women's narratives strongly link environmental justice to other social justice concerns, such as jobs, housing, and crime. Environmental justice comes to mean the need to resolve the broad social inequities of race. For Native American women, environmental justice is bound up with the sovereignty of the indigenous peoples.[34]

Such different positionalities create interesting interpretive tensions within the environmental justice movement across the themes of class, race, gender, and national identity. Bullard summarizes evidence to show, for example, that people of color are much more vulnerable to environmental hazards even when controlling for social status and class and concludes that the injustice is fundamentally a race and not a class problem.[35]

5. The racial and discriminatory aspects to the problem become highlighted for a very particular reason. In the case of exposure to toxic wastes and hazardous landfills, there is a symbolic dimension, a kind of "cultural imperialism" embedded in the whole issue—Are we not presuming that only trashy people can stomach trash? The question of stigmatization of "the other" through, in this instance, association of racially marked others with pollution, defilement, impurity, and degradation becomes a part of the political equation. If, as Douglas claims, "some pollutions are used as analogies for expressing a general view of the social order," and if "pollution beliefs can be used in a dialogue of claims and counter-claims to status," then claims about pollution as "matter out of place" cannot be separated from claims about the impurities and dangers of "people out of place."[36] The environmental justice movement typically pushes discussion far beyond the scientific evidence on, for example, health effects, cost-benefit schedules, or "parts per billion" and onto the thorny, volatile, and morally charged terrain of symbolic violence, "cultural imperialism," and personalized revolt against debasement of the colonialized "other."

These conditions of production of an environmental justice movement in the United States account for some of its central features. To begin with, the focus on particular kinds of pollution—toxins and dangerous contaminants—

loads the discussion toward symbolic questions, making clear that the issue is as much about "claims and counter-claims to status," as it is about pollution per se. This is what gives the movement so much of its moral force and capacity for moral outrage. But the corollary, as Szasz points out, is that the movement relies heavily upon symbolic politics and powerful icons of pollution incidents.[37] Toxins in someone's basement at Love Canal in Buffalo, New York, is a much more powerful issue from this perspective, even though it involves a very small number of people, than the diffuse cloud of ozone concentrations in major cities that affects millions every summer throughout much of the United States. In the case of Love Canal, there was an identifiable enemy (a negligent corporation), a direct and unmistakable effect (nasty liquids in the basement, sick children, and worried mothers), a clear threat to public trust in government (the Board of Education was particularly negligent), a legal capacity to demand personal compensation, an undefinable fear of the unknown, and an excellent opportunity for dramatization that the media could and did use with relish. In the case of ozone concentration, the enemy is everyone who drives, governments have very little mandate to intervene in people's driving habits, the effects are diffuse, demands for compensation hard to mount, and the capacity for dramatization limited, making for very little media coverage. The resultant bias in choice of targets permits critics to charge that the emphases of the environmental justice movement are misplaced, that its politics is based on an iconography of fear, and that the movement has more to do with moral outrage than the science of impacts. Such criticisms are often justifiable by certain standards (such as those espoused by mainstream environmentalists), but precisely for that reason are largely beside the point.

The refusal to cast discussion in monetary terms, to take another example, reflects an intuitive or experiential understanding of how it is that seemingly fair market exchange always leads to the least privileged falling under the disciplinary sway of the more privileged and that *costs* are always visited on those who have to bow to money discipline, whereas *benefits* always go to those who enjoy the personal authority conferred by wealth. There is an acute recognition within the environmental justice movement that the game is lost for the poor and marginalized as soon as any problem is cast in terms of the asymmetry of monetary exchange. Money is always a form of social power and an instrument of discipline in social relations rather than a neutral universal equivalent with which to calculate "welfare-enhancing benefits."

The environmental justice movement has, by and large, rejected the idea that money should make the environment go round. But this means that it also has to do battle with the liberal illusion about market freedoms in general (and neoliberal politics in particular) and its pervasive effects, as well as with direct forms of ecological harm. In so doing, some have indeed been led into backward-looking praise for the medieval world (a golden age of integration with nature, when human societies trod so lightly on the earth that all was well between humans and nature) and sideward-looking admiration for those marginalized peoples who have not yet been fully brought within the global political economy of technologically advanced and bureaucratically rationalized capitalism.

The affirmation of the "sacredness of Mother Earth" and other rhetoric of that sort is, I want to suggest, both problematic and empowering. It is empowering precisely because it permits issues to be judged in terms of moral absolutes, of good and evil, right and wrong. By posing matters in terms of the defilement, violation, or even "rape" of a sacred Mother Earth, the environmental justice movement adopts a nonnegotiable position of intense moral rectitude untouchable by legal, scientific, or other rationalistic discourses. It permits the assertion, in quasi-religious language, of the widespread view that the proper approach is to ask, in Lois Gibbs's words, "what is morally correct?" rather than "what is legally, scientifically and pragmatically possible?"[38]

It also permits, through the medium of social protest, the articulation of ideas about a moral economy of collective provision and collective responsibility as opposed to a set of distributive relations within the political economy of profit. Although the "moral economy" being proposed is definitely not that of the traditional peasant, the very grounding of the discourse in a language of sacredness and moral absolutes creates a certain homology among, say, struggles over exposure to environmental hazards in urban areas, nativist beliefs of the relation to nature, and peasant movements throughout the developing world such as that of the Chipko or the Amazon rubber tappers.[39] It is therefore not surprising to find that "the fundamental right to political, economic, cultural and environmental self-determination of all peoples" is asserted as one of the principles of environmental justice.

It is precisely through this discursive strategy that links can then be found between the environmental justice movement as shaped within the specific conditions of the United States, and the broader movement throughout the world concerning "the environmentalism of the poor." These movements fundamentally concern either the defense of livelihoods and of communal access to "natural" resources threatened by commodification, state takeovers, and private property arrangements, or more dynamic movements (both in situ and migratory) arising as a response to ecological scarcities, threats to survival, and destruction of long-standing ways of life.[40] But, as with the environmental justice movement, the symbolic dimension, the struggle for empowerment, for recognition and respect, and above all for emancipation from the oppressions of material want and domination by others, inevitably has a powerful role to play, making the environmentalism of the poor focus upon survivability in all of its senses.

From this standpoint, it is not hard to understand the fierce critique of "sustainable development" and "ecological modernization" (in its corrupted form) launched by Sachs: "The eco-cratic view likes universalist ecological rules, just as the developmentalist liked universalist economic rules. Both pass over the rights of local communities to be in charge of their resources and to build a meaningful society. The conservation of nature [should be] intimately related to rights of communal ownership, traditional ways of knowing, cultural autonomy, religious rituals, and freedom from state-centered development."[41]

Doctrines of cultural autonomy and dispersion, of tradition and difference, nevertheless carry with them a more universal message that permits a loose alliance of forces around alternative strategies of development (or even, in some instances, growth) that focus as much upon diversity and geographical difference as upon the necessary homogeneities of global market integrations. What seems to be at work here is the conversion of ideals learned through intense ecologically based "militant particularism" into some universal principles of environmental justice.[42] The environmental justice movement, like the labor movement before it, "has tried to connect particular struggles to a general struggle in one quite special way. It has set out, as a movement, to make real what is at first sight the extraordinary claim that the defence and advancement of certain particular interests, properly brought together, are in fact the general interest."[43]

This connection is nowhere more apparent than in the shift from "Not-in-my-backyard" politics to "Not-in-anyone's-backyard" principles in the United States:

Environmental philosophy and decision making has often failed to address the justice question of who gets help and who does not; who can afford help and who cannot; . . . why industry poisons some communities and not others; why some contaminated communities get cleaned up but others do not; and why some communities are protected and others are not protected. . . . The grassroots environmental justice movement . . . seeks to strip away the ideological blinders that overlook racism and class exploitation in environmental decision making. From this critical vantage point, the solution to unequal environmental protection is seen to lie in the struggle for justice for all Americans. No community, rich or poor, black or white, should be allowed to become an ecological "sacrifice zone." Saying "NO" to the continued poisoning of our communities of color is the first step in this struggle. Yet our long-range vision must also include institutionalizing sustainable and just environmental practices that meet human needs without sacrificing the land's ecological integrity. If we are to succeed, we must be visionary as well as militant. Our very future depends on it.[44]

But as a movement embedded in multiple "militant particularisms," it has to find a way to cross that problematic divide between action that is deeply embedded in local experience, power conditions, and social relations and a much more general movement. And like the working-class movement, it has proven, in Williams's words, "always insufficiently aware of the quite systematic obstacles which stood in the way."[45] The move from tangible solidarities felt as patterns of social bonding in affective and knowable communities to a more abstract set of conceptions with universal meaning involves a move from one level of abstraction—attached to place—to quite different levels of abstraction capable of reaching across a space in which communities could not be known in the same unmediated ways. Furthermore, principles developed out of the experience of Love Canal or the fight in Warren County do not necessarily travel to places where environmental and social conditions are radically different. And in that move from the particular to the general something is bound to be lost. In comes, Williams notes, "the politics of negation, the politics of differentiation, the politics of abstract analysis." And these, whether we like them or not, are "now necessary even to understand what [is] happening."[46]

But it is exactly here that some of the empowering rhetoric of environmental justice itself becomes a liability. Appealing to "the sacredness of Mother Earth," for example, does not help arbitrate complex conflicts over how to organize material production and distribution in a world grown dependent upon sophisticated market interrelations and commodity production through capital accumulation. The demand to cease the production of *all* toxins, hazardous wastes, and radioactive materials, if taken literally, would prove disastrous to the public health and well-being of large segments of the population, including the poor. And the right to be free of ecological destruction is posed so strongly as a negative right that it appears to preclude the positive right to transform the Earth in ways conducive to the well-being of the poor, the marginalized, and the oppressed. To be sure, the environmental justice movement does incorporate positive rights, particularly with respect to the rights of all people to "political, cultural and environmental self-determination," but at this point the internal contradictions within the movement's propositions become blatant. And that is a serious problem as long as the contradictions remain unacknowledged and not brought into creative tension.

At this conjuncture, therefore, all of those militant particularist movements around the world that loosely come together under the umbrella of environmental justice and the environmentalism of the poor are faced with a critical choice. They can either ignore the contradictions, remain within the confines of their own particularist militancies—fighting an incinerator here, a toxic waste dump there, a World Bank dam project somewhere else, and commercial logging in yet another place—or they can treat the contradictions as a fecund nexus to create a more transcendent and universal politics. If they take the latter path, they have to find a discourse of universality and generality that unites the emancipatory quest for social justice with a strong recognition that social justice is impossible without environmental justice (and vice versa). But any such discourse has to transcend the narrow solidarities and particular affinities shaped in particular places—the preferred milieu of most grassroots environmental activism—and adopt a politics of abstraction capable of reaching out across space, across the multiple environmental and social conditions that constitute the geography of difference in a contemporary world that capitalism has intensely shaped to its own purposes over the past two hundred years.[47]

The abstractions cannot rest solely upon a moral politics dedicated to protecting the sanctity of Mother Earth. They have to deal in the material and institutional issues of how to organize production and distribution in general, how to confront the realities of global power politics, and how to displace the hegemonic powers of capitalism not simply with dispersed, autonomous, localized, and essentially communitarian solutions (apologists for which can be found on both right and left ends of the political spectrum), but with a rather more complex politics that recognizes how environmental and social justice must be sought by a rational ordering of activities at different scales. The reinsertion of the idea of "rational ordering" indicates that such a movement will have no option, as it broadens out from its militant particularist base, but to reclaim for itself a nonco-opted and nonperverted version of the theses of ecological modernization. On the one hand, that means subsuming the highly geographically differentiated desire for cultural autonomy and dispersion, for the proliferation of tradition and difference, within a more universalizing politics. But on the other hand, it means making the coupled quest for environmental and social justice central rather than peripheral concerns. The effect is then to make the environmental movement recognize that class-, gender-, and race-oppression issues are fundamental to its own politics.

For that to happen, the environmental justice movement has to radicalize the ecological modernization discourse itself. And that requires confronting the fundamental underlying processes (and their associated power structures, social relations, institutional configurations, discourses, and belief systems) that simultaneously generate environmental and social injustices. The fundamental problem in today's world is that of unrelenting capital accumulation and the extraordinary asymmetries of money and political power that are embedded in that process. Alternative modes of production, consumption, and distribution as well as alternative modes of environmental transformation have to be explored if the discursive spaces of the environmental justice movement and the theses of ecological modernization are to be conjoined in a program of radical political action. Only in that way can the Left find a foundation for its distinctive form of environmental politics and seek to reshape simultaneously social and environmental relations.

Notes

My analysis of ecological modernization owes much to the pleasure of supervising Maarten Hajer's dissertation work in Oxford. That work has now been published as Maarten Hajer, *The Politics of Environmental Discourse: Ecological Modernization and the Policy Process* (Oxford, 1995).

1 William Leiss, *The Domination of Nature* (Boston, 1994); Carolyn Merchant, *The Death of Nature: Women, Ecology and the Scientific Revolution* (New York, 1990).

2 On ecological distribution, see J. Martinez-Alier and M. O'Connor, "Economic and Ecological Distribution Conflicts," in *Getting Down to Earth: Practical Applications of Ecological Economics,* ed. R. Costanza, O. Segura, and J. Martinez-Alier (Washington, D.C.: 1996). On political ecology, see Friedrich Engels, *Dialectics of Nature* (New York, 1940); Alfred Schmidt, *The Concept of Nature in Marx* (London, 1971); Neil Smith, *Uneven Development: Nature, Capital and the Production of Space* (Oxford, 1974); Reiner Grundmann, *Marxism and Ecology* (Oxford, 1991); Raymond Williams, *Resources of Hope* (London, 1989); Joan Martinez-Alier, *Ecological Economics: Energy, Environment and Society* (Oxford, 1987).

3 John Bellamy Foster, *The Vulnerable Planet: A Short Economic History of the Environment* (New York, 1994). The citations that follow are from pages 12 and 142 respectively.

4 Even James Lovelock, creator of the Gaia hypothesis, is intensely antagonistic to planetary managerialism and resolutely refutes any appeal to the idea that the Earth is fragile. See Lovelock, "The Earth Is Not Fragile," in *Monitoring the Environment,* ed. Bryan Cartledge (Oxford, 1992).

5 Greg Easterbrook, *A Moment on the Earth: The Coming Age of Environmental Optimism* (New York, 1995); Julian Simon, *The Ultimate Resource* (Princeton, NJ, 1981).

6 Barry Commoner, *Making Peace with the Planet* (New York, 1990). I have always found it odd that Commoner combines a strong Marxist concern for the social control of production with an ideology in which "nature knows best."

7 Foster, *Vulnerable Planet,* 118–124.

8 I have criticized this idea more fully in David Harvey, "The Nature of Environment: The Dialectics of Social and Environmental Change," *Socialist Register* (1993): 1–51. See also David Harvey, *Justice, Nature and the Geography of Difference* (Oxford, 1996).

9 Dorcetta Taylor, "Can the Environmental Movement Attract and Maintain the Support of Minorities?" in *Race and the Incidence of Environmental Hazards,* ed. Bunyan Bryant and Paul Mohai (Boulder, CO, 1992), 39.

10 World Commission on Environment and Development (Brundtland Report), *Our Common Future* (Oxford, 1987).

11 Emil Zola, *Money* (Gloucestershire, UK, 1991), 65.

12 Cited in Smith, *Uneven Development,* 64.

13 Zola, *Money,* 117, 140.

14 Ibid., 75.

15 Emil Zola, *l'Argent* (Paris, 1967), 224–225 (my translation).

16 Donald Worster, *Rivers of Empire: Water, Aridity and the Growth of the American West* (New York, 1985).

17 Richard Lewontin, "Organism and Environment," in *Learning, Development and Culture,* ed. Harold Plotkin (Chichester, UK, 1982).

18 Samuel Hays, *Conservation and the Gospel of Efficiency: The Progressive Conservation Movement, 1890–1920* (Cambridge, UK, 1959).

19 See Hajer, *Politics;* Albert Weale, *The New Politics of Pollution* (Manchester, UK, 1992).

20 Besides Hajer, *Politics,* see Karen Litfin, *Ozone Discourses: Science and Politics in Global Environmental Cooperation* (New York, 1994).

21 Joan Martinez-Alier, "Ecology and the Poor: A Neglected Dimension of Latin American History," *Journal of Latin American Studies* 23 (1990): 621–639.

22 World Commission on Environment and Development, *Common Future.*

23 Samuel Hays, *Beauty, Health and Permanence: Environmental Politics in the United States, 1955–85* (Cambridge, UK, 1987).

24 Donella Meadows, Dennis Meadows, Jorgen Rangers, and William Behrens, *The Limits to Growth* (New York, 1972); World Commission on Environment and Development, *Common Future.*

25 *The Economist,* 3 June 1995, 57.

26 David Harvey, "Population, Resources and the Ideology of Science," *Economic Geography* 50 (1974): 256–277.

27 *The Economist,* 3 June 1995, 57.

28 Wolfgang Sachs, ed., *Global Ecology: A New Arena of Political Conflict* (London, 1995), xv.

29 Bunyan Bryant and Paul Mohai, eds., *Race and the Incidence of Environmental Hazards* (Boulder, CO, 1992); Robert Bullard, ed., *Confronting Environmental Racism: Voices from the Grassroots* (Boston, 1993); Robert Bullard, ed., *Unequal Protection: Environmental Justice and Communities of Color* (San Francisco, 1994).

30 Lois Gibbs, *Love Canal: My Story* (Albany, NY, 1982); Adeline Levine, *Love Canal: Science, Politics and People* (New York, 1982); Andrew Szasz, *Ecopopulism: Toxic Waste and the Movement for Environmental Justice* (Minneapolis, 1994).

31 Dorcetta Taylor, "Environmentalism and the Politics of Inclusion," in Bullard, *Confronting.*

32 Karl Grossman, "The People of Color Environmental Summit," in Bullard, *Unequal Protection.*

33 Robert Gottlieb, *Forcing the Spring: The Transformation of the American Environmental Movement* (Washington, DC, 1993).

34 Celene Krauss, "Women of Color in the Front Line," in Bullard, *Unequal Protection,* 270.

35 Bullard, *Confronting,* 21. See also the comments by Richard Moore in Paul Almeida, "The Network for Environmental and Economics Justice in the Southwest: Interview with Richard Moore," *Capitalism, Nature, Socialism* 5, no. 1 (1994): 21–54.

36 Mary Douglas, *Purity and Danger: An Analysis of the Concepts of Pollution and Taboo* (London, 1984), 3.

37 Szasz, *Ecopopulism.*

38 Cited in William Greider, *Who Will Tell the People?* (New York, 1993), 214.

39 Ramachandra Guha, *The Unquiet Woods: Ecological Change and Peasant Resistance in the Himalayas* (Berkeley, CA, 1989); Susanna Hecht and Alexander Cockburn, *The Fate of the Forest: Developers, Destroyers and Defenders of the Amazon* (New York, 1990).

40 Dharam Ghai, D. Vivian, and Jessica Vivian, eds., *Grassroots Environmental Action: People's Participation in Sustainable Development* (London, 1995); Sachs, *Global Ecology.*

41 Sachs, *Global Ecology.*

42 The term comes from Raymond Williams. I have expanded on its meaning and utility in Harvey, *Justice,* chap. 1.

43 Williams, *Resources.*

44 Bullard, *Confronting,* 206.

45 Williams, *Resources,* 115.

46 Williams, *Loyalties* (London, 1985), p. 293.

47 I am not, of course, the only one to make such an argument. Gottlieb, in *Forcing the Spring,* prepares the way historically for this kind of perspective, and useful theoretical arguments are advanced by Enrique Leff, *Green Production: Towards an Environmental Rationality* (New York, 1995); David Pepper, *Eco-Socialism: From a Deep Ecology to Social Justice* (London, 1994), particularly chap. 5; and Grundmann, *Marxism and Ecology.* Some of the political difficulties facing such a project in the United States are taken up in Jim O'Connor, "A Red Green Politics in the U.S.?" *Capitalism, Nature, Socialism* 5, no. 1 (1994): 1–19. The most obvious difficulty is confronting the historical divide between anarchist decentralized antistatism (with its contemporary offshoots of social ecology and bioregionalism) and the more systematic and organized tradition of Marxism.

Noam Chomsky

Free Trade and Free Market:

Pretense and Practice

Just as Jane Kelsey's illuminating study of "the New Zealand experiment" was about to appear,[1] the Royal Institute of International Affairs in London published the seventy-fifth anniversary issue of its journal, *International Affairs*, with survey articles on major issues of the day. One is devoted to "experiments" of the kind to which New Zealand is subjecting itself, and their intellectual roots. The author, Paul Krugman, is a leading figure in international and development economics.[2] He makes five central points, quite pertinent in this context.

His first point is that knowledge about economic development is very limited. Much of economic growth has to be attributed to the "residual"— "the measure of our ignorance," as Robert Solow calls it. In the best-studied case, the United States, two-thirds of the rise in per capita income falls within this category. Similarly, the Asian NICs provide "no obvious lessons," having followed "varied and ambiguous" paths that surely do not conform to what "current orthodoxy says are the key to growth." Krugman recommends "humility" in the face of the limits of understanding, and caution about "sweeping generalizations."

Krugman's second point is that, nevertheless, sweeping generalizations are constantly offered by policy intellectuals and planners (including many economists). Furthermore, they provide the doctrinal support for policies that are implemented, when circumstances allow.

Third, the "conventional wisdom" is unstable, regularly shifting to something else, perhaps the opposite of the latest phase—though its proponents are again brimming with confidence as they impose the new orthodoxy.

Fourth, it is commonly agreed in retrospect that the policies didn't "serve their expressed goal" and were based on "bad ideas."

Finally, it is usually "argued that bad ideas flourish because they are in the interest of powerful groups. Without doubt that happens. . . ."

That it happens has been a commonplace at least since Adam Smith condemned the mercantilist theories designed in the interests of the "merchants and manufacturers" who were "the principal architects" of Britain's policies, mobilizing state power to ensure that their own interests were "most peculiarly attended to," however "grievous" the impact on others, including the people of England. It not only happens, but does so with impressive consistency. Today's "New Zealand experiment" breaks no new ground when "the benefits [of the policies] rapidly accrued to the corporate sector" that had the "manifest . . . strategic influence" in their design, and "political actors stack the deck in favor of constituents who are intended beneficiaries."[3]

That is the heart of the matter, and I think it calls for some restatement of Krugman's conclusions. The "bad ideas" may not serve the "expressed goal," but they typically turn out to be very *good* ideas for their proponents. There have been quite a few experiments in economic development in the modern era, and though it is doubtless wise to be wary of sweeping generalizations, still they do exhibit some regularities that are hard to ignore. One is that the designers seem to come out quite well, though the experimental subjects, who rarely sign consent forms, quite often take a beating.

The first such experiment was carried out shortly after Smith wrote, when the British rulers in India instituted the "permanent settlement" of 1793, which was going to do wondrous things. The results were reviewed by a British Enquiry Commission forty years later. It concluded that "The settlement fashioned with great care and deliberation has to our painful knowledge subjected almost the whole of the lower classes to most grievous oppression," leaving "misery" that "hardly finds a parallel in the history of commerce," the director of the Honorable Company added, as "the bones of the cotton-weavers are bleaching the plains of India."

But the experiment can hardly be written off as a failure. Governor-General Lord Bentinck noted that "the 'Permanent Settlement,' though a failure in many other respects and in most important essentials, has this great advantage, at least, of having created a vast body of rich landed proprietors deeply interested in the continuance of the British Dominion and having complete command over the mass of the people," whose growing misery is therefore less of a problem than it might have been. British investors didn't lose out either. Apart from the enormous wealth that flowed to individuals and companies, India was soon financing 40% of Britain's trade deficit while providing a protected market for its manufacturing exports; contract laborers for British possessions from the Caribbean, to Africa, to Ceylon and Malaysia "replacing earlier slave populations," the *Cambridge Economic History of India* notes; troops for Britain's colonial and European wars; and the opium that was the staple of Britain's exports to China—not quite by the operations of the free market, just as the sacred principles were overlooked when the useful substance was barred from England.[4]

In brief, the first great experiment was a "bad idea" for the subjects, but not for the designers and local elites associated with them. That coincidence has recurred with curious regularity until the present day. The consistency of the record is no less impressive than the flights of rhetoric hailing the latest "showcase for democracy and capitalism" and "testing area for scientific methods of development" as a remarkable "economic miracle"—and the consistency of what the rhetoric conceals.

The most recent example is Mexico. It was highly praised for its strict observance of the rules of the "Washington consensus" that guides the thinking of New Zealand's technocrats, and offered with pride as a model for others as wages collapsed, the poverty rate rose almost as fast as the number of billionaires, foreign capital flowed in (mostly speculative, or for exploitation of super-cheap labor kept under control by the brutal "democracy"), and the other familiar concomitants of "showcases" and "miracles." Also familiar is the denouement, the collapse of the house of cards in December 1994, as had been predicted by observers who chose not to watch what was happening through the distorting prism of the "bad ideas" that "flourish because they are in the interest of powerful groups."

The historical record offered some further lessons. In the eighteenth century, the differences between the first and third worlds were far less sharp than they are today. Two obvious questions arise:

1. Which countries developed, and which not?
2. Can we identify some operative factors?

The answer to the first question is fairly clear. Outside of Western Europe, two regions developed: the United States and Japan—that is, the two regions that managed to escape European colonization. Japan's colonies are another case, in no small part because Japan, though a brutal ruler, did not rob its colonies but developed them, at about the same rate as Japan itself.

What about Eastern Europe? In the fifteenth century, Europe began to divide, the West developing and the East becoming its service area, the original third world. The divisions deepened into early in this century, when Russia extricated itself from the system. Despite Stalin's awesome atrocities and the huge destruction of the two World Wars, the USSR did undergo significant industrialization, as did its satellites. It is the "second world," not part of the third world—or was, until 1989. Into the early 1960s, the documentary record reveals, the great fear of Western planners was that Russia's economic growth would allow it to catch up with the West and that the "demonstration effect" would induce others to pursue a course of "economic nationalism." With the cold war over, most of Eastern Europe is returning to the status quo ante: regions that were part of the industrial West are regaining that status, while typical third-world structures are being restored in the traditional service areas.

The world is more complicated than any simple description, but this is a pretty good first approximation, which tells us more about the question at hand, and also about the cold war. What it suggests is supported by the observation that, although John F. Kennedy's "monolithic and ruthless conspiracy" dedicated to world conquest is now a fading memory, the Pentagon budget remains at normal cold war levels and is now increasing, facts that help a rational person to draw some conclusions about the role of the Soviet threat in the thinking of planners; and Washington's international policies have undergone little more than tactical adjustment and rhetorical revision now that past pretexts can no longer be reflexively dusted off when needed, more facts that help a rational person gain some understanding of the nature of the cold war.

Returning to question 1, it seems that development has been contingent on freedom from "experiments" based on the "bad ideas" that were very good ideas for the designers and their collaborators. The ability to fend off such measures does not guarantee economic development, but does seem to have been a prerequisite for it.

Let's turn to question 2. How did Europe and those who escaped its clutches succeed in developing? Part of the answer seems exceptionless: by radically violating approved free market doctrine. That conclusion holds from England to the East Asian growth area today, surely including the United States, "the mother country and bastion of modern protectionism," economic historian Paul Bairoch observes in his recent study of myths concerning economic development. The most extraordinary of these, he concludes, is the belief that protectionism impedes growth: "It is difficult to find another case where the facts so contradict a dominant theory," in a conclusion supported by many other studies.[5]

Reviewing their program of economic development after World War II, a group of prominent Japanese economists point out that they rejected the neoclassical economic counsel of their advisers, choosing instead, the editor observes, a form of industrial policy that assigned a predominant role to the state, a system that is "rather similar to the organization of the industrial bureaucracy in socialist countries and seems to have no direct counterpart in the other advanced Western countries" (Tokyo University economist Ryutaro Komiya). "The 'ideology' of industrial policy during this [early postwar] period was not based on neoclassical economics or Keynesian thinking, but was rather neomercantilist in lineage," one contributor adds, and "also was distinctly influenced by Marxism." Market mechanisms were gradually introduced by the state bureaucracy and industrial-financial conglomerates as prospects for commercial success increased. The defiance of orthodox economic precepts was a condition for the Japanese miracle, the economists conclude.

Turning to Japan's former colonies, the first extensive study of the U.S. Aid mission in Taiwan discovered that the U.S. advisers and Chinese planners, "although versed in Anglo-American economics," disregarded the doctrines and the orders from Washington. The U.S. technical experts in Taiwan chose "to jettison free-market nostrums from the start and collaborate with Chinese officials" in developing a "state-centered strategy," as Taiwan resumed the development of the colonial period. Policy was based on the principle, which still holds, that it must "depend upon the active participation of the government in the economic activities of the island through deliberate plans and its supervision of their execution."[6] Meanwhile, U.S. officials were "advertising

Taiwan as a private enterprise success story," much as the World Bank does today with increasing desperation while analysts concerned with the facts detail the crucial and continuing role of the "entrepreneurial state," functioning differently from South Korea but with no less of a guiding hand.[7]

The central role of state management and initiative in late-developing economies has been well known since the work of Alexander Gerschenkron; it need only be added that the same is true from the earliest moments of the industrial revolution. In these domains, few propositions seem as well-founded empirically.

An ancillary question is how the third world became what it is today. Bairoch provides a plausible if partial answer: "There is no doubt that the Third World's compulsory economic liberalism in the nineteenth century is a major element in explaining the delay in its industrialization," and, in the dramatic and very revealing case of India, the "process of de-industrialization" that converted the industrial workshop and trading center of the world to a deeply impoverished agricultural society, suffering a sharp decline in real wages, food consumption, and availability of other simple commodities from the eighteenth century, a "misfortune that is unprecedented in the world's economic history," the most detailed modern study concludes.[8]

"India was only the first major casualty in a very long list," Bairoch observes, including "even politically independent Third World countries that were forced to open their markets to Western products." Meanwhile, Western societies protected themselves from market discipline, and developed—with correlations to market interference that are not easy to disregard, as Bairoch and others observe.

Putting the details aside, it seems fairly clear that one reason for the sharp divide between today's first and third worlds is that much of the latter was subjected to "experiments" that rammed free market doctrine down their throats, whereas today's developed countries were able to resist such measures.

That brings us to another feature of modern history that is hard to miss, in this case at the ideological level. Free market doctrine comes in two varieties. The first is the official doctrine that is taught to and by the educated classes and imposed on the defenseless. The second is what we might call "really existing free market doctrine": For thee, but not for me, except for temporary advantage; I need the protection of the nanny state, but you must learn responsibility under the harsh regimen of "tough love." Those in a position to make choices typically adopt the second version of free market doctrine, the one that has been a prerequisite to development, so the historical record suggests, though not a sufficient condition for it.

Pursuing the inquiry further, we quickly discover that the effects of state intervention in the economy are much underestimated in standard accounts, which focus narrowly on such special cases as protectionism. The category is far broader.

To select one obvious case, the early industrial revolution relied on cheap cotton. It was not exactly kept cheap and available by worship of the market—rather, by the expulsion or extermination of the indigenous population of the American South along with slavery, later a near functional equivalent. There were, furthermore, other cotton producers at the time. Prominent among them was India, under colonial rule, so that its resources flowed to England while its own considerably more advanced textile industry was destroyed by the harsh and self-conscious application of "really existing free market doctrine." Another case is Egypt, which was initiating industrial development at the same time as America's New England, but was barred from that course by British force—on the quite explicit grounds that Britain would brook no competition or independent development. New England, in contrast, was able to follow the path of the mother country, barring cheaper British textiles by very high tariffs, as Britain had done to India. Without such measures, half of the emerging textile industry of New England would have been destroyed, the sole inquiry into the topic by an economic historian concludes, with the obvious effects on the many industrial spinoffs.[9]

It is curious that the central question of American economic history seems to be virtually off the agenda, apparently regarded as "politically incorrect."

To be sure, Britain did finally turn to liberal internationalism—in 1846, after 150 years of protectionism, violence, and creation of a strong and efficient state had enabled it to gain more than twice the per capita industrialization of any competitor, so that a "level playing field" looked fairly safe. By 1846, India exported no cotton goods at all, and had to import cloth from England, over four times as much as ten years earlier. England had, at last, become preeminent in textile production, having succeeded in de-industrializing India by force. "It is striking," Mukerjee observes, "that English economists and statesmen became adherents of the doctrine of free trade as the surest way to the wealth of nations after the rise of the Lancashire cotton industry through the tariff and prohibition against French goods, Irish woolen goods and Indian silk and cotton imports." The measures that Britain undertook were extreme, going well beyond extremely high protective tariffs. The contention of ideologues that Adam Smith "convinced England of the merits of free international trade" (George Stigler, Nobel laureate in economics of the University of Chicago) cannot withstand even the slightest exposure to empirical fact.[10]

In 1846, Britain did finally turn to liberal internationalism, though not without significant reservations. Thus, 40 percent of British textiles continued to go to colonized India, and much the same was true of British exports generally. In the latter part of the nineteenth century, British steel was blocked from U.S. markets by very high tariffs that enabled the United States to develop its own steel industry; the noted pacifist Andrew Carnegie was able to construct the world's first billion-dollar corporation thanks to high tariffs, naval contracts, and resort to state violence to block labor organization and impose virtual tyranny on manufacturing towns. But India and other colonies were still available, as they were when British steel was later priced out of international markets. India again is a particularly interesting case: it produced as much iron as all of Europe in the late eighteenth century; British engineers were still studying Indian steel manufacturing techniques in 1820 "in order to help English steel makers close the technological gap with India," a Harvard military historian observes; and Bombay was producing locomotives at competitive levels when the railway boom began. But "really existing free market doctrine" destroyed these sectors of Indian industry just as it demolished India's textile industry, along with its advanced shipbuilding industry and others that had made it the world's leading center of manufacture before the British takeover. The United States and Japan, in contrast, could adopt Britain's model of radical violation of market principles. And when Japanese competition proved to be too much to handle, England simply called off the game: the Empire was effectively closed to Japanese exports, one significant part of the background of World War II in the Pacific. Indian manufacturers asked for protection at the same time—but against England, not Japan. No such luck, under really existing free market doctrine.[11]

A century after England turned to liberal internationalism—temporarily, and with reservations—the United States followed the same course, for much the same reasons. By 1945, after 150 years of extreme protectionism, violence, and formation of an efficient developmental state, the United States had become by far the richest and most powerful country in the world and, like

England before it, suddenly came to perceive the merits of liberal internationalism on a "level playing field." But, again, with crucial reservations.

One was that, like Britain, Washington used its power to bar independent development elsewhere. Latin America was permitted "complementary" but not "competitive" development, a harsh condition imposed upon this "testing area for scientific methods of development" in accord with "American capitalism." Aid to newly independent Egypt and (in complex ways) India was conditioned on similar principles. Attempts to violate the rules have often elicited extreme violence—under cold war pretexts when they were available, others when they were not.

Another crucial reservation was (and remains) domestic. One fundamental component of free trade theory is that public subsidies are disallowed. But the American business world and leading economists expected a return to the Great Depression when pent-up consumer demand from the war was exhausted and business leaders were aware that advanced industry "cannot satisfactorily exist in a pure, competitive, unsubsidized, 'free enterprise' economy" and that "the government is their only possible savior" (*Fortune, Business Week*). Business leaders quickly settled on the Pentagon system as the optimal device to impose the costs on the public while profits are privatized, for sensible reasons. It was understood that social spending could play the same stimulative role, but it is not a direct subsidy to the high-tech corporate sector, and it has inherent unwelcome features. Social spending has democratizing effects: people have opinions about where a hospital or school should be, but not about air defense systems that lay the groundwork for commercial computers. And social spending tends to be redistributive. Military spending has none of these defects, and is also easy to sell, at least as long as democratic forms can be deprived of substance by deceit and manipulation. Truman's Air Force Secretary Stuart Symington put the matter forthrightly in January 1948: "The word to talk was not 'subsidy'; the word to talk was 'security.'" As industry representative in Washington, he regularly demanded enough procurement funds in the military budget to "meet the requirements of the aircraft industry," as he put it. One consequence is that "civilian aircraft" is now the country's leading export, and the huge travel and tourism industry, aircraft-based, is the source of major profits and a hefty favorable trade balance in services. The same pattern prevails in computers, electronics generally, metallurgy, biotechnology, telecommunications and information processing, in fact just about every dynamic sector of the economy.[12]

It is a bit hard to keep a straight face when "evangelical libertarian intellectuals and free-market economists" praise the "conservative free-market governments in the U.S. and elsewhere," admiring "Anglo-Saxon laissez-faire."[13] Such posturing may pass in the doctrinal institutions, but would simply elicit ridicule in the corridors of power, corporate or state.

The story continues to the present. There was no need to explain "really existing free market doctrine" to the Reaganites, who were masters at the art, extolling the glories of the market to the poor at home and the service areas abroad while boasting proudly to the business world that Reagan had "granted more import relief to U.S. industry than any of his predecessors in more than half a century" (Secretary of the Treasury James Baker, who was far too modest; in fact, it was more than all predecessors combined, as the Reaganites doubled import restrictions).[14] Meanwhile, the administration stepped up the transfer of public funds to private power, primarily through the Pentagon system. Had these extreme measures of market violation not been pursued, it is doubtful that such central sectors of industry as steel, automotive, machine tools, and semiconductors would have survived Japanese competition or been able to forge ahead in emerging technologies, with widely proliferating effects throughout the economy. That experience illustrates once again that "the conventional wisdom" is "full of holes," Alan Tonelson points out in reviewing the Reaganite record of market interference in *Foreign Affairs*.[15] But the conventional wisdom retains its virtues as an ideological weapon to discipline the defenseless.

There is also no need to explain the doctrines to the leader of today's "conservative revolution" in Washington, Newt Gingrich, who sternly lectures seven-year-old children on the evils of welfare dependency while winning the national prize in bringing federal subsidies to his rich constituents, thanks to such paragons of free enterprise as Lockheed, the major employer in his district, and others like it. Or to the Heritage Foundation, which crafts the budget proposals for the congressional "conservatives," and therefore called for (and obtained) an increase in the Pentagon budget beyond Clinton's increase to ensure that the "defense industrial base" remains solid, protected by the nanny state and offering dual-use technology to its beneficiaries, to enable them to dominate commercial markets. Clinton's expansion of the Pentagon budget, quickly topped by the congressional "libertarians," was his immediate response to the "popular mandate for conservatism" in November 1994, and was supported by an overwhelming one-sixth of the population.

But all understand very well that democracy is a nuisance to be ignored as long as possible, and that free enterprise means that the public pays the costs under various guises, bearing the risks if things go wrong, while profit is privatized. And in pursuit of these ends, decision making is to be transferred as much as possible from the public arena to unaccountable private tyrannies, and "locked in" by treaties that undermine the potential threat of democracy.

New Zealand's Law Commission is on target in observing that a crucial feature of the international trade treaties is that they "limit in substance the power of the New Zealand Parliament."[16] That is a good part of their function. In the United States, it is no longer possible to produce the euphoric predictions about the benefits that Nafta will surely bring, so it is now tacitly conceded by sophisticated elites that the advocates of Nafta were lying all along. The Clinton administration "forgot that the underlying purpose of NAFTA was not to promote trade but to cement Mexico's economic reforms," *Newsweek* correspondent Marc Levinson loftily declares in *Foreign Affairs,* failing only to add that the contrary was loudly claimed to ensure the passage of Nafta, while the critics who emphasized this "underlying purpose" were efficiently excluded from the debate.[17] The main goal of Nafta, we can now concede, was not to achieve the highly touted wonders of "trade" and "jobs," always illusion, but to ensure that Mexico would be "locked in" to the reforms that had made it an "economic miracle" (for U.S. investors and Mexican elites), deflecting the danger detected by a Latin America Strategy Development Workshop at the Pentagon in September 1990: that "a 'democracy opening' in Mexico could test the special relationship by bringing into office a government more interested in challenging the U.S. on economic and nationalist grounds." Despite the rich variety of means available to deter the threat of democracy, the powerful cannot be certain that the plague may not break out somewhere.

Of course, the United States is not alone in its conceptions of "free trade," even if its ideologues lead the cynical chorus. The doubling of the gap between rich and poor countries from 1960 is substantially attributable to protectionist measures of the rich, the UN Development Report concluded in 1992. The practices persist through the Uruguay Round, the 1994 UNDP report observes, concluding that "the industrial countries, by violating the principles of free trade, are costing the developing countries an estimated $50 billion a year—nearly equal to the total flow of foreign assistance"—much of it publicly subsidized export promotion.[18] To illustrate with a different measure, a recent study of the top 100 transnationals in the *Fortune* list found that "virtually all appeared to have sought and gained from industrial and/or trade policies [of their home government] at some point," and "at least 20 . . . would not have survived as independent companies if they had not been saved in some way by their governments." One is Gingrich's favorite cash cow, Lockheed, saved from collapse by $2 billion federal loan guarantees provided by the Nixon administration. Again, New Zealand breaks no new ground as its libertarians bail out Electricorp when it gets in trouble.[19]

There is a great deal more to say about these matters, but some conclusions seem fairly clear: as in the days of Smith and later Ricardo, the approved doctrines are carefully crafted and employed for reasons of power and profit. There is no new departure when the "New Zealand experiment" takes the form of "socialism for the rich" as part of the international "triumph of the market" based on a system of global corporate mercantilism in which "trade" consists in substantial measure of centrally managed intrafirm transactions and interactions among huge institutions, totalitarian in essence, designed to undermine democratic decision making and to safeguard the masters from market discipline; a system in which "Oligopolistic competition and strategic interaction among films and governments rather than the invisible hand of market forces condition today's competitive advantage and international division of labor in high-technology industries."[20] It is the poor and defenseless who are to be instructed in the stern doctrines of market discipline.

From the origins of the industrial revolution, there have been repeated efforts to implement within the industrial societies themselves the kinds of "experiments" imposed elsewhere, but with only limited success. The first was in England in the early nineteenth century, when the doctrines of "neo-liberalism" were forged as an instrument of class warfare: specifically, the doctrine that one only harms the poor by efforts to help them, and that people have no rights other than what they can gain in the labor market, contrary to the mistaken assumptions of precapitalist society, which upheld a misguided "right to live." Those who cannot survive under harsh market discipline may enter the workhouse-prison or, preferably, go somewhere else— not impossible in those days, as North America and parts of the Pacific were being cleared of the native scourge. These are virtual laws of nature, Ricardo and others solemnly explained, as certain as the principle of gravitation.

With the triumph of right thinking at the service of British manufacturing and financial interests, the people of England were "forced into the paths of a utopian experiment," Karl Polanyi wrote in a classic work, the most "ruthless act of social reform" in all of history, which "crushed multitudes of lives." But a problem arose. The stupid masses, unable to comprehend the compelling logic of the science, began to draw the conclusion that if we have no right to live, then you have no right to rule. The British army had to cope with riot and disorder, and soon an even greater threat took shape: "factory laws and social legislation, and a political and industrial working class movement sprang into being . . . to stave off the entirely new dangers of the market mechanism."[21] Chartism and socialist organizing posed even greater terrors. The science, which is fortunately supple, took new forms as elite opinion shifted in response to uncontrollable popular forces, discovering that the "right to live" had to be preserved under a social contract of sorts.

That story too has been repeated over the years, in the United States as well, and in other industrializing societies. Today the social contract that has been gained by popular struggle is once again under attack, primarily in the Anglo-American societies. That is one aspect of what the business press calls "capital's clear subjugation of labor . . . for the past 15 years."[22] The new experiments, as always, are accompanied by confident proclamations, which merit all the respect they deserved in the past.

Recalling again how little is understood, one has to evaluate with care and caution the "neoliberal economies and philosophy [that have] dominated intellectual discourse, radiating out primarily from the United States,"[23] with due attention to the rationale of the argument (such as it is) and to the lessons of past and present history, among them, the cynicism of the intellectual discourse intended to veil "really existing free market doctrine." It makes little sense to ask what is "right" for the United States (or India, or New Zealand . . .), as if these were entities with shared interests and values. Within the realm of practical choice, that is rarely true. And what may be right for people in the United States, given their unparalleled advantages, could well be wrong for others who have a much narrower scope of choices, which have to be made in the light of particular historical and sociocultural contingencies. We can, however, reasonably anticipate that what is right for the people of the United States (or India, or New Zealand . . .) will only by the remotest accident conform to what is preferred by the "principal architects of policy," for much the reasons that Adam Smith understood very well.

Notes

This article was originally published electronically in the *Electronic Journal of Radical Organization Theory* 2, no. 1 (1996), at http://www.mngt.waikato.ac.nz/depts/sm&l/journal/ejrot.htm. We are grateful to its editors.

1 Jane Kelsey is associate professor of Law at the University of Auckland. Her *The New Zealand Experiment: A World Model for Structural Adjustment* (1995) was published under the title *Economic Fundamentalism* in the British version by Pluto. She is also the author of *A Question of Honor* and *Rolling Back the State.* Kelsey's original title refers to the adoption of a version of neoliberalism in New Zealand, one of the few cases on record when neoliberal doctrine was adopted without external pressure or outright coercion, in this case, by a rich country. Kelsey's verdict is negative, unlike that of the international business world. This article was part of a symposium in New Zealand on her study.

2 Paul Krugman, "Cycles of Conventional Wisdom on Economics Development," *International Affairs* 71, no. 4 (October 1995).

3 Kelsey, *New Zealand Experiment,* 8, 72–73.

4 For references, see my *Year 501* (Boston, 1993). Also C. A. Bayly, *The New Cambridge History of India* (Cambridge, UK, 1988).

5 Paul Bairoch, *Economics and World History* (Chicago, 1993). For more detail on the U.S. case, see Alfred Eckes, *Opening America's Market: U.S. Foreign Trade Policy since 1776* (Chapel Hill, NC, 1995).

6 K. Y. Win (1953), cited in Nick Cullaher, "The U.S. and Taiwanese Industrial Policy," *Diplomatic History* 20, no. 1 (1996).

7 Ryutaro Komiya et al., *Industry Policy of Japan* (Tokyo, 1984); Cullaher, "The U.S. and Taiwanese Industrial Policy"; Vincent Wei-ching Wang, "Developing the Information Industry in Taiwan," *Pacific Affairs* 68, no. 4 (winter 1995–96).

8 R. Mukerjee, *The Economic History of India: 1600–1800* (Allahabad, 1967). See Bayly for a briefer review and confirmatory evidence. Also Dietmar Rothermund, *An Economic History of India,* 2d ed. (London, 1993); and Bipan Chandra, *Modern India* (Delhi, 1971).

9 Mark Bils, "Tariff Protection and Production in the Early U.S. Cotton Textile Industry," *Journal of Economic History,* no. 4 (1984).

10 George Stigler, introduction to the University of Chicago bicentennial edition of Smith's *Wealth of Nations* (1976). On his misrepresentations of Smith's text, see Chomsky, *Year 501.*

11 See references of note 4; Stephen Peter Rosen, "Military Effectiveness," *International Security* 19, no. 4 (1995).

12 For references, see my *Year 501* and *World Orders Old and New* (New York, 1994). Also Frank Kofsky, *Harry Truman and the War Scare of 1948* (New York, 1993).

13 Kelsey, *New Zealand Experiment,* 10, 17, 19.

14 Baker cited by Fred Bergsten, *Financial Times,* 19 August 1993.

15 Alan Tonelson, *Foreign Affairs,* July–August 1994.

16   Kelsey, *New Zealand Experiment,* 104.

17   Marc Levinson, *Foreign Affairs,* March–April 1996.

18   For discussion, see Eric Toussaint and Peter Drucker, eds., *IMF/World Bank/ WTO, Notebooks for Study and Research* 24, no. 5 (1995; International Institute for Research and Education, Amsterdam).

19   Winfried Ruigrok, *Financial Times* (London), 5 January 1996; Kim McQuaid, *Uneasy Partners* (Baltimore, 1994); Kelsey, *New Zealand Experiment,* 124.

20   OECD, 1992. See Dieter Ernst and David O'Connor, *Competing in the Electronics Industry* (Pinter, 1992), cited by Laura Tyson, *Who's Bashing Whom?* (Institute for International Economics, Washington, 1992).

21   Karl Polanyi, *The Great Transformation* (1944; reprinted, Boston, 1957), 78.

22   John Liscio, "Is Inflation Tamed? Don't Believe It. We're Getting Close to the Edge Again," *Barron's,* 15 April 1996.

23   Kelsey, *New Zealand Experiment,* 17.

Masao Miyoshi

In Place of a Conclusion

Most of the papers collected in this volume were delivered at the Globalization and Culture Conference held November 9–12, 1994, at Duke University, which was organized by Ariel Dorfman, Fredric Jameson, Walter Mignolo, Alberto Moreiras, and me. A majority of the papers were later revised, and a few were replaced with other papers by the same authors. The conference was primarily a symposium of scholars and writers, but it was also pedagogic. It had a large audience of the general public and graduate students not only from Duke but from as far as California and Canada. The conference, of course, had the requisite question-and-answer period after each session. Realizing, however, the usual difficulty for the audience to participate in discussion, the organizers provided graduate students with a forum on the day after the conference to which only graduate students were invited. There were some organizers present at the forum, but they—we—agreed among ourselves to be as passive as the audience is forced to be at a large-scale conference such as this one; our point was to give the graduate students a chance to speak instead of to listen.

About forty students attended, and many spoke, most of them disciplining themselves to fit their comments to the allotted space of time, only a few minutes. The remarks on the conference, its substance and form, were in many ways provocative. Instead of responding, however, we tried to listen: we had had our time on the floor, this was their turn. I don't know what the students thought of each other's comments, but as far as I was concerned, they were as insightful and articulate as the conference panelists; that is, some more so than others, of course, and some were more sensitive to their audience's possible responses than were others. I also experienced the pain of sitting silent when I wanted to interject—just as they must have felt on the preceding days. We asked the students at the meeting to send us a few paragraphs describing their thoughts and responses. What follows are the comments we received from eight students, some of whom have since joined college and university faculties.

(There were several students who came as a group from the University of Montreal. They were students of the late Bill Readings, of the Department of Comparative Literature, the University of Montreal, who was killed at thirty-four in a plane crash a few weeks earlier. For them the conference provided a chance to mourn together the death of their teacher, for whom they had developed profound love and respect. They also sought together to reaffirm their determination to continue the studies of the subjects that Bill and the conference shared. I hope the conference—and this volume—has served in some measure to strengthen their alliance and hope.)

There was a bizarre moment during the conference when, after the Transnational Culture and Consumerism panel asked for questions and debate, the lighting on the platform made it difficult for the panelists to see the hands raised in the auditorium. Many in the auditorium believed they were being intentionally marginalized and suggested that the panelists were trying to shut down genuine debate. The situation was the result of a simple misunderstanding, but it also represented one of the earliest moments of what I saw as the "conspiracy effect" that seemed to hover over the conference. Somehow, somewhere, it was often suggested, someone was trying to keep some of us silent. Whereas critical reflection on procedures, arrangements, and so on often strengthened the conference, it often revealed an odd pathology, a desire for alienation, rather than a resistance to alienation. There is a mood, more discernible in my generation (the twenty-something crowd), that is symptomatic of globalization. Many who attempt to grasp the loci of authority in late capitalism end up feeling more passive, more defeated than they did prior to such intellectual and political engagement. The conspiracy effect (on several occasions the organizers were portrayed as a kind of *deus absconditus*) suggests that God is not dead but continues to take the form of a supranational ego-ideal: We must do something about this (we say conscientiously), and a voice behind the screen or in the holy glow of the lighted platform replies, You may not.

Powerlessness is both a self-imposed and symptomatic trait of the subjects of global capitalism, and I would like to suggest that we breathe a bit of fresh air (there must be at least a little left) and generate an alternative "mood" (without Prozac) that both recognizes the range of external forces and also helps create a pessimism of strength. Such a strategy would not signal a retreat and call to arms for "militant particularisms" (Harvey's term) but rather an expansion of our cyborglike consciousness. This consciousness would resist the condition of seriality or the sense that neither the self nor the group at hand has any real power to effect change, that someone else far away is always preventing it. Instead, it would map and affirm its own limited powers in the larger network of seemingly inhuman, cybernetic global social relations.

It was proposed in the Graduate Student Forum that we need to stay away from "abstract" or "theoretical" thinking and get to work on "real," "concrete," "local" struggles, as if thought and action could ever provide two separate modes of living. This proposal ran counter to most of the discussions in the conference-at-large, which pushed toward a heightened grasp of dialectical strategies. As a panelist remarked, "resistance is not only possible but is inevitable," and I would add that the postmodern subject confronts, among other things, the threefold form of a "conspiracy effect": the development of Big Science (the discovery of the Archimedean Point), the increasingly mobile and transnational corporations (which now appear to be in the realm of the Sublime), and the retreat into the self in a privatized, bourgeois lifeworld. The conspiracy effect that marked the internal disputes of the conference may have been an inevitable manifestation of the global pressures we tried to confront in our debates.

A genuine political disturbance, then, may need to take such modern and postmodern developments into account when mapping the individual subject onto the global substance. It may turn out that we are something like Spinoza's worm, which, living in the blood, is only capable of regarding "each individual particle as a whole, not as a part," and has "no idea as to how all the parts are modified by the overall nature of the blood." Global capitalism is not, however, Spinoza's Infinity, and, in any case, if it sometimes *feels* that way, this can only be grounds for greater curiosity and collective motion rather than for inertia or misplaced anxiety wrought by the effect of an ineffable conspiracy.

Benjamin Bertram
University of California at San Diego

I will focus on three words: *localization, differentiation,* and *articulation.* The "local" presents a major challenge to theorizing globalization and culture. Because the current globalization process entails the further implement of a neocolonial project, how different communities and peoples that constitute what we call the "local" assume or reassume their positions and roles in confronting that process commands more attention. It is the "local" (largely represented by localities within the vast area formerly named the "South," "underdeveloped," "developing," "satellite," or "periphery") that compels a significant shift in our mode of theorizing. By this I mean that we need to relocate ourselves both physically and theoretically, that is, to move away from "dwelling" at the very center of the world's political, economic, and cultural powers to grounding ourselves somewhere outside of it, and to move away from anchoring our analysis largely on Western theoretical parameters to building our abstraction upon lived realities of local communities. In other words, to understand the "local" we must "localize" ourselves. To go beyond the contours of discourse and of global production and trade, we must participate in the political, social, and cultural worlds outside the academy. I share a panelist's critique of the university and academic elitism, and a number of participants' urge to link academic work to political action.

The shift is imperative if we want to connect theory to practice and if we really hope to contribute to sociocultural transformation. Both would demand a style of research, theorizing, and conducting conferences different from the conventions of the "Ivory League." I see "localizing" our research and theorization as the only way by which we can radically change theorization of globalization and culture from becoming another Western academic babble. Indeed, if circumstances make it difficult for us to fulfill the obligations of the "organic intellectual," at least we should try to be grounded intellectuals.

The limitation of a Western-centered fashion of theorization is reflected in the all-encompassing notions of the global and local circulating in talks about globalization and culture. In particular, I find that the celebration of local resistance (usually referred to as cultural production and hybrid products) often deprives the local (or localizing the global) of its complexity. If we admit that contemporary globalization in its most general sense is a twofold process involving universalization of particularism and particularization of universalism, the dichotomy of domination/resistance would not be enough to delineate the disjunctures and the multifarious outcome of globalizing-localizing dynamics.

Although we know that the global is largely represented by capitalism and the West, we do need to differentiate local resistance and cultural hybridity. This necessitates, theoretically, the breakdown of totalizing narratives of the local into several levels of analysis and, empirically, a closer examination of local cultural production and representations. We need to look into the polysemy of cultural hybridization and, following this, to differentiate resistance and submission, resistance-in-submission, and submission-in-resistance. All these forms of local response to global cultural flows can produce hybrids. For example, in China's cultural production today, the fusion of foreign and local cultural forms constitutes at least three intersecting discourses: the official discourse of modernity, where hybrid cultural texts operate to promote high modernism and consumer capitalism; the discourse of commercial culture, where China's newly emergent cultural industries are engaged in producing hybrids to compete with Western and Hong Kong transnationals for local and regional markets; and a third form of hybridization, in which individual cultural producers utilize hybridized forms to resist the state, the commercialization of culture, and Western domination. In analyzing each of these forms we encounter difficulty drawing clear lines between compliance and resistance.

In connection to this, I want to use the anthropological concept of *articulation* to conceptualize consequences of globalizing-localizing dynamics and complex local situations. Formulated by Marxist anthropologists in the early 1980s, the "theory of articulation" tries to uncover concrete manifestations of the hierarchical coexistence of different modes of production in the "third world" as a result of global capitalist expansion. The emphasis is that under globalization, both local and larger spatial arenas are transformed. Although the local is more likely to undergo more drastic change, the change may not necessarily happen in a predetermined direction. As uncovered by feminist anthropologists, local social formations may have determining influence (not necessarily positive) on the way capitalism affects local production systems and social relations.

Now recognized by some as "one powerful model of cultural change that attempts to relate dialectically the local to larger spatial arenas," articulation allows one to explore the richly unintended consequences of globalization, where loss occurs alongside invention. One of the consequences is the hybridization of local sociocultural formations. The local under the "assault" of global capitalism can evolve into a mesh of social and cultural formations normally conceived as belonging to different types of societies. This is the case in contemporary China, where feudalism, totalitarianism, and consumer capitalism are coming to form a peculiar social totality as the country further integrates into global systems of production and consumption. Articulation, then, forces us not to neglect the multiple movements and acts taking place in processes of localizing the global, while we trace occurrences of assimilation imposed on the local by global capitalism.

Xiaoping Li
York University

One of the ongoing concerns of the conference was the question of feminism and its role in resisting the effects of globalization, a concern that was brought up in various contexts but was rarely itself the subject of prolonged discussion. Another more thoroughly explored question was that of how resistance can be strategized within an increasingly globalized economy. What strikes me as particularly crucial in response to this conference is the fact that the interrelatedness of these two questions becomes apparent when, first of all, the importance of feminist and sexuality-based critiques of global capitalism is acknowledged at the level of ideology, and second, when white, first-world feminism is critiqued for its complicity with global power structures not only in its exclusivity but also in relation to the type of knowledge it produces about women. In both cases, these critiques of the ideological production of identities are quite different from an identity politics that would further the cause of a particular group but leave unquestioned persisting colonial structures of power that promote the interests of a particular class through the exploitation of (often racialized) others.

In her improvised talk, Nawal el Saadawi stated that "there is no global feminism," even though, as a speaker noted in the opening panel, globalization has led to increasing levels and new forms of the exploitation of women. Saadawi began to explore the reasons for the lack of a truly global feminism in her description of how feminists in the United States know nothing about Egyptian women's movements. I would like to expand on Saadawi's comments by arguing that this ignorance on the part of U.S. feminists arises out of an ideologically produced sense of "distance" from what, as a result of this false sense of distance, has been termed the third world. It is this distance that allows for the gestures of altruism that are central to the construction of alterity (i.e., the desire to export, from the first world, "modern" knowledge about women), thus preventing white, first-world feminism from realizing what David Harvey might call its "implicatedness" in a global system. In other words, this decidedly provincial feminism needs to know about the different priorities and needs of other women's movements not in order to "help" third-world women liberate themselves from what is often represented in the West as a traditional and "backward" patriarchy, but to better understand the various ways exploitation is deployed through the axis of gender within global capitalism, from unpaid and unacknowledged domestic labor to factory workers of transnational corporations with production sites in the third world. Most important, this knowledge on the part of white feminists in the first world should not be understood as knowledge about "the other" but, instead, as part of a broader understanding of the conditions of their own existence.

Not only does feminism need to become global in scope and self-definition, but critiques of globalization also need to address issues of gender and sexuality as central concerns, and not as separate issues. Otherwise, these critiques will fail to provide an accurate account of the ways in which capitalism not only exploits women, but also uses ideological notions of "womanhood," in conjunction with compulsory heterosexuality, to mobilize the Family as an ideological state apparatus that perpetuates the reproduction of the labor relations and conditions that allow globalization to take place.

Amie Parry
University of California at San Diego

Interwoven with discussions at the conference of the increasing domination of the world's cultural and geographical spaces by transnational capitalism and consumerism were questions of resistance to these forces. The treatment of land—as a source of profit, a location of ecosystems, or a foundation of identity—is one realm in which to examine the contents and contours of globalization. The terms in which David Harvey discussed ecology provide a useful framework for addressing not only the environment, but also politics, economics, and culture.

Harvey defined four particular kinds of environmentalism, one of which is especially interesting when thinking about the possibilities and problems of local resistance to global capitalism. As presented in Harvey's talk, the phenomenon of connecting the environment to cultural, national, or ethnic identity sounds a warning about the exclusionary potential of local efforts of resistance, environmental or otherwise. At the same time, the struggle for local autonomy offers a potentially strong source of resistance to the homogenizing and destructive elements of global capitalism. How, then, can people engage in such local acts of resistance without falling prey to their own specificity, or succumbing to the particular danger that Harvey and others have called eco-fascism? That is, how might grassroots and government-driven environmentalisms draw their strength not from the fostering of national, ethnic, or cultural ties to a given piece of land, but rather from a larger sense of the global effects of their actions, and especially the global causes of their particular crises? When do local or national efforts to gain political autonomy lead into a specificity that becomes exclusionary? This tension between local identities and global forces was a prevalent force in the talks and conversations of the conference, appearing not only in Harvey's environmentalism, but also in Noam Chomsky's advocacy of local activism, Nawal el Saadawi's visions and critiques of women's movements, and Geeta Kapur's discussions of Indian regionalism. These and other speakers explored the complex edges and currents of the tenuous balance between localism and globalization, bringing up the not easily answered question of local activism's ability to draw strength from what Michael Harte termed global lines of affiliation, from a connection to and awareness of transnational resistance to transnational capitalism.

Jennifer Jordan
University of California at San Diego

In his paper delivered to the conference's final panel, David Harvey argued persuasively for two political imperatives that fit together uncomfortably at best: a strategic necessity of "foundational beliefs" in political conflicts, and a need to create coordination among "militant particularisms," while respecting their particularity, in any program of resistance to globally entrenched injustice. His argument that these two imperatives might become compatible if "foundational beliefs" are conceived, paradoxically, in an indefinite future tense, if "we" try "to be pre-" rather than "post-," was interesting, but is complicated by the suggestion he made earlier that we'd all just missed the historical bus, so to speak, because regionalization has replaced globalization as the geographic logic of TNC power. I'm entirely unqualified to comment on the accuracy of this observation; rather, what interests me is the implication that historical comprehension can't keep up with the urgency of the need for resistance, that the speed and subtlety of political and economic mutation means that actions derived directly from descriptive beliefs risk "intervening" in situations that no longer exist. It would seem to me that the articulation of local struggles or "militant particularisms" is far too urgent a project to be made to depend upon the truth value of possibly anachronistic information.

Matthew Hyland
Université de Montréal

At the reception area just outside the hall where the conference was being held, I came upon a curious flyer advertising an international essay competition. The essay question read: "How can nations or individuals internationalize without sacrificing their cultural identity?" Sponsored by *Intersect Japan*, an international business magazine, AT&T, and Matsushita Electric Corporation of America, the competition would award the first-place winner a $5,000 cash prize. Next to several academic journals and the conference reader, the innocent flyer seemed oddly out of place. But then again, corporations and universities have always had a lot in common, not the least of which being the questions they ask. One reason for this is that questions are produced not simply by individuals, but by history. And our own historical moment of late capitalism, in which political and economic decision-making power has been quickly transferring from nation-states to transnational corporations, has prepared us (both in the university and in the corporate boardroom) to ask—with great urgency—the question of how culture functions within this emerging network of globalization.

If the nation-state is declining, is there a new global imaginary being produced? What is the network of production and consumption that shapes this new transnational space, this new transnational imaginary? What will happen to older national identities and those who still have much invested in the nation as a site of resistance? Who will profit and who will lose from globalization? These were the questions contested by many of the conference's participants. As the conference developed, what seemed clear was that, although transnational corporations are the driving force of economic production, on the level of consumption the nation-state is far from dead. In fact, cultural/national identity is one of the most valuable products transnational corporations sell. But why does the nation as an imaginary construct need to be resold like so many newly improved products that are now bigger, more effective, and extra-strength? And how is this repackaging done?

These last two questions return us to the flyer. Can we not view the contest itself as just another way to "resell" the nation? Here I am referring to the post–cold war cultural exchange industry, that is, a network of international organizations that focus on exchange, education, and goodwill. From education-abroad programs to humanitarian aid to international essay contests, there is a growing industry of private and public groups who, with the best of intentions, conduct cultural exchange. But if we bracket the intentions and focus on the function of this emerging industry, the complicity with transnational corporatism is striking. Instead of answering the flyer's question, then, we might want to ask why and how the question can be asked in the first place. Thus, not only can we protect against locking ourselves into a discourse in which we are compelled to fetishize a singular "cultural identity" and celebrate an internationalizing process, but we can also interrogate the very desire on behalf of the sponsors to pose the question. The most appropriate answer to the essay question would surely be one that rewrites the question itself, as say, How can we think about the process of transnationalism without reifying the notions of national and cultural identity? Of course, this may not win us the $5,000 prize, but it will take us a long way in understanding how transnational corporatism uses the nation to conceal its own power.

Eric Cazdyn
University of California at San Diego

After listening to and reading the work of the conference presenters, I believe two points stand out as important in any approach to the question of globalization and culture. First, we need to be aware of the dangerous occlusion of some axes of identity—sexuality, gender, accessibility—when we look at others—economics (class), race, geography. Second, we must understand that global economic forces now make certain types of isolation virtually impossible—economically and culturally—and that this fact must be understood in all of its manifestations. For instance, much more needs to be said about the complementary relationship that this new world-system has with the advent of multiculturalism and attempts in the United States (though much more advanced in Canada, the U.K., and Europe) to integrate—sometimes colonize—the cultural production of other countries. At the same time that the West is seeking to begin an investigation of the cultural production of the rest of the world—whether Benetton ads or David Byrne's mambo CDs—it is also attempting to "internationalize" its businesses, universities, and agencies. For example, it is now difficult to find an issue of a business magazine that doesn't warn about the inevitable need to become international in focus. Though this awareness of the world is a fairly new one for the United States, how the United States responds to both multiculturalism and internationalization may be key to the future of both globalization and culture.

Shelton Waldrep
Duke University

Although Allan Bloom mourned the fact that what he called "the adventure of a liberal education" no longer had a hero, Bill Readings thought that this presented us with certain definite advantages. For if such an adventure had neither "a student hero to embark upon it, nor a professor hero as its end," if no one was in a position anymore to "imagine him or herself . . . as the instantiation of the cultivated individual [the liberal, reasoning subject] that the entire great machine labors night and day to produce," then it appeared clear to him that there was no point for any of us students in waiting for any kind of permission to be granted to us by the institution—whether in the form of a degree or a teaching position—or still, in virtue of some idea of "maturity," to start thinking about the university and to attempt, as he was, to think our own way "out of an impasse between militant radicalism and cynical despair." As far as he was concerned, he certainly saw no reason why he should wait—as he so well wrote—"for the twilight of [his] career, to write a book upon the University." I am glad he did not. For shortly after finishing *The University in Ruins*, Bill Readings, professor at the Department of Comparative Literature of the Université de Montréal, died tragically at the age of thirty-four, in the October 31st Chicago plane crash.

So we are left with his suggestion that we should not wait to begin our own reflection on this matter. For one thing, he would warn us that the current debate on the status of the university by and large missed the point because it failed to think the university in a transnational framework, "preferring to busy itself with either nostalgia or denunciation." On the contrary, we should consider seriously that, "if the nation-state no longer is the primary instance of the reproduction of global capitals, then 'Culture'—as the symbolic and political counterpart to the project of integration pursued by the nation state—has lost its purchase." Then, he suggested, we should try to imagine the university "after" culture, to think in terms of an "institutional pragmatism," of a "tactical use of the space of the University while recognizing that space as a historical anachronism." We should adopt an attitude of incredulity about the university as an institution, an attitude of "committed unbelief" that would help us in "trying to imagine what it would mean to be in the University without being able to believe in the University, in either its actual or its ideal form."

But what this also means is that the university can no longer understand its mission as the safeguard and propagation of national culture. It actually witnesses a major reduction of the ideological stakes involved in what gets taught or produced as knowledge within its confines. More concretely, this means that "the wider social role of the University as an institution is now up for grabs; it is no longer clear what the place of the University is within society, nor what the exact nature of that society is, and the changing institutional form of the University is something that intellectuals cannot afford to ignore." Most especially, in a context of globalization, which names "the generalized imposition of the rule of the cash-nexus in place of the notion of national identity as determinant of all aspects of investment in social life," there is a serious need to distinguish between the notions of *accountability* and *accounting*. Although it appears clear that "it is imperative that the University respond to the demand for accountability," we should at the same time refuse that "the debate over the nature of its responsibility be conducted solely in terms of the language of accounting," which threatens to offer itself as the only possible standard by which to judge the university as an institution.

In view of the circumstances of his death, it seems particularly pertinent that Bill Readings would draw our attention to the fact that, "As a state ideological apparatus, the University had a cultural position roughly equivalent to that of a national airline." The national airline appears as "an instance of the state's attempt to realize itself by guaranteeing the hegemony of the *political* over the *economic*": "Rather than being crudely subjected to the profit motive, the national airline is subsidized by the nation state." What happens with the declining importance of the nation-state is the crucial question here; we should consider the refusal of the U.S. government to provide sufficient state subsidy to Pan-American airlines as indicative of "the irrelevance of such a political vision of the state to the current global economic order of TNCs." According to the same logic, the abolition of state subsidies to universities and national airlines is presented as likely to increase "efficiency" and ensure a return to "profitability."

In the present economic context of severe competition and deregulation, to what extent—and to whom—can airlines and other "national" corporations such as universities be accountable for their policies other than through a logic of accounting that balances net profit against lost planes and customers, or assigns ashes and junk mail the same cash value in the postal system?

Marie Lessard
Université de Montréal

Index

Contributors

Fredric Jameson is Professor of Comparative Literature and French and Chair of the Literature Program at Duke University. His most recent books include *Postmodernism, or, The Cultural Logic of Late Capitalism* (1990), *The Geopolitical Aesthetic* (1992), *Seeds of Time* (1994), *The Cultural Mutation: Selected Writings on the Postmodern* (1997), and *Brecht and Method* (forthcoming).

Masao Miyoshi is Hajime Mori Professor of Japanese, English, and Comparative Literature at the University of California, San Diego. His coedited book *Learning Places: Area Studies, Cultural Studies, Ethnic Studies, Gender Studies, and Other Disciplines* is forthcoming in 1999.

Noam Chomsky is Institute Professor at the Massachusetts Institute of Technology. His recent publications include *Language and Problems of Knowledge: The Managua Lectures* (1998), *World Orders Old and New* (1996), and *Global Contradictions: Answers to Key Political Questions of Our Time* (1997).

Ioan Davies is Professor of Sociology and Social and Political Thought at York University.

Manthia Diawara is Director of African Studies at New York University and editor of *Black Renaissance*. He recently directed a 58mm film, *Rouce in Reverse.*

Enrique Dussel is from Argentina, but has been in exile in Mexico since 1975. He is currently Professor of Ethics in the Philosophy Department of the Metropolitan Authonomous University in Mexico City. He is author of *Philosophy of Liberation* (2nd Ed., 1990), *Ethics and Community* (2nd Ed., 1993), *The Invention of the Americas* (1995), and *The Underside of Modernity: Apel, Ricoeur, Taylor, Rorty and the Philosophy of Liberation* (1996).

David Harvey is Professor of Geography at Johns Hopkins University. He is the author of *The Condition of Postmodernity* (1989) and *Justice, Nature, and the Geography of Difference* (1996).

Sherif Hetata is a writer, medical doctor, and one of the prominent figures in the left-wing movement in Egypt. He is the author of five novels, two travelogues, an extensive study of health and development in Egypt, and several books on Egyptian politics. His most recent work is an autobiography in three volumes.

Geeta Kapur is an art critic, author, and founding editor of the *Journal of Art and Ideas*. She has curated exhibitions of contemporary Indian art and has written and lectured widely on Indian and international art. Her most recent work is *When Was Modernism: Essays on Contemporary Cultural Practice in India* (1998).

Liu Kang is Associate Professor of Comparative Literature at Pennsylvania State University. He is the author of *Marxism and Aesthetics: Chinese Marxists and Their Contemporaries* (forthcoming from Duke) and *Bakhtin's Cultural Theory* (1995). He is also coeditor of *Politics, Ideology, and Literary Discourse in Modern Chinese* (1993).

Joan Martinez-Alier is Professor of Economics and Economic History at the Autonomous University of Barcelona. He is author of *Ecological Economics: Energy, Society, and Environment* (1987) and, with Ramchandra Guha, *Varieties of Environmentalism* (1997).

Walter D. Mignolo is Professor and Chair in Romance Studies and Professor in the Program in Literature and Cultural Anthropology at Duke University. He is author of *The Darker Side of the Renaissance: Literacy, Territoriality, and Colonization* (1995) and editor, with Elizabeth Hill Boone, of *Writing without Words: Alternative Literacies in Mesoamerica and the Andes* (Duke, 1994). His new book, *Local Histories/Global Designs: Essays in Colonial Legacies, Subaltern Knowledges, and Border Thinking*, is forthcoming.

Alberto Moreiras is Associate Professor of Romance Languages and Literature at Duke University, where he also serves as Director of the Latin American Cultural Studies Program. His publications include *Interpretacion y diferencia* (1991) and two forthcoming books (from Duke), *Third Space: Literary Mourning in Latin America* and *The Exhaustion of Difference: Paradigms of Latinamericanism*.

Paik Nak-chung is Professor of English at Seoul National University and founding editor of the Korean literary journal, *Creation and Criticism*. He has published six books of literary and social criticism in Korean and five volumes translated into Japanese.

Leslie Sklair teaches Sociology at the London School of Economics. His recent publications include *Sociology of the Global System* (1995), and articles in *Review of International Political Economy, Political Power, and Social Theory*, and *International Journal of Urban and Regional Research*.

Subramani is Professor of Literature at the University of the South Pacific.

He is the author of *South Pacific Literature: From Myth to Fabulation* and *The Fantasy Eaters*. His most recent book is *Altering Imagination*.

Barbara Trent is an Oscar-winning filmmaker, former welfare mother, seasoned activist, and trail blazer for change. She is the Film Director/Co-Director of the Empowerment Project.

Library of Congress Cataloging-in-Publication Data
The cultures of globalization / edited by Fredric Jameson and Masao
Miyoshi.
    p.   cm.
   Includes index.
   ISBN 0-8223-2157-2 (cloth : alk. paper). — ISBN 0-8223-2169-6
(pbk. : alk. paper)
   1. Cultural relations.   2. International economic relations.
I. Jameson, Fredric.   II. Miyoshi, Masao.
HM101.C399   1998
303.48′2—dc21   97-44373